REGISTERED HOMES ACT
MANUAL

AUSTRALIA
The Law Book Company
Brisbane . Sydney . Melbourne : Perth

CANADA
Carswell
Ottawa . Toronto . Calgary . Montreal . Vancouver

Agents
Steimatzky's Agency Ltd., Tel Aviv;
N.M. Tripathi (Private) Ltd., Bombay;
Eastern Law House (Private) Ltd., Calcutta;
M.P.P. House, Bangalore;
Universal Book Traders, Delhi;
Aditya Books, Delhi;
MacMillan Shuppan KK, Tokyo;
Pakistan Law House, Karachi, Lahore.

REGISTERED HOMES ACT MANUAL

by

Richard M. Jones, M.A.

*Solicitor, C.Q.S.W. Deputy Director of
Social Services, Mid Glamorgan County Council*

Second Edition

LONDON
SWEET & MAXWELL
1993

Published in 1993 by
Sweet and Maxwell Limited of
South Quay Plaza, 183 Marsh Wall,
London E14 9FT
Phototypeset by LBJ Enterprises Ltd. of Aldermaston and Chilcompton.
Printed and bound in Great Britain by Butler & Tanner Ltd., Frome and London

No natural forests were destroyed to
make this product: only farmed
timber was used and re-planted.

ISBN 0-421-48020-3

A catalogue record for this book is available from the British Library

*All rights reserved. No part of
this publication may be reproduced
or transmitted, in any form or by any means, electronic,
mechanical, photocopying, recording or
otherwise, or stored in any retrieval system
of any nature, without the written permission
of the copyright holder and the publisher, application
for which shall be made to the publisher.*

© Sweet & Maxwell Ltd.
1993

PREFACE

This edition follows its predecessor by bringing together in an annotated form the Registered Homes Act 1984 (as amended), and related subordinate legislation, Government circulars and guidance notes. The most significant development since the publication of the previous edition has been the passing of the Registered Homes (Amendment) Act 1991 which establishes a modified form of regulatory control for residential care homes with fewer than four residents ("small homes"). The requirements of Part I of the 1984 Act which are applied to small homes with modifications are:

(i) the registration authority may waive the whole or part of the registration fee or annual fee (ss.5(2A), 8(2));
(ii) the certificate of registration need not be on public display (s.5(6));
(iii) registration may only be refused if a person involved in the running of the home is not a fit person (s.9(2)); and
(iv) people running small homes are required to complete an annual return and send it to the registration authority and a failure to do so is a ground on which registration may be cancelled (ss.8(A), 10(*bb*)).

The law is stated as at September 1, 1993.

Richard Jones
Penarth
September, 1993

CONTENTS

	Page
Preface	v
Table of Cases	ix

PART 1
Registered Homes Act 1984 ... 1

PART 2
Residential Care Homes Regulations 1984 ... 85
Nursing Homes and Mental Nursing Homes Regulations 1984 ... 105

PART 3
Registered Homes Tribunal Rules 1984 ... 117

PART 4
Circular No. HC (81)8—Registration and Inspection of Private Nursing Homes and Mental Nursing Homes (Including Hospitals) ... 125
Circular No. LAC (84)15—Registration of Residential Homes and Registered Homes Tribunals ... 132
Circular No. HC (84)21—Registration and Inspection of Private Nursing Homes and Mental Nursing Homes (Including Private Hospitals) ... 155
Circular No. LAC (91)4—Disclosure of Criminal Background: Proprietors and Managers of Residential Care Homes and Nursing Homes ... 164
Circular No. LAC (92)10—Registered Homes (Amendment) Act 1991 and Residential Care Homes (Amendment) (No. 2) Regulations ... 171
Circular No. LAC (92)24—Local Authority Contracts for Residential and Nursing Home Care: NHS Related Aspects ... 183

Index ... 185

TABLE OF CASES

Avon County Council v. Lang [1990] C.O.D. 365.... 1–036, 1–038, 1–040, 1—042, 1—092

Coombs v. Hertfordshire County Council (1991) 89 L.G.R. 774; [1991] EGCS 47; *The Times*, April 26, 1991...... 1–041, 1–088, 2–009
Cotgreave v. Cheshire County Council, *The Times*, July 9, 1992..... 1–013, 1–040

Dodds v. Walker [1981] 1 W.L.R. 1027; (1981) 125 S.J. 463; [1981] 2 All E.R. 609; (1981) 32 P.&C.R. 131, H.L.; affirming [1980] 1 W.L.R. 1061; (1980) 124 S.J. 575; [1980] 2 All E.R. 507; (1980) 40 P.&C.R. 487; (1980) 255 E.G. 53, C.A....... 1–045, 1–078, 1–090, 1-191, 1–205

Green v. D.P.P. (1991) 155 J.P. 816; (1991) 155 J.P.N. 474; *The Times*. May 9, 1991, D.C... 1–106
Green v. Moore [1982] Q.B. 1044; [1982] 2 W.L.R. 671; (1982) 126 S.J. 79; [1982] 1 All E.R. 428; (1982) 74 Cr.App.R. 250; [1982] Crim.L.R. 233, D.C... 1–106
Grove v. Eastern Gas Board [1952] 1 K.B. 77; [1951] 2 T.L.R. 1128; 116 J.P. 15; 95 S.J. 789; [1951] 2 All E.R. 1051, C.A.; affirming [1951] 2 K.B. 586................................. 1–105, 1–210

Hare v. Gocher [1962] 2 Q.B. 641; [1962] 3 W.L.R. 339; 126 J.P. 396; 106 S.J. 531; [1962] 2 All E.R. 763; 13 P.& C.R. 298; 60 L.G.R. 278, D.C.. 1–218
Harrison v. Cornwall County Council, 90 L.G.R. 81; *The Times*, August 1, 1991............................... 1–013, 1–117, 3–030
Heydon's case (1584) 3 Co.Rep. 72; Moore, K.B. 128; 76 E.R. 637.. 1–087
Hillingdon London Borough Council v. McLean, 88 L.G.R. 49; (1989) 153 J.P.N. 594; (1989) 153 L.G.Rev. 790; (1989) 153 J.P. 564... 1–067
Hinchcliffe v. Sheldon [1955] 1 W.L.R. 1207; 120 J.P. 13; 99 S.J. 797; [1955] 3 All E.R. 406, D.C................................. 1–106

Isle of Wight County Council v. Humphreys (1991) 90 L.G.R. 186..1–040, 1–176

Jones v. Director of Public Prosecutions, *The Times*, June 4, 1992, D.C...... 1–030

Lewis v. Cox [1984] 3 W.L.R. 875; (1984) 128 S.J. 596; (1984) 148 J.P. 601; [1984] 3 All E.R. 672; (1984) 80 Cr.App.R. 1; [1984] Crim.L.R. 756; (1984) 81 L.S.Gaz. 2538, D.C................ 1–106
London and Clydeside Estates Ltd. v. Aberdeen District Council [1980] 1 W.L.R. 182; (1979) 124 S.J. 100; [1979] 3 All E.R. 876; (1979) 39 P.&C.R. 549; 253 E.G. 1011, H.L.................. 1–088

London and Globe Finance Corporation Ltd., *Re* [1903] 1 Ch. 728; 72
  L.J. Ch. 368; 88 L.T. 194; 51 W.R. 651; 19 T.L.R. 314; 10 Mans.
  198. 1–148
Lyons *v.* East Sussex County Council (1988) 152 J.P. 488; (1988) 86
  L.G.R. 369; (1988) 152 L.G.Rev. 674; [(1988) 138 New L.J. 277],
  C.A.; affirming *The Times*, July 27, 1987, D.C. . . . 1–066, 1–068, 1–087,
                                                 1–088, 1–180, 1–206, 3–024

Mattarroa *v.* East Sussex County Council, May 1, 1987. 1–055

Otter *v.* Norman [1989] A.C. 129; (1989) 153 L.G.Rev. 11, H.L. 1–013

Palmer *v.* Caledonian Railway Co. [1892] 1 Q.B. 823; 61 L.J.Q.B.
  552; 66 L.T. 771; 40 W.R. 562; 8 T.L.R. 502; 36 Sol.Jo. 425, C.A. . . . . . .
                                                                    1–268

R. *v.* Birmingham City Council, *ex p.* Ferrero (1991) 10 Tr.L.R. 129;
  (1991) 155 J.P. 721; (1991) 155 J.P.N. 522; (1991) 155 L.G.Rev.
  645; (1991) 3 Admin.L.R. 613; *The Independent*, May 24, 1991; *The
  Times*, May 30, 1991, C.A.; reversing (1990) 9 Tr.L.R. 148;
  (1990) 154 J.P. 601; (1990) 154 J.P.N. 508. . . . . 1–060, 1–167, 1–225
R. *v.* Home Secretary, *ex p.* Khawaja. *See* R. v. Secretary of State for
  the Home Department, *ex p.* Khera.
R. *v.* Humberside County Council, *ex p.* Bogdal [1992] C.O.D. 467;
  The Times, June 1, 1992. . . . . 1–055, 1–085, 1–225
R. *v.* Leicester County Council, *ex p.* Thompson, unreported, April 19,
  1991. 1–225
R. *v.* National Insurance Commissioner, *ex p.* Secretary of State for
  Social Services [1981] 1 W.L.R. 1017; (1981) S.J. 376; [1981] 2
  All E.R. 738, C.A. 1–117
R. *v.* Secretary of State for the Home Department, *ex p.* Khera; R. v.
  Secretary of State for the Home Department, *ex p.* Khawaja
  [1984] A.C. 74; [1983] 2 W.L.R. 321; (1982) 127 S.J. 137; [1983]
  1 All E.R. 765; [1982] Imm.A.R. 139, H.L.; affirming *sub nom.* R.
  v. Secretary of State for the Home Department, *ex p.* Khawaja
  [1992] 1 W.L.R. 625; (1982) 126 S.J. 294; [1982] 2 All E.R. 523,
  C.A.. 1–087
Rice *v.* Connolly [1966] 2 Q.B. 414; [1966] 3 W.L.R. 17; 130 J.P. 322;
  110 S.J. 371; [1966] 2 All E.R. 649, D.C. 1–106

Sharpe *v.* Wakefield [1891] A.C. 173; [1886–90] All E.R. Rep. 651; 60
  L.J.M.C. 73; 64 L.T. 180; 55 J.P. 197; 39 W.R. 561; 7 T.L.R.
  389, H.L. 1–040
Stevens (G.E.) (High Wycombe) *v.* High Wycombe Corporation
  [1962] 2 Q.B. 547; [1961] 3 W.L.R. 228; 125 J.P. 464; 105 S.J.
  570; [1961] 2 All E.R. 738; 13 P.&C.R. 106; 59 L.G.R. 390;
  [1961] R.V.R. 737. 1–130
Swallow *v.* London County Council [1916] 1 K.B. 224; [1914–15] All
  E.R. Rep. 403; 85 L.J.K.B. 234; 114 L.T. 368; 80 J.P. 164; 32
  T.L.R. 181; 14 L.G.R. 301; 25 Cox C.C. 295, D.C. 1–106
Swindells *v.* Cheshire County Council, *The Times*, February 18, 1993,
  D.C. 1–013, 1–040

W. (Minors) (Wardship: Evidence), *Re* [1990] 1 F.L.R. 203; [1990] F.C.R. 286; [1990] Fam. Law. 216; (1990) 154 J.P.N. 363; *The Times*, November 10, 1989, C.A.. 3–026
Warwickshire County Council *v.* McSweeney, unreported, December 8, 1988.. ....1–004, 1–040, 1–067, 1–091, 1–092, 1–176, 1–207
Welham *v.* D.P.P. [1961] A.C. 103; [1960] 2 W.L.R. 669; 124 J.P. 280; 104 S.J. 308; [1960] 1 All E.R. 805; 44 Cr.App.R. 124, H.L.; affirming *sub nom.* R. *v.* Welham [1960] 2 Q.B. 445; [1960] 2 W.L.R. 533; 124 J.P. 156; 104 S.J. 108; [1960] 1 All E.R. 260; 44 Cr.App.R. 79, C.A.. 1–148
Wooding *v.* Secretary of State for Social Services [1984] 1 W.L.R. 348; (1984) 128 S.J. 130; [1984] 1 All E.R. 593; (1984) 81 L.S.Gaz. 740; (1984) 134 New L.J. 236, H.L.. 1–117

PART 1

REGISTERED HOMES ACT 1984

(1984 c. 23)

Tables of Derivations and Destinations can be found at the end of the Act.

ARRANGEMENT OF SECTIONS

PART I

RESIDENTIAL CARE HOMES

Registration and conduct of residential care homes

SECT.
1. Requirement of registration.
2. Offence of carrying on home without registration.
3. Registration of managers, etc., and persons in control.
4. Registration in respect of small home registered under Part II.
5. Registration—general.
6. Death of only person registered in respect of home.
7. Inspection of registers.
8. Annual fee for registration.
8A. Annual return in respect of small home.
9. Refusal of registration.
10. Cancellation of registration.
11. Urgent procedure for cancellation of registration, etc.
12. Ordinary procedure for registration, etc., under Part I.
13. Right to make representations.
14. Decision of local authority.
15. Appeals.
16. Regulations as to conduct of residential care homes.
17. Inspection of homes.
18. Defences.

Provisions supplementary to Part I

19. Meaning of "relative".
20. General interpretation.

PART II

NURSING HOMES AND MENTAL NURSING HOMES

Interpretation

21. Meaning of "nursing home".
22. Meaning of "mental nursing home".

Registration and conduct of nursing homes and mental nursing homes

23. Registration of nursing homes and mental nursing homes.
24. Prohibition of holding out premises as nursing home, maternity home or mental nursing home.
25. Refusal of registration.
26. Regulations as to conduct of nursing homes and mental nursing homes.
27. Supplementary regulations.

28. Cancellation of registration.
29. Additional registration conditions.
30. Urgent procedure for cancellation of registration, etc.
31. Ordinary procedure for registration, etc., under Part II.
32. Right to make representations.
33. Decision of Secretary of State.
34. Appeals.
35. Inspection of mental nursing homes and visiting of patients.
36. Effect of cancellation or death on mental nursing home registration.

Miscellaneous and supplemental

37. Power to exempt Christian Science homes.
38. Ancillary provisions of Mental Health Act 1983.

PART III

REGISTERED HOMES TRIBUNALS

39. Preliminary.
40. Constitution of panels for chairmen and members.
41. Constitution of tribunals—general.
42. Tribunal for appeals relating to nursing homes (including maternity homes) and mental nursing homes.
43. Procedure of tribunals.
44. Staff for tribunals.
45. Fees, allowances and expenses.

PART IV

OFFENCES

46. Failure to register.
47. Failure to affix certificate of registration.
48. Breach of conditions as to registration.
49. Contravention of regulations.
50. Contravention of section 24.
51. Obstruction.
52. Bodies corporate and their officers.
53. Proceedings.

PART V

SUPPLEMENTARY

54. Service of documents.
55. Interpretation—general.
56. Regulations and orders.
57. Consequential amendments, transitional provisions, savings and repeals.
58. Extent.
59. Short title and commencement.

SCHEDULES

1. Consequential amendments.
2. Transitional provisions and savings.
3. Repeals.

An Act to consolidate certain enactments relating to residential care homes and nursing homes and Registered Homes Tribunals, with amendments to give effect to recommendations of the Law Commission.

[June 26, 1984]

General Note

Background

Pt. I of this consolidating measure provides for the registration, conduct and inspection of **1–002**
"residential care homes" (including small homes) which are establishments providing both board and personal care for persons who are in need of care by reason of old age, disablement, dependence on alcohol or drugs, or mental disorder. In their original form the provisions in Pt. I derive partly from the National Assistance Act 1948 and partly from the Mental Health Act 1959. Those provisions, together with subsequent amendments, were consolidated in the Residential Homes Act 1980. That Act was supplanted by a new code set out in Pt. I of Sched. 4 to the Health and Social Services and Social Security Adjudications Act 1983, and it is that Schedule which provides the most recent source of Pt. I.

Pt. II covers similar ground in respect of nursing homes and mental nursing homes. The original legislation on nursing homes was the Nursing Homes Registration Act 1927. This was followed by Pt. VI of the Public Health Act 1936 and the Nursing Homes Act 1963. The regulation of mental nursing homes began with the Mental Health Act 1959. Legislation relating to both sets of homes was consolidated in the Nursing Homes Act 1975. The 1975 Act was substantially amended by the Health Service Act 1980 and Pt. II of Sched. 4 to the Health and Social Services and Social Security Adjudications Act 1983. The 1983 Act did not repeal the whole of the legislation about nursing homes and mental nursing homes as it did for residential care homes, and so Pt. II reproduces the amended version of the 1975 Act.

Pt. III reproduces Pt. III of Sched. 4 to the 1983 Act, which established Registered Homes Tribunals to hear appeals relating to residential care homes, nursing homes and mental nursing homes. These tribunals superseded the tribunals previously constituted under the Child Care Act 1980 to hear appeals in respect of certain voluntary and private children's homes. Provisions relating to the registration of such homes can now be found in the Children Act 1989, ss.60(4), 63(11), Scheds. 5, 6.

Pt. IV creates a number of offences which relate to both registered and unregistered homes, and Pt. V contains supplementary provisions.

This Act, which incorporates the recommendations made by the Law Commission in Cmnd. 9115, is analysed by David Carson, "Registering Homes: Another Fine Mess?" [1985] *Journal of Social Welfare Law* 67–84 and by R. Brooke Ross, "Safeguarding and Promoting the Welfare of Residents? The Contribution of the Registered Homes Act in England and Wales" [1989] *Journal of Social Welfare Law* 262–276. The Social Services Inspectorate of the Department of Health has produced two reports on the operation of this Act: *Inspection of the Implementation of the Registered Homes Act 1984: Stage 1 The Impact on Registration Authorities* (1986) and *Certain Standards: Inspection of the Implementation of the 1984 Registered Homes Act* (undated). A British Association of Social Workers publication, *The Impact of the 1984 Registered Homes Act* (1986), looks at the effect that the Act has had on the workload of social services departments. Also see B. Holmes and A. Johnson, *Cold Comfort: The Scandal of Private Rest Homes* (Souvenir Press, 1988), which contains a first-hand account of conditions in a randomly selected number of residential care homes and Royal College of Nursing, *A Scandal Waiting to Happen?* (1992), which focuses on the provision of nursing care for elderly people in residential and nursing homes. Publications on the operation of the Registered Homes Tribunals are listed in the General Note to Pt. III of this Act.

The government has produced four documents in the "Caring for Quality" series which are intended to offer guidance and information on standards in residential care to registration authorities, proprietors, managers and users. They are *Guidance on Standards for Residential Homes for Elderly People* (HMSO, 1990); *Guidance on Standards for Residential Homes for People with a Physical Disability* (HMSO, 1990); *Guidance on Standards for the Residential Care Needs of People with Specific Mental Health Needs* (HMSO, 1992) and *Guidance on Standards for the Residential Care Needs of People with Learning Disabilities* (HMSO, 1992). For a model which has been devised by the Social Services Inspectorate to enable agencies responsible for providing residential care, and agencies concerned with inspection, to make qualitative evaluations of the performance of residential care homes, see *Homes are for Living In* (HMSO, 1989). Also see *Standards for the Residential Care of Elderly People with Mental Disorders* (HMSO, 1993) which focuses on those issues which are of particular importance in ensuring a good quality of care for elderly people with mental disorders.

Registration of small homes

In its original form this Act excluded from the requirement of registration an establishment **1–003**
which provided board and personal care for fewer than four persons, not including the persons carrying on the establishment and the staff in the establishment and their relatives. An opposition amendment to the Health and Services and Social Security Adjudications Bill to insert "3" and leave out "4" in the relevant provision of that measure was resisted by the government on the ground that "there would be a risk of bringing into registration homes of a primarily domestic character which were manifestly not intended to be brought within the

registration system and where it would be generally agreed that an institutional type of treatment with a registration system would be ... inappropriate and bureaucratically oppressive. It could also raise practical problems of enforcement which would undermine the capacity of local authorities to carry out their job properly for larger homes" (*per* the Under-Secretary of State for Health and Social Security, Standing Committee B, March 17, 1983, cols. 209, 210). The inability of local authorities, as registration authorities, to regulate these homes led to concern being expressed about the quality of care that some residents were receiving. There was also "some evidence of people who have been found unsuitable to run larger homes and declared unfit to do so continuing in business by reducing the numbers of residents to three per home and spreading them over a larger number of homes" (*per* Baroness Gardner of Parkes, *Hansard*, H.L. Vol. 529, col. 74). The government responded to these concerns through the Registered Homes (Amendment) Act 1991 which establishes a modified form of regulatory control for homes with fewer than four residents: see ss.1(4), (4A), (4B), 5(2A), 8(2), 8A, 9(2) and 10(*bb*) of this Act. Advice on the registration and inspection of small homes is contained in Department of Health Circular No. LAC (92)10.

Dual registration

1–004 The Residential Homes Act 1980 excluded from registration by local authorities any premises requiring registration as a nursing home or as a mental nursing home under the Nursing Homes Act 1975. A feature of this Act is that the restriction on dual registration has been removed and in certain circumstances an establishment has to be registered both as a residential care home and as a nursing or mental nursing home (see ss.1(3), (5)(*a*) and 23(2)). This change has been brought about partly because of the difficulty in distinguishing between the provision of personal care (s.1(1)) and nursing care (s.21(1)(*a*)), and partly because of a wish to avoid residents having to be transferred from one establishment to another as their physical condition deteriorates. The distinction between personal care and nursing care is considered in the note on "personal care" in s.1(1).

Although the whole of an establishment will be jointly registered, this need not prevent the two different types of care being provided in separate parts of the establishment, *e.g.* in a separate wing. Dual registration would also allow for a range of care, including terminal care, to be provided in the patient's own room. Guidance on dual registration is contained in paras. 3 to 13 of Annex B to DHSS Circular No. HC (84)21.

The effect of the dual registration provisions of this Act can be summarised as follows:
  (i) a residential care home which provides nursing care for one or more of its residents will have to be registered as a nursing home under Pt. II of this Act (s.1(3));
  (ii) a residential care home which provides nursing or other medical treatment for one or more mentally disordered patients will have to be registered as a mental nursing home under Pt. II (s.1(3));
  (iii) a residential care home which is also registered as a nursing home or mental nursing home must have either a doctor or a nurse as the "person in charge" of the home (s.25(1)(*f*));
  (iv) a nursing home or mental nursing home which is used solely as such is not registrable as a residential care home (s.1(5)(*a*));
  (v) a nursing home or mental nursing home which provides just board and personal care for four or more of its patients will also have to be registered as a residential care home under Pt. I (s.23(2));
  (vi) a nursing home or mental nursing home which provides just board and personal care for fewer than four of its patients must also register either as a residential care home or as a small home (s.4); and
  (vii) with a dually registered home the person registered in respect of it as a residential care home may be different from the person registered in respect of it as a nursing home (*cf.* ss.3 and 31(1)).

When an establishment is registered both as a residential care home and as a nursing home or mental nursing home, two registration authorities will be involved: the local social services authority (s.20(1)) and the health authority (s.23(3)). There is clearly a need for the authorities to co-operate over the registration procedures and to carry out joint inspections when this is called for. Local authorities and health authorities are required to establish joint consultative committees under s.22 of the National Health Service Act 1977 to advise the authorities on the planning and operation of services of common concern, and this machinery could be used to facilitate co-operation under this Act. The need for close co-operation between the two authorities and the desirability of joint inspections has been emphasised by the government in para. B7 of the Guidance Notes attached to DHSS Circular No. LAC (84)15. It has been reported that Bolton Social Services Department and Local District Health Authority have introduced a scheme under which private homes providing both care and nursing can be inspected and registered under a single process; see *Social Services Insight*, November 6, 1987, p. 8. Also see the reference to s.26(3)(*c*) of the National Health Service Act 1977 made in the note on "personal care" in s.1.

Codes of practice and registration authority guidance

Legal regulation can only be partially effective in controlling standards in institutions. As **1–005**
Klein and Day have pointed out there is a

> "crucial distinction between 'inputs' and 'outputs': between standards measured in terms of appropriate staffing levels and a suitable physical environment as against standards seen as the production of adequate levels of care of quality of life . . . Presumably, the 'input' standards are chosen on the assumption that these will promote, in turn, a desirable quality of care or life for consumers. But even if they are a necessary condition (which may be questionable), they are certainly not a sufficient condition. It is, for example, quite possible to imagine a nursing home for the elderly which has extremely high hotel standards and good staffing ratios, but where the atmosphere is repressive and where the clients are sunk in passive gloom" ("Two sides of the same coin" [1984] *Health and Social Services Journal* 285).

As only "inputs" lend themselves to legal regulation the government commissioned the Centre for Policy on Ageing to produce a code of practice for residential care homes and the National Association of Health Authorities to produce a handbook on the registration and inspection of nursing homes. The residential care homes publication is called *Home Life: a Code of Practice for Residential Care* (1984), copies of which can be obtained from Bailey Brothers and Swinfen Ltd., Warner House, Folkestone, Kent CT19 6PH. The nursing home handbook, *Registration and Inspection of Nursing Homes*, is obtainable from the NAHA, Birmingham Research Park, Vincent Drive, Birmingham B15 2SQ. Three supplements to this handbook have also been published.

Apart from fostering good practice in residential care homes and nursing homes, the two documents have also influenced the registration and inspection process. Speaking of the code for residential care homes, the Minister for Health said that

> "[its] principal effects will be twofold. First, those who carry out the inspections of registered homes will have regard to the code of practice in deciding what standards of care they should look for when inspecting a home and deciding whether to renew its licence. Secondly, the code will give guidance to local authorities about conditions that should be applied to the licence that registered homes have. By that I mean the legal conditions of registration for a particular home which a local authority might apply. We would imagine that the inspectors will consult the code of practice which will give them guidance about what legally binding conditions they might properly apply to a home and will apply them in appropriate cases. There will thus be a legally binding obligation on homes to conduct their affairs in a way that complies with the code of practice" (Standing Committee B to the Health and Social Services and Social Security Adjudications Bill, March 29, 1983, col. 387).

The two documents are also used as reference points by Registered Homes Tribunals when hearing appeals under this Act. "[*Home Life*] is not a statute to be rigidly applied without full consideration of all the circumstances. It is a guide to good practice to be applied as the foreword states 'positively and sensitively, in a way which makes sense in local circumstances and has regard to the standards achieved in [the authorities'] own homes' " (*Registered Homes Tribunal Decision* No. 11). Also note *Decision* No. 27 where the Tribunal said that the "purpose of the [NAHA] model guidelines is to provide some guidance, which, while not binding, should be given its appropriate weight."

Although neither *Home Life* nor the NAHA handbook is legally binding, the Secretaries of State for Social Services and Wales have asked "local authorities in carrying out their duties in relation to [residential care homes] to regard [*Home Life*] in the same light as the general guidance that we issue from time to time under our powers in s.7 of the Local Authority Social Services Act 1970" (*Home Life*, p. 7). Ministers have also stated that they "welcome the publication of the new handbook on registration and inspection produced by the . . . NAHA" (DHSS Circular No. HC (84)21, para. 8).

The approach adopted by Registered Homes Tribunals towards Guidelines produced by registration authorities can be gleaned from the following extract from *Decision* No. 127:

> "As to Guidelines, the Tribunal has these observations to make. They are, of course, minimum requirements in respect of important aspects of the conduct of residential Homes. However, they are simply that; they should not be inflexible and they do not have the force of law, although they are of persuasive authority. They provide a starting point. Local authorities are right to have formulae for Home-owners as guidance or ground rules. It is not only reasonable but essential that they constantly strive to improve standards. However, all minimum requirements are fraught with difficulties and in particular there will always be hard cases which come on the division if numerical formulae are used. Guidelines are to be afforded the appropriate weight, that is to say they are of great interest and importance in the maintenance and improvement of standards, and in many cases they are of persuasive authority. *Home Life*, for example, is of great persuasive authority. However, they should not be regarded as laying down any rules of particular application which the Tribunal is bound to follow. Having said this,

the Tribunal is very mindful of the fact that such Guidelines are designed properly to seek to encourage the up-grading of residential care Homes and to improve standards for the ultimate benefit and protection of all residents. This sentiment is entirely endorsed by the Tribunal which considers it right and proper for local authorities to aim to improve standards of care wherever possible."

Also see *Decision* No. 148 where the Tribunal, after emphasising that a policy document or guidelines produced by a registration authority must be interpreted flexibly, said that:

"a public authority which is entrusted with a discretion must exercise that discretion, and is not entitled to fetter its discretion by adopting rules from which it will never depart. And when exercising its discretion it must have regard to all relevant considerations which apply to the particular case it is considering. The law has reached this conclusion for a very good reason. When Parliament entrusts a public authority with a discretion, the public expects, and is entitled to expect, that the authority's skill and experience will be brought to bear on each individual case that comes before the authority."

In *Decision* No. 148 the Tribunal, on criticising the registration authority's failure to consult with home-owners before adopting new guidelines, said that "not only is it obviously desirable that a registration authority should take Home-owners into its confidence before making decisions that may seriously affect them, but there may well be a legal duty to consult". It is submitted that as there is no legal requirement for a registration authority to produce guidelines, there can be no legal duty to consult.

In *Decision* No. 86 the Registered Homes Tribunal said that:

"the lack of national guidelines of material standards, particularly with regard to space standards for residents, and also qualifications of senior staff in residential care Homes, would appear to be causing difficulties, because neighbouring authorities are adopting different standards, thereby creating indefensible anomalies. It is hoped that the DHSS in consultation with the Local Authority Associations will be able to agree national guidelines in the light of experience gained since the Registered Homes Act 1984 came into effect."

Registration and inspection

1–006 On November 11, 1990, the Secretary of State for Health published directions requiring local authorities to set up inspection units to inspect local authority residential care homes and homes registered under this Act, and to establish Advisory Committees in support of this activity. The directions were issued as an Annex to Department of Health Circular No. LAC (90)13. *Caring for People—Community Care in the Next Decade and Beyond: Policy Guidance* (HMSO, 1990), a government publication issued under s.7(1) of the Local Authority Social Services Act 1970 which places a duty on local authorities to act under the general guidance of the Secretary of State, outlines the requirement of all inspections undertaken by inspection units to be conducted in a consistent and even-handed manner. A report of the work of inspection units in ten local authorities can be found in Social Services Inspectorate, *Social Services Department Inspection Units: The First Eighteen Months* (HMSO, 1993).

"Authorities are reminded that the registration and inspection system is intended not only to ensure appropriate standards but also to enable constructive advice to be offered to help raise the quality of care. It also offers the opportunity to engage the co-operation of the private and voluntary sectors in developing a local strategy for residential and community care" (DHSS Circular No. LAC (88)15, para. 6).

In an Annex to *Tribunal Decision* No. 3 Mr. J. Hanson urged registration authorities to agree a registration procedure which enables private or voluntary homes to obtain a decision about a registration before incurring expenditure. The Annex reads as follows:

"NOTE ON THE REGISTRATION PROCEDURE ADOPTED BY CLWYD COUNTY COUNCIL

1. The procedural arrangements applied by the Clwyd County Council for the registration of residential care homes need immediate amendment.
2. It was clear that under the present procedures, any private or voluntary organisation proposing to establish a home, or extend an existing one, could not obtain any indication as to whether their proposals would be approved until the actual facilities were made available. This can—and did in the case of Care Concern—involve significant expenditure, often of a capital nature.
3. The decision in Clwyd County Council to register or otherwise is taken by Members and officers do not give any indication as to whether proposals by a private or voluntary agency are likely to be approved. Presumably, they do not feel able to do so because the decision is reserved to Members.
4. Elsewhere in England and Wales, it is often the Members who decide upon the revocation of a registration or a refusal but the decision about registration is delegated to officers who are then in a better position to indicate what an outcome is likely to be.

5. But whatever the procedure, no voluntary or private agency should have to incur excessive or significant expenditure before being given an indication as to whether the resultant scheme will be approved.

6. Where Members decide to make decisions about registration, they should be prepared to do so upon the submission of plans and proposals at a stage where excessive expenditure has not been committed. It is a relatively simple procedure to attach a condition to such decisions that certain requirements must be met.

7. In Clwyd, the position regarding delegation may need review but if Members continue to reserve to themselves the decision making powers under the Registered Homes Act 1984 (which, of course, they have a perfect right to do) they should agree a procedure which enables a private or voluntary home to obtain a decision about registration before incurring significant expenditure."

It is submitted that while it is highly desirable for owners to be given an indication as to whether their proposals are likely to be approved, it is not permissible for registration authorities to follow the advice contained in para. 6 of Mr Hanson's Annex. Registration can only be granted subject to the conditions set out in s.5(3) of this Act and it is therefore not possible for a registration certificate to contain a condition that certain requirements must be met by a specified date. Neither is it permissible for a registration authority to register an owner "in principle": see the General Note to s.5.

Community health services for residents of residential care and nursing homes

Local authority and National Health Service responsibilities, from April 1993, for funding community health services for residents of residential care and nursing homes who have been placed in those homes by local authorities are set out in Department of Health Circular No. LAC (92)24.

1–007

Rehabilitation of Offenders Act 1974

Under the Rehabilitation of Offenders Act 1974 (Exceptions) Order 1975 (S.I. 1975 No. 1023), arts. 3(*a*)(iii), 4(*b*), and 5, Sched. 1, Pt. III, paras. 6(*b*), 7 and Sched. 3, paras. 11(*b*), 12, the following provisions of the Rehabilitation of Offenders Act 1974 do not apply to procedures or proceedings under this Act:

1–008

(i) s.4(1) which relates to the way in which offenders whose convictions have become "spent" under the 1974 Act are to be treated and prohibits reference to such convictions in judicial proceedings. The effect of this exception is that "spent" convictions can be referred to in proceedings under this Act;

(ii) s.4(2) which is concerned with questions put to a person about his, or some other person's, "spent" convictions otherwise than in the course of judicial proceedings. The effect of this exception is that questions about a person's "spent" convictions can be put when the suitability of that person to run or to be employed in a residential care home, nursing home or mental nursing home is being assessed; and

(iii) s.4(3)(*b*) which provides that a conviction that becomes "spent" or a failure to disclose such a conviction shall not be a ground for dismissing a person from his employment. The effect of this exception is that a "spent" conviction, or failure to disclose such a conviction, can be used as a ground for dismissing a person from his employment in a home to which this Act applies.

The 1975 Order is applied to this Act by virtue of the Interpretation Act 1978, ss.17(2), 23(2). Also see the note on reg. 2 of the Residential Care Homes Regulations 1984 (S.I. No. 1984 No. 1345).

EXTENT

This Act does not apply in Scotland or Northern Ireland (s.58(1)). The application of this Act to the Isles of Scilly is governed by s.58(2), (3).

1–009

COMMENCEMENT

The Registered Homes Act 1984 (Commencement) Order 1984 (S.I. 1984 No. 1348) brought into force on January 1, 1985 all the provisions of this Act except s.1 so far as it relates to an establishment which is a school referred to in s.1(5)(f). Section 1, so far as it relates to such an establishment, was brought into force by the same Commencement Order on January 1, 1986.

TRANSITIONAL PROVISIONS

These are set out in Sched. 2 and S.I. 1984 No. 1345, reg. 4(2).

PARLIAMENTARY DEBATES

Hansard: H.L. Vol. 446, col. 485; Vol. 447, col. 142; Vol. 451, cols. 203 and 632; H.C. Vol. 61, col. 552.

The Bill was considered by the Joint Committee on Consolidation Bills (Sixth Report).

PART I

RESIDENTIAL CARE HOMES

GENERAL NOTE

1–010 Registration authorities for the purposes of this Part are the councils of non-metropolitan counties, metropolitan districts, the London Boroughs, the Common Council of the City of London and the Council of the Isles of Scilly: see ss.20(1), (2) and 1 of the Local Authority Social Services Act 1970. By virtue of s.2 and Sched. 1 to the 1970 Act the functions of a registration authority must be referred to the authority's social services committee.

Registration and conduct of residential care homes

Requirement of registration

1–011 **1.**—(1) Subject to the following provisions of this section, registration under this Part of this Act is required in respect of any establishment which provides or is intended to provide, whether for reward or not, residential accommodation with both board and personal care for persons in need of personal care by reason of old age, disablement, past or present dependence on alcohol or drugs, or past or present mental disorder.

(2) Such an establishment is referred to in this Part of this Act as a "residential care home."

(3) Registration under this Part of this Act does not affect any requirement to register under Part II of this Act.

[(4) Registration under this Part of this Act is not required in respect of a small home—

  (*a*) if the only persons for whom it provides or is intended to provide residential accommodation with both board and personal care are persons carrying on or intending to carry on the home or employed or intended to be employed there or their relatives, or

  (*b*) in such other cases as may be prescribed by the Secretary of State.

(4A) In this Part a "small home" means an establishment which provides or is intended to provide residential accommodation with both board and personal care for fewer than 4 persons, excluding persons carrying on or intending to carry on the home or employed or intended to be employed there and their relatives.

(4B) The references in subsections (4) and (4A) to the persons for whom residential accommodation is or is intended to be provided relate only to persons who are in need of personal care by reason of old age, disablement, past or present dependence on alcohol or drugs, or past or present mental disorder.]

(5) Registration under this Part of this Act is not required in respect of any of the following—

  (*a*) any establishment which is used, or is intended to be used, solely as a nursing home or mental nursing home;

  (*b*) any hospital as defined in section 128 of the National Health Service Act 1977 which is maintained in pursuance of an Act of Parliament;

  (*c*) any hospital as defined in section 145(1) of the Mental Health Act 1983;

  [(*d*) any community home, voluntary home or children's home within the meaning of the Children Care Act 1989];

  (*f*) subject to subsection (6) below, any school, as defined in section 114 of the Education Act 1944;

  (*g*) subject to subsection (7) below, any establishment to which the Secretary of State has made a payment of maintenance grant under regulations made by virtue of section 100(1)(*b*) of the Education Act 1944;

(h) any university or university college or college, school or hall of a university;

(j) any establishment managed or provided by a government department or local authority or by any authority or body constituted by an Act of Parliament or incorporated by Royal Charter.

(6) An independent school within the meaning of the Education Act 1944 is not excluded by subsection (5) above if the school provides accommodation for 50 or less children under the age of 18 years and is not for the time being approved by the Secretary of State under section 11(3)(a) of the Education Act 1981.

(7) An establishment to which the Secretary of State has made a payment of maintenance grant under regulations made by virtue of section 100(1)(b) of the Education Act 1944 is only excluded by subsection (5) above until the end of the period of 12 months from the date on which the Secretary of State made the payment.

AMENDMENTS

Subss. (4), (4A) and (4B) were substituted by the Registered Homes (Amendment) Act 1991, s.1(2).

In subs. (5), para. (d) was substituted for paras. (d) and (e) by the Children Act 1989, s.108(5), Sched. 13, para. 49.

DEFINITIONS

personal care: s.20(1).
disablement: s.20(1).
mental disorder: s.21.
nursing home: s.21.
mental nursing home: s.22.
relative: s.19.

GENERAL NOTE

This section provides a definition of those establishments which are required to be registered as residential care homes (including small homes) under the Act. It also permits an establishment to be registered both as a residential care home and as a nursing home or mental nursing home. If an establishment meets the criteria for registration it must be registered as a residential care home irrespective of what it might call itself, *e.g.* a hotel, boarding house, rest home, hostel, bed and breakfast establishment, or holiday home. 1–012

A registered residential care home which accommodates children is not a children's home for the purposes of Pt. VIII of the Children Act 1989 and does not therefore require to be registered under that Act (*ibid.* s.63(1)(5)).

For a description of the extent and nature of private residential care, see Malcolm Johnson, "Privatising Residential Care—A Review of Changing Practice and Policy" in H. Laming *et al.*, *Residential Care for the Elderly: Present Problems and Future Issues* (Policy Studies Institute, 1984), pp. 52–62 and Bob Hudson, "The rise and rise of private care" [1990] *Health Services Journal* 1520, 1521. A detailed case study of private residential care in Devon can be found in D. Phillips *et al.*, *Home from Home: Private Residential Care for Elderly People* (Social Services Monographs, University of Sheffield, 1988).

Subs. (1)

Registration: It is the person that is registered and not the premises: see the note on s.5(2). 1–013

Establishment: "The Tribunal considered s.1 of the 1984 Act which refers to an 'establishment' which must include all accommodation within that establishment. In determining the type and numbers of residents to be housed in the establishment for which it is or will be registered some rooms may be deemed to be suitable for a limited number of residents, but this does not mean that there are separate units within the establishment nor does it create a 'registered room.' It is the establishment which is registered" (*Decision* No. 130). It is possible for two physically separate establishments to exist on one site, each being registered under this Act: see *Tribunal Decision* No. 109. In *Decision* No. 146 the Tribunal concluded that a house and a lodge, "being within the same curtilage, and providing respectively and exclusively the accommodation and the board for the residents, cannot be regarded as anything other than one establishment". On appeal, the judge held that the Tribunal was fully entitled to reach such a conclusion: see *Harrison* v. *Cornwall County Council* (1991) 90 L.G.R. 81 at 97, C.A. Also see *Swindells* v. *Cheshire County Council, The Times,* February 18, 1993, D.C., where a bungalow was situated in the grounds of a house and shared "the same services, call bell, nursing staff and pathway" with the house. The Divisional Court held that the house and bungalow were one establishment and not two.

Reward or not: In *Decision* No. 13, the Tribunal has said that the financial viability of running a residential care home as a business is not a matter for consideration by a Registered Homes Tribunal. Compare this decision with *Decision* No. 136 where the Tribunal examined the financial viability of running a home when considering whether the joint owners of a nursing home were "fit persons" for the purposes of this Act and with *Decision* No. 14 where the Tribunal indicated that it would be prepared to take into account economic factors when considering the question whether a double room should be reduced to a single room. It is submitted that as neither this Act nor the Regulations made under it covers factors such as the economic viability of running a home as a business, such matters should not be considered by a Tribunal hearing an appeal under Pt. I or II of this Act. This was the approach adopted by the Tribunal in the following passage from *Decision* No. 109:

"So far as the financial concerns of the Appellants are relevant to the considerations of the Tribunal, reference was made to *Decision* Number 13 . . . heard on 10 March 1986 at the paragraph headed 'considerations' on page 2 of the Decision. This Tribunal accept the point that as s.1(1) of the 1984 Act includes the words 'whether for reward or not' and neither the 1984 Act nor the 1984 Regulations refer to the costs of running a Home nor the viability of the same as a business, that the financial aspect of the Home cannot be a matter which is taken into account by the Tribunal in deciding the heads of appeal nor can any comment be made in respect thereof. It is proper to add that both in the Guidelines and in *Home Life*, the attention of prudent management is drawn to those who are proposing to run Homes, but the Tribunal must be concerned with the life, health and well-being of the residents for whom care is the paramount consideration."

This approach did not find favour with the Tribunal in *Decision* No. 217. In this case the registration authority's statement of reasons supporting its decision to refuse an application for registration included the allegation that the home in question was marginally funded. On this point the Tribunal found that the registration authority "must prove on balance that the funding is so marginal that for the purposes of s.9 it renders the Appellant financially unfit or that the Home is unfit because the accommodation, staffing facilities or services are short for lack of finance". In addition to the reason given above, there are two further reasons to suggest that the approach adopted by the Tribunal in *Decision* No. 217 is misconceived. First, nowhere in this Act is the concept of financial unfitness recognised. Secondly, if the Tribunal finds on the evidence that a Home is unfit because the "accommodation, staffing facilities or services are short", then that finding is sufficient in itself for the purpose of an appeal. The fact that a shortfall in provision might, or might not, be due to a lack of finance is irrelevant.

Residential accommodation: Although this section does not cover accommodation provided for homeless people "many homeless people suffer from drug or alcohol abuse or the aftermath of mental disorder. If there are [such people] in a home or an establishment where they receive personal care, that establishment will be registrable on those grounds" (*per* the Under-Secretary of State for Wales, Standing Committee B on the Health and Social Services and Social Security Adjudications Bill, March 17, 1983, col. 206).

If residential accommodation is provided it does not matter whether the residents intend to stay for a long or short time (*Swindells* v. *Cheshire County Council, supra*). People who attend at a residential care home only during the day are not "resident" there (*Cotgreave* v. *Cheshire County Council, The Times*, July 9, 1992, D.C.): see further the note on s.5(3).

Board: This is defined in the *Oxford English Dictionary* as "food served at the table; daily meals provided in a lodging or boarding house according to stipulation; the supply of daily provisions". It would therefore appear to be the case that "board" is provided if the residents of a home are supplied with food which they cook for themselves. The Residential Care Homes Regulations 1984 are ambiguous on this point: compare reg. 10(1)(*l*) which refers to the supply of "properly prepared" food with reg. 10(1)(*k*) which is concerned with the provision of "facilities for residents to prepare their own food and refreshments". In *Otter* v. *Norman* [1988] 2 All E.R. 897, the House of Lords held that the provision of a daily "continental breakfast" was more than *de minimis* and constituted "board" for the purposes of s.7 of the Rent Act 1977. Note that the board *must* be accompanied by personal care if the establishment is to be registrable.

Personal care: This may include assistance with the residents' bodily functions: see s.20(1) and *Harrison* v. *Cornwall County Council* (1991) 90 L.G.R. 81, C.A. The Act is silent as to what other forms of assistance come within the scope of "personal care". The fact that residents are being cared for in residential accommodation would appear to suggest that what is being contemplated is no more than the sort of care that would be provided in a private home by a caring relative. This is the approach adopted by the DHSS in para. 3 of "Residential Homes for the Elderly: A Memorandum of Guidance" which was issued with Circular No. LAC (77)13:

"Residential Homes are primarily a means of providing a greater degree of support for those elderly people no longer able to cope with the practicalities of living in their own homes even with the help of the domiciliary services. The care provided is limited to that appropriate to a residential setting and is broadly equivalent to what might be provided by a competent and caring relative able to respond to emotional as well as physical needs. It includes for instance help with washing, bathing, dressing; assistance with toilet needs; the administration of medicines and, when a resident falls sick, the kind of attention someone would receive in his own home from a caring relative under guidance of the general practitioner or nurse member of the primary health care team. However, the staff of a Home are not expected to provide the professional kind of health care that is properly the function of the primary health care services. Nor should residential Homes be used as nursing homes or extensions of hospitals."

An approach based on the model of the caring relative does, of course, beg the question of what level and intensity of care a caring relative can be expected to provide. This question is especially relevant to the problem of attempting to differentiate between the "personal care" that is provided to the residents of a residential care home, and the "nursing" care that is given to patients in a nursing home or mental nursing home: see ss.21(1) and 22(1). The dictionary definition of a nurse is "a person, generally a woman, who attends or waits upon the sick; now especially one properly trained for this purpose" (*Oxford English Dictionary*), which is almost as wide as the definition most commonly used in the professional literature; see the note on "nursing" in s.21(1). As attending or waiting upon the sick is a task that almost every caring relative will perform at one time or another, what is the distinction between the type of nursing that would be allowable in a residential care home which is not also registered as a nursing home, and other nursing? It is suggested that registration authorities might wish to approach this problem by drawing a distinction between "household nursing" and "professional nursing". "Household nursing", which would be permissible in residential care homes, would cover those tasks which a caring relative could reasonably be expected to perform with the benefit of guidance from a general practitioner. They might include the taking of temperatures, changing simple dressings, the management of incontinence, and the dispensing of medication prescribed by a general practitioner. "Professional nursing", which could only be given in a registered nursing home or mental nursing home, would cover all other types of nursing including any technical procedures which require invasion of the body, *e.g.* injections, the use of specialised equipment, and general therapeutic procedures that would be beyond the competence of a caring relative, *e.g.* the management of bed sores. This approach, which relies on an examination of function rather than an identification of the status of the person providing the care, avoids having to classify establishments as nursing homes solely because a professionally qualified nurse who acts in a caring capacity either runs the establishment or is employed by it.

Advice to health authorities on the distinction between "personal care" and "nursing" is contained in paras. 3.48 to 3.50 of Pt. I of the NAHA Handbook, *Registration and Inspection of Nursing Homes*. The distinction, it is stated, "may in the end be a subjective decision, but it is thus firmly based on the professional advice of the designated senior nurse of the Registering Health Authority". The factors which should be taken into account by the designated senior nurse in reaching a decision on whether a person requires care or nursing are said to be, first, a situation where a resident's general health deteriorates to a level that needs constant nursing care and, secondly, where a resident's health is such that one or more of a range of procedures is required periodically over 24 hours. The procedures include the administering of medication by injection, frequent attention as a result of double or single incontinence and the dressing of an open or closed wound. The Handbook advises health authorities to exercise a degree of flexibility in their decision making in the light of the fact that the health of those receiving residential care may fluctuate from time to time. Para. 3.50 states that "a sudden deterioration in a resident's health, requiring extra nursing care, may not in itself mean that registration as a nursing home is appropriate".

In *Tribunal Decision* No. 40, one of the issues of contention was whether a residential care home was providing nursing care. A witness for the health authority referred to the NAHA advice and confirmed that, in his view, the distinction between a resident and a patient is based on the advice given by the designated senior nurse applying the formula set out in the Handbook. Evidence on behalf of the appellant was given by the general practitioner to all but one of the residents who took the view that "the responsibility for the care of a resident was that of a general practitioner and nursing care could be assessed by the district nurse attached to the practice if that should prove necessary". In its conclusions the Tribunal stated that the registration authority "was justified in its approach". Also see *Decision* No. 110 where the joint owner of a residential care home, who was a qualified nurse, gave an unsupervised injection of morphine to a resident. Although the question whether the home should have also been registered as a nursing home under Pt. II of this Act was not taken at the appeal, one of the expert members attached the following footnote to the Tribunal's decision:

"This appeal has served to highlight the extreme caution which needs to be exercised concerning the provision of 'nursing' care in a residential care Home setting. A degree of such nursing may be required and practised. However, it must be dealt with under the closest supervision. The role of the G.P., District Nurse, hospital staff, etc., is of very great importance, particularly in a sector where semi-skilled or unskilled staff are employed."

A definition of nursing home care and the circumstances in which such care may be necessary is contained in Annex 3 to *Managing Care: Guidance on assessment and the provision of social and community care* (Welsh Office, April 1991) which reads as follows:

"This Annex sets out some key components of nursing skills which may be deployed in assessment or treatment and care. A nursing home provides the kind of care which requires the skills of a qualified nurse or the supervision of a qualified nurse. NURSING SKILLS include the following:—

* Assessment of nursing needs and identification of problems which need skill intervention.
* Prescribing nursing care and delegating tasks to other members of the nursing team.
* Evaluating the effectiveness of the care prescribed.
* Teaching carers basic tasks which enhance their contribution to care.
* Communicating with the appropriate General Practice(s) and the other support services as and when required.
* Maintaining as far as possible the optimum level of health preventing deterioration, and when necessary providing terminal care.

NURSING CARE may be necessary in circumstances such as the following:—

Where a patient's general health deteriorates to a level that needs constant nursing care.

Where a patient's health is such that one or more of the following procedures is required periodically during 24 hours:—

* administration of medication by injection;
* dressing to an open or closed wound;
* feeding requiring nursing skills;
* basic nursing care of the type given to a bedfast or predominantly bedfast person;
* frequent attention as a result of double or single incontinence;
* intensive rehabilitation measures following surgery or debilitating disease which is likely to continue for more than a short period;
* management of complex prostheses or appliances;
* management of complex psychological or aggressive states requiring medical supervision.

The above list is neither comprehensive nor prescriptive. Such nursing interventions can be undertaken in a variety of settings including the patient's own home. However, when a registered home offers such services as a part of the facilities available and provided in the home, then the home which provides such services is a nursing home and must be registered under Part II of the Registered Homes Act 1984."

The term "personal care" includes counselling and general social work support. Thus, for example, a hostel for alcoholics which provided residents with counselling to help them overcome their addiction would come within the registration provisions of this Part. However, psychotherapeutic support to mentally disordered persons given by trained counsellors under medical supervision could only be provided in a mental nursing home: see s.22.

If an establishment is run as a nursing home or mental nursing home without it being registered as such, an offence is committed under s.23(1). Whenever a local social services authority considers that a residential care home might be providing nursing care which comes within the scope of "professional nursing" the district health authority should be consulted, and a joint inspection of the home carried out where this is felt to be appropriate. Note that the district health authority has a duty to make available to a local authority the services of any medical practitioner, dentist or nurse employed by it for the purpose of enabling the local authority to discharge its social services functions: see s.26(3)(c) of the National Health Services Act 1977. In *Tribunal Decision* No. 95 the registration authority assessed the dependency of the resident of a residential care home and found that she was in need of nursing care. The registration officer of the authority was informed that the resident's relatives did not wish her to be moved. The authority, on considering this plea, allowed the resident to stay. Although the motives that led the authority to take this decision are quite understandable, this Act does not provide for such a flexible approach in the absence of the home being dually registered.

A particular difficulty might arise with establishments which provide holiday accommodation for persons who are in the dependent categories. If personal care as well as board is provided the establishment would need to be registered as a residential care home or as a small home. Registration authorities might consider approaching this area of provision by only registering those establishments which provide "holiday" board and personal care to residents on a regular basis, although it has to be said that there is no statutory authority to permit this: see David Carson, "Registering Homes: Another Fine Mess" [1985] J.S.W.L. at 72.

Persons in need: If a child becomes a resident of the home the relevant registration authority and District Health Authority must be informed: see reg. 13 of the Residential Care Homes Regulations 1984. Regulations 14(2) and 16 are also concerned with child residents.

Old age: "We do not think that it is necessary or even prudent to define old age for the purposes of the registration system. We have a general conception of old age, but whether or not a person receives personal care in a residential home does not depend on the attainment of a specific age, but on his need for such care" (*per* the Under-Secretary of State for Wales, Standing Committee B on the Health and Social Services and Social Security Adjudications Bill, March 17, 1983, col. 201). The Wagner Review of Residential Care has recommended that religious or secular communities, which continue to provide a home for members who have become old or infirm, should not be deemed to be within the scope of this Act: see *A Positive Choice* (NISW, 1988), p. 59.

In *Decision* No. 204 the Tribunal adopted "the common-sense" meaning of the term "elderly" which is "generally accepted (*e.g.* by consultant geriatricians and by the Office of Population Census and Surveys), as meaning 'over retirement age', which means in effect over 65 for men and women".

Dependence on alcohol or drugs: The following advice to local authorities on registering establishments which are rehabilitating drug and alcohol misusers is contained in paras. 12 to 16 of DHSS Circular No. LAC (86)6:

"Particular attention needs to be given to the aims of establishments for the rehabilitation of people who have a dependency on drugs or alcohol and to apply the guidance with sensitivity to that kind of establishment. *Home Life* at subs.4.7 indicated how the general advice might be modified in relation to them. Experience of the effects of the Registered Homes Act 1984 on these establishments suggests the need for guidance additional to that provided in *Home Life*.

Home Life was written largely with elderly, physically handicapped and mentally disordered people in mind, many of whom have high dependency needs or require home-like surroundings. Those being rehabilitated from drug or alcohol misuse constitute rather different client groups. Unlike some of the others who may be likely to spend a longer time in residential accommodation—perhaps the remainder of their lives—misusers will be resident in rehabilitation houses for what will invariably be a temporary period, varying between three and 18 months.

Sharing rooms is sometimes an important aspect of their rehabilitation. It is important to encourage them to be more open to share and to be able to plan with others. It may not be necessary for the mobile residents in drug and alcohol rehabilitation houses, who are quite capable of using bathroom facilities, to have individual wash basins, provided there are adequate facilities available elsewhere in the building.

Since domestic work such as cleaning and cooking may be undertaken by residents as part of their rehabilitation, staffing levels may be different from those considered appropriate for some other groups. Some drug rehabilitation programmes require a rigid routine restricting contact with relatives and friends to help the resident break with the drug lifestyle and those connected with it. Such restrictions on freedom would form part of the 'contract' entered into by the resident on admission and would be reviewed regularly.

Again with staffing the objectives of the establishment need to be looked at to decide to what extent staff need to be there throughout the 24 hours. Where the residents' independence and decision-making is being developed as part of a rehabilitative programme it may be desirable *not* to have staff there for 24 hours a day, *provided* there are satisfactory arrangements for a member of staff to be contacted easily and available quickly in an emergency. Authorities should see that the arrangements are clearly set out for the staff and the residents."

Mental disorder: For a study of the provision of residential care homes for mentally handicapped people, see L. Hoyes and L. Harrison, "An Ordinary Life—Or an Imitation", *Community Care*, February 12, 1987, pp. 20–23.

It is an offence for a man to have unlawful sexual intercourse with a woman who is a mentally disordered patient and who is in his guardianship or otherwise in his custody or care as a resident in a residential care home as defined in this section: see Mental Health Act 1959, s.128(1)(*b*). Also note that under s.127(2) of the Mental Health Act 1983 it is an offence "for any individual to ill-treat or wilfully to neglect a mentally disordered patient who is for the time being subject to his guardianship . . . or otherwise in his custody or care".

Subs. (2)

Residential care home: A residential care home does not have to call itself by that name. It can continue to be known by whatever name it was using prior to registration, provided that it does not call itself a nursing home when it is not registered as such (s.23(1)). On the other hand, an establishment which is not required to be registered under this Act can call itself a residential care home.

1–014

Note that when s.2(5) of the Disabled Persons (Services, Consultation and Representation) Act 1986 is brought into force, the authorised representative of a disabled person residing in a residential care home may at any reasonable time visit him there and interview him in private.

Subs. (3)

1–015 Subs. (3), together with subs. (5)(*a*) and s.23(2), have the effect of requiring an establishment to be registered both as a residential care home and as a nursing home or mental nursing home if the establishment satisfies the relevant registration criteria: see the note on dual registration in the General Note to this Act.

Part II of this Act: i.e. ss.21 to 38.

Subs. (4)

1–016 This provision relieves from the requirement of registration small homes where the only residents are the persons running the home, their employees or their relatives.

Not required: Under s.4 a nursing home or mental nursing home which is registered under Part II of this Act has the option of registering as a residential care home or as a small home, if it is providing board and personal care for fewer than four residents in the dependent categories: see further paras. 23 and 24 of Annex A to Department of Health Circular LAC (92)10.

Small home: Is defined in subs. (4A).

Personal care: See subs. (4B).

Relatives: As defined in s.19.

Such other cases: See reg. 24 of the Residential Care Homes Regulations 1984.

Subs. (4A)

1–017 From April 1, 1993 (the commencement date of the Registered Homes (Amendment) Act 1991), it will be an offence to operate an unregistered small residential home which is not exempt from the requirement to register. Where an application has been made by that date the home will be deemed to be registered until such time as the application has been determined and any appeal rights exhausted: see s.2(3) of the 1991 Act.

Small home: This definition covers establishments caring for people under adult placement schemes: see paras. 15 to 17 of Annex A to Department of Health Circular No. LAC (92)10. Concern has been expressed over the consequences of this development: see Polly Neate, "No Room Under the Umbrella", *Community Care,* February 13, 1992, pp.20, 21.

Fewer than four persons: There is no requirement for the establishment to be "solely" or "mainly" used as a small home. If there are fewer than four persons in the dependent categories who are receiving board and personal care, the whole of the establishment is registerable as a small home even though the majority of residents are not receiving board and personal care.

Excluding . . . relatives: Relatives are excluded even though they might be in receipt of board and personal care.

Subs. (5)

1–018 Subsection (5) specifies the establishments which are not required to be registered as residential care homes.

For exemptions relating to homes registered under the Children Act 1989 and certain schools, see paras. 19 to 21 of Annex A to Department of Health Circular No. LAC (92)10.

Para. (a)

1–019 *Nursing home:* Only nursing homes and mental homes that are used *solely* for that purpose are excluded. If such a home provides board and personal care for less than four persons it has an option as to whether it registers as a residential care home or as a small home (s.4). If four or more persons fall into this category the home must also be registered as a residential care home (s.23(2)).

Para. (b)

1–020 *Hospital:* Defined in the 1977 Act as:

"(*a*) any institution for the reception and treatment of persons suffering from illness,

(*b*) any material home, and

(*c*) any institution for the reception and treatment of persons during convalescence or persons requiring medical rehabilitation,

and includes clinics, dispensaries and out-patient departments maintained in connection with any such home or institution."

Maintained in pursuance of an Act of Parliament: Thus privately run hospitals are excluded from the definition.

Para. (c)

1–021 *Community home, voluntary home or children's home:* These terms are defined in ss.53(1), 60(3) and 63 of the Children Act 1989.

Para. (f)

1–022 The effect of this paragraph and subs. (6) is to exempt from registration schools within the meaning of the Education Act 1944, except independent schools with 50 or fewer children which are not approved by the Secretary of State for Education and Science under s.11(3)(*a*) of the Education Act 1981. Such a school would need to be registered as a residential care home if it provides personal care for more than four boarders in the dependent categories. This paragraph did not come into force until January 1, 1986 (S.I. 1984 No. 1348).

Para. (g)
The effect of this paragraph and subs. (7) is to exempt from registration educational establishments which have received during the previous 12 months maintenance grants from the Secretary of State for Education and Science under s.100(1)(*b*) of the Education Act 1944. A list of such establishments is contained in Pt. I of Annex 1 to DHSS Circular No. (84)15.

1–023

Para. (j)
Provided . . . by a local authority: These establishments are listed in Pt. II of Annex 1 to DHSS Circular No. LAC (84)15.
Royal Charter: The fact that a body described itself as "Royal" does not necessarily mean that it is a body incorporated by Royal Charter. The Wagner Review of Residential Care has recommended that establishments operating under Royal Charter should be brought within the scope of this Act: see *A Positive Choice* (NISW, 1988), p. 59.

1–024

Subs. (6)
Age of 18 years: A person attains a particular age at the commencement of the relevant anniversary of the date of his birth: see the Family Law Reform Act 1969, s.9.

1–025

Subs. (7)
12 months from the date: Excluding the date on which the Secretary of State made the payment (*Dodds* v. *Walker* [1981] 1 All E.R. 609, H.L.). "Month" means a calendar month (Interpretation Act 1978, s.5, Sched. 1).

1–026

Offence of carrying on home without registration
2. If any person carries on a residential care home without being registered under this Part of this Act in respect of it, he shall be guilty of an offence.

1–027

DEFINITION
residential care home: s.1(1), (2).

GENERAL NOTE
A person who carries on an unregistered residential care home without being registered in respect of it commits an offence under this section. Therefore, if a residential care home is sold as a going concern, the registration does not run with it as the new owner will have to seek registration on his own account. An owner does not have to give notice to the registration authority that he is about to cease running his home. If a registration authority has reasonable cause to suspect that an unregistered residential care home is operating in its area it could use its power to enter and inspect the establishment: see s.17.
A conviction for an offence under this section does not automatically enable the registration authority to cancel the registration under s.9(*a*) on the ground that the convicted person is not a fit person to be concerned in carrying on a residential care home: see *Tribunal Decisions* No. 37 and 118.
Person: Or corporation (Interpretation Act 1978, s.5, Sched. 1). Re-registration is not required where there is a change in the ownership or control of a company already registered under this Act. The registration authority would need to be informed of such changes to satisfy itself that the company continues to be a "fit person". Also see the note on "person" in s.23(1).
If the person in control of the home is a company, note reg. 19(2) of the Residential Care Homes Regulations 1984.
Carries on: Both the manager and the person or organisation which controls the establishment are to be treated as carrying on the home (s.3).
This Part of this Act: i.e. ss.1 to 20.
Offence: Which, on conviction, could lead to a fine of up to level 5 on the standard scale (s.46(1)). For offences by corporations and their officers, see s.52.

1–028

Registration of managers, etc., and persons in control
3. Where the manager or intended manager of a residential care home is not in control of it (whether as owner or otherwise) both the manager or intended manager and the person in control are to be treated as carrying on

1–029

or intending to carry on the home and accordingly as requiring to be registered under this Part of this Act.

DEFINITION
residential care home: s.1(1), (2).

GENERAL NOTE

1–030   This section provides that where a residential care home is managed by one person and that person is not in control of it (whether as owner or otherwise), both the manager and the person in control of it are to be treated as carrying on the home and, accordingly, both are required to be registered in respect of it. Although there is no requirement for an applicant in respect of a residential care home to hold a professional qualification, registration can be refused on the ground that the applicant is not a "fit person" to be concerned with the running of such a home: see s.9(a) and *Tribunal Decision* No. 86, noted below.

A person can manage more than one home. In *Decision* No. 185 the Tribunal, in confirming the appropriateness of a person managing three homes, made the following general comments:

"Although the Tribunal has said in this particular case and on these very particular and special facts that the manager of two of these Homes could manage a third, this is not to say that it advocates or even necessarily approves of a manager managing two or more Homes. It must be reiterated that each case must be looked at on its merits. It might be totally inappropriate, for example, for the manager of a Home for elderly, incontinent and/or otherwise heavily dependent residents, to be manager of another Home at the same time, particularly one some distance from the other. The present decision is in no way a 'precedent' for the conclusion that, as a matter of general application, managers may manage more than one Home at a time."

The reasons why, in this case, the Tribunal considered that the registration authority should move away from its "one Home one manager" policy were:
(1) each home was very small;
(2) the homes were relatively close to each other;
(3) the residents were not in a high dependent category;
(4) most residents were mobile;
(5) the homes were well run by caring and dedicated people, and
(6) the appellants had enjoyed a long and constructive relationship with the registration authority.

In *Tribunal Decision* No. 94 the marriage breakdown between joint proprietors totally destroyed meaningful communication between the couple which had the effect of adversely affecting the residents in their care. Although no requirement exists for proprietors to disclose their marital status, or any change which might occur in that status, the Tribunal considered that "such a breakdown between partners of any kind, *i.e.* married persons or otherwise, should have been disclosed [to the registration authority]".

If the person in control of the home or, as the case may be, the manager of it intends to be absent from the home for more than a month, the registration authority has to be informed: see reg. 15 of the Residential Care Homes Regulations 1984. Where the person in control of the home is not also the manager of the home he must visit the home on the occasions specified in reg. 19 of the 1984 Regulations.

Manager: In *Decision* No. 48, the Tribunal was concerned with the interpretation of the term "manager". The Tribunal concluded its decision by stating:

"We are conscious of the fact that the parties to this Appeal were hoping that we should be able to give some guidance as to the meaning of 'manager' for the benefit of other local authorities or persons seeking registration under the Act; we do not feel able to do this. Each case must be decided on its merits looking in particular at the functions of the proposed manager, the hours spent on the premises, the employment structure of the Home and in the light of those and other facts giving the word manager its normal everyday meaning making a decision as to whether that person is 'the manager' or not."

In *Decision* No. 185 the Tribunal said that regs. 9(3) and 10 of the Residential Care Homes Regulations 1984 assisted them in understanding the meaning of "manager". Beldam L.J., speaking in *Jones* v. *Director of Public Prosecutions, The Times,* June 4, 1992, D.C., said that exercising control was a requirement of "managing".

In *Decision* No. 86 the registration authority refused to register a person as the manager of a residential care home on the ground that she was unfit because she did not comply with a requirement set out in its operational manual that the person in day to day control of the home should be in possession of a recognised qualification. Although the Tribunal supported the authority in its effort to raise the standard of independent homes in their area and considered that the requirement for qualifications was desirable for all senior staff who are to be appointed, they considered that it was reasonable to make an exception and depart from the strict qualification requirement because the person in question was experienced, had undertaken training, was continuing to attend courses, and had shown herself to be capable of undertaking the duties of manager. The Tribunal described this case as "not a precedent to be followed without due caution and careful consideration". A lack of sufficient qualifications was a ground for refusing to register a manager in *Tribunal Decision* No. 196.

The definition of "manager" in *Home Life*, p. 13 as someone who "may be the responsible person in charge of day-to-day care, or may be concerned solely with business or financial affairs of the home" was relied on by the Tribunal in *Decision* No. 135. In this case the Tribunal decided that the manager of the residential care element of a dually registered home for 30 patients and 30 residents was not an unfit person because of the fact that he had no qualifications relating to social work or residential care and because his main role was to manage the business affairs of the home. The Tribunal also found that the manager had a "significant involvement in the day to day delivery of care" by virtue of the fact that he had regular contact with the matron of the nursing home and was fully involved in the social activities of residents. It is submitted that this decision relates to the particular facts of the case and is of no general application. For the training, qualifications and experience required of the "responsible person in charge of the day-to-day running" of a residential care home, see para. 5.9 of *Home Life*.

Owner: This refers to the ownership of the business which controls the operation of the home. The owner of the business need not necessarily own the building in which the business is carried on. There can be more than one owner (Interpretation Act 1978, s.6(c)).

Person: Or corporation (Interpretation Act 1978, s.5, Sched. 1). Also see the note on "person" in s.2.

Registered: The functions of the person registered in respect of a home are set out in regs. 9 and 10 of the Residential Care Homes Regulations 1984.

[Registration in respect of small home registered under Part II

4.—(1) A person who— 1–031
(a) is required to be registered under this Part in respect of a small home, and
(b) is registered under Part II of this Act in respect of the same premises,

may apply to be registered under this Part as if the home were not a small home.

(2) If he does so the provisions of this Part have effect as in relation to a home which is not a small home.]

AMENDMENT
This section was substituted by the Registered Homes (Amendment) Act 1991, s.1(3).

DEFINITION
small home: ss.1(4A), 20(1).

GENERAL NOTE

This section provides the registered owner of a nursing home or mental nursing home which 1–032
provides board and personal care, but not nursing care, to less than four residents with the option of registering the premises under this Part as if the number of such residents exceeded four. If the owner exercises this option he would be covered against situations where the number of such residents accommodated in the home fluctuated above and below the limit of four provided for in the definition of "small home" in s.1(4A). If the option is not exercised an application for registration as a small home must be made.

A nursing home or mental nursing home which is registered in this way prior to the coming into force of the Registered Homes (Amendment) Act 1991 is governed by s.2(4) of that Act:
"Where immediately before the appointed day [of April 1, 1993] a person is registered in respect of an establishment by virtue of section 4 of the Registered Homes Act 1984 (optional registration in respect of small homes also registered under Part II), the registration shall have effect thereafter as if granted on an application made under section 4 as substituted by this Act. This applies whether or not the establishment is one in respect of which registration is required by virtue of this Act."
Also see paras. 23 and 24 of Annex A to Department of Health Circular No. (92)10.

Subs. (1)

Person: Or corporation (Interpretation Act 1978, s.5, Sched. 1). 1–033
Part II: i.e. ss.21 to 38.

Subs. (2)

Provisions of this Part have effect: If the application is refused the person carrying on the home 1–034
will commit an offence under s.2, if he continues to provide board and personal care for residents.

Registration—general

1–035 **5.**—(1) An application for registration under this Part of this Act shall be made to the registration authority and shall be accompanied by a registration fee of such amount as the Secretary of State may by regulations prescribe.

(2) Subject to sections 9, 12 and 13 below, on receipt of an application for registration and of the registration fee the registration authority shall register the applicant in respect of the home named in the application and issue to him a certificate of registration.

[(2A) In the case of an application for registration in respect of a small home, the registration authority may waive the whole or part of the registration fee; and in such a case the references in subsections (1) and (2) above to the registration fee shall be construed as references to such registration fee (if any) as may be payable.]

(3) It shall be a condition of the registration of any person in respect of a residential care home that the number of persons for whom residential accommodation with both board and personal care is provided in the home at any one time (excluding persons carrying on or employed at the home and their relatives) does not exceed such number as may be specified in the certificate of registration; and the registration may also be subject to such other conditions (to be specified in the certificate) as the registration authority consider appropriate for regulating the age, sex or category of persons who may be received in the home.

(4) The registration authority may from time to time—
   (*a*) vary any condition for the time being in force in respect of a home by virtue of this Part of this Act; or
   (*b*) impose an additional condition,

either on the application of a person registered in respect of it or without such an application.

(5) If any such condition for the time being in force in respect of a home by virtue of this Part of this Act is not complied with, any person registered in respect of the home shall be guilty of an offence.

(6) The certificate of registration issued in respect of [a home other than a small home] shall be kept affixed in a conspicuous place in the home; and if default is made in complying with this subsection, any person registered in respect of the home shall be guilty of an offence.

AMENDMENT
Subs. (2A) and the words in square brackets in subs.(6) were inserted by the Registered Homes (Amendment) Act 1991, s.1(4).

DEFINITIONS
registration authority: s.20(1), (2).
prescribe: s.20(1).
residential care home: s.1(2), (2).
personal care: s.20(1).
small home: ss.1(4A), 20(1).

TRANSITIONAL PROVISIONS
See regs. 4 and 6(2) of the Residential Care Homes Regulations 1984.

GENERAL NOTE

1–036 This section provides that an application for registration in respect of a residential care home must be made to the local social services authority for the area in which the home is situated, and must, subject to subs. (2A), be accompanied by the prescribed fee. On receipt of the application the authority can either make a proposal to refuse it (s.9) or to grant it subject to conditions (subs. (3)). The authority is also given a power to amend the conditions of an existing registration (subs. (4)). Where the authority proposes to refuse the application, or to amend an existing registration, or to grant an application subject to conditions which have not been agreed with the applicant, written notice of the proposal and the reasons for it must be given to the applicant or to the registered person (s.12) who must be given an opportunity to make representations to the authority about the proposal (s.13). A decision of the registration authority may be appealed against to a Registered Homes Tribunal (s.15(1)).

The person registered in respect of a residential care home commits an offence if he fails to comply with a condition of registration (subs. (5)) or if he fails to place the certificate of registration in a conspicuous place (subs. (6)). The conditions that can be attached to a registration and enforced through this section are limited to matters relating to age, sex, category or number of persons who are to reside at the home. Other matters are covered by the Residential Care Homes Regulations 1984: see especially regs. 6, 10, 11, 13, 14, 15, 16 and 19. A breach of these regulations can be enforced under the procedure set out in reg. 20.

In *Decision* No. 153 the Tribunal made the following attempt to "analyse and define" registration:

"Registration, for the purposes of the Registered Homes Act 1984, is the culmination of a process designed to ensure, in the considered opinion of a local authority exercising its statutory powers under the Act and subordinate legislation, that the person/s whose name/s appear/s on the registration certificate and on the register has/have satisfied all the requirements of the authority as to the fitness of those persons named, and as to the suitability and fitness of the premises to be used as the registered care home. A register is a public record, being an official or formal written list, regularly kept and maintained, recording names/events/transactions. It can be a book in which such a list is written or included. Registration is an inscription or entry in such a register."

In *Tribunal Decision* No. 185 the registration authority had purported to register an owner "in principle". The Tribunal described this practice as follows:

"This appears to be a device used by the Respondents whereby a 'middle way' is adopted. In effect owners are registered in advance of certain requirements to be complied with, for example, when fire precautions have been completed. At that stage they would be given a certificate. Owners could, of course, demand a certificate, and similarly they could be prosecuted for running a Home without such a certificate. However, the philosophy of the Respondents appears to be that they will not prosecute under s.2, and that, whilst of course they would not generally agree to a Home running without a certificate, yet in these special cases, a judgment having been taken that the residents are in no immediate risk (for example as fire precautions are not completed), they recognise the practicality and reality of the situation."

The practice of registering "in principle" was described by the Tribunal as being "curious" and "very unsatisfactory". It is also, it is submitted, of dubious legality. As was pointed out by the Tribunal in *Decision* No. 153, registration is the cumulation of a process. This Act does not provide for a "halfway house" of registration "in principle" and registration authorities would be most unwise to collude with the operation of unregistered homes.

The responsibilities of registration authorities under this Act were considered in the following passage from *Tribunal Decision* No. 66:

"It is of the greatest importance that all registration authorities should appreciate that registration is by no means a formality. This is clear from . . . ss.5, 9, 12 and 13 which set out the grounds on which a registration authority is entitled to refuse or to impose conditions on registration, and from [reg. 2 and Sched. 1 to the Regulations] which require an applicant for registration to supply a large quantity of information. The legislature's intention in conferring these powers and imposing these duties is obvious—to endeavour to ensure that no Home is registered and therefore entitled to admit residents unless the danger of it turning out to be an unsatisfactory Home has been eliminated as far as possible. Bearing this in mind, registration officers should regard it as part of their duty to counsel applicants in depth before recommending registration. Particularly, they should investigate with applicants the matters which, as experience has shown, most frequently give rise to difficulties after registration. The financial viability of the project ranks high among these difficulties, as there can be no doubt that many cases of poorly equipped and maintained Homes, understaffing, regimented routines and failure to keep adequate records stem from lack of money necessary to provide an adequate service for residents."

For an account of the role of registration officers in attempting to maintain a quality of care in residential care homes, see N. Grindrod, A. Leigh and S. Smith, "Private Care, Public Concern", *Community Care*, January 1, 1987, pp. 18, 19.

The residents of a residential care home cannot by agreement relieve the person carrying on the home or the registration authority of his statutory duties. This is not to say that the residents' agreement should be ignored: see *Tribunal Decision* No. 55.

"A registering authority must have regard not only to the present situation but also to a situation which may well arise with the passage of time in any Home": see *Tribunal Decision* No. 33 and *Avon County Council* v. *Lang* [1990] C..D. 365, noted under subs. (3).

Subs. (1)

1-037 *Application for registration:* Which must contain the information specified in the Residential Care Homes Regulations 1984: see reg. 2 and the note thereto. The registration authority should involve itself with prospective proprietors well before a formal application for registration is made. The matters which could be discussed during pre-registration consultation are set out in s.6 of *Home Life: A Code of Practice for Residential Care*: see the General Note to this Act. A description of the pre-registration procedure adopted by Dorset County Council can be found in [1984] *Health and Social Services Journal* 287. Also see the British Association of Social Workers publication, *Practice Notes for Social Workers and Registration Officers Working with the Private and Voluntary Residential Sector* (1984), which, at para. 3.2.3., gives guidance to registration officers on the points that they should discuss with prospective proprietors and Jenyth Worsley, *Good Care Management: A Guide to Setting Up and Managing a Residential Home* (ACE Books, 1992), an Age Concern publication which offers guidance to proprietors and managers. "Authorities should respond to prospective applicants' queries as far as they reasonably can, while ensuring that the registration fees are paid as soon as responding to an enquiry would amount to a stage in the processing of an application" (DHSS Circular No. LAC (88)15, para. 5). The need for registration authorities to adopt a registration procedure which enables an applicant to obtain a decision about a registration before incurring expenditure was emphasised by Mr J. Hanson in his Annex to *Tribunal Decision* No. 3: see the General Note to this Act under *Registration and inspection*.

The application is made in respect of a particular home: see s.2. In *Decision* No. 12 the Tribunal found as a question of law that a person cannot be registered in respect of a property which he does not own and in which he cannot carry on a residential care home.

Made to the registration authority: "When an application has been duly made in accordance with s.5(1) . . . we consider that an entitlement to a decision immediately arises having regard to the terms of s.5(2)": see *Tribunal Decision* No. 88.

Registration fee: See reg. 3 of the Residential Care Homes Regulations 1984. An annual fee is also payable under *ibid.* reg. 5.

Subs. (2)

1-038 *Subject to section 9:* The registration authority can refuse to register the applicant on any or all of the grounds set out in s.9.

Registration fee: The registration authority is under no obligation to register an applicant who has not paid the registration fee.

Shall register: Note the mandatory terms of this provision. In *Decision* No. 197 the Tribunal said that the registration authority by s.5(2) "were under a duty to register unless there were good reasons for not doing so. However, from the evidence adduced, the Respondents appear to have acted contrary to this tenet; they seems to have sought reasons as to why the Appellant's Home should be registered, not justification as to why it should NOT be registered".

The register must be available for public inspection (s.7) and contain the information specified in Sched. 3 to the Residential Care Homes Regulations 1984.

If the applicant appeals to a Registered Homes Tribunal against a condition which the registration authority proposes to attach to the registration, registration cannot take place until the appeal is either determined or abandoned (s.14(3)).

The applicant: It is the person that is registered and not the premises. "The Act speaks, throughout, of the registration of persons 'in respect of' a Home; it does not, as its short title may be taken to imply, require or contemplate the registration of premises": *per* the Tribunal in *Decision* No. 171.

Certificate of registration: Which must be displayed in a conspicuous place (subs. (6)). The registration authority does not have the power to issue a temporary certificate of registration. A certificate of registration once issued does not remain in force for any particular period, but remains in force until such time, if ever, as it is varied or discharged or added to in pursuance of the powers contained in this Act: see *Avon County Council* v. *Lang* [1990] C.O.D. 365.

> "A registration certificate is a document confirming registration of the owner/manager of the Home, and showing to the world the numbers of persons for whom residential care is provided. It can also contain conditions such as the authority considers appropriate for regulating the age, sex or category of persons who may be received in the Home. It must be issued by the authority . . . for display in the Home in order to show to anyone visiting the Home that the person/s named thereon is/are legally authorised to run the Home and that it is, as a consequence, a registered Home within the Act. It is evidence that the person/s named are registered persons. Failure to affix such a certificate in the Home constitutes an offence under s.47": *per* the Tribunal in *Decision* No. 153.

Subs. (2A)

1-039 *Waive the whole or part of the registration fee:* See paras. 6 and 7 of Annex A to Department of Health Circular No. LAC (92)10.

Subs. (3)

In *Avon County Council* v. *Lang, supra*, Rose J. stated that as the contents of a certificate of registration are capable of forming the basis of a criminal offence the conditions attached to a certificate must be in a simple and concise form and free from uncertainty or ambiguity. His Lordship held that it was not permissible for a registration authority to state in a registration certificate that the number of residents permitted by the registration might vary on the happening of a specified contingency. An example of this approach would be the use of a formula such as "eleven residents permitted but this to be reduced to ten when Mrs X. leaves". It would be equally impermissible to state in a registration certificate that the number of residents would depend upon the occupancy of a double bedroom, *e.g.* a registration for 22/23 residents (see *Tribunal Decisions* No. 106 and 179).   **1–040**

Rose J. also held in the *Lang* case that a registration authority (and a Tribunal on appeal), when exercising its powers under this provision, is entitled to take into account the particular circumstances of potential as well as actual residents. The decision that gave rise to this appeal is *Tribunal Decision* No. 99. In its concluding remarks the Tribunal stated that it appreciated

"the conflicting considerations often faced by a registration authority; on the one hand it is expected positively and confidently to apply its policies without suspicion of weakness or favouritism, but on the other hand it has to do so in a sensible way that takes account of the circumstances of each individual case, and therefore may appear to be discriminatory. The final decision must always be a matter of judgment and not, as it rather appears to have been in this case, one of purely arithmetical calculation".

Shall be a condition: There have been two High Court decisions relating to the imposition of conditions on a first registration under this subsection and the variation of existing conditions under subs. (4). They are *Warwickshire County Council* v. *McSweeney* (unreported, December 8, 1988, *per* Roch J.) and *Isle of Wight County Council* v. *Humphreys* (1991) 90 L.G.R. 186, *per* Hutchison J. The combined effect of these decisions is:

(1) the imposing of conditions is a derogation from the primary duty of the registration authority to grant a registration application unless one of the grounds of refusal set out in s.9 exists. Consequently the provisions which give the registration authority power to impose a condition must be interpreted restrictively (*McSweeney*);

(2) the correct interpretation of subss. (3) and (4) of this section is that the power to impose conditions is limited to those cases set out in subs. (3). The power of the registration authority to attach conditions to the registration is therefore limited to regulating the age, sex or category of persons who may be cared for in the home (*McSweeney*);

(3) a registration authority when exercising its powers under this section in relation to the imposition of conditions on a first registration or the variation of existing conditions is not bound in law to base its decision on the criteria for the refusal of a registration set out in s.9 (*Humphreys*); and

(4) if a registration authority has determined upon a general policy on the registration of homes in their area they must state it publicly for the information of all concerned and must, despite their policy, apply their minds properly to the circumstances of each individual case in order to decide whether the policy should be applied in that particular case or whether there are grounds for reaching a decision at variance with the policy (*Humphreys*).

In the *Humphreys* case the registration authority had a policy of refusing to agree to the variation of the conditions of registration of homes so as to increase the number of residents, on the ground that there was no need for more beds in its area and that to allow an increase would be detrimental to both owners and residents. In upholding the right of the authority to have regard to this policy when either imposing or considering a variation of a condition Hutchison J. considered the question, "By what yardstick is the authority's entitlement to impose conditions as to numbers to be judged?" His Lordship suggested

"that the answer is likely to be found by having regard to the general principles governing the exercise of a discretionary power by bodies in whom discretion, apparently unfettered, is imposed . . . The authority must act not capriciously but within the rules of reason and justice, not according to private opinion . . . according to law and not humour. It is to be, not arbitrary, vague and fanciful, but legal and regular. Those well known words, it will probably be recognised, come from the speech of Lord Halsbury L.C. in *Sharpe* v. *Wakefield* [1891] A.C. 173 at 179".

If the authority proposes to grant the application subject only to conditions which the applicant specified in his application, or which have been subsequently agreed with the applicant, the requirement for the authority to give the applicant notice of the proposal is dispensed with (s.12(2)) and the decision to grant the application has immediate effect (s.14(3)). Note that in *Decision* No. 27, the Tribunal said that "an authority should not impose requirements which are too far out of line with those of most authorities in the country. If an authority does go down this road it should be prepared to justify its requirements with convincing evidence when it is taken to appeal": also see *Decision* No. 61, noted below.

The judgment in the *McSweeney* case does not affect a registration authority's powers to specify requirements under reg. 20(1)(a) of the Residential Care Homes Regulations 1984 or reg. 15(4) of the Nursing Homes and Mental Nursing Homes Regulations 1984.

Numbers of persons: In *Decision* No. 127 the Tribunal made the following observations on the registration authority's guidelines which stated that the maximum number of residents in a residential care home should be 30:

"The Tribunal is satisfied that the Respondent's policy, founded on its collective experience and strong belief that the quality of care is enhanced and promoted by smaller, rather than larger, units (which, in its opinion, ensure the individuality of residents, provide better interaction between residents, and residents and staff, provide a more stimulating environment and continuity of care for residents and blend into the neighbourhood), is a good one, and generally to be encouraged. However, the guideline of 30 as a maximum number (recognising the need for homes to be economically viable) is, the Tribunal feels, unnecessarily inflexible and fails to take account of other factors, for example, that in a hotel-mode Home there can be small group living arising naturally from the numbers of residents, and that there does not necessarily need to be a move towards smaller Homes to achieve this. So much depends on the choice of the residents, particularly those who are less dependent."

In this case the Tribunal allowed an appeal to increase the number of residents from 40 to 46. In *Decision* No. 61 the Tribunal found that there was nothing in this Act or the Regulations to suggest that a registration authority had an implied power to impose a condition limiting the number of residents in a home to "twelve patients plus two on a review basis". The purported purpose of the condition was to keep the use of two rooms as double rooms under review. Such a condition would fall foul of the principle established in *Avon County Council* v. *Lang, supra.* Also see the note on reg. 10(1)(b) of the Residential Care Homes Regulations 1984.

For whom residential accommodation is provided: In *Cotgreave* v. *Cheshire County Council, The Times,* July 9, 1992, the Divisional Court held that elderly people who came with their carers only during the day to a residential care home were not "resident" there. Their presence in the home did not therefore count for the purpose of determining whether the number of residents in the home exceeded the figure contained in the certificate of registration.

People whose stay in the accommodation is temporary are to be treated as resident there: *Swindells* v. *Cheshire County Council, The Times,* February 18, 1993, D.C. *Per* Staughton L.J.:

"The application of the Act cannot, in my judgment, vary according to the intention of the person who is occupying accommodation. Many of the people who are persuaded by relatives to enter residential care homes are not themselves at all sure that they want to stay there very long; and some quite soon form an intention to leave as soon as they can. That is not a matter of importance to the application of the Act. It is the accommodation which has to be residential; and if residential accommodation is provided it does not matter whether the occupier intends to stay for a long or a short time."

Does not exceed such number: The annual fee payable by the person in control of the home is based on this number: see reg. 5(1) of the Residential Care Homes Regulations 1984. In *Decision* No. 143 the Tribunal confirmed the decision of the registration authority to reduce the maximum number of residents permitted to live in the home, so as to conform with its policy guidelines, when the home changed hands.

Category: In *Decision* No. 63 the Tribunal doubted the validity of a condition which limited the use of a residential care home for mentally handicapped people "resident within the administrative county of West Glamorgan". It is submitted that such a condition would be invalid and incapable of enforcement as the categories of residents set out in para. (3)(g) of Sched. 1 to the Residential Care Homes Regulations 1984 are limited to questions relating to the age and physical and psychological disabilities of residents.

Subs. (4)

1–041   This provision enables the registration authority to vary a condition of registration or to impose an additional condition. The variation or imposition can be made on an application by the registered proprietor or without such an application. In the former case there is no appeal to a Registered Homes Tribunal under s.15 upon a refusal by the registration authority to agree to the variation or imposition: see below. The registration authority's power to vary or impose a condition is governed by the decisions of the High Court in the *McSweeney* and *Humphreys* cases, noted under subs. (3).

The registration authority may: The authority has a discretion not to alter the status quo.

Vary . . . or impose: On a variation or imposition proposed by the authority, notice of the authority's proposal and the reasons for it must be given to the registered person (s.12(4), (5)). Thereafter the provisions of ss.13 to 15 apply. A registration authority has no power to charge a fee when agreeing to vary a condition of registration on the application of the registered person: see the note to reg. 3 of the Residential Care Homes Regulations 1984.

Additional condition: Only the type of condition referred to in subs. (3) may be attached to the registration, whether by agreement between the parties or otherwise. There is therefore no lawful authority for the imposition, *inter alia*, of conditions relating to the prohibition of fee increases or the development of the site: see *Tribunal Decisions* No. 68 and 88.

Application of a person registered: In Coombs v. Hertfordshire County Council (1991) 89 L.G.R. 774, Kennedy J., in affirming the decision of the Tribunal in *Decision* No. 115, held that on an application by a registered proprietor pursuant to this provision to vary a condition of registration (or to impose an additional condition), there is no right of appeal to a Registered Homes Tribunal under s.15(1)(*a*) upon a refusal by the registration authority to agree to the variation (or imposition). Section 15(1)(*a*) only provides a right of appeal in respect of a proposal *by the registration authority* to vary a condition of registration or to impose an additional condition. The only recourse available to a registered proprietor on a refusal by a registration authority to agree to his proposal for a variation or imposition is to make a fresh application to the registration authority to register the establishment. If the application is refused the decision of the registration authority could be tested by means of an application to the Tribunal. When a registration authority refuses an application to vary a condition, on the application of the registered person, the grounds on which it may refuse to vary the condition are those set out in s.9: see *Tribunal Decision* No. 125.

Subs. (5)

Condition: The conditions attached to a registration should be unambiguous because a prosecution will not succeed unless it can be shown that there has been a clear breach of a condition: see *Avon County Council* v. *Lang* [1990] C.O.D. 365, noted under subs. (3).

1–042

Guilty of an offence: Which, on conviction, could attract a fine of up to level 4 on the standard scale (s.48). For a defence, see s.18.

Subs. (6)

Conspicuous place: It is submitted that the certificate of registration should be fixed in a place where it can be easily seen by staff, residents and visitors.

1–043

Guilty of an offence: Which, on conviction, could attract a fine of up to level 2 on the standard scale, and a further fine of £5 for each day on which the offence continues after conviction (s.47(1)). For a defence, see s.18.

Death of only person registered in respect of home

6. Where—

1–044

(*a*) one person only is registered under this Part of this Act in respect of a residential care home; and

(*b*) that person dies,

his personal representatives or his widow or any other relative of his may for a period not exceeding four weeks from his death, or such longer period as the registration authority may sanction, carry on the home without being registered in respect of it.

DEFINITIONS
   residential care home: s.1(1), (2).
   relative: s.19.
   registration authority: s.20(1).

GENERAL NOTE

This section enables persons to continue to run a residential care home for a limited period on the death of a sole registered proprietor. If a registered person became incapable of running a home in an acceptable manner as a result of illness, the registration authority would have to consider taking steps to cancel the registration under s.10(*a*).

1–045

Widow: Or widower (Interpretation Act 1978, s.6).

Four weeks from his death: The date of the death of the registered person should be disregarded in calculating this period (*Dodds* v. *Walker* [1981] 2 All E.R. 609, H.L.).

Inspection of registers

7. The registers kept by a registration authority for the purposes of this Part of this Act shall be available for inspection at all reasonable times, and any person inspecting any such register shall be entitled to make copies of entries in the register on payment of such reasonable fee as the registration authority may determine.

1–046

DEFINITION
   registration authority: s.20(1), (2).

General Note

1–047   Each registration authority is required to keep registers of those establishments which it has registered as residential care homes. This section provides that these registers must be available for inspection and copying by the public. The particulars which are to be set out in the registers are specified in reg. 7 and Sched. 3 to the Residential Care Homes Regulations 1984. Although a registration authority may charge a person a fee for making a copy of the register, no fee can be charged for an inspection of the register.

At all reasonable times: In the context of this section it would be reasonable to make the registers available during office hours.

Annual fee for registration

1–048   **8.** [(1)] The Secretary of State may by regulations—
(a) require persons registered in respect of residential care homes to pay an annual fee of such amount as the regulations may specify; and
(b) specify when the fee is to be paid.

[(2) In the case of registration in respect of a small home, the registration authority may waive the whole or part of the annual fee; and in such a case the reference in section 10(b) below to the annual fee shall be construed as a reference to such annual fee (if any) as may be payable.]

Amendment
Subs. (2) was inserted by the Registered Homes (Amendment) Act 1991, s.1(5).

Definitions
residential care home: s.1(1), (2).
small home: ss.1(4A), 20(1).

General Note

Subs. (1)

1–049   *Regulations:* See reg. 5 of the Residential Care Homes Regulations 1984.
Annual fee: A separate registration fee is also under s.5(2).

Subs. (2)

1–050   *Waive the whole or part of the annual fee:* See paras. 6 and 7 of Department of Health Circular No. LAC (92)10.

[Annual return in respect of small home

1–051   **8A.**—(1) The Secretary of State may by regulations require a person registered under this Part in respect of a small home to make an annual return to the registration authority.

(2) Provision may be made by the regulations as to the contents of the return and the period in respect of which and date by which it is to be made.]

Amendment
This section was inserted by the Registered Homes (Amendment) Act 1991, s.1(6).

Definition
small home: ss.1(4A), 20(1).

General Note

1–052   *Regulations:* See the Residential Care Homes Regulations 1984, reg. 25 and Sched. 4.
Annual return: See Department of Health Circular No. LAC (92)10, Annex A, para. 11 and Appendix 2.

Refusal of registration

1–053   **9.** [(1)] The registration authority may refuse to register an applicant for registration in respect of a residential care home if they are satisfied—
(a) that he or any other person concerned or intended to be concerned in carrying on the home is not a fit person to be concerned in carrying on a residential care home;

(b) that for reasons connected with their situation, construction, state of repair, accommodation, staffing, or equipment, the premises used or intended to be used for the purposes of the home, or any other premises used or intended to be used in connection with it, are not fit to be used; or

(c) that the way in which it is intended to carry on the home is such as not to provide services or facilities reasonably required.

[(2) The registration authority may refuse to register an applicant for registration in respect of a small home only if they are satisfied that he or any other person concerned or intended to be concerned in carrying on the home is not a fit person to be concerned in carrying on a residential care home.]

AMENDMENT
Subs. (2) was inserted by the Registered Homes (Amendment) Act 1991, s.1(7).

DEFINITIONS
registration authority: s.20(1), (2).
residential care home: s.1(1), (2).
small home: ss.1(4A), 20(1).

GENERAL NOTE
This section, which "exists for the protection of both present and future occupants of a residential care Home" (*Tribunal Decision* No. 103), sets out the criteria which enable a registration authority to refuse to register an applicant for registration in respect of a residential care home. The grounds for refusal can be categorised as matters relating to the person or persons intended to carry on the home, the nature and condition of the premises, the nature of the services intended to be provided and the way in which the home is to be conducted. Registration in respect of a small home can only be refused if the registration authority is satisfied that the applicant or any other person concerned with running the home is not a fit person (subs. (2)). When a registration authority proposes to refuse a registration application it must give the applicant notice of the proposal (s.12(3)) and the reasons for it (s.12(5)). The applicant then has 14 days to inform the authority whether he wishes to make representations about the proposed refusal (s.13(1)). If the applicant does not wish to make representations the authority can proceed to refuse the application (s.13(2)(*b*)). If the applicant does wish to make representations the authority cannot make a final decision on the proposal until it has considered the applicant's representations (s.13(2)(*a*)), as long as they are made within a reasonable time (s.13(3)).

1–054

In *Decision* No. 102 the Tribunal considered two possible interpretations of this section:

"The first is that s.9 gives a registration authority only one opportunity to refuse to register an applicant for registration, which opportunity it may exercise on any or all of the grounds set out in subss. (*a*), (*b*) and (*c*). The second interpretation is that the section gives an authority three opportunities for refusal, which it may exercise *seriatim* on the grounds set out in subss. (*a*), (*b*) and (*c*)."

It is submitted that the Tribunal was correct in preferring the first interpretation. The consequences of this interpretation are that

"when an authority gives the reasons for its decision as required by r.5(2) [of the Registered Homes Tribunal Rules 1984], it nails its colours to the mast, and if the mast is shot away on appeal it cannot fall back on new colours and a new mast. In other words the authority's statement of reasons carries the corollary that it has no other reasons for refusal and will therefore register if its reasons are held [to be] inadequate or unjustified on appeal".

A registration authority's decision to refuse an application for registration takes effect immediately (s.14(3)). An appeal against the decision can be made to a Registered Homes Tribunal (s.15(1)).

May: When exercising its discretion under this section the registration authority must have regard to all relevant considerations which apply to the particular case it is considering and must not fetter its discretion by adopting rules from which it will never depart: see *Decision* No. 148 where the Tribunal said that "the public expects, and is entitled to expect, that a registration authority will use its skill and experience to examine each case individually in order to assess [the applicant's] fitness. If an authority does not do this, public expectations are disappointed because suitable applicants may be rejected without examination".

"It seems to us that the use of the word 'may' in s.9 must be construed as being purely permissive. We do not accept that the word means, in the context, 'may or may not' for we very much doubt that Parliament would have intended to confer a discretion in favour of registration in circumstances where a registration authority must first have become satisfied of unfitness in terms of para. (*a*) or (*b*), or of an inadequacy of the kind and degree described by para. (*c*)" (*Tribunal Decision* No. 103).

Satisfied: It is for the registration authority to be positively satisfied as to the matters contained in para. (*a*), (*b*) or (*c*) and not for the applicant to convince the authority: see *Tribunal Decision* No. 141.

Refuse to register: The authority must give the applicant written notice of its decision together with a note explaining his right of appeal to a Tribunal (s.14(1), (2)). A record of the reasons for the decision should be made at the time when it is made, so that in the event of an appeal the authority will be able to comply with r. 5(2) of the Registered Homes Tribunal Rules 1984.

Para. (a)

1–055
He or any other person: On an appeal to a Registered Homes Tribunal, it is for the registration authority to establish to the Tribunal's satisfaction on the balance of probabilities that the relevant person is unfit and not for that person to prove that he is fit: see *Tribunal Decision* No. 136. The person can be a corporation (Interpretation Act 1978, s.5, Sched. 1).

Concerned in carrying on the home: In *R. v. Humberside County Council, ex p. Bogdal* (1992) 11 B.M.L.R. 46 at 54, Brooke J. said that a person could be fit to be involved in the home in a small way but not fit to "carry on" the home and that the registration authority needs "to be satisfied about the person who will be carrying on the home in the sense that he or she will have control or direction of the home". A person "concerned in carrying on the home" could include a person who is concerned with financial and administrative arrangements through being a partner in the business of running the home, even though he was not involved in the day to day care of residents: see *Tribunal Decision* No. 35. Also see *Decision* No. 114 where the Tribunal found that the separation of a husband from his wife was an "artificial and a temporary expedient" to distance himself from the running of the home. The occasional provision of small services to residents was deemed to be insufficient evidence of any real involvement in the running of the home in *Decision* No. 84.

Fit person: Having regard to the fact that the objective of a residential care home is to provide care which is broadly equivalent to what a competent and caring relative would provide: see the note on s.1(1). In *Decision* No. 191, the Tribunal stated that a conclusion that an applicant is not a fit person "directly concerns the capacity of a person, as distinct from matters concerning the physical features of premises and the adequacy of a person's intentions with regard to the manner of carrying on a Home (which are matters dealt with under s.9(*b*) and (*c*))". Note, however, that in *R. v. Humberside County Council, ex p. Bogdal, supra,* Brooke J. said that he was persuaded that it could well be the way that it was intended to carry on a home under s.9(*c*) which might influence the way an authority decided fitness of a person under s.9(*a*). In *Bogdal* an application for registration was made in conjunction with a company which specialised in running care homes. Registration was agreed on the understanding that the applicant would play only a subsidiary and background role. Responsibility for running the home was to be that of the company acting through a manager and an assistant. His Lordship refused an application for a judicial review of the decision of the registration authority to cancel the registration of the applicant on the departure of the company. Also see *Tribunal Decision* No. 141 where an inexperienced owner's action in employing an experienced consultant on a management support contract influenced the Tribunal in rejecting the registration authority's submission that the applicant was not a fit person because he lacked awareness of a proper relationship between owner and manager.

Because of the potential serious consequences for all concerned following a finding of unfitness the Tribunal, in *Decision* No. 182, said that it would expect registration authorities "to present a clear, consistent and structured case, supported by reliable and creditable evidence".

Department of Health Circular No. LAC (91)4 sets out the procedure for checking with the police the possible criminal background of applicants for registration as owners or managers of residential care homes. The Rehabilitation of Offenders Act 1974 does not apply to applicants for registration: see the General Note to this Act. A failure to disclose a conviction in an application form for registration was a factor in determining that the applicant was not a "fit person" in *Decisions* No. 151 and 200. To aid registration authorities in their task of judging the fitness of applicants, the Department of Health keeps a list of persons and companies whose registration in respect of a residential care home, a nursing home, a mental nursing home, or a children's home has been cancelled after the commencement of this Act. The Department of Health sends a copy of the current list to each registration authority at quarterly intervals. Registration authorities have been asked to notify the Department of every occasion when a registration has been cancelled and also when a magistrate has made an order under s.11. Notification has been given in para. 7 of Department of Health Circular No. LAC (89)12 that the list is being extended to include the names of people whose application for registration has been refused on or after September 1, 1989, on the ground that he was not a fit person to run a home. It is not sufficient for a registration authority to declare that an applicant is not a "fit person" solely on the ground that his name appears on the Department of Health list: full reasons must be given. If the applicant intends to accommodate children in the home, the authority can also make use of the "Consultancy Service" operated by the Department. This service could inform the authority if anything were known about the applicant which would point to his unsuitability for having a position of authority over children: see further DHSS Circular No. HC (84)21, Annex B, para. 35.

In *Decision* No. 76 the Tribunal, offered the following general comments on the meaning of "fit person":

> "There is no statutory definition of a 'fit' or 'unfit' person. It is probably much easier to recognise the quality of fitness than to attempt to define it. However, the words 'trust', 'integrity', 'uprightness', 'honourable', and 'truthful' spring to mind. A fit person is one who can be trusted, in whom one has confidence, who acts according to high principles. It follows that a person will be unfit if he or she is untrustworthy or dishonest. The Act requires that a proprietor of a care Home be such a fit person, since the elderly people in their care are often frail and vulnerable and the person in control of them is in a powerful position to exploit that frailty. It is imperative that residents' well-being must be assured and that they must be protected from harm. It is a high standard that the law requires . . ."

The issue of trust was also emphasised by the Tribunal in *Decision* No. 209:

> "Dictionaries turn up various synonyms for integrity and honesty: soundness, uprightness, accuracy, truth, sincerity, virtue, honour, being of good principle, probity, faith, straightforward, open, true, frank, trusty, reliable, genuine and so on. Trust goes to the very heart of the relationship which should exist between a proprietor and manager, between the manager and the most vulnerable residents, between the manager and those vulnerable peoples' relatives, who trust the manager to look after and care for them. This is self evident, since the welfare of those defenceless and susceptible residents are so much at the mercy of those who care for them. Any failure to exercise truth and honesty could have dire consequences for residents. Perhaps most importantly of all, the question of the honesty and integrity of a manager is vital to the relationship which exists between such a person and the local authority. Local authorities are under a statutory duty to protect those who cannot protect themselves. They must be able to trust people who have been registered. They are able to make few visits to Homes generally, and must be able totally to rely on the veracity of records, accounts, statements, to which they are referred, for example, staffing rotas, accounts of accidents, medication—in short, on what the manager (or her staff under for authority and control) says or writes."

The "absolute necessity" of proprietors of registered homes of all kinds having the highest principles of probity and candour regarding matters connected with the running of the home was emphasised by the Tribunal in *Decision* No. 131 and in *Decision* No. 110 the Tribunal said that "fitness . . . in the sense used in the Act, must imply more than competence at a job". In *Decision* No. 1 the Tribunal, in deciding that a person was not a "fit person", said that "our main concern was the vulnerability of residents in a residential care home, the extent they have to rely on the staff, and the very high standard of integrity required of the staff". Also see *Decision* No. 189 where the appellant had been convicted of two counts of obtaining money from the Department of Social Security by deception. In this case the Tribunal said that:

> "both the registration authorities and this Tribunal have an over-riding responsibility to ensure that only persons of integrity are entrusted with the care of elderly and vulnerable residents. This is necessary to ensure not only that there is no danger of residents being financially prejudiced, but also to ensure that those running a Home can be trusted in all matters of its administrations."

McCowan J., in the unreported case of *Mattarooa v. East Sussex County Council*, May 1, 1987, said that reg. 9 of the Residential Care Homes Regulations 1984, which is concerned with the conduct of homes, "throws some light on the expression in the Act 'fit person' which, as I have indicated, is undefined". Also see paras. 5.9 and 6.4 of *Home Life*.

In *Decision* No. 37 the Tribunal said that a conviction under s.2 of this Act for carrying on a home without registration did not automatically mean that the convicted person cannot be allowed to be concerned with the running of a residential care home. However, a "conviction [under s.2] goes to the credibility of a person" (*Tribunal Decision* No. 118). A conviction "has to be considered in the content of whether to allow the applicant to run the . . . Home would be likely to affect adversely the interests of the residents" (*Tribunal Decision* No. 6), although it is not necessary to establish a connection between the crime and the possible adverse effect it might have on the care and well-being of the residents (*Tribunal Decision* No. 76). Also note *Decision* No. 88 where the Tribunal said that it would be wrong to hold that a conviction for dishonesty spoke for itself and was sufficient reason to find that a person was not a "fit person". In over-ruling the registration authority's intention to deregister an owner who had been convicted of theft from a nursing home the Tribunal said that "it was proper to enquire into the broad circumstances of and surrounding the offences as well as the past history of [the applicant] and other matters to enable us to assess her fitness or otherwise in terms of s.9(*a*)".

The question whether a registration authority is entitled to regard an applicant for registration as being unfit because he faces a serious criminal charge came before the Tribunal in *Decision* No. 137. The Tribunal accepted the applicant's submission that this section:

"does not put the onus on an applicant to establish his fitness. The registration authority must be positively satisfied of his unfitness before it is entitled to refuse to register him, and because of the fundamental principle that everyone is presumed innocent until proved guilty, an authority cannot be so satisfied simply because an applicant has been charged with serious offences. The principle that a person is presumed innocent until proved guilty is not an empty phrase. It contains the truth that many people charged with crimes are acquitted, sometimes because they are completely, not just technically, innocent."

Also note *Decision* No. 213 where the Tribunal said that the quashing of a conviction on appeal restores the presumption of innocence and that in such circumstances "there is no distinction to be drawn between the quashing of the conviction and an acquittal".

In *Decision* No. 122 one of the reasons cited by the registration authority to support its contention that the appellant was not a fit person was the fact that licensing justices had refused to grant him a licence on the ground that he was not a fit and proper person to hold the licence. The Tribunal concluded that:

"the finding of the magistrates as to the unfitness of the appellant is evidence on which it can rely. In reaching this decision it does not go behind the justice's decision nor seek to discover what was in their minds when they reached this decision. The Tribunal's decision is based on the written and oral evidence at the Tribunal hearing of the officers who were in court at the relevant time and who gave evidence, which the Tribunal believed, that the Appellant was not on the premises at all times, as he had promised when originally being given the licence."

A decision of a Registered Homes Tribunal confirming a registration authority's judgment that a person is not fit to carry on a particular residential care home does not automatically render that person as being unfit to run any other home that he or she might own. However, in *Decision* No. 93 the Tribunal said that "it is clearly relevant in considering the fitness of a person to run one Home to consider his conduct in running another". Also note *Decision* No. 77 where the Tribunal allowed an appeal against a refusal to register in respect of an applicant who had lost a previous appeal against deregistration (*Decision* No. 22) on the ground that she was not a "fit person".

Examples of situations where Registered Homes Tribunals have found that a person is not a "fit person" include convictions of theft from employers (*Decisions* No. 1 and 10); convictions of obtaining property by deception which related directly to a patient in a nursing home (*Decision* No. 180); entering into financial arrangements with mentally handicapped persons which were not to their benefit and which were inconsistent with the way in which anyone to be entrusted with the care of individuals should conduct themselves (*Decision* No. 74); a lack of management skills and an unwillingness to spend on staff to ensure adequacy and continuity, together with the failure to keep proper records of staff (*Decision* No. 93); a history of misconduct, including the sexual harassment of members of staff of a local authority establishment (*Decision* No. 101); a past history of participation in a failed business enterprise (*Decision* No. 114); the making and production to a registration authority of a false record with intent to deceive (*Decision* No. 131); a "total disregard for the law . . . a total disregard for, and ignorance of, the duties and responsibilities associated with being a person in control of a residential care Home . . . [and] a total lack of understanding of the importance of the registration process" (*Decision* No. 122); a contravention of s.5(3) by admitting additional residents into inadequate accommodation together with a failure to keep adequate records and unsatisfactory financial dealings with residents (*Decision* No. 130); shortcomings in regard to staffing and a deplorably low standard of general administration of the home (*Decision* No. 144); a failure to comply with the Regulations in relation to the administration and storage of drugs and the reckless administration of an unprescribed drug (*Decision* No. 110); a failure to keep adequate records and to comply with the fire authority's requirements (*Decision* No. 62); a lack of managerial skills (*Decision* No. 53); a person who was employed full time as a teacher lying about his availability to attend at the home (*Decision* No. 66); using deception to introduce hospital patients to a home (*Decision* No. 41); too great a degree of regimentation, unacceptable methods of control and training of residents, an obsession with routine and hygiene, set and rigid ideas of management, a lack of patience and sensitivity, and a lack of a sufficient understanding of the needs of residents (*Decision* No. 45); an owner being in debt and without means (*Decision* No. 177); dealing with residents "in a manner which was far too authoritarian without sufficient regard to their individual requirements and without regard to their need for independence and meaningful activity and without sufficient regard to maintaining their status as independent adults" (*Decision* No. 9); and where the person had a history of depressive illness and it was felt by the Tribunal that the chances of a re-occurrence of the illness were high (*Decision* No. 18). In *Decision* No. 6 the Tribunal did not cancel the registration of a proprietor who had served a two-month prison sentence on being found guilty of two counts of personation at a Parliamentary election. The Tribunal based its decision on its findings that the proprietor acted more out of inexperience than out of deliberate intention to obtain votes, that she had gained no personal benefits from the crime, and that the residents would not be adversely affected by the proprietor continuing to be registered.

Para. (b)

Situation: Home Life, at para. 3.2, states that: **1–056**
"many residential care homes have been sited inappropriately. Registration authorities, in dealing with all new applications, should therefore ensure that the location and the surrounding environment are suited to the stated aims of the establishment, and at the same time provide a setting which enables the home to blend into the neighbourhood. The accessibility of local facilities, community health services and public transport should be considered fully prior to registration."

The question whether registration should be refused because of the isolated position of the property was considered by the Tribunal in *Decision* No. 64. The Tribunal said that:
"the second ground for refusing registration is the isolated location of the property. The Tribunal visited the property and there is no doubt that it is isolated, set in remote countryside and far from habitation. The Respondents are quite right to be concerned. Proximity to local facilities is important if residents are to have the maximum opportunity to have normal contact with the community. In practice, however, this proximity needs to be immediate if frail and less than fully ambulant people are to take advantage of it. For most in this category a distance of even a quarter of a mile may be a severe deterrent. The Tribunal therefore had to consider whether the respondents were justified in regarding the isolated location as sufficient grounds for refusal to register. The private sector does offer choice, and the Tribunal does not accept the view of the Respondents, that, in practice, few, if any, residents make personal choice in the matter of residential care homes. There will undoubtedly be some who will enjoy, and deliberately choose, an isolated rural location, particularly in a house with considerable grounds. If too few make that choice, the enterprise will fail, but potential failure arising from an inadequate research of the market should not be a reason for refusal. The Appellant is to be congratulated on achieving an understanding with the local bus company to provide scheduled services from the end of [the home's] drive. Should this fail, and it may, the provision of a mini-bus service becomes very important. On balance therefore the Tribunal concluded that the isolated location of [the home] is not sufficient reason, of itself, to justify a refusal of registration. It will be up to the Appellant to show during the first year of operation that she has fully grasped the issue of isolation and has sought to alleviate it."

Emphasis on the desirability of potential residents having the choice of living in a rural environment was also made by the Tribunal in *Decision* No. 2, but in *Decision* No. 5, an appeal against a refusal to register was turned down on the ground that, having regard to the situation of the premises, the residents would be unduly restricted in their independence and ability to move freely outside the house. It is submitted that the Tribunal in *Decision* No. 145 identified the correct approach to the issue of location when it concluded that "those who occupy residential care Homes are entitled to the opportunity to preserve their independence for as long as possible". In this case the registration authority successfully argued that the distance between the home and ordinary amenities was so great that residents would be denied their independence of choice in relation to their use of those amenities and that the residents could not become part of the local community. Also see *Decision* No. 49 where the Tribunal allowed a home to be located on a cramped and uneven site located next to a commercial bus station and which suffered from a degree of isolation from local amenities. The Tribunal has yet to develop a consistent approach to the question of location.

Accommodation: Recommendations from the DHSS on the provision of residential accommodation for elderly, mentally handicapped and physically handicapped people are contained in Local Authority Building Notes No. 2 and 8, and Circulars No. LASSL (75)19 and LAC (86)1. Also note the following advice contained in paras. 9 and 10 of DHSS Circular No. LAC (86)6:

"Circular LAC (86)1 was issued in January to clarify the status of Local Authority Note No. 2—'Residential Accommodation for Elderly People'. The circular reviews the design guidance available to authorities and reiterates the need for flexibility in design matters, above all in the matter of whether bedrooms should be provided on the basis of single or more-than-single occupancy. The circular also includes a reminder that the Building Note is intended to apply more to newly built premises than to converted or adapted premises. Decisions on the size and occupancy of bedrooms will need to take account not only of the design and construction of the premises but also of the levels of dependency of prospective residents and their likely needs for privacy and care. These are points made also in paragraphs 2.5 and 3.1 of *Home Life* which stress the need for guidance on physical features to be interpreted flexibly in case of older buildings and suggest that special reasons should be expected when there are more than two people to a bedroom. Both the guidance notes issued with LAC (84)15 (paragraph A41) and *Home Life* indicated that the standards in the Housing Corporation's 'Design and Contract Criteria—Shared Housing Supplement' would generally be acceptable where establishments to which it applied were registered as residential care homes."

A "Draft Guide to Fire Precautions in Existing Residential Care Premises", prepared by H.M. Inspectorate of Fire Services, was issued with DHSS Circular No. LAC (83)4.

In *Decision* No. 143 the issue before the Tribunal was whether on a change of ownership the maximum number of residents in the home should be reduced in line with the registration authority's policy guidelines. On confirming the authority's decision the Tribunal said that if the situation at the time of change of ownership was allowed to prevail, that authority's "task of bringing all the Homes under its jurisdiction up to an acceptable standard would become much more difficult, because other Home-owners would no doubt demand the same privilege". The Tribunal went on to state that "the evidence of financial loss [to the applicant] does not outweigh the desirability of supporting the [registration authority's] efforts to apply its guidelines to all home owners in an even-handed manner".

In *Tribunal Decision* No. 73 an appeal against the refusal of a registration authority to register a residential care home for 10 persons with a mental and physical handicap which was to be located on the same site, though separated from, an existing residential care home for 20 mentally handicapped persons was dismissed on the ground that the increase in numbers is "more than likely to result in a perception of the site as a whole as a place of institutional care". The Tribunal considered that the inclusion of para. 8 in the Local Authority Building Note No. 8 in 1973 where the maximum number of residents then recommended was put at 24 must "now be regarded as well overtaken by the events in more modern thought". However, the Tribunal stated that they did not hesitate to uphold the principle expounded by that paragraph.

In *Decision* No. 3 the registration authority had refused an application to extend the number of registered persons at The Village, Llangwyfan, from 107 to 124. The Tribunal, by a majority, rejected the appeal against this decision on the grounds, *inter alia*, that the Village is already too large to be run as anything other than an impersonal institution, such a régime cannot enable each resident to achieve his or her potential, and that too great a distance from the resident's family can lead to a loss of sufficient contact with friends, family and social workers.

On a significantly different scale, the issue of the number of residents to be accommodated came before the Tribunal in *Decision* No. 216. In dismissing an appeal against the decision of the registration authority to refuse an application for registration which would have had the effect of increasing the numbers of persons with learning difficulties accommodated in the home from six to twelve, the Tribunal said that:

"[this] significant increase in size would not be masked from the local community by the arrangements proposed and would lead to a perception of the premises as a place of institutional care. This perception could exist not only in the minds of those in the outside world but, we find, in the minds of the residents themselves. As a consequence it would be a factor inhibiting their integration into the community and would tend to emphasise the fact that they are in some way set apart from the rest of society. This factor we find is of greater importance than the element of choice which we accept would be fostered by the proposals, if adopted. Those in the local community, with whom the residents would need to integrate and live relatively normal day to day lives, would realistically label such residents as coming from 'the Home' and this negative stereotyping, . . . would act as a barrier to integration."

A phased reduction in bed occupying from three-bed to two-bed rooms has been ordered by the Tribunal in some cases: see, for example, *Decision* No. 25.

For tribunal decisions relating to multiple occupancy bedrooms, see the note to reg. 10(1)(*b*) of the Residential Care Homes Regulations 1984.

Staffing: A registration authority has a discretion to define standards of both qualifications and also experience for staff in residential care homes. Also see the notes on "manager" in s.3 and the notes on reg. 10(1)(*a*) of the Residential Care Homes Regulations 1984.

Equipment: In *Decision* No. 126 the Tribunal confirmed the decision of the registration authority to cancel the registration of a residential care home where the proprietors had installed an internal system of closed circuit television. The members of the Tribunal said that they:

"are convinced that the very existence of closed circuit television in a residential care Home is prima facie objectionable. We were not convinced of this by the argument based on the perception of residents subject to paranoia or those who might be particularly sensitive to their environment, although that might be an important consideration in some other case. But we take the view that whereas an individual can respect a space that is temporarily and for whatever reason private, a camera cannot do so. A camera has no sensitivity—it cannot look away. So far as residents are concerned the eye of a camera, whether in use or not, presents a hard unblinking stare, without sympathy or understanding or other expression, and for many is likely to engender an uncomfortable feeling of being watched. Moreover it seems to us repugnant that any personal idiosyncrasies of elderly people should be capable of being observed in what is their home by the gaze of a machine and reproduced on a screen."

In connection with it: Which would include separate staff accommodation.

Para. (c)

Intended to carry on the home: In *Tribunal Decision* No. 190 the appellant submitted that if action is proposed under this provision:

"the question is, what is the proprietor's intention as to the future? That is not to say that all information as to the past should be excluded, since sometimes what happened in the past can be the only reliable indication of what might occur in the future. However, the Tribunal should direct its mind to what is likely to happen to the Home in the future."

The Tribunal adopted this submission.

Reasonably required: Registration authorities are given guidance on the services and facilities that should be provided in residential care homes in *Home Life: A Code of Practice for Residential Care*: see the General Note to this Act.

1–057

Subs. (2)

Fit person: "Making the fitness of the persons running the Home the sole ground for the refusal of registration, strikes a balance between the complete absence of controls and placing excessive burdens on the operators of small homes and on local authorities. It addresses widely felt concerns about unsuitable people running small homes, including people who have been found unfit to run larger ones, and also brings operators of such homes within the scope of the arrangements described in Circular LAC (91)4 for checks with the police on the possible criminal background of applicants" (Department of Health Local Authority Social Services Letter (91)7, para. 3).

1–058

Cancellation of registration

10. The registration authority may cancel the registration of a person in respect of a residential care home—

(*a*) on any ground which would entitle them to refuse an application for his registration in respect of it;

(*b*) on the ground that the annual fee in respect of the home has not been paid on or before the due date; or

[(*bb*) in the case of a small home, on the ground that the annual return has not been duly made in accordance with regulations under section 8A above; or]

(*c*) on the ground—

(i) that he has been convicted of an offence under this Part of this Act or any regulations made under it in respect of that or any other residential care home;

(ii) that any other person has been convicted of such an offence in respect of that home; or

(iii) that any condition for the time being in force in respect of the home by virtue of this Part of this Act has not been complied with.

1–059

AMENDMENT

Para. (*bb*) was inserted by the Registered Homes (Amendment) Act 1991, s.1(8).

DEFINITIONS

registration authority: s.20(1), (2)).
residential care home: s.1(1), (2).
small home: ss.1(4A), 20(1).

GENERAL NOTE

This section provides a registration authority with grounds for cancelling the registration of a person in respect of a residential care home. When an authority proposes to cancel a registration it must give the registered person notice of the proposal (s.12(4)) and the reasons for it (s.12(5)). The registered person then has 14 days within which he may notify the authority that he wishes to make representations about the proposed cancellation (s.13(1)). If the registered person does not wish to make representations the authority can proceed to

1–060

cancel the registration (s.13(2)(*b*)). If he does wish to make representation the authority cannot make a final decision on the proposed cancellation until it has considered the representations (s.13(2)(*a*)) as long as they are made within a reasonable time (s.13(3)).

A registration authority which considers that the length of this procedure would put the life, health or well-being of the residents seriously at risk can make an application to a magistrate under s.11.

If the registered person decides not to exercise his right of appeal to a Registered Homes Tribunal against a decision to cancel his registration (s.15(1)), the decision will not take effect until 28 days after he was notified by the authority that it had been made (ss.14(3)(*a*), 15(3)). If an appeal is made the decision will not take effect until the appeal is either determined or abandoned (s.14(3)(*b*)). A registered person is not entitled to use judicial review to challenge the registration authority's decision to cancel the registration until the appeals procedure before the Registered Homes Tribunal has been exhausted (*R.* v. *Birmingham City Council, ex p. Ferrero* (1991) 89 L.G.R. 977).

The difficulties that face registration authorities in taking action against the proprietors of a home when complaint has been made about poor practice are discussed by Emlyn Cassam, "Home Sweet Home", *Social Services Insight*, May 1, 1987, pp. 12–14.

Person: Or corporation (Interpretation Act 1978, s.5, Sched. 1).

May: The authority has a discretion. If the authority does cancel the registration it should record its reasons for so doing at the time when the decision is made, so that in the event of an appeal against the decision the authority can comply with r. 5(2) of the Registered Home Tribunal Rules 1984.

If the registration authority considers that the concerns that are prompting it to consider invoking the procedure under this section are capable of being redressed within a finite period, it could defer its decision to that date. This course of action was taken by the registration authority in *Tribunal Decision* No. 190.

As an alternative to cancelling a registration the authority could consider varying a condition of the registration or imposing an additional condition (s.5(4)).

Para. (a)

1–061 *Refuse an application:* See the notes on s.9.

Para. (b)

1–062 *Annual fee:* See s.8.

Para. (bb)

1–063 *Regulations:* See the Residential Care Homes Regulations 1984, reg. 25, Sched. 4.

Para. (c)

1–064 *Offences under this Part:* See ss.2, 5(5), (6), 16(2) and 17(6).

Has been convicted: It should be noted that a breach of the Regulations which is not followed by a prosecution and conviction is not a ground for cancelling the registration.

Any condition for the time being in force: The authority could cancel a registration on this ground even though it has not prosecuted for a breach of the condition under s.5(5).

Has not been complied with: For an example of a Registered Homes Tribunal confirming the cancellation of a registration under this ground, see *Decision* No. 146.

Urgent procedure for cancellation of registration, etc.

1–065 **11.**—(1) If—

(*a*) the registration authority apply to a justice of the peace for an order—
  (i) cancelling the registration of a person in respect of a residential care home;
  (ii) varying any condition for the time being in force in respect of a home by virtue of this Part of this Act; or
  (iii) imposing an additional condition; and
(*b*) it appears to the justice of the peace that there will be a serious risk to the life, health or well-being of the residents in the home unless the order is made,

he may make the order, and the cancellation, variation or imposition shall have effect from the date on which the order is made.

(2) An application under subsection (1) above may be made *ex parte* and shall be supported by a written statement of the registration authority's reasons for making the application.

(3) An order under subsection (1) above shall be in writing.

(4) Where such an order is made, the registration authority shall serve on any person registered in respect of the home, as soon as practicable after the making of the order,—
   (a) notice of the making of the order and of its terms; and
   (b) a copy of the statement of the authority's reasons which supported their application for the order.

DEFINITIONS
   registration authority: s.20(1), (2).
   residential care home: s.1(1), (2).

GENERAL NOTE

This section provides for a single magistrate to make an order cancelling or amending the registration of a residential care home. An application to the magistrate to cancel can only be made on one or other of the grounds for cancellation set out in s.10, the first of which relates back to s.9, and in *addition* it must appear to the magistrate that there "will be a serious risk to the life, health or well-being of the residents in home unless the order is made": *Lyons* v. *East Sussex County Council* (1988) 86 L.G.R. 369, C.A. In this case members of the Court indicated that there is no reason why, if a registration authority has material before it which it believes justifies an application to a justice of the peace under this section, but recognises that it may fail either in its application to the justice or an appeal against the justices to a tribunal under s.15, it should not simultaneously adopt the alternative route of indicating under s.12 that it proposes to cancel the registration. If the justice refuses to make the order the ordinary route procedure under s.12 can be followed. If the justice makes the order and there is an appeal to the tribunal, which allows the appeal, the ordinary route can again be followed. "By this stage presumably the travellers on that route will be well under way and there may be, by that stage, an appeal also against the confirmation by the authority of its proposal under s.14": *per* Glidewell L.J. at 379. The Court stressed that an appeal against an order under this section must be heard as quickly as possible and that if there are going to be two appeals, one against an order made under this section and one against a decision of the registration authority to adopt a proposal to cancel under s.14, the one should not delay the other. This is provided for in r. 13(1), (3) of the Registered Homes Tribunal Rules 1984 (S.I. 1984 No. 1346). In endorsing the alternative route procedure the Master of the Rolls said that he hoped that "where a local authority was satisfied that it should apply under s.11, it would normally also institute the s.12 procedure, thereby giving the Tribunal the widest possible scope for dealing with the justice of the matter": *supra*, at 381. He described the powers of this section as being "Draconian in the extreme". The advantages of using the alternative route procedure are illustrated by *Tribunal Decision* No. 187 where the registration authority relied exclusively on the powers contained in this section.

1–066

If a magistrate grants an order cancelling the registration of a person in respect of a residential care home, the effect of such an order is to make illegal the continued operation of the home. There is no provision for restoration of the registration pending an appeal to a Registered Homes Tribunal. An order under this section does not empower the registration authority to close the home and remove the residents, nor does it provide the authority with the powers to manage and run the home. As continued operation of the home would render the persons carrying on the home liable to prosecution under s.2, they will doubtless wish to co-operate with the registration authority in its attempt to make alternative arrangements for the care of the residents. The officers of the registration authority would have a right of access to the premises and the residents by virtue of their powers of inspection under s.17. If persons carrying on the home exhibit a reluctance to co-operate with the authority it could consider requesting the local community physician to make an application to the magistrates' court for an order either under s.47 of the National Assistance Act 1948 or s.1 of the National Assistance (Amendment) Act 1951. These sections enable the court to order the removal of a person from his place of residence on the grounds that:
   (i) the person is suffering from grave chronic disease or, being aged, infirm or physically incapacitated, is living in insanitary conditions; and
   (ii) the person is unable to devote to himself, and is not receiving from other persons, proper care and attention; and
   (iii) his removal is necessary, either in his own interests or for preventing injury to the health of, or serious nuisance to, other persons.

The procedure under this section is limited to situations where the home in question is registered under this Act. If a home is unregistered and urgent action is required to protect residents the registration authority could either apply to the High Court for an injunction to close the home or utilise the National Assistance Act procedure, mentioned above. It has been reported that Croydon Social Services, as registration authority, successfully sought a High Court injunction to close a home which it had refused to re-register on the ownership of the home changing hands. Although the new owners had lodged an appeal with the Registered Homes Tribunal against the decision not to register, the hearing was not going to be held for some considerable time and the registration authority had a grave ongoing concern about standards of management at the home: see *Community Care*, February 12, 1987, p. 3.

In *Decision* No. 166 the Tribunal offered the following observations on this section:

"The powers of s.11 are Draconian and it is axiomatic that they should never ever be contemplated without the gravest and most serious thought. The Tribunal is absolutely convinced that respondent authorities, knowing of the dreadful upset to residents, to the problems with resettling them, to the inevitable problems which arise with the relatives, to the enormous administrative difficulties involved, to the possibility of adverse comments in the press and to the time and expense which closures of this nature cause, would never ever proceed with such a step unless they felt it to be absolutely imperative. They are under a duty delegated to them by Parliament to protect and ensure the welfare of all people in their care, people who, because of age or disability, are particularly vulnerable. Therefore, if they believe, after taking into consideration all the serious consequences, that such a step is necessary to ensure that protection, they must take it. Even if they are subsequently found to have been wrong, this in no way should derogate from their duty to act."

It is not possible for the registration authority to apply to a magistrate for an order under this section and at the same time institute proceedings for a contravention of the Residential Care Homes Regulations 1984: see *ibid.* reg. 20(3).

If the Registered Homes Tribunal concludes that the magistrate was wrong to make the order of cancellation it would not be open to the Tribunal, when directing under s.15(5) that the order shall cease to have effect, to make a finding that the person running the home was not a "fit person" under ss.9 and 10: see *Lyons* v. *East Sussex County Council*, *The Times*, July 27, 1987, *per* Farquharson J.

For an account of the use of the procedure under this section and a subsequent Registered Homes Tribunal hearing, see David Tombs, "An Open and Shut Case", *Social Services Insight*, June 14, 1986, pp. 12–14. The circumstances that have been grounds for seeking an order under this section are described by R. Brooke Ross, "Emergency Powers under the Registered Homes Act", *Social Work Today*, February 4, 1988, p. 25 and by H. and S. Harman, *No Place Like Home* (NALGO, 1989), pp. 50–67. The operation of this section is also examined by M. Hinchcliffe, "Emergency Closure of Old People's Homes" [1992] 156 *Justice of the Peace Journal* 360–362.

Subs. (1)

1–067 *Registration authority:* The decision to make an application under this section should not be taken by a junior officer.

Person: Or corporation (Interpretation Act 1978, s.5, Sched. 1).

Condition . . . in respect of a home: The power of the magistrate to vary a condition or to impose an additional condition has been limited by the decision of the High Court in *Warwickshire County Council* v. *McSweeney* (unreported, December 8, 1988), which is noted under s.5(3).

Appears to the justice of the peace: On the day on which the application is made. An order should not be made under this section on the ground that certain anticipated events will occur in the future: see *Tribunal Decision* No. 129.

Serious risk: In *Hillingdon London Borough Council* v. *McLean* (1989) 88 L.G.R. 49, Phillips J. held that the risk to residents in residential care must be sufficiently serious to justify cancelling the registration, not merely serious in the abstract, for the court to make an order under this section:

"The question for the magistrate and, therefore, for the Tribunal was not simply: 'is there a serious risk to life, health or well-being of the residents?' but: 'will there be a serious risk if I do not make the order?' In practice, I do not see how any Tribunal could consider the question whether there would be a serious risk if the order were not made without comparing the degree of risk and the consequences of the order, whatever that order might be."

In this case Phillips J. also held that the Tribunal which heard the appeal from the magistrate's order had not erred in law by failing to consider *Home Life* in depth when examining the issue whether the practice in the home involved serious risk to life, etc., and that the Tribunal was right to look ahead to what was likely to happen if the order were not made by having regard to the proprietor's plans for the future.

In *Decision* No. 82 the Tribunal said that "there is no statutory definition of 'serious risk'. Clearly the Act envisages the urgent procedure being used only in exceptional circumstances since the application can be made *ex parte*". In this case the Tribunal upheld the magistrate's decision to cancel the registration on the ground that the evidence before it disclosed physical, mental and verbal abuse of residents and that such abuse would have continued if the home had not been closed. Also note *Decision* No. 98 where the Tribunal found that what the appellant did with regard to a resident "was the very antithesis of many of the basic principles commended in paragraph 4.6.2 of *Home Life*—a publication the Appellant apparently had never possessed nor even consulted until after her registration was cancelled; which in turn we view as an omission symptomatic of her proud complacency and evident determination to manage the home without the benefit of consultation or advice on important matters". In *Decision* No. 133 the Tribunal confirmed an order under this section because a "persistence in understaffing" together with a "clear lack of understanding" by the appellant of "what was required to ensure proper care of [the residents] led to a situation where their health and well-being were seriously at risk". The concept of responsible risk taking is set out in para. 1.2.8 of *Home Life*.

Life, health or well-being: The words used are disjunctive and a registration authority would be justified in taking action under this section if any of these matters are thought to be seriously at risk.

Shall have effect from the date: The person registered or carrying on the home would then be liable to be prosecuted under either s.2 or 5(5), if the order of the magistrate was not complied with.

Subs. (2)

Ex parte: There is no requirement for the registration authority to inform the registered person that an application is to be made under this (s.12(4)). "It is clear that the application may be made either *ex parte* or *inter partes*, but we have been informed, and we were not surprised to learn, that normally if this procedure is followed the majority of applications are made *ex parte*, and indeed if it is really urgent that is sensible": *East Sussex County Council* v. *Lyons, supra, per* Glidewell L.J. at 374. In *Decision* No. 174 the Tribunal said that a "justice of the peace is put in a difficult position in urgent applications that are made *ex parte* as he cannot but accept the information given by an authority. This makes it all the more essential that a balanced picture should be given in the statement of reasons put before him".

1–068

Written: See the note on s.15(2).

Reasons: Which would include a statement of the nature of the risk to residents, together with the authority's reasons for considering that the risk was serious enough to justify use of the urgent procedure.

Subs. (4)

Serve on any person registered: Who can appeal against the order to a Registered Homes Tribunal (s.15(1)(b)).

1–069

Notice: For the service of notices, see s.54.

Ordinary procedure for registration, etc., under Part I

12.—(1) Subject to subsection (2) below, where— **1–070**
   (*a*) a person applies for registration under this Part of this Act; and
   (*b*) the registration authority propose to grant his application,
the authority shall give him written notice of their proposal and of the conditions subject to which they propose to grant his application.

(2) The registration authority need not give notice of such a proposal if they propose to grant the application subject only to conditions which—
   (*a*) the applicant specified in the application; or
   (*b*) the authority and the applicant have subsequently agreed.

(3) The registration authority shall give an applicant notice of a proposal to refuse his application.

(4) Except where they make an application under section 11 above, the registration authority shall give any person registered in respect of a residential care home notice of a proposal—
   (*a*) to cancel the registration;
   (*b*) to vary any condition for the time being in force in respect of the home by virtue of this Part of this Act; or
   (*c*) to impose any additional condition.

(5) A notice under this section shall give the registration authority's reasons for their proposal.

DEFINITIONS
   registration authority: s.20(1), (2).
   residential care home: s.1(1), (2).

GENERAL NOTE

1–071 The general procedures for dealing with a registration application and for cancelling, refusing or amending a registration are set out in this section and in ss.13 and 14. An urgent procedure for cancelling or amending a registration in exceptional circumstances is contained in s.11.

If the registration authority proposes to grant an application for registration subject to conditions (s.5(3)), the authority must normally give the applicant written notice of the proposal (subs. (1)) and the reason for it (subs. (5)). If, however, the authority proposes to grant an application subject only to conditions which the applicant specified in his application, or which have been subsequently agreed with the applicant, the requirement to give notice of the proposal is dispensed with (subs. (2)) and the decision to grant the application takes effect immediately (s.14(3)).

Notice of a proposal to refuse a registration (subs. (3)) or to cancel or amend a registration (subs. (4)) must be given to the applicant or registered person, together with a statement of the authority's reasons for the proposal (subs. (5)).

Notices issued under this section are subject to the provision of s.13.

Subs. (1)

1–072 *Person:* Or corporation (Interpretation Act 1978, s.5, Sched. 1).
Applies for registration: See s.5.
This Part of this Act: i.e. ss.1 to 20.
Written: See note on s.15(2).
Notice: For the service of notices, see s.54.

Subs. (3)

1–073 *Refuse his application:* On one of the grounds contained in s.9.

Subs. (4)

1–074 This provision, unlike subss. (1) to (3) of this section, is concerned with the situation after registration has been obtained and deals with the possibility of the registration being cancelled or there being a variation of it or the imposition of an additional condition.
Cancel the registration: See s.10.
Vary any condition . . . impose any additional condition: See s.5(4).

Subs. (5)

1–075 *Reasons:* The reasons for the decision should be recorded at the time when the decision is made, so that in the event of an appeal the authority can comply with r.5(2) of the Registered Homes Tribunal Rules 1984. In *Decision* No. 101 the Tribunal held that the registration authority was bound by the contents of the statement of reasons that it had issued under this provision and refused to introduce a fresh ground of complaint at the hearing which the appellant had not had the opportunity to answer.

Right to make representations

1–076 **13.**—(1) A notice under section 12 above shall state that within 14 days of service of the notice any person on whom it is served may in writing require the registration authority to give him an opportunity to make representations to them concerning the matter.

(2) Where a notice has been served under section 12 above, the registration authority shall not determine the matter until either—
  (*a*) any person on whom the notice was served has made representations concerning the matter; or
  (*b*) the period during which any such person could have required them to give him an opportunity to make representations has elapsed without their being required to give such an opportunity; or
  (*c*) the conditions specified in subsection (3) below are satisfied.

(3) The conditions mentioned in subsection (2) above are—
  (*a*) that a person on whom the notice was served has required the registration authority to give him an opportunity to make representations to them concerning the matter;
  (*b*) that the registration authority have allowed him a reasonable period to make his representations; and

(c) that he has failed to make them within that period.

(4) Representations may be made, at the option of the person making them, either in writing or orally.

(5) If he informs the registration authority that he desires to make oral representations, they shall give him an opportunity of appearing before and of being heard by a committee or sub-committee of the registration authority.

DEFINITION

registration authority: s.20(1), (2).

GENERAL NOTE

1–077 This section provides a right to make representations against a proposal notified in accordance with the provisions of s.12. If the person who has been notified decides to exercise his right to make representations the authority cannot normally come to a decision on the proposal until it has considered the representations (subs. (2)(a)). The authority can proceed to make a final decision on the proposal if the person concerned fails to make his representations within a reasonable period (subs. (3)).

The procedure for hearing representations under this section should not take the form of an appeal against the decision of the registration authority because the authority will only have reached the stage of stating that it *proposes* to reach a particular decision: see s.12. The representations should address the reasons that the registration authority has given to justify its proposal: see s.12(5). This was the approach adopted in *Decision* No. 79 where the Tribunal rejected a submission of counsel that, as a matter of law, the right to make representations under this section included the right to call witnesses and cross-examine any witnesses called by the registration authority. The Tribunal took the view that "there was a fundamental difference in the right to make representations and what would in effect be a full hearing of the matter and the right to represent".

The manner in which the registration authority receives representation is subject to the rules of natural justice which require, *inter alia*, that all material facts taken into consideration by the authority should be revealed. In *Decision* No. 7 the Tribunal said that registration authorities "must act in a judicial manner following the accepted standards of natural justice". It is submitted that s.15 does not give the Tribunal power to consider the manner in which the decision was reached at the representations hearing under this section. An allegation of a flawed decision-making process can only be challenged in the High Court on an application for judicial review. This was the approach taken by the Tribunal in *Decision* No. 163. The Tribunal in *Decision* No. 29 did purport to accept jurisdiction to review the decision-making process. In this case the official who had received the representations had also signed the letter proposing cancellation. The Tribunal found that there had been no breach of natural justice because the official's sole function was to record the representations and pass them onto the registration authority; she had no decision-making powers and did not take any part in the registration authority's decision.

Subs. (1)

1–078 *Within 14 days of service:* Excluding the date of service (*Dodds* v. *Walker* [1982] 2 All E.R. 609, H.L.).

Notice: As to the serving of notices, see s.54.

Writing: See the note on s.15(2).

Registration authority: The members who made the proposal should not constitute the committee which is established to hear the representations: see the General Note to s.14.

Representations: Which can be made orally or in writing (subs. (4)).

Subs. (2)

Para. (a)

1–079 *The period:* Of 14 days from the service of the notice (subs. (11)).

Subs. (3)

Para. (b)

1–080 *Reasonable period:* What is a reasonable period would, to a certain extent, depend upon the complexities of the issues involved. It is suggested that the registration authority should indicate to the person who wishes to make representations the period within which the authority is prepared to receive them.

Subs. (4)

1–081 *In writing or orally:* These are alternatives and the person concerned must notify the registration authority of the preferred option.

Subs. (5)

1–082   *Oral representations:* Unlike r.6 of the Registered Homes Tribunals Rules 1984, this provision does not provide for a right to legal representation. In *Decision* No. 148, the Tribunal, acting on the assumption that this provision leaves the registration authority with a discretion whether or not to allow an applicant to be represented, said that "we are firmly of the view the discretion ought normally to be exercised in favour of the applicant. The hearing is of great importance to the applicant, and it is important that he or she be treated with scrupulous fairness".

Committee or sub-committee: Which would be the council's social services committee or a sub-committee of that committee: see the note on s.20.

Decision of local authority

1–083   **14.**—(1) If the registration authority decide to adopt the proposal, they shall serve notice in writing of their decision on any person on whom they were required to serve notice of their proposal.

(2) A notice under this section shall be accompanied by a notice explaining the right of appeal conferred by section 15 below.

(3) A decision of a registration authority, other than a decision to grant an application for registration subject only to such conditions as are mentioned in section 12(2) above or to refuse an application for registration, shall not take effect—

(a) if no appeal is brought, until the expiration of the period of 28 days referred to in section 15(3) below; and

(b) if an appeal is brought, until it is determined or abandoned.

DEFINITION
registration authority: s.20(1), (2).

GENERAL NOTE

1–084   This section sets out the procedure to be followed by a registration authority when it decides to adopt a proposal to grant or refuse an application for registration or to cancel or amend a registration. It also provides that an authority's decision on a proposal shall not take effect until either the expiration of the 28-day period within which an appeal against the decision may be made (s.15(3)) or, if an appeal is made, until it is determined or abandoned. This delay does not apply where the authority is granting the registration application subject only to conditions which have been specified by the applicant, or which have been subsequently agreed between the authority and the applicant. Nor does it apply when a registration application is being refused.

The undesirability of a similarly constituted committee of the registration authority making a proposal under s.12 and making a decision under this section was mentioned by the Tribunal in *Decision* No. 88. This practice received further criticism in *Decision* No. 161 where the Tribunal urged that "similar instances be altogether avoided henceforth by all registration authorities". This statement was endorsed by the Tribunal in *Decision* No. 199.

Subs. (1)

1–085   *Notice:* The notice should contain reference to the particular sections of this Act on which the registration authority can rely: see *R. v. Humberside County Council, ex p. Bogdal* (1992) 11 B.M.L.R. 46. For the serving of notices, see s.54.

Writing: See the note on s.15(2).

On any person: Who will either be the applicant or the registered person.

Person: Or corporation (Interpretation Act 1978, s.5, Sched. 1).

Appeals

1–086   **15.**—(1) An appeal against—

(a) a decision of a registration authority; or

(b) an order made by a justice of the peace under section 11 above,

shall lie to a Registered Homes Tribunal.

(2) An appeal shall be brought by notice in writing given to a registration authority.

(3) No appeal against a decision or order may be brought by a person more than 28 days after service on him of notice of the decision or order.

(4) On an appeal against a decision of a registration authority the tribunal may confirm the decision or direct that it shall not have effect.

(5) On an appeal against an order made by a justice of the peace the tribunal may confirm the order or direct that it shall cease to have effect.

(6) A tribunal shall also have power on an appeal against a decision or order—
- (*a*) to vary any condition for the time being in force in respect of the home to which the appeal relates by virtue of this Part of this Act;
- (*b*) to direct that any such condition shall cease to have effect; or
- (*c*) to direct that any such condition as it thinks fit shall have effect in respect of the home.

(7) A registration authority shall comply with any direction given by a tribunal under this section.

DEFINITION
registration authority: s.20(1).

GENERAL NOTE

This section establishes a right of appeal to a Registered Homes Tribunal against a decision of a registration authority or an order made by a magistrate under s.11, sets out the procedure for appealing, and identifies the powers of tribunals. It is submitted that this section does not give the Tribunal power to consider the manner in which the decision was reached as the Tribunal is only vested with jurisdiction once the decision is made. This was the approach taken in *Decision* No. 166 where it was said that it "is not for the Tribunal to comment on how the decision [of the registration authority] was made" and in *Decision* No. 199 where the Tribunal said that it "cannot look behind the fact of deregistration". Also see the General Note to s.13.

1–087

In *Lyons* v. *East Sussex County Council, The Times*, July 27, 1987, Farquharson J. answered questions about the burden and standard of proof in appeals to tribunals and about the admissibility of evidence. His Lordship held that:

"on the basis of 'he who asserts must prove' the burden of proof on an appeal before the tribunal will rest on the authority which is seeking to maintain the justices' order to cancel or their own decision under s.12(4). While the tribunal has power to regulate its own procedure, the sensible course in these circumstances is for the authority to present its case first so that an appellant is not taken by surprise, although he will have had a statement of the case under s.11(4) or alternatively notice under s.12(3) or (4). It is, I am informed, the practice of some tribunals to request the parties to exchange affidavits or proofs of evidence before the hearing. This is obviously desirable and much to be encouraged so as to avoid unnecessary adjournments. Such an exchange should, of course, be made long enough before the hearing to enable the parties to prepare evidence to meet the case against them.

So far as the standard of proof is concerned, it is for the authority to satisfy the tribunal of the truth of their allegations on the balance of probabilities. The degree of probability will depend on the gravity of the issue which the tribunal is called upon to decide. Lord Scarman's words in *R.* v. *Home Secretary, ex p. Khawaja* [1984] 1. A.C. 74 at 113 were cited in argument: 'The flexibility of the civil standard of proof suffices to ensure that the court will require the high degree of probability which is appropriate to what is at stake.' [N.B. In *Decision* No. 162 the main issue in dispute was an allegation that the owner had engaged in sexual intercourse with a mentally handicapped resident. The Tribunal said that "in a case such as this, with such serious repercussions, on an analogy with child abuse cases or ones of fraud, a very high standard of proof is required, more akin to the criminal standard". In *Decision* No. 187 the Tribunal, on hearing an appeal against a s.11 closure order, made the following comment: "To find serious risk, which results in the awful trauma for everyone concerned in the immediate closing down of a home, there must be a very high degree of probability."]

The last question in the case relates to the admission of evidence which although relevant was either (a) not included in the authority's statement of reasons although available at the time or (b) related to events which occurred after the application to the justice of the peace. In criminal appeals such evidence would generally be excluded but here one has to consider, as [counsel] puts it, the mischief against which the legislation is directed. He relied upon *Heydon's Case* (1584) 3. Co.Rep. 7a. The scheme of the Act, as already observed, is to provide protection to particular groups of society who are in need of it. Accordingly, evidence which has previously been overlooked, or not included in the authority's statement on the application to the justice of the peace, should, because of the urgency of the matter, still be admitted if it assists the tribunal in arriving at its conclusion. Equally, relevant evidence may later become available about, for example, the disposition and character of the person running the home which relates to his fitness to do so; once again it would be desirable that such evidence is available to the tribunal in the interests of those whom the Act is seeking to protect. I emphasise, however, that decisions on these questions are really for the tribunal itself. Under the regulations it is not bound by the strict rules of evidence which apply to the courts and it will really act on the basis of what is fair. I need hardly add that such evidence should never be presented at the appeal unless notice has been given to the other side."

These findings were confirmed by the Court of Appeal: see (1988) 86 L.G.R. 369. In *Decision* No. 195, the Tribunal commented upon the treatment of evidence on the hearing of an appeal against a s.11 order:

"the Respondents accept that if they are to persuade us to dismiss the emergency procedure appeal, they must prove, on the balance of probabilities but to a very high standard, sufficient of the grounds put to the magistrates to establish that there would have been a serious risk to the life, health or well-being of the residents if the order had not been made. This is the correct view in the interests of justice. The emergency procedure is *ex parte* and Draconian. It would be wrong by having too relaxed an approach to the rules of evidence to allow the Respondents to prove a subsequent serious risk to the life, health or well-being of the residents which could not be made out at the time of the order."

In *Decision* No. 26 the Tribunal made the following comments about the lack of a preliminary hearing in the Registered Homes Tribunal Rules 1984:

"It should be noted that the procedure of the Tribunal does not allow for any preliminary hearing for the purpose of giving directions. The Parties must therefore ensure in good time before a hearing before a Tribunal takes place that the issues between them are clearly defined. That any photograph, plans, or sketches are agreed. That there is discovery of documents. That any medical, experts and technical reports have been disclosed, and (if possible) agreed. All those preliminary steps and any others which the parties may consider necessary must be dealt with between the parties in plenty of time before the hearing so that this may go forward without any technical point of procedure arising at the hearing. The Parties must each one of them put their house in order."

The merit of the Registered Homes Chairman of the Tribunal meeting with the legal representatives of the parties prior to the hearing is emphasised in para. 4.8 of the Department of Health's *Registered Homes Tribunals Procedure* (1989):

"In certain cases, it will sometimes be advantageous, from the point of view of the length of the hearing and consequent expense to the parties, for the Chairman, with their consent, to meet before the hearing with their legal representatives. The purpose of this preliminary meeting is to see how best savings in time and cost could be achieved, for example, to see whether any agreement as to the matters in issue can be reached, or to resolve procedural matters which might otherwise be argued at length during the actual hearing. The Secretariat will arrange this at the request of the parties where the Chairman considers it appropriate."

In *Decisions* No. 16 and 29 the Tribunal emphasised that, on the hearing of an appeal, the needs of future as well as present residents must be considered. This approach which, it is submitted, is correct did not appear to commend itself to the Tribunal in *Decision* No. 24 where the Tribunal confined itself to considering the needs of present residents when addressing the adequacy of night cover arrangements. For comment on the power of the Tribunal to take into account economic factors when considering an appeal, see the note on "reward or not" in s.1(1).

For the procedure to be followed at Registered Homes Tribunal hearings, see the notes to r. 9 of the Registered Homes Tribunals Rules 1984.

Subs. (1)

1–088 *Appeal:* In *Decision* No. 105 the Tribunal found "that s.15(1) does not expressly prescribe who has the right of appeal. By necessary implication the right of appeal lies in the person/s against whom the registration authority made its decision . . . ". It is possible for an appeal to be pursued even if, before the hearing date, the appellant has disposed of the property: see *Decision* No. 67 where the appellant brought the appeal in an attempt to clear his name. In *Decision* No. 107 the Tribunal said that, to have jurisdiction to hear an appeal in circumstances where the home has been sold, the appellants had to be the owners of the property at the time when the decision of the registration authority was made and at the time when the notice of appeal was submitted.

A decision of a registration authority: Made subsequent to a proposal by the registration authority of the kind specified in s.12. Therefore, on an application by a registered proprietor pursuant to s.5(4) to vary a condition of registration or to impose an additional condition, there is no right of appeal to a Registered Homes Tribunal upon a refusal by the registration authority to agree to the variation or imposition as there has been no proposal under s.12 capable of adoption and therefore no decision from which to appeal: see *Coombs* v. *Hertfordshire County Council* (1991) 89 L.G.R. 774, noted under s.5(4). The jurisdiction of the Tribunal does not arise until the registration authority has decided to adopt a proposal and has given written notice of that decision in accordance with s.14(1). In *Decision* No. 63 the Tribunal accepted jurisdiction in circumstances where this procedure had not been followed but where neither party desired an adjournment and both accepted the jurisdiction of the Tribunal. Also see *Decision* No. 105 where the Tribunal, relying on the decision of the House of Lords in *London and Clydeside Estates Ltd.* v. *Aberdeen District Council* [1980] 1 W.L.R. 182, proceeded to hear an appeal in circumstances where there were discrepancies between the set of conditions cited in the proposal and the set of conditions contained in the decision. The Tribunal found that the fact of the discrepancies had not prejudiced either party.

In *Decision* No. 135 the Tribunal made the following comment on the scope of this section: "If the Tribunal considered the procedural steps leading up to the decision, it would be acting *ultra vires* its statutory powers and usurping the functions of the High Court in hearing a judicial review. It is well established in law that if there are procedural defects in breach of the rules of natural justice, it would only be in wholly exceptional circumstances that the case should not continue to be heard on the merits. If there are defects . . . these can be 'cured' by an appeal. A complaints procedure has been made available by statute. It is an appeal *de novo* and the Tribunal can start all over again hearing evidence on both sides, dealing with the matter on the merits."

Order made by a justice of the peace under section 11: On hearing an appeal against an equivalent order made under s.30, the Tribunal in *Decision* No. 187 said that "it had to consider whether the risk at the relevant time was so serious as to justify an *ex parte* application to the magistrate for an immediate closure, to consider whether the risk at that time was any more serious than concerns/risks the Respondents had already been aware of". It is submitted that this is not the approach that a Registered Homes Tribunal should adopt on hearing an appeal from a s.11 or s.30 cancellation. The sole issue before the Tribunal should be whether the magistrate was justified on the evidence in cancelling the registration on the ground that if such an order was not made there would be a serious risk to the life, health or well-being of the residents.

In *Lyons* v. *East Sussex County Council* (1988) 86 L.G.R. 369, the question before the Court was whether, upon an appeal from an order made by a magistrate under s.11, if the Registered Homes Tribunal finds that the evidence adduced proves that the appellant is not a fit person to be concerned in carrying on a residential care home but fails to prove any serious risk to the life, health or well-being of the residents in the home, the Tribunal should confirm the order of the justice of the peace or direct that it should not have effect. The Court of Appeal confirmed the answer given by Farquharson J. (see *The Times*, July 27, 1987) that the Tribunal should not confirm the order unless it is satisfied of the serious risk described in s.11. For an appeal that succeeded because the magistrate was given, and must have relied upon, facts which could not be substantiated at the appeal hearing, see *Tribunal Decision* No. 133.

Registered Homes Tribunals: General provisions relating to these Tribunals are to be found in Pt. III of this Act. The function of a Registered Homes Tribunal hearing an appeal is to conduct a complete rehearing of the decision, and not merely to review it. The Tribunal can therefore consider matters which came to light after the original decision was made: see the General Note to this section.

Subs. (2)

Notice: Which should state concisely the grounds of appeal. The notice should not set out the evidence that will be relied on at the hearing. **1–089**

Writing: Includes typing, printing, lithography, photography and other modes of representing or reproducing words in a visible form (Interpretation Act 1978, s.5, Sched. 1).

Registration authority: "It will assist the Registered Homes Tribunals Secretariat in arranging an early hearing if you also send a copy direct to them at the same time. Their address is:
Room B1601
Alexander Fleming House
Elephant & Castle
London SE1 6BY
Telephone: 01–407 5522 Ext. 7721 or 6253; Fax 01–407 2765" (*Registered Homes Tribunals Procedure* (Department of Health, 1989), para. 2.2).

Subs. (3)

Person: Or corporation (Interpretation Act 1978, s.5, Sched. 1). **1–090**

28 days after service: i.e. excluding the date of service (*Dodds* v. *Walker* [1981] 2 All E.R. 609, H.L.).

Subss. (4), (5)

Confirm the decision or direct that it shall not have effect: The Registered Homes Tribunal does not have power to allow an appeal in part only. This means that a joint appeal must be either allowed or dismissed and no distinction can be drawn between the joint appellants. In *Decision* No. 69 the Tribunal said that: **1–091** "we can conceive of cases where it would be desirable to debar one joint owner but not the other from being further concerned in the management of residential homes. This result could, we think, be achieved in a proper case by allowing a joint appeal but exercising the Tribunal's power under s.15(6)(c) to impose a condition that the joint owner who has been found unfit be no longer permitted to be concerned in the management of the home. Such cases will be rare, because almost always where joint owners or managers are concerned the one whose personal actions have not come under criticism will be found to be at fault for inaction, in not preventing the actions of his spouse, partner or business associate."

This device has now been disallowed by virtue of the decision in the *McSweeney* case, noted below.

The powers of a Registered Homes Tribunal on hearing an appeal are limited to either confirming the decision or directing that it shall not have effect. If an appeal has been lodged and the parties subsequently come to an agreement which obviates the need for a hearing, the Tribunal does not have jurisdiction to make an order incorporating the terms of the agreement. (Note, however, that in *Decision* No. 157 the Tribunal did make such an order which it described as being "legally unobjectionable".) A withdrawal of the appeal under r.12 of the Registered Homes Tribunal Rules 1984 would be ineffective as this course of action would leave the decision of the registration authority standing. In these circumstances the most appropriate course of action would be for the registration authority to notify the Registered Homes Tribunal that they would call no evidence in support of their statement of reasons. The Tribunal would then have no option but to allow the appeal. This course of action was followed in *Tribunal Decisions* No. 151, 165 and 176.

In *Tribunal Decision* No. 193 the parties, after an adjournment of the hearing, agreed that the appellants would "formally withdraw" their appeals. The Tribunal stated that it "was satisfied" that the agreement "was in the best interests of both parties and of the patients and residents in the two homes". It is submitted that there is no requirement for a Registered Homes Tribunal to satisfy itself that the withdrawal of an appeal is in the best interests of any person affected by the decision and that in such circumstances the Tribunal would have no option other than to dismiss the appeal.

An appeal cannot be allowed on the understanding that a future development might take place which would render the premises fit to be used: see *Tribunal Decision* No. 175.

Subs. (6)

1-092   *Power:* It is submitted that the Registered Homes Tribunal decision has immediate effect.

Any such condition: The use of these words in subparas. (b), (c) refer to the conditions which can be imposed by virtue of this Part of this Act which are limited to those categories set out in s.5(3): see *Warwickshire County Council* v. *McSweeney* (unreported, December 8, 1988, *per* Roch J.). "Section 15(6)(c) cannot be read as giving the Tribunal power to impose any condition that it thinks fit when it allows an appeal because, if that were right, then the Tribunals would have a wider power of imposing condition than would the registration authority . . . That would clearly be undesirable . . .": Transcript, p. 10. Also note the *obiter* comment of Rose J. in *Avon County Council* v. *Lang* [1990] C.O.D. 365 that it is "common ground that the power of a Tribunal to impose or vary conditions is coterminate with the power of the regulating authority". In *Decision* No. 149 the Tribunal would have liked to have allowed an appeal on condition that the appellants undertook to complete certain work within a specified time. In the absence of such a power the Tribunal stated, in allowing the appeal, that any further delays in undertaking the work "would certainly justify a renewed proposal to deregister the home". The Tribunal also suggested a timetable within which they expected the work to be done.

In *Decision* No. 113 the Tribunal rejected a submission from the registration authority that the Tribunal has no jurisdiction to impose a condition under s.15(6)(c) unless the appeal is against the imposition of a condition.

Regulations as to conduct of residential care homes

1-093   **16.**—(1) The Secretary of State may make regulations as to the conduct of residential care homes, and in particular—

    (a) as to the facilities and services to be provided in such homes;

    (b) as to the numbers and qualifications of staff to be employed in such homes;

    (c) as to numbers of suitably qualified and competent staff to be on duty in such homes;

    (d) as to the records to be kept and notices to be given in respect of persons received into such homes;

(e) as to the notification of events occurring in such homes;
(f) as to the giving of notice by a person of a description specified in the regulations of periods during which any person of a description so specified proposes to be absent from a home;
(g) as to the information to be supplied in such a notice;
(h) making provision for children under the age of 18 years who are resident in such homes to receive a religious upbringing appropriate to the religious persuasion to which they belong;
(j) as to the form of registers to be kept by registration authorities for the purposes of this Part of this Act and the particulars to be contained in them; and
(k) as to the information to be supplied on an application for registration.

(2) Regulations under this section may provide that a contravention of or failure to comply with any specified provision of the regulations shall be an offence against the regulations.

DEFINITION
residential care home: s.1(1), (2).

GENERAL NOTE
The Secretary of State has made the Residential Care Homes Regulations 1984 (S.I. 1984 No. 1345). These Regulations, which provide registration authorities with a mechanism for ensuring that a home is, and continues to be, suitable for registration, can be enforced either through the courts (subs. 2)), or through cancelling the registration of a residential care home on a ground which constitutes a breach of the Regulations. For example, inadequate staffing levels (see reg. 10(1)(a)) could be a ground for cancelling a registration under ss.9(b), 10(a). The Regulations themselves also contain a procedure for securing compliance (reg. 20). A conviction for an offence against the Regulations provides a ground for cancelling the registration of a home: see s.10(c)(i).

1–094

Subs. (1)
Conduct of residential care homes: See reg. 9 of the Residential Care Homes Regulations 1984.

1–095

Para. (h)
Under the age: See the note on s.1(6).

1–096

Subs. (2)
Offence against the regulations: Which, on conviction, could attract a fine of up to level 4 on the standard scale (s.49). A defence is provided by s.18.

1–097

Inspection of homes

17.—(1) Any person authorised in that behalf by the Secretary of State may at all times enter and inspect any premises which are used, or which that person has reasonable cause to believe to be used, for the purposes of a residential care home.

1–098

(2) Any person authorised in that behalf by a registration authority may at all times enter and inspect any premises in the area of the authority which are used, or which that person has reasonable cause to believe to be used, for those purposes.

(3) The powers of inspection conferred by subsections (1) and (2) above shall include power to inspect any records required to be kept in accordance with regulations under this Part of this Act.

(4) The Secretary of State may by regulations require that residential care homes shall be inspected on such occasions or at such intervals as the regulations may prescribe.

(5) A person who proposes to exercise any power of entry or inspection conferred by this section shall if so required produce some duly authenticated document showing his authority to exercise the power.

(6) Any person who obstructs the exercise of any such power shall be guilty of an offence.

DEFINITIONS
   residential care home: s.1(1), (2).
   registration authority: s.20(1), (2).

GENERAL NOTE

1–099 This section gives a person authorised by the registration authority or by the Secretary of State a power to enter and inspect premises which are used, or which that person has reasonable cause to believe to be used, for the purposes of a residential care home. A power to enter and inspect mental nursing homes is given by s.35, and a power to enter and inspect nursing homes is given by reg. 10 of the Nursing Homes and Mental Nursing Homes Regulations 1984. Where an establishment is registered both as a residential home and as a nursing home or mental nursing home the two registration authorities will need to work closely together, and should carry out joint inspections where this felt to be appropriate: see the General Note to this Act.

An inspection carried out under this section can be made at any time of the day or night and advance notice of the inspection does not have to be given. For the inspection of small homes, see paras. 9 and 10 of Annex A to Department of Health Circular No. LAC (92)10.

Section 80 of the Children Act 1989 provides the Secretary of State with an additional power to inspect any residential care home required to be registered under this Act and used to accommodate children (subs. (1)). This power is supplemented by a power to inspect the children (subs. (6)) and by powers to direct the person carrying on the home to provide specific information (subss. (4) and (5)), to inspect records (subs. (7)) and to enter the home (subs. (8)). It is an offence intentionally to obstruct entry (subs. (10)) and if entry is refused a warrant can be obtained under s.102 of the 1989 Act. Section 86 of the 1989 Act places a duty on the person carrying on a residential care home to notify the relevant local authority about children that are being accommodated in the home. The local authority has a duty to safeguard the children's welfare (subs. (3)) and also has a duty under s.24 of the 1989 Act to provide such children with advice and assistance with a view to providing for their long-term welfare. An owner who provides day care for children under the age of eight in a residential care home is exempted from the registration requirements of Pt. X of the 1989 Act which deals with childminding and day care for young children: see *ibid.* s.71(1)(*b*) and Sched. 9, para. 4(1)(*d*).

Guidance on the inspection process is given to registration authorities by the British Association of Social Workers' *Practice Notes for Social Workers and Registration Officers Working with the Private and Voluntary Residential Sector* (1984), paras. 3.2.5 *et seq.*, by *Home Life: A Code of Practice for Residential Care* (1984), para. 6.11, by the NAHA handbook, *Registration and Inspection of Nursing Homes*, paras. 3.1 *et seq.*, and by Annex 3 and paras. A46 to A53 of the Guidance Notes attached to DHSS Circular No. LAC (84)15. Also see Paul Ridout, "20 Tips for Registration Officers", *Care Weekly*, April 6, 1990, pp. 12, 13.

Although the Department of Health has recommended that the registered person should be given a copy of the inspection report or be made aware in writing of its principal contents so that he would know how well he was performing and whether any deficiencies needed to be remedied, there is no requirement for the authority to adopt this desirable procedure. Mary A. Mendleson has recommended that all American nursing homes that receive federal money should post the latest inspection report prominently in the home and provide copies of the report to potential applicants as this "would make available to those most concerned the inspector's judgement on the home, and would also enable someone reading the posted report to contrast what the inspector said with the reality around him" (*Tender Loving Greed* (1974), p. 224).

A training package for inspection staff, *Making Sense of Inspection: Registered Homes Act 1984: Training Course for Registration and Inspection Staff* which was commissioned by the Department of Health and the Welsh Office has been produced by the Polytechnic of North London, Ladbroke House, 62–66 Highbury Grove, London N5 2AD.

Subs. (1)

1–100 *Secretary of State:* Also see the Secretary of State's power of inspection under the Children Act 1989, noted above.

Subss. (1), (2)

1–101 *At all times:* And not necessarily at "reasonable" times.

"Inspections should occur more often—at nights and during weekends when staff shortages are the worst, not just during weekdays—and should not be announced in advance. The desire to have records and key nursing home staff present is the reason for giving advance notice of inspections and for holding them during weekdays. Many violations go undiscovered when inspections are conducted only in this way, however": Robert N. Brown, "An Appraisal of the Nursing Home Enforcement Process" [1975] *Arizona Law Review* 328.

Enter and inspect: A person who obstructs an authorised person in the exercise of his power under this section commits an offence under subs. (6). The authorised person is not empowered to use force in his attempt to gain entry to the premises. Note that under reg. 10(1)(*o*) of the Residential Care Homes Regulations 1984 the person who is registered in respect of a home must make arrangements for an authorised person to interview in private any resident.

Reasonable cause to believe: It is an offence under s.2 for a person to carry on a residential care home without being registered.

Subs. (2)

Any person authorised . . . by a registration authority: The registration authority could authorise an officer of the health authority to join with the registration officer in carrying out a joint inspection of a residential care home. This could be useful where there is a doubt whether the home is correctly registered or where advice is needed on the arrangements that the home has made for the control of medicines. Registration authorities and health authorities could use the joint consultative committees established under s.22 of the National Health Service Act 1977 to agree on a general procedure for such inspections.

1–102

Subs. (3)

Records: See Sched. 2 to the Residential Care Homes Regulations 1984.

1–103

Subs. (4)

Require: Registration authorities are required to inspect residential care homes not less than once every year: see reg. 18(1) of the Residential Care Homes Regulations 1984.

1–104

Subs. (5)

If so required produce: The power to enter and inspect can be exercised even if there is nobody on the premises to whom the document can be produced: see Sommervell L.J., speaking on a similar provision in the Gas Act 1948, in *Grove* v. *Eastern Gas Board* [1951] 2 All E.R. 1051 at 1053, C.A.

1–105

Subs. (6)

Obstructs: Cases on the offence of obstructing a constable in the execution of his duty suggest that an offence under this provision: (1) need not involve physical violence (*Hinchcliffe* v. *Sheldon* [1955] 1 W.L.R. 1207); (2) is not committed on a mere refusal to answer questions (*Rice* v. *Connolly* [1966] 2 Q.B. 414) or on advising a person not to answer questions (*Green* v. *D.P.P.* [1991] Crim. L.R. 782, D.C.); and (3) might be committed if a verbal warning of an impending inspection was given (*Green* v. *Moore* [1982] 2 W.L.R. 671). There is also authority to support the contention that an offence is committed if the defendant's conduct makes it more difficult for an authorised person to carry out his duties: see the dictum of Lord Goddard C.J. in *Hinchcliffe* v. *Sheldon* at 1210 which was followed by the Divisional Court in *Lewis* v. *Cox* [1984] 3 W.L.R. 875. In *Swallow* v. *London County Council* [1916] 1 K.B. 224, a case on the Weights and Measure Act 1889, it was held that, in the absence of a legal duty to act, standing by and doing nothing did not amount to an obstruction.

1–106

Offence: Which, on conviction, can attract a fine of up to level 4 on the standard scale (s.51(1)). A defence is provided by s.18.

Defences

18.—(1) In any proceedings for an offence under this Part of this Act, subject to subsection (2) below, it shall be a defence for the person charged to prove—

1–107

(*a*) that the commission of the offence was due to a mistake or to reliance on information supplied to him or to the act or default of another person, an accident or some other cause beyond his control; and

(*b*) that he took all reasonable precautions and exercised all due diligence to avoid the commission of such an offence by himself or any person under his control.

(2) If in any such case the defence provided by subsection (1) above involves the allegation that the commission of the offence was due to the act

or default of another person or to reliance on information supplied by another person, the person charged shall not, without leave of the court, be entitled to rely on that defence unless, within a period ending 7 clear days before the hearing, he has served on the prosecutor a notice in writing giving such information identifying or assisting in the identification of that other person as was then in his possession.

GENERAL NOTE

1–108 This section provides a defence to prosecutions brought under s.2, 5(6), 16(2) or 17(6) of this Act. It is submitted that it also applies to prosecutions brought under the Residential Care Homes Regulations 1984.

Subs. (1)

1–109 *Offence under this Part of this Act: i.e.* under s.2, 5(5),(6), 16(2) and 17(6).
Person: Or corporation (Interpretation Act 1978, s.5, Sched. 1).

Subs. (2)

1–110 *Notice:* As to the serving of notices, see s.54.
Writing: See the note on s.15(2).

Provisions supplementary to Part I

Meaning of "relative"

1–111 19.—(1) In this Part of this Act "relative" means any of the following—
   (*a*) husband or wife;
   (*b*) son or daughter;
   (*c*) father or mother;
   (*d*) brother or sister;
   (*e*) grandparent or other ascendant;
   (*f*) grandchild or other descendant;
   (*g*) uncle or aunt;
   (*h*) nephew or niece.
   (2) In deducing any relationship for the purposes of subsection (1) above—
   (*a*) any relationship by affinity shall be treated as a relationship by consanguinity, any relationship of the half-blood as a relationship of the whole blood, and the stepchild of any person as his child; and
   (*b*) an illegitimate person shall be treated as the legitimate child of his mother and reputed father.
   (3) In this section "husband" and "wife" include a person who is living with a person carrying on or intending to carry on a residential care home as that person's husband or wife, as the case may be, and who has been so living for a period of not less than 6 months.
   (4) A person, other than a relative, with whom a person carrying on or intending to carry on a residential care home ordinarily resides, and with whom that person has been ordinarily residing for a period of not less than 5 years, shall be treated for the purposes of this Part of this Act as if he were a relative.

DEFINITION
   residential care home: s.1(1), (2).

GENERAL NOTE

1–112 This section defines the term "relative". A relative of a sole proprietor of a residential care home can run the home for a limited period on the death of that person under s.6. Relatives are excluded from the calculation of the number of persons in a home for the purposes of ss.1(4) and 5(3).

Subs. (1)

1–113 *Relative:* Of any age.

Husband or wife: See subs. (3).

Son or daughter: An adopted child is treated as if he were the child of his adoptive parents (Adoption Act 1976, s.39) and an illegitimate child is treated as if he were the legitimate child of his mother and reputed father (subs. (2)(*b*)).

Subs. (2)

Affinity: A relationship by marriage. 1–114
Consanguinity: A blood relationship.

Subs. (4)

Ordinarily resides: This provision does not require the persons who have been residing 1–115
together for five years or more to have had an emotional attachment to each other. It covers members of religious communities needing care: see para. 18 of Annex A to Department of Health Circular No. LAC (92)10.

Five years: Temporary separations resulting, for example, from separate holidays being taken, should be disregarded in calculating this period. The persons concerned need not have lived together in the same place during this period.

General interpretation

20.—(1) In this Part of this Act— 1–116
"disablement", in relation to persons, means that they are blind, deaf or dumb or substantially and permanently handicapped by illness, injury or congenital deformity or any other disability prescribed by the Secretary of State;

"personal care" means care which includes assistance with bodily functions where such assistance is required;

"prescribed" means prescribed by regulations under this Part of this Act;

"registration authority", in relation to a residential care home, means, subject to subsection (2) below, the local social services authority for the area in which the home is situated;

["small home" has the meaning given to it by section 1(4A) above.]

(2) The Council of the Isles of Scilly is the registration authority in relation to a residential care home in the Isles.

AMENDMENT
The definition of small home was inserted by the Registered Homes Act 1991, s.1(9).

DEFINITIONS
residential care home: s.1(1), (2).
social services authority: s.55.

GENERAL NOTE

Subs. (1)

Disablement: No regulations have been made prescribing other disabilities for the purposes of 1–117
this definition.

Personal care: The Tribunal's conclusion in *Decision* No. 146 that this phrase "embraces care in many forms, emotional or psychiatric as well as physical" was approved by the Court of Appeal in *Harrison* v. *Cornwall County Council* (see below).

Bodily functions: In *R.* v. *National Insurance Commissioner, ex p. Secretary of State for Social Services* [1981] 2 All E.R. 738 at 741, C.A., Lord Denning M.R. defined "bodily functions" as including

"breathing, hearing, seeing, eating, drinking, walking, sitting, sleeping, getting in and out of bed, dressing, undressing, eliminating waste products, and the like, all of which an ordinary person, who is not suffering from any disability, does for himself. But they do not include cooking, shopping or any of the other things which a wife or daughter does as part of her domestic duties: or generally which one of the household normally does for the rest of the family".

Subsequently the House of Lords held in *Woodling* v. *Secretary of State for Social Services* [1984] 1 All E.R. 593 that the phrase "bodily functions" is a restricted and precise one, narrower than, for example, "bodily needs".

The fact that residents of a residential care home do not require and do not receive "assistance with bodily functions" does not prevent them from being persons who require or who are provided with "personal care" within the meaning of this Part of this Act (*Harrison* v. *Cornwall County Council* (1991) 90 L.G.R. 81).

Local social services authority: Matters relating to the discharge by a social services authority of its functions under this Act stand referred to the authority's social services committee (Local Authority Social Services Act 1970, s.2, Sched. 1). Each resident should be informed of the name and address of the registration authority: see reg. 17(2) of the Residential Care Homes Regulations 1984. "Authorities should keep separate accounts of their costs and incomes arising from the Registered Homes Act 1984": DHSS Circular No. LAC (88)15, para. 7.

Small home: Advice on the registration and inspection of small homes is contained in Department of Health Circular No. LAC (92)10.

Part II

Nursing Homes and Mental Nursing Homes

General Note

1–118 The Secretary of State has delegated his registration functions under this Act to district health authorities by virtue of the National Health Service Functions (Directions to Authorities and Administration Arrangements) Regulations 1991 (S.I. 1991 No. 554), regs. 3, 5 and 7. These functions cannot be further delegated by the district health authority.

The National Association of Health Authorities has produced a handbook, *Registration and Inspection of Nursing Homes* (1985). The

"aims of the handbook are twofold. First, it is to provide advice to District Health Authorities on their responsibilities in relation to registration and inspection of nursing homes and to be a source of reference to relevant legislation. Secondly, it seeks to provide model guidelines to assist District Health Authorities in carrying out the duties delegated to them by the Secretary of State": *ibid.* p.v.

This publication has been welcomed by the government: see DHSS Circular No. HC (84)21, para. 8. A supplement to the handbook was published in 1988.

The following guidance to health authorities on the exercise of their registration functions is contained in paras. 7 to 16 of DHSS Circular No. HC (86)5:

"Guidance

1–119 The review demonstrated that authorities had adopted different approaches to registration and inspection. In the light of the report of the review the following guidance is commended to all authorities.

Some authorities undertake a great deal of work in dealing with detailed pre-registration inquiries which do not result in a formal application for registration. It is for authorities to determine at what stage a formal application for registration is required, but the costs of detailed pre-registration work should be borne in mind in deciding when a formal application, together with the fee, should be submitted. A cost effective approach adopted by a few authorities is provision of an information package on nursing home registration for intending applicants, for which a charge is made to cover costs.

While authorities have a duty to co-operate with other statutory bodies that have an interest in private nursing homes, it is the responsibility of the applicant to obtain satisfactory reports from other statutory bodies. Authorities should advise applicants of the standards to be met and the various reports and certificates required, but the applicant himself should arrange for these to be obtained. Similarly, it is the responsibility of the applicant or person-in-charge to check with the United Kingdom Central Council for Nursing, Midwifery and Health Visiting (UKCC) the registration of all qualified nurses, including those employed from nurses' agencies.

Where unsatisfactory situations are identified during inspections of registered homes, health authorities should consider making use of the powers in Regulation 6 of the Nursing Homes and Mental Nursing Homes Regulations 1984 to vary the conditions of registration. Any notice issued under Regulation 6 should be identifiable as such to avoid possible misunderstanding on the part of recipients. Where unsatisfactory conditions are identified and persist, legal proceedings should be contemplated.

The 1984 Regulations provide for changes to be made in the conditions of registration without the home being required to go through the full registration procedure again. Such variations may be requested by either the "person registered" or the registering authority. Where the authority wishes to change the conditions there should be full prior discussions with the home. Varying a condition of registration to bring into use an extension to registered premises may not be appropriate, and this provision should be used for minor changes only. It is for authorities to decide whether a proposed variation is substantial, but when this is the case, the person registered has to apply for re-registration.

Authorities are reminded that it is up to them to ensure that they make the most efficient and economical use of their resources in fulfilling their statutory responsibilities in respect of registration and inspection. A minimum of two inspections in every period of 12 months must be made. In some cases, more than two inspections will be necessary, but authorities should consider carefully the need for additional visits and the size of the inspecting team required for any individual home. Authorities are requested to pay special attention to the need to avoid routine extra visits and excessive numbers of inspectors which will not, in normal circumstances, be justified. It is recognised, however, that, particularly with newly registered premises, the development role of inspection staff, for example in the area of nursing care, may mean that some additional visits will be essential.

Appeals

1–120 In submitting a notice of an appeal in respect of a nursing home to the Department, authorities are asked to include details of whether the appeal is against the refusal of an application, a condition of registration, or the cancellation of a registration. Authorities should also indicate whether the appeal is against the Order of a Justice of the Peace under the urgent procedure.

Authorities are reminded that, in issuing a notice to an applicant or person registered proposing to grant registration subject to conditions, refuse registration, cancel, vary or apply additional conditions to an existing registration, 14 days must be given for the applicant to make written or oral representations about any matter which he wishes to dispute. No decision to refuse or cancel registration or impose conditions should be made until the applicant has made representations or until the 14-day period has elapsed. No appeal can be entered against the decision of the health authority until that decision has actually been taken.

Inspection of unregistered premises

1–121 Homes providing care for less than four people are exempt from registration under Part I of the Registered Homes Act 1984 [*This is no longer the case—R.M.J.*], but not under Part II. They therefore come within the Secretary of State's Direction that authorities must seek to identify unregistered premises believed to be providing nursing care, and if nursing care is provided, the premises must be registered as a nursing home.

Contractual arrangements

1–122 Some private nursing homes admit NHS patients under contractual arrangements with health authorities. These beds are subject to inspection in the same way as those provided for private patients and should be subject to the same standards as are required for other beds in private nursing homes."

Interpretation

Meaning of "nursing home"

21.—(1) In this Act "nursing home" means, subject to subsection (3) 1–123 below—
    (*a*) any premises used, or intended to be used, for the reception of, and the provision of nursing for, persons suffering from any sickness, injury or infirmity;
    (*b*) any premises used, or intended to be used, for the reception of pregnant women, or of women immediately after childbirth (in this Act referred to as a "maternity home"); and
    (*c*) any premises not falling within either of the preceding paragraphs which are used, or intended to be used, for the provision of all or any of the following services, namely—
       (i) the carrying out of surgical procedures under anaesthesia;
       (ii) the termination of pregnancies;
       (iii) endoscopy;
       (iv) haemodialysis or peritoneal dialysis;
       (v) treatment by specially controlled techniques.
(2) In subsection (1) above "specially controlled techniques" means techniques specified under subsection (4) below as subject to control for the purposes of this Part of this Act.

(3) The definition in subsection (1) above does not include—
(a) any [health service hospital, within the meaning of the National Health Service Act 1977, or any] other premises maintained or controlled by a government department or local authority or any other authority or body instituted by special Act of Parliament or incorporated by Royal Charter;
(b) any mental nursing home;
(c) any sanatorium provided at a school or educational establishment and used, or intended to be used, solely by persons in attendance at, or members of the staff of, that school or establishment or members of their families;
(d) any first aid or treatment room provided at factory premises, at premises to which the Offices, Shops and Railways Premises Act 1963 applies or at a sports ground, show ground or place of public entertainment;
(e) any premises used, or intended to be used, wholly or mainly—
   (i) by a medical practitioner for the purpose of consultations with his patients;
   (ii) by a dental practitioner or chiropodist for the purpose of treating his patients; or
   (iii) for the provision of occupational health facilities,
   unless they are used, or intended to be used, for the provision of treatment by specially controlled techniques and are not excepted by regulations under paragraph (g) below;
(f) any premises used, or intended to be used, wholly or mainly as a private dwelling; or
(g) any other premises excepted from that definition by regulations made by the Secretary of State.

(4) The Secretary of State may by regulations specify as subject to control for the purposes of this Part of this Act any technique of medicine or surgery (including cosmetic surgery) as to which he is satisfied that its use may create a hazard for persons treated by means of it or for the staff of any premises where the technique is used.

(5) Without prejudice to the generality of section 56 below, regulations under subsection (4) above may define a technique by reference to any criteria which the Secretary of State considers appropriate.

(6) In this section "treatment" includes diagnosis and "treated" shall be construed accordingly.

DEFINITION
mental nursing home: s.22.

AMENDMENT
In subs. (3) the words in square brackets were substituted by the National Health Service and Community Care Act 1990, s.66(1), Sched. 9, para. 27.

GENERAL NOTE

1–124 This section defines those establishments which are required to be registered as nursing homes under this Act. If a person carries on an unregistered nursing home he commits an offence under s.23(1). It is also an offence for a person to call an establishment a nursing home when it is not registered as such (s.24(1)).

An establishment which is used solely as a nursing home is not a "residential care home" and is therefore not required to be registered under Pt. I of this Act: see s.1(5)(a). A nursing home which provides board and personal care, but not nursing care, for residents must also be registered under Pt. I of this Act. If fewer than four such residents are being cared for, the registered person can exercise the option provided for in s.4.

A registered nursing home which accommodates children is not a children's home for the purposes of Pt. VIII of the Children Act 1989 and does not therefore require to be registered under that Act (*ibid.* s.63(1), (5)).

Subs. (1)

Para. (a)

Any premises: Which could range from a large acute private hospital to a small nursing home providing long-term care. **1–125**

Reception of: The *Shorter Oxford English Dictionary* definition of "receive" in relation to a place or building reads as follows: "to admit (a person); to give accommodation or shelter to." It is therefore submitted that this paragraph and para. (*b*) exclude premises where patients are not kept in overnight.

Nursing: A definition of nursing home care and the circumstances in which such care may be necessary is contained in Annex 3 to the government publication *Managing Care*. Annex 3 is reproduced in the note on "pesonal care" in s.1(1). The most commonly used definition of nursing is the one contained in Virginia Henderson and Gladys Nite, *Principles and Practice of Nursing* (6th ed., 1978), p. 34: "Nursing is primarily helping people (sick or well) in the performance of those activities contributing to health, or its recovery (or to a peaceful death) that they would perform unaided if they had the necessary strength, will or knowledge. It is likewise the unique contribution of nursing to help people to be independent of such assistance as soon as possible." This definition is concerned with the activities of trained nurses and registration authorities might find it useful to make a distinction between "household nursing" and "professional nursing" when they are considering whether the ongoing care which is being provided to residents amounts to either "personal care" or "nursing" care: see the note on "personal care" in s.1(1). If the registration authority believes that some of the patients of a nursing home might be receiving "personal care" rather than "nursing" care it should arrange with the relevant local authority to undertake a joint inspection of the home: see the note on *Dual registration* in the General Note to this Act.

Para. (b)

Reception of: See the note on para. (*a*). Premises registered under this paragraph need not necesarily have to provide nursing care for the women accommodated in the home. **1–126**

The definition of a maternity home includes a number of establishments, often referred to as "mother and baby homes", which provide care and support for teenage mothers. Registration and inspection of these homes should be carried out in consultation with the relevant local authority: see further DHSS Circular No. HC (81)8, para. 49. The registered person must keep a case record of each child born to a patient in a maternity home: see the Nursing Home and Mental Home Regulations 1984, reg. 7(5), (6), Sched. 4.

Para. (c)

While the definitions in paras. (*a*) and (*b*) exclude the registration of premises where patients are not kept in overnight, the definition contained in this paragraph would include such premises. Note that the services mentioned in this paragraph could be provided without the assistance of nursing care and that the patients who receive such services need not necessarily be sick, injured or infirm: *cf.* para. (*a*). **1–127**

The termination of pregnancies: A registered nursing home that intends to admit patients for the termination of pregnancies must obtain the prior approval of the Secretary of State under the Abortion Act 1967, s.1(3): see further DHSS Circular No. HC (81)8, para. 15.

Specially controlled techniques: See subss. (2) and (4).

Subs. (2)

This Part of this Act: i.e. ss.21 to 38. **1–128**

Subs. (3)

Para. (a)

Hospital: Which includes a hospital or other premises maintained or controlled by the service authority of a visiting force or by a headquarters: see the Visiting Forces and International Headquarters (Application of Law) Order 1965 (S.I. 1965 No. 1536), art. 12(2), Sched. 3. **1–129**

Para. (f)

Premises: This paragraph is designed to exempt any person who uses dialysis equipment in his own home (DHSS Circular No. HC (81)8, Annex A, para. 5(*f*)). **1–130**

Mainly: It is submitted that this means "more than half".

Private dwelling: "Means occupation as the dwelling-house of a private person or occupied by a person in his private capacity as opposed to being occupied for business purposes": *per* Diplock J. in *G.E. Stevens (High Wycombe) Ltd.* v. *High Wycombe Corporation* [1962] 2 Q.B. 547 at 554.

Para. (g)

1-131 *Regulations:* No regulations have been made under this provision.

Subs. (4)

1-132 *Regulations:* Reg. 3 of the Nursing Homes and Mental Nursing Homes Regulations 1984 (S.I. 1984 No. 1578) specifies techniques of medicine or surgery involving the use of class 3B or class 4 laser products as subject to control for the purposes of this section. Class 3B and class 4 laser products are defined by reference to British Standard 4803:83 which is published by the British Standards Institution and can be obtained from the B.S.I., Linford Woods, Milton Keynes, MK14 6LE. Also see DHSS Circular No. HC (84)15 which gives advice to registration authorities on the registration and inspection of premises using lasers for medical and surgical purposes, a Department of Health document, *Guidance on the Safe Use of Lasers in Medical Practice*, copies of which are available from HMSO, and regs. 7(2) and 13 of the 1984 Regulations which deal with the keeping of records and the conduct of nursing homes using specially controlled techniques.

Any premises: Note that the premises mentioned in subs. (3)(*e*) are not exempt from registration if they are used for treatments involving class 3B or class 4 lasers.

Meaning of "mental nursing home"

1-133 **22.**—(1) In this Act "mental nursing home" means, subject to subsection (2) below, any premises used, or intended to be used, for the reception of, and the provision of nursing or other medical treatment (including care, habilitation and rehabilitation under medical supervision) for, one or more mentally disordered patients (meaning persons suffering, or appearing to be suffering, from mental disorder), whether exclusively or in common with other persons.

(2) In this Act "mental nursing home" does not include any hospital as defined in subsection (3) below, or any other premises managed by a government department or provided by a local authority.

(3) In subsection (2) above, "hospital" means—

(*a*) any health service hospital within the meaning of the National Health Service Act 1977; and

(*b*) any accommodation provided by a local authority and used as a hospital by or on behalf of the Secretary of State under that Act.

DEFINITION
mental disorder: s.55.

GENERAL NOTE

1-134 This section defines those establishments which are required to be registered as mental nursing homes under this Act. Special provisions relating to mental nursing homes are contained in ss.35 and 36. An establishment which is used solely as a mental nursing home is not a "residential care home" and is, therefore, not required to be registered under Pt. I of this Act: see s.1(5)(*a*). A mental nursing home which provides board and personal care, but not nursing care, for residents must also be registered under Pt. I of this Act. If fewer than four such residents are being cared for, the registered person can exercise the option provided for in s.4.

A registered mental nursing home which accommodates children is not a children's home for the purposes of Pt. VIII of the Children Act 1989 and does not therefore require to be registered under that Act (*ibid.* s.63(1), (5)).

If the requirements of s.23(3)(*c*), (5) are complied with, a registered nursing home can admit patients who are detained under the Mental Health Act 1983, except those patients who are being transferred from prison by virtue of orders made under ss.46, 47 and 48 of that Act. Under the 1983 Act a mental nursing home that admits detained patients has virtually all the powers and duties which are possessed by psychiatric hospitals. This means that the registered person must, *inter alia*, check that the documents authorising the detention of the patient are in order, ensure that the patient has a "responsible medical officer", give the patient details of his legal status, and consider whether to renew the authority to detain the patient. These and other responsibilities are discussed in Brenda Hoggett, *Mental Health Law* (3rd ed., 1990, Sweet Maxwell) and Richard Jones, *Mental Health Act Manual* (3rd ed., 1991, Sweet and Maxwell). A failure to deal with the relevant provisions of the 1983 Act may call into question the registered person's fitness to run a mental nursing home.

The Mental Health Act Commission, approved social workers, the registration authority, and a maintaining health authority have certain powers in relation to patients who are detained in mental nursing homes under the Mental Health Act 1983: see the note on s.35.

Under s.127(2) of the 1983 Act it is an offence "for any individual to ill-treat or wilfully to neglect a mentally disordered patient who is for the time being subject to his guardianship . . . or otherwise in his custody or care": see the note to s.127.

Subs. (1)

1–135 *Mental nursing home:* This definition does not cover establishments providing day care only. Guidance on the facilities to be provided by a mental nursing home is given in para. 50 of DHSS Circular No. HC (81)8.

Nursing: See the note on "personal care" in s.1(1).

Habilitation: "The action of enabling or endowing with ability or fitness" (*Oxford English Dictionary*). An illustration of the distinction between habilitation and rehabilitation was given by Mr. Terry Davis M.P. at the Special Standing Committee on the Mental Health (Amendment) Bill:

" 'habilitation' would cover those cases in which someone, probably a child, was so severely mentally impaired that he had never learnt certain social skills such as being able to eat or communicate in some way. The remedying of that impairment cannot be called 'rehabilitation' because that person never had those skills, so one has to use 'habilitation' in its technical sense" (June 22, 1982, col. 646).

Mentally disordered patients: In para. 47 of DHSS Circular No. HC (81)8 the following advice is given to registration authorities:

"Private nursing homes catering for elderly people may often accommodate some people who are mentally confused, but this need not necessarily involve registration as a mental nursing home. In such cases the authority will need to keep under consideration the number of such patients and the seriousness of their condition. Where the possibility of additional registration as a mental nursing home arises this should be fully discussed with those responsible for the home."

The difficulty here is to identify the distinction between "mentally confused" and "mentally disordered" patients, because, on a strict interpretation of the definition of "mental disorder" contained in s.55, a "confused" mind is probably a "disordered" mind. Many confusional states in the elderly are caused by infections and are generally short-lived once the underlying condition has been diagnosed and treated. It is submitted that establishments which nurse persons who are suffering from these temporary conditions should not be required to be registered as mental nursing homes. If, however, the establishment is nursing elderly persons who are suffering from a significant degree of intellectual deterioration and memory impairment arising from one of the organic dementias, registration as a mental nursing home would be required because dementia clearly comes within the category of "any other disorder or disability of mind" contained in the definition of mental disorder.

Subss. (2), (3)

1–136 These subsections exclude National Health Service hospitals and other government and local authority establishments from the requirements to register as mental nursing homes.

Hospital: The definition of "hospital" is contained in s.128 of the National Health Service Act 1977.

Registration and conduct of nursing homes and mental nursing homes

Registration of nursing homes and mental nursing homes

1–137 **23.**—(1) Any person who carries on a nursing home or a mental nursing home without being registered under this Part of this Act in respect of that home shall be guilty of an offence.

(2) Registration under this Part of this Act does not affect any requirement to register under Part I of this Act.

(3) An application for registration under this Part of this Act—

(*a*) shall be made to the Secretary of State;

(*b*) shall be accompanied by a fee of such amount as the Secretary of State may by regulations prescribe;

(*c*) in the case of a mental nursing home, shall specify whether or not it is proposed to receive in the home patients who are liable to be detained under the provisions of the Mental Health Act 1983.

(4) Subject to section 25 below, the Secretary of State shall, on receiving an application under subsection (3) above, register the applicant in respect of the home named in the application, and shall issue to the applicant a certificate of registration.

(5) Where a person is registered in pursuance of an application stating that it is proposed to receive in the home such patients as are described in subsection (3)(c) above—

(a) that fact shall be specified in the certificate of registration; and

(b) the particulars of the registration shall be entered by the Secretary of State in a separate part of the register.

(6) The certificate of registration issued under this Part of this Act in respect of any nursing home or mental nursing home shall be kept affixed in a conspicuous place in the home, and if default is made in complying with this subsection, the person carrying on the home shall be guilty of an offence.

DEFINITIONS
nursing home: s.21.
mental nursing home: s.22.

GENERAL NOTE

1–138   This section provides for applications for the registration of nursing homes and mental nursing homes to be made to registration authorities, makes it an offence to carry on an unregistered nursing home or mental nursing home, and provides that in certain circumstances a home has to be registered both as a nursing home or mental nursing home and as a residential care home. It also makes special provision for the registration of mental nursing homes which intend to care for patients who are detained under the Mental Health Act 1983.

The Secretary of State has directed district health authorities to inspect premises which are not registered as a nursing home or a mental nursing home where there is reason to believe that the premises should be so registered: see the note on s.27. If an inspection reveals that premises should be registered, the owner should be told to submit an immediate application and warned of the consequences of continued non-registration.

Subs. (1)

1–139   *Person:* Or corporation (Interpretation Act 1978, s.5, Sched. 1). Re-registration is not required where there is a change in the ownership or control of a company already registered under this Act. The company should inform the registration authority of such a change to enable the authority to satisfy itself that the company continues to be a "fit person": see paras. 34 and 35 of DHSS Circular No. HC (81)8.

If the registered person or, if he is not in charge of the home, the person who is in charge of it, proposes to be absent from the home for over a month, the registered person must inform the registration authority: see reg. 9 of the Nursing Homes and Mental Nursing Homes Regulations 1984.

Who carries on: The registered person cannot transfer the registration to another person.

Nursing home or a mental nursing home: A home cannot be registered as a nursing home and as a mental nursing home.

This Part: i.e. ss.21 to 38.

Offence: See ss.46(2) and 53(1). As to offences by corporations and their officers, see s.52. Note the power of the Secretary of State to exempt Christian Science homes from the provisions of this Part (s.37).

Subs. (2)

1–140   *Does not affect:* If a nursing home provides both board and personal care for more than four persons in the categories mentioned in s.1(1), it will have to apply to the local social services authority for registration as a residential care home. If the nursing home provides board and personal care for less than four persons, s.4 provides the home with an option as to whether it applies for registration as a residential care home. Also see the note on *Dual registration* in the General Note to this Act.

Subss. (3), (4), (5)

1–141   *Secretary of State:* See the General Note to this Part.

Subs. (3)

1–142   *Application:* Information which the registration authority will require from the applicant is set out in Sched. 2 to the Nursing Homes and Mental Nursing Homes Regulations 1984. The Rehabilitation of Offenders Act 1974 does not apply to procedures under this Act: see the General Note to this Act.

Fee: See Sched. 3 to the Nursing Homes and Mental Nursing Homes Regulations 1984 (S.I. 1984 No. 1578). Once the home has been registered the registered person is required to pay an annual fee by virtue of s.27(e).

Detained . . . under the Mental Health Act 1983: If the mental nursing home is caring for patients who are liable to be detained under the 1983 Act at the time when the registration authority cancels the home's registration under s.28, or when the registered person dies, the registration of the home will continue for a temporary period under s.36. Under s.23(3) of the 1983 Act patients who are detained in mental nursing homes may be discharged from their detention by the registration authority, or by the health authority which is maintaining them there.

Subs. (4)

Register: The registration can be made subject to conditions: see s.29.

1–143

The applicant: Under this Act the functions of the "person registered" and the "person in charge" of the home (s.25(1)(*f*)) are separate even though they might be performed by the same person. The "person registered" is the person who applied for registration. He is responsible to the registration authority for ensuring that the requirements of this Act and the Regulations are fulfilled, and his name appears on the registration certificate. There is no requirement in the Act for him to be professionally qualified. The "person in charge", who does not have to be registered, is the person who has responsibility for the day-to-day running of the home and for the care of patients. He must be a registered medical practitioner, a qualified nurse, or, in the case of a maternity home, a registered midwife. Under s.25(1)(*a*), the registration authority will need to ensure that both the "person registered" and the "person in charge" are fit persons to carry out their respective functions. An applicant for registration could be a corporation, in which case the authority will need to consider the fitness of the persons who control the company. The authority could refuse registration under s.25(1)(*a*), on the ground that, by reason of the unfitness of the persons who control the company, the company is not a "fit person" to carry on the nursing home.

Under s.145(1) of the Mental Health Act 1983, the person or persons registered in respect of a nursing home take on the functions of "the managers" of the home under that Act. Also note that by virtue of s.12(5)(*d*), (*e*) of the 1983 Act, a medical practitioner who is on the staff of a mental nursing home or who has a financial interest in the home cannot provide a medical recommendation for the purpose of supporting an application for the compulsory admission of a patient to that home under Pt. II of that Act.

Subs. (5)

Proposed to be received in the home: The fact that the applicant has stated that he proposes to receive patients who are detained under the Mental Health Act 1983 in his home does not mean that, once the home has been registered, either all or any of the patients must be subject to detention at any given time. A mental nursing home cannot admit patients who have been transferred from prison under ss.46, 47 and 48 of the 1983 Act.

1–144

Subs. (6)

Conspicuous place: It is submitted that the certificate of registration should be fixed in a place where it can be easily seen by staff, residents and visitors.

1–145

Offence: Which, on conviction, could attract a fine of up to level 2 on the standard scale, and to a further fine of up to £5 for each day on which the offence continues after conviction (s.47(2), (3)). As to persons who may take proceedings in respect of an offence under this subsection in relation to a nursing home, see s.53(1).

Prohibition of holding out premises as nursing home, maternity home or mental nursing home

24.—(1) A person who, with intent to deceive any person,—

1–146

(*a*) applies any name to premises in England or Wales; or

(*b*) in any way so describes such premises or holds such premises out,

as to indicate, or reasonably be understood to indicate, that the premises are a nursing home or maternity home, shall be guilty of an offence unless registration has been effected under this Part of this Act in respect of the premises as a nursing home.

(2) A person who, with intent to deceive any person,—

(*a*) applies any name to premises in England or Wales; or

(*b*) in any way so describes such premises or holds such premises out,

as to indicate, or reasonably be understood to indicate, that the premises are a mental nursing home, shall be guilty of an offence, unless registration has been effected under this Part of this Act in respect of the premises as a mental nursing home.

DEFINITIONS

nursing home: s.21.

maternity home: s.21(1)(*b*).
mental nursing home: s.22.

GENERAL NOTE

1–147 This section makes it an offence for a person who is not registered under this Part intentionally to set out to deceive any person by describing or holding out premises to be a nursing home, maternity home or mental nursing home. Proprietors of residential care homes should therefore take care not to describe their establishments as nursing homes if they are to avoid prosecution. A person found guilty of an offence under this section could be fined up to level 3 on the standard scale (s.50).

Subss. (1), (2)

1–148 *Person:* Or corporation (Interpretation Act 1978, s.5. Sched. 1).

To deceive: Is to induce a person to believe that a thing is true which is false, or to believe a thing to be false which is true, contrary to what the person practising the deceit believes to be the case (*Re London and Globe Finance Corporation Ltd.* [1903] 1 Ch. 728 at 732, *per* Buckley J., as modified by the observations of Lord Radcliffe in *Welham* v. *D.P.P.* [1961] A.C. 103 at 126, 127).

Describes: Either in the name that is given to the home, in publicity material, or in oral communication.

Holds such premises out: It would therefore be an offence for a person to produce publicity material about a home which is not registered under this Part which either explicitly or implicitly refers to the provision of nursing care. It is submitted that the apparently widespread practice of unqualified proprietors and managers of residential care homes calling themselves "matron" could place the proprietor at risk of contravening this section: see B. Holmes and A. Johnson, *Cold Comfort* (Souvenir Press, 1988), p. 26.

This Part of this Act: i.e. ss.21 to 38.

Offence: For offences committed by corporations and their officers, see s.52.

Refusal of registration

1–149 **25.**—(1) The Secretary of State may refuse to register an applicant in respect of a nursing home or a mental nursing home if he is satisfied—

(*a*) that the applicant, or any person employed or proposed to be employed by the applicant at the home, is not a fit person (whether by reason of age or otherwise) to carry on or be employed at a home of such a description as that named in the application; or

(*b*) that, for reasons connected with situation, construction, state of repair, accommodation, staffing or equipment, the home is not, or any premises used in connection with the home are not, fit to be used for such a home; or

(*c*) that the home is, or any premises used in connection with the home are, used, or proposed to be used, for purposes which are in any way improper or undesirable in the case of such a home; or

(*d*)–(*e*) [*Repealed by the National Health Service and Community Care Act* 1990, *s.*66(2), *Sched.* 10.]

(*f*) that the home is not, or will not be, in the charge of a person who is either a registered medical practitioner or a qualified nurse or, in the case of a maternity home, a registered midwife; or

(*g*) that the condition mentioned in subsection (3) below is not, or will not be, fulfilled in relation to the home.

(2) In subsection (1) above "qualified nurse", in relation to a home, means a nurse possessing such qualifications as may be specified in a notice served by the Secretary of a State on the person carrying on or proposing to carry on the home.

(3) The condition referred to in subsection (1) above is that such numbers of nurses possessing such qualifications and, in the case of a maternity home, such number of registered midwives as may be specified in a notice served by the Secretary of State on the person carrying on or proposing to carry on the home are on duty in the home at such times as may be specified.

(4) In preparing any notice under subsection (2) or (3) above, the Secretary of State shall have regard to the class and, in the case of a notice under subsection (3) above, the number of patients for whom nursing care is or is to be provided in the home.

DEFINITIONS
nursing home: s.21.
mental nursing home: s.22.
maternity home: s.21(1)(*b*).

TRANSITIONAL PROVISIONS
See Sched. 2, paras. 1, 2.

GENERAL NOTE

This section sets out the criteria which enable a registration authority to refuse to register an applicant for registration in respect of a nursing home or mental nursing home. When an authority intends to refuse a registration application it must give the applicant notice of the proposal (s.31(2)) and the reasons for it (s.31(4)). The applicant then has 14 days within which he may notify the authority that he wishes to make representations about the proposal (s.32(1)). If the applicant does not wish to make representations the authority can proceed to refuse the application (s.32(2)(*b*)). If the applicant does wish to make representations the authority cannot make a final decision until it has considered the representations (s.32(2)(*a*)), as long as they are made within a reasonable time (s.32(3)).

A registration authority's decision to refuse an application takes immediate effect (s.33(3)). An appeal against the decision can be made to a Registered Homes Tribunal (s.34(1)).

Registration authorities are given advice on their power to refuse or cancel a registration in paras. 26 and 27 of DHSS Circular No. HC(81):

1–150

"The authority has power to cancel registration or to refuse to register a home. Cancellation is clearly a final resort. In most cases where problems arise they can be identified quickly through frequent and effective inspection, and resolved by discussion. Decisions to refuse or cancel a registration should only result after the authority has concluded that there has been a serious breach of the registration requirements and that the 'person registered' was either unwilling or unable to meet and maintain the standards required.

It is important that authorities establish clear procedures for dealing with registration problems and especially the refusal or cancellation of a registration. When difficulties arise which may lead to refusal or cancellation, the authority should ensure, at the outset, that the applicant or 'person registered' is given a clear explanation, in writing, of the requirements they are failing to fulfil and the steps to be taken to rectify the situation. This statement should indicate a timescale for meeting the requirements, giving the applicant or 'person registered' reasonable time to fulfil the requirements."

Subs. (1)

Secretary of State: See the General Note to this Part.
May: The registration authority has a discretion.
Refuse to register: If the registration authority decides to adopt the proposal to refuse an application it must send the applicant written notice of its decision, together with a note explaining the applicant's right of appeal to a Registered Homes Tribunal (s.33).

1–151

Para. (a)

Applicant: Which could be a corporation (Interpretation Act 1978, s.5, Sched. 1). If the applicant is a corporation, the registration authority will need to satisfy itself as to the fitness of those in control. Under s.52, the officers of a corporation as well as the corporation itself are deemed to be guilty of an offence where an offence has been committed.

1–152

Note that it is the applicant, and not the premises, that is registered. The applicant does not have to be in charge of the home, and nor can he be unless para. (*f*) is satisfied.

Employed: In *Decision* No. 39 the Tribunal took the view that the term "employed" meant that the person concerned was engaged or employed within the dictionary meaning and that the expression is not limited to gainful employment. In this case the Tribunal found that a person was a person employed within the meaning of this section because of his close financial association with the company which was the "person registered" in respect of the home, his need from time to time to protect this financial interest by dealing with the Department of Social Security and with the relatives of residents, his signing cheques on behalf of the company, and his proximity to the whole enterprise by virtue of his wife's close association with the company as its former managing director and secretary.

Fit person: An analysis of the meaning of "fit person" and examples of situations where the Registered Homes Tribunal has found that a person is not a "fit person" for the purposes of Pt. I of this Act are contained in the note to s.9(*a*).

In *Decision* No. 154 the Tribunal emphasised that:
> "anybody running a nursing home must be reliable, trusting, caring and of integrity, and be able to set the example and the standard of care in the home. Some of the elements of a fit person were those capable of coping under pressure, showing patience and total commitment to the job and of intelligence. It was also essential to understand and to prepare a policy of the administration of drugs and to look after the care of the vulnerable and defenceless persons who were likely to become patients in the home."

Department of Health Circular LAC (91)4: HC (91)16 sets out the procedure for checking with the police the possible criminal background of applicants for registration as owners or managers of nursing homes and mental nursing homes. The Rehabilitation of Offenders Act 1974 does not apply to applicants for registration: see the General Note to this Act. To aid authorities in their task of judging the fitness of applicants, the Department of Health keeps a list of persons and companies whose registration in respect of a residential care home, a nursing home, a mental nursing home or a children's home has been cancelled after the commencement of this Act. Notification has been given in para. 7 of Health Notice HN (89)19 that the list is being extended to include the names of people whose application for registration has been refused on or after September 1, 1989, on the ground that he was not a fit person to run such a home. If the applicant intends to accommodate children in the home, the authority can also make use of the "consultancy service" operated by the Department. It is submitted that a registration authority must give reasons for refusing to register an applicant under this provision and that it is not a sufficient reason for the authority to state baldly that an applicant is not a fit person by reason of his appearing on the Department of Health list.

Para. (b)

1–153   *Fit:* The provision of facilities and services are governed by reg. 12 of the Nursing Homes and Mental Nursing Homes Regulations 1984 and reference should be made to the notes thereto.

Para. (c)

1–154   *Improper or undesirable:* This provision gives the registration authority power to investigate the therapeutic régime that the applicant proposes to adopt.

Para. (f)

1–155   *In charge of:* The "person in charge" of a home need not necessarily reside at the home. See the note on s.23(4), for a discussion of the separate functions of the "person registered" and the "person in charge" of the home. Where the "person registered" employs someone as "person in charge" of the home, re-registration would not be required if the "person in charge" was changed, although the registration authority could consider cancelling the registration if it did not regard the new employee as a fit person. If the home is dually registered as a nursing home and as a residential care home the person who is the "manager" of the home will have to be registered if he is not in control of it: see s.3. The "person in charge" and the "manager" could be the same person.

The National Association of Health Authorities recommends that "a person designated as being 'in charge' of a nursing home does *not* hold a similar position in any other nursing home. It also recommends that the 'person-in-charge' works a minimum of 35 hours per week in respect of the home": para. 2.8 of the 1988 supplement to the handbook, *Registration and Inspection of Nursing Homes.*

Qualified nurse: See para. 43 of DHSS Circular No. HC (81)8 and subs. (2).

Subs. (2)

1–156   *Such qualifications as may be prescribed:* See the Direction issued by the Secretary of State for Social Services in September 1984 which is reproduced in the note on s.27.

Subss. (3), (4)

1–157   These subsections give registration authorities "discretion in determining the numbers and qualifications of nursing staff in a home, and when they should be on duty. In exercising that discretion authorities are under a statutory duty to have regard to the category and number of patients for whom the premises are to be used. These conditions will vary considerably—a hospital carrying out major surgery or a home accommodating very elderly and frail patients will need 24 hour nursing cover whereas a clinic carrying out surgery on a day care basis only will obviously not. Once determined these staffing requirements will also be a condition of registration set out in a notice under subs. (3), which may not be reduced without the permission of the authority. Where the premises are fully occupied the nurse staffing must be maintained at least at the level specified in the notice": DHSS Circular No. HC (81)8, para. 42.

Subs. (3)

Condition: Which could be varied under the procedure set out in the Nursing Homes and Mental Nursing Homes Regulations 1984, reg. 6. Non-compliance with the condition could lead to the registration being cancelled under s.28.

As may be specified: The registration authority has a discretion when it comes to determining the number of nurses or midwives who are to be specified in the notice. Note that a condition made under this provision does not have to be specified in the certificate of registration (*cf.* s.29(1)). Advice on nursing qualifications and staffing levels is contained in the 1988 supplement to the NAHA Handbook, *Registration and Inspection of Nursing Homes*, pp. 8–11.

Notices: See s.54.

1–158

Regulations as to conduct of nursing homes and mental nursing homes

26. The Secretary of State may make regulations as to the conduct of nursing homes and mental nursing homes, and such regulations may in particular—

(*a*) make provision as to the facilities and services to be provided in such homes;

(*b*) make provision as to the giving of notice by a person registered in respect of such a home of periods during which he or, if he is not in charge of the home, the person who is in charge of it, proposes to be absent from the home;

(*c*) specify the information to be supplied in such a notice;

(*d*) provide for the making of adequate arrangements for the running of such a home during a period when the person in charge of it is absent from it;

(*e*) provide that a contravention of or failure to comply with any specified provision of the regulations shall be an offence against the regulations.

1–159

DEFINITIONS

nursing home: s.21.
mental nursing home: s.22.

GENERAL NOTE

Regulations made under this section may make provision in respect of the additional matters set out in s.35(3).

Regulations: See the Nursing Homes and Mental Nursing Homes Regulations 1984 (S.I. 1984 No. 1578). A failure to comply with these regulations is an offence (reg. 15). and the fact that a person has been convicted of such an offence provides a ground for cancelling the registration (s.28(*d*)). A procedure for securing compliance with the regulations is set out in reg. 15(4).

1–160

Para. (e)

Offence: Which, on conviction, could attract a fine of up to level 4 on the standard scale (s.49).

1–161

Supplementary regulations

27. The Secretary of State may make regulations—

(*a*) with respect to the registration of persons under this Part of this Act in respect of nursing homes and mental nursing homes, and in particular with respect to—
 (i) the making of applications for registration; and
 (ii) the refusal and cancellation of registration;

(*b*) with respect to the keeping of records relating to nursing homes and mental nursing homes, including records relating to the detention and treatment of persons detained under the Mental Health Act 1983 in a mental nursing home;

(*c*) with respect to the notification of events occurring in nursing homes and mental nursing homes;

1–162

(d) with respect to entry into and the inspection of premises used or reasonably believed to be used as a nursing home;
(e) requiring persons registered under this Part of this Act to pay an annual fee of such amount as the regulations may specify;
(f) specifying when the fee is to be paid;
(g) providing that a contravention of or failure to comply with any specified provision of the regulations shall be an offence against the regulations.

DEFINITIONS
nursing home: s.21.
mental nursing home: s.22.

GENERAL NOTE

1–163 *Regulations:* See the Nursing Homes and Mental Nursing Homes Regulations 1984. (S.I. 1984 No. 1578).

Para. (d)

1–164 *Inspection . . . nursing home:* Regulations relating to the inspection of mental nursing homes are made under s.26, as extended by s.35(3).
Reasonably believed to be used: The following direction was made by the Secretary of State for Social Services in September 1984 (see Annex C to Circular No. HC (84)(21):
"The Secretary of State for Social Services, in exercise of the powers conferred on him by section 17 of the National Health Service Act 1977 and all other powers enabling him on that behalf, hereby gives the following Directions:—
1. Each District Health Authority is hereby directed, in the exercise of the functions relating to nursing homes and mental nursing homes which it has been directed to exercise:—
    (1) to secure that there shall be inspected any premises in its district which are not registered as a nursing home or a mental nursing home under Part II of the Registered Homes Act 1984 and which it has reason to believe should be so registered;
    (2) to specify in any notice served under section 25(2) of the Registered Homes Act 1984, as a qualification which a nurse shall possess, that the nurse shall be registered in Part 1, 3, 5, 8 or 10 of the register maintained under the Nurses, Midwives and Health Visitors Act 1979.
2. The Nursing Homes (Qualifications of Nurses) Directions 1981 are hereby revoked."

Para. (g)

1–165 *Offence:* Which, on conviction, would attract a fine up to level 4 on the standard scale (s.49). A conviction for a failure to comply with the Regulations is a ground for cancelling the registration: see s.28(d).

Cancellation of registration

1–166 **28.** The Secretary of State may at any time cancel the registration of a person in respect of a nursing home or mental nursing home—
(a) on any ground which would entitle him to refuse an application for the registration of that person in respect of that home;
(b) on the ground that the person has been convicted of an offence against the provisions of this Part of this Act relating to nursing homes or mental nursing homes, or on the ground that any other person has been convicted of such an offence in respect of that home;
(c) on the ground that any condition for the time being in force in respect of the home by virtue of this Part of this Act has not been complied with;
(d) on the ground that that person has been convicted of an offence against regulations made under section 26 or 27 above;
(e) on the ground that the annual fee in respect of the home has not been paid on or before the due date.

DEFINITIONS
nursing home: s.21.
mental nursing home: s.22.

GENERAL NOTE

1–167 This section provides a registration authority with grounds for cancelling the registration of a person in respect of a nursing home or mental nursing home. When an authority intends to cancel a registration it must first give the registered person notice of the proposal (s.31(2)) and the reasons for it (s.3(4)). The registered person then has 14 days within which he may notify the authority that he wishes to make representations about the proposal (s.32(1)). If the registered person does not wish to make representations the authority can proceed to cancel the registration (s.32(2)(b)). If the registered person does wish to make representations the authority cannot make a final decision on the proposal until it has considered the representations (s.32(2)(a)), as long as they are made within a reasonable time (s.32(3)). If the authority believes that the length of this procedure would put the life, health or well-being of the patients seriously at risk it could make an application to a magistrate under s.30.

If the registered person decides not to exercise his right to appeal to a Registered Homes Tribunal against the decision to cancel his registration (s.34(1)) the decision will not take effect until 28 days after he was notified by the authority that it had been made (ss.33(3)(a), 34(3)). If an application is made to a Tribunal the decision will not take effect until the appeal is either determined or abandoned (s.33(3)(b)). A registered person is not entitled to use judicial review to challenge the registration authority's decision to cancel the registration until the appeals procedure before the Registered Homes Tribunal has been exhausted (*R. v. Birmingham City Council, ex p. Ferrero* (1991) 89 L.G.R. 977).

If the registration authority cancels the registration of a mental nursing home at a time when the home is caring for patients who are liable to be detained under the Mental Health Act 1983, the registration of the home will continue for a temporary period under s.36.

The Department of Health keeps a list of persons whose registration has been cancelled under this section. The procedure is set out in DHSS Circular No. HC (84)21, Annex B, paras. 23 to 34. Also see the extract from DHSS Circular No. HC (81)8 reproduced in the General Note to s.25.

Secretary of State: See the General Note to this Part.
Person: Or corporation (Interpretation Act 1978, s.5, Sched. 1).
May: The registration authority has a discretion. As an alternative to cancelling a registration, the authority could consider varying a condition of the registration or imposing a new condition under s.29(3).

Para. (a)

1–168 *Refuse an application:* See the notes on s.25. This provision would, for example, enable a registration authority to cancel the registration of a mental nursing home which was found to be operating an improper behaviour modification régime: see s.25(1)(c).

Para. (b)

1–169 *Offence against the provisions of this Part:* See ss.23(1), (6), 24(1), (2), 29(4), and 35(5), (6). A conviction by the registered person in respect of *any* nursing home or mental nursing home is a sufficient ground for cancellation.

Any other person: Even if that person is no longer concerned with the running of the home. A conviction by "any other person" is a sufficient ground for cancellation only if the conviction is *in respect of the home in question.*

Para. (c)

1–170 *Any condition for the time being in force:* The registration authority could cancel a registration on this ground even though it has not exercised its powers to prosecute for a breach of the condition under s.29(4).

Para. (d)

1–171 *Offence against regulations:* See reg. 15 of the Nursing Homes and Mental Nursing Homes Regulations 1984. The conviction need not necessarily relate to the home in question. Note that a breach of the Regulations which is not followed by a prosecution and conviction is not a ground for cancelling the registration.

Para. (e)

1–172 *Annual fee:* See Sched. 3 to the Nursing Homes and Mental Nursing Homes Regulations 1984.

Additional registration conditions

1–173 **29.**—(1) It shall be a condition of the registration of any person in respect of a nursing home or mental nursing home that the number of persons kept at any time in the home (excluding persons carrying on, or employed in, the home, together with their families) does not exceed such number as may be specified in the certificate of registration.

(2) Without prejudice to subsection (1) above, any such registration may be effected subject to such conditions (to be specified in the certificate of registration) as the Secretary of State may consider appropriate for regulating the age, sex or other category of persons who may be received in the home in question.

(3) The Secretary of State may make regulations—
   (a) as to the variation of any condition for the time being in force in respect of a nursing home or mental nursing home by virtue of this Part of this Act; and
   (b) as to this imposition of additional conditions.

(4) If any conditions for the time being in force in respect of a home by virtue of this Part of this Act is not complied with, the person carrying on the home shall be guilty of an offence.

DEFINITIONS
   nursing home: s.21.
   mental nursing home: s.22.

GENERAL NOTE

1–174   This section provides for the registration of a nursing home or mental nursing home to be made subject to conditions, enables regulations to be made to allow for the variation of a condition of registration and for the imposition of additional conditions and makes non-compliance with a condition of registration an offence. See s.25(3) for the imposition of a condition regulating the number of qualified nurses or registered midwives required to be on duty at the home at any given time.

Subs. (1)

1–175   *Shall be a condition:* The number of residents in a nursing home or mental nursing home must not exceed the number which may be specified in the certificate of registration. The registration authority must give notice to the applicant of any condition which it proposes to attach to the registration (s.31(1)) and the reasons for it (s.31(4)). This notice will specify that the applicant has 14 days within which he may require the authority to give him the opportunity to make representations about the proposal (s.32(1)). If the applicant does not wish to make representations the authority can proceed to grant the application (s.32(2)(b)). If the applicant does wish to make representations the authority cannot make a final determination on the proposal until it has considered the representations (s.32(2)(a)), as long as they are made within a reasonable time (s.32(3)).

A registration authority's decision to grant an application subject only to conditions which have been agreed with the applicant takes effect immediately (s.33(3)). If a condition has not been agreed between the authority and the applicant, and the applicant decides not to exercise his right to appeal to a Registered Homes Tribunal (s.34(1)) the decision will not take effect until 28 days after he was notified by the authority that it has been imposed (ss.33(3)(a), 34(3)). If an application is made to a Tribunal the decision will not take effect until the appeal it either determined or abandoned (s.33(3)(b)).

Number of persons: See *Tribunal Decision* No. 61, noted under s.5.
Families: Compare with "relatives" in s.5(3).
Certificate of registration: See s.23(4).

Subs. (2)

1–176   *Conditions:* The registration authority's power to impose conditions on an initial registration under this subsection or to vary or impose conditions under subs. (3) is governed by the decisions of the High Court in *Warwickshire County Council* v. *McSweeney* (unreported, December 8, 1988, *per* Roch J.), and *Isle of Wight County Council* v. *Humphreys* (1991) 90 L.G.R. 186, noted under s.5(3).

Subs. (3)

1–177   *Regulations:* See reg. 6 of the Nursing Homes and Mental Nursing Homes Regulations 1984. Regulations under para. (b) imposing additional conditions have not been made.

Variation . . . imposition: Notice of the authority's proposal and the reasons for it must be given to the registered person (s.31(3), (4)). Thereafter the provisions of ss.32 to 34 apply. The registration authority will need to consider whether the variation of the condition should be reflected in the number of nurses that are required to be on duty at the home: see s.25(3). Also see the note on subs. (2).

Subs. (4)

Offence: Which, on conviction, could attract a fine of up to level 4 on the standard scale (s.48). For offences by a corporation and its officers, see s.52.

1–178

Urgent procedure for cancellation of registration, etc.

30.—(1) If— 1–179
  (a) the Secretary of State applies to a justice of the peace for an order—
    (i) cancelling the registration of a person in respect of a nursing home or mental nursing home;
    (ii) varying any condition for the time being in force in respect of a home by virtue of this Part of this Act; or
    (iii) imposing an additional condition; and
  (b) it appears to the justice of the peace that there will be a serious risk to the life, health or well-being of the patients in the home unless the order is made,
he may make the order, and the cancellation, variation or imposition shall have effect from the date on which the order is made.

(2) An application under subsection (1) above may be made *ex parte* and shall be supported by a written statement of the Secretary of State's reasons for making the application.

(3) An order under subsection (1) above shall be in writing.

(4) Where such an order is made, the Secretary of State shall serve on any person registered in respect of the home, as soon as practicable after the making of the order,—
  (a) notice of the making of the order and of its terms; and
  (b) a copy of the statement of the Secretary of State's reasons which supported his application for the order.

DEFINITIONS
  nursing home: s.21.
  mental nursing home: s.22.

GENERAL NOTE

This section provides for a single magistrate to make an order cancelling or amending the registration of a nursing home or mental home on being satisfied that there would be a serious risk to the life, health, or well-being of the patients in the home if the order was not made. An order made under this section has immediate effect. The grounds upon which an application can be made to a magistrate and the procedure to be adopted by the registration authority were considered by the Court of Appeal in *Lyons* v. *East Sussex County Council* [1988] 86 L.G.R. 369: see the note on s.11. 1–180

"The question of the arrangements for care of patients affected by a Section 30 order will have concerned the registering authority during the approach to the making of an order, and all necessary action should be arranged so that patients are cared for": NAHA handbook, *Registration and Inspection of Nursing Homes*, Pt. I, para. 3.33c.

Subs. (1)

Secretary of State: See the General Note to this Part. 1–181
Person: Or corporation (Interpretation Act 1978, s.5, Sched. 1).
This Part of this Act: i.e. Pt. II (ss.21 to 38).
Serious risk: See the note on s.11.
Shall have effect from the date on which the order is made: From then on the registered person would be liable to be prosecuted under either s.23(1) or 29(4) if he failed to comply with the order.

Subs. (2)

Ex parte: The registration authority need not inform the registered person that it intends to apply to a magistrate under this section. 1–182
Written: See the note on s.15(2).

Reasons: Which would include an account of the nature of the risk to patients and the authority's justification for considering that the risk involved is serious enough to justify that use of this procedure.

Subs. (4)

1–183 *Serve on any person registered:* Who can appeal against the order to a Registered Homes Tribunal (s.34(1)(*b*)).
Notice: See s.54.

Ordinary procedure for registration, etc., under Part II

1–184 **31.**—(1) Where—
(*a*) a person applies for registration in respect of a nursing home or mental nursing home; and
(*b*) the Secretary of State proposes to grant his application,
the Secretary of State shall give him written notice of this proposal and of the conditions subject to which he proposes to grant his application.

(2) The Secretary of State shall give an applicant notice of a proposal to refuse his application.

(3) Except where he makes an application under section 30 above, the Secretary of State shall give any person registered in respect of a nursing home or mental nursing home notice of a proposal—
(*a*) to cancel the registration;
(*b*) to vary any condition for the time being in force in respect of the home by virtue of this Act; or
(*c*) to impose any additional condition.

(4) A notice under this section shall give the Secretary of State's reasons for his proposal.

DEFINITIONS
nursing home: s.21.
mental nursing home: s.22.

GENERAL NOTE

1–185 The general procedure for dealing with a registration application and for cancelling, refusing or amending a registration is set out in this section and in ss.32 and 33. An urgent procedure for cancelling or amending a registration is contained in s.30.

Subs. (1)

1–186 *Person:* Or corporation (Interpretation Act 1978, s.5, Sched. 1).
Applies for registration: See s.23.
Secretary of State: See the General Note to this Part.
Written: See the note to s.15(2).
Notices: Notices issued under this section are subject to the provisions of s.32. As to the service of notices, see s.54.
Conditions: A decision to grant an application for registration subject only to conditions agreed between the applicant and the registration authority is effective from the date when the authority informs the applicant of its decision to register (s.33(3)).

Subs. (2)

1–187 *Refuse his application:* On one of the grounds set out in s.25.

Subs. (3)

1–188 *Cancel the registration:* See s.28.
Vary any condition . . . impose any additional condition: See s.29(3).

Right to make representations

1–189 **32.**—(1) A notice under section 31 above shall state that within 14 days of service of the notice any person on whom it is served may in writing require the Secretary of State to give him an opportunity to make representations to him concerning any matter which that person wishes to dispute.

(2) Where a notice has been served under section 31 above, the Secretary of State shall not determine any matter in dispute until either—
  (a) any person on whom the notice was served has made representations to him, concerning the matter; or
  (b) the period during which any such person could have required the Secretary of State to give him an opportunity to make representations has elapsed without the Secretary of State being required to give such an opportunity; or
  (c) the conditions specified in subsection (3) below are satisfied.
(3) The conditions mentioned in subsection (2) above are—
  (a) that a person on whom the notice was served has required the Secretary of State to give him an opportunity to make representations to him concerning the matter;
  (b) that the Secretary of State has allowed him a reasonable period to make his representations; and
  (c) that he has failed to make them within that period.
(4) The representations may be made, at the option of the person making them, either in writing or orally.
(5) If he informs the Secretary of State that he desires to make oral representations, the Secretary of State shall give him an opportunity of appearing before and of being heard by a person appointed by the Secretary of State.

GENERAL NOTE

This section establishes a right to make representations to a registration authority in respect of a proposal which has been notified in accordance with the provisions of s.31. If the person who has been so notified decides to exercise his right to make representations, the registration authority cannot normally come to a decision on the proposal until it has considered the representations (subs. (2)(a)). The authority can proceed to make a final decision on the proposal if the person fails to make his representations within a reasonable period (subs. (3)).

See the note on s.13, for the procedure that should be adopted by a registration authority when receiving representations under this section. Paragraph 3.6 of the 1988 supplement to the NAHA handbook, *Registration and Inspection of Nursing Homes*, states that "the person(s) to hear (or receive) the representations should not be an officer of the authority involved in the advising of the proposals. Some authorities have found it helpful to appoint a sub-committee of members either ad hoc or as a standing body to advise the authority and/or hear representations on its behalf".

1–190

Subs. (1)

Within 14 days of service: Excluding the day of service (*Dodds* v. *Walker* [1981] 2 All E.R. 609, H.L.).
  Service of the notice: See s.54.
  Person: Or corporation (Interpretation Act 1978, s.5, Sched. 1).
  Secretary of State: See the General Note to this Part.
  Representations: Which can be made orally or in writing (subs. (4)).

1–191

Subs. (2)

Para. (a)

Has made representations: The person has a reasonable period within which he can make his representations (subs. (3)).

1–192

Para. (b)

The period: Of 14 days from the service of the notice (subs. (1)).

1–193

Subs. (3)

Reasonable period: What is a "reasonable period" would, to a certain extent, depend on the complexity of the issues involved. It is suggested that the registration authority should indicate to the person who wishes to make representations the period within which the authority is prepared to receive them.

1–194

Subs. (4)

In writing or orally: These are alternatives and the person concerned must notify the registration authority of the preferred option.

1–195

Subs. (5)

1–196 *Person appointed:* Or persons appointed (Interpretation Act 1978, s.6). The person appointed, who should not have had any previous dealings with the case, could be a member or officer of the registration authority or be some other suitably qualified person.

Decision of Secretary of State

1–197 **33.**—(1) If the Secretary of State decides to adopt the proposal, he shall serve notice in writing of his decision on any person on whom he was required to serve notice of the proposal.

(2) A notice under this section shall be accompanied by a note explaining the right of appeal conferred by section 34 below.

(3) A decision of the Secretary of State, other than a decision to grant an application for registration subject only to conditions agreed between the applicant and the Secretary of State or to refuse an application for registration, shall not take effect—

(a) if no appeal is brought, until the expiration of the period of 28 days referred to in section 34(3) below; and

(b) if an appeal is brought, until it is determined or abandoned.

GENERAL NOTE

1–198 The section sets out the procedure to be followed by the registration authority when it decides to adopt a proposal to grant an application for registration, or to refuse, cancel or amend a registration. It also provides that the authority's decision shall not take effect either until the expiration of the 28-day period within which an appeal against the decision may be made (s.34(3)) or, if an appeal is made, until it is determined or abandoned. This delay does not apply where the authority is granting a registration application subject only to conditions which have been agreed between the authority and the applicant or where a decision has been made to refuse an application.

Subs. (1)

1–199 *Secretary of State:* See the General Note to this Part.
Serve: See s.54 for the service of notices under this Act.
Notice in writing: See the note on s.15(2).
On any person: Who will either be the applicant or the registered person: see s.31.

Appeals

1–200 **34.**—(1) An appeal against—

(a) a decision of the Secretary of State under this Part of this Act; or

(b) an order made by a justice of the peace under section 30 above,

shall lie to a Registered Homes Tribunal.

(2) An appeal shall be brought by notice in writing given to the Secretary of State.

(3) No appeal against a decision or order may be brought by a person more than 28 days after service on him of notice of the decision or order.

(4) On an appeal against a decision of the Secretary of State the tribunal may confirm the decision or direct that it shall not have effect.

(5) On an appeal against an order made by a justice of the peace the tribunal may confirm the order or direct that it shall cease to have effect.

(6) A tribunal shall also have power on an appeal against a decision or order—

(a) to vary any condition for the time being in force in respect of the home to which the appeal relates by virtue of this Part of the Act;

(b) to direct that any such condition shall cease to have effect; or

(c) to direct that any such condition as it thinks fit shall have effect in respect of the home.

(7) The Secretary of State shall comply with any directions of a tribunal given under this section.

General Note

This section establishes a right of appeal to a Registered Homes Tribunal against a decision of a registration authority or an order made by a magistrate under the urgent procedure, sets out the procedure for appealing, and identifies the powers of Tribunals. For an account of Tribunal procedure, see the General Note to s.15. **1–201**

Subs. (1)

A decision: To impose or vary a condition of registration (s.29(3)), to refuse an application for registration (s.25), or to cancel a registration (s.28). **1–202**
An order made by a justice of the peace: See the note on s.15(1)(b).
Registered Homes Tribunal: General provisions relating to these Tribunals are contained in Pt. III of this Act.

Subs. (2)
Writing: See the note on s.15(2). **1–203**

Subss. (2), (7)
Secretary of State: See the General Note to this Part. **1–204**

Subs. (3)
Person: Or corporation (Interpretation Act 1978, s.5, Sched. 1). **1–205**
28 days after service: i.e. 28 days excluding the day on which the notice was serviced (*Dodds* v. *Walker* [1981] 2 All E.R. 609, H.L.).
Service . . . of notice of the decision or order: Under s.30(4) or 33(1).

Subss. (4), (5)
May confirm: The Registered Homes Tribunal has a discretion. An appeal cannot be allowed on the understanding that a future development might take place which would render the premises fit to be used: see *Tribunal Decision* No. 175. The Tribunal can admit evidence that became available after the registration authority reached its decision: see *Lyons* v. *East Sussex County Council* (1988) 86 L.G.R. 369, noted in the General Note to s.15. The question of what course of action is appropriate in a situation where the parties have come to an agreement after an appeal has been lodged is considered in the note on s.15(4), (5). **1–206**

Subs. (6)
Direct that any such condition as it thinks fit: "Such condition" refers back to "any condition for the time being in force" in para. (a). Conditions can only be imposed by a registration authority if they come within the categories set out in s.29(2). A Registered Homes Tribunal's discretion is similarly limited: see the decision of Roch J. in *Warwickshire County Council* v. *McSweeney* (unreported, December 8, 1988), noted under s.15(6). **1–207**

Inspection of mental nursing homes and visiting of patients

35.—(1) Subject to the provisions of this section, any person authorised in that behalf by the Secretary of State may at any time, after producing, if asked to do so, some duly authenticated document showing that he is so authorised, enter and inspect any premises which are used, or which that person has reasonable cause to believe to be used, for the purposes of a mental nursing home, and may inspect any records kept in pursuance of section 27(*b*) above. **1–208**

(2) A person authorised under subsection (1) above to inspect a mental nursing home may visit and interview in private any patient residing in the home who is, or appears to be, suffering from mental disorder—
  (*a*) for the purpose of investigating any complaint as to his treatment made by or behalf of the patient; or
  (*b*) in any case where the person so authorised has reasonable cause to believe that the patient is not receiving proper care;
and where the person so authorised is a medical practitioner, he may examine the patient in private, and may require the production of, and inspect, any medical records relating to the patient's treatment in that home.

(3) Regulations made under section 26 above may make provision with respect to the exercise on behalf of the Secretary of State of the powers conferred by this section, and may in particular provide—

(a) for imposing conditions or restrictions with respect to the exercise of those powers in relation to mental nursing homes which, immediately before November 1, 1960, were registered hospitals as defined in subsection (4) below, and

(b) subject as aforesaid for requiring the inspection of mental nursing homes under subsection (1) above to be carried out on such occasions, or at such intervals, as the regulations may prescribe.

(4) In subsection (3)(a) above, "registered hospital" means a hospital registered as mentioned in section 231(9) of the Lunacy Act 1980.

(5) Any person who refuses to allow the inspection of any premises, or without reasonable cause refuses to allow the visiting, interviewing or examination of any person by a person authorised in that behalf under this section or to produce for the inspection of any person so authorised any document or record the production of which is duly required by him, or otherwise obstructs any such person in the exercise of his functions, shall be guilty of an offence.

(6) Without prejudice to the generality of subsection (5) above, any person who insists on being present when requested to withdraw by a person authorised as aforesaid to interview or examine a person in private shall be guilty of an offence.

DEFINITIONS
mental nursing home: s.22.
mental disorder: s.55.

GENERAL NOTE

1–209 This section gives power to a person authorised by the registration authority to enter and inspect premises which are used, or which that person has reasonable cause to believe to be used, for the purpose of a mental nursing home. A power to enter and inspect nursing homes is given by reg. 10 of the Nursing Homes and Mental Nursing Homes Regulations 1984 (S.I. 1984 No. 1578). Each home must be inspected at least twice a year (*ibid*. reg. 11).

Section 80 of the Children Act 1989 provides the Secretary of State with an additional power to inspect any mental nursing home required to be registered under this Act and used to accommodate children (subs. (1)). This power is supplemented by a power to inspect the children (subs. (6)) and by powers to direct the person carrying on the home to provide specific information (subss. (4) and (5)), to inspect records (subs. (7)) and to enter the home (subs. (8)). It is an offence intentionally to obstruct entry (subs. (10)) and if entry is refused a warrant can be issued under s.102 of the 1989 Act. Section 86 of the 1989 Act places a duty on the person carrying on a mental nursing home to notify the relevant local authority about children who are being accommodated in the home. The local authority has a duty to safeguard the children's welfare (subs. (3)) and also has a duty under s.24 of the 1989 Act to provide such children with advice and assistance with a view to providing for their long-term welfare. An owner who provides day care for children under the age of eight in a mental nursing home is exempted from the registration requirements of Pt. X of the 1989 Act which deals with childminding and day care for young children: see *ibid*. s.71(1)(b) and Sched. 9, para. 4(1)(d).

Local social services authorities are empowered to inspect residential care homes under s.17. Where an establishment is registered both as a mental nursing home and as a residential care home the District Health Authority and the local social services authority should consider whether they should undertake joint inspections: see the General Note to this Act.

Under s.120(1), (4) of the Mental Health Act 1983, the Mental Health Act Commission and persons authorised by the Commission have power to visit and interview in private patients who are detained under the provisions of that Act in mental nursing homes. Also note that under s.115 of the 1983 Act an approved social worker of the local social services authority may enter and inspect a mental nursing home, if he has reasonable cause to believe that a mentally disordered patient is not under proper care.

Patients who are detained in mental nursing homes under the 1983 Act may be discharged from the power detaining them by the registration authority or by the health authority maintaining them at the home (see s.23(3) of the 1983 Act). To assist them in the exercise of this power, s.24(3), (4) of that Act provides the authorities with a power to visit and examine patients and to require the production of relevant documents.

Subs. (1)

1–210 *Any person authorised:* See the General Note to this section and the note on s.17(2).

Secretary of State: See the General Note to this Part.

After producing, if asked to do so: The power to enter and inspect can be exercised even if there is nobody on the premises to whom the document can be produced: see Sommervell L.J., speaking on a similar provision in the Gas Act 1948, in *Grove* v. *Eastern Gas Board* [1951] 2 All E.R. 1051 at 1053, C.A.

At any time: Advance notice of the inspection does not have to be given. Also see the note on s.17(1).

Enter and inspect: See the General Note to s.17. A person who obstructs an authorised person in the exercise of his power under this section commits an offence under subs. (5). The authorised person is not empowered to use force in his attempt to gain entry to the premises.

Reasonable cause to believe to be used: The Secretary of State has issued a direction requiring registration authorities to enter and inspect unregistered premises believed to be functioning as a mental nursing home: see the note on s.27.

Subs. (2)

Interview . . . examine in private: Anyone who fails to withdraw when asked to do so by the authorised person commits an offence (subs. (5)). Under reg. 12(1)(*t*) of the Nursing Homes and Mental Nursing Homes Regulations 1984 the person registered must provide adequate interview facilities.

Investigating any complaint: The Mental Health Act Commission can investigate complaints made by, or in respect of, detained patients: see s.120(1)(*b*) of the Mental Health Act 1983.

1–211

Subs. (3)

Regulations: See reg. 11 the Nursing Homes and Mental Nursing Homes Regulations 1984.

1st November 1960: The date on which all the provisions of the Mental Health Act 1959 not then in operation were brought into force.

1–212

Subs. (5)

Obstructs: See the note on s.17(4).

1–213

Subss. (5), (6)

Offence: Which, on conviction, could lead to imprisonment for up to three months or to a fine of up to level 4 on the standard scale, or to both (s.51(2)). A local social services authority may institute proceedings under these provisions (s.53(2)). For offences by a corporation and its officers, see s.52.

1–214

Effect of cancellation or death on mental nursing home registration

36.—(1) This section applies to any mental nursing home the particulars of the registration of which are entered in the separate part of the register referred to in paragraph (*b*) of section 23(5) above, and in subsections (2) and (3) below "patient" means a person suffering or appearing to be suffering from mental disorder.

(2) If the registration of any such home is cancelled under section 28 above at a time when any patient is liable to be detained in the home under the provisions of the Mental Health Act 1983, the registration shall, notwithstanding the cancellation, continue in force until the expiry of the period of two months beginning with the date of the cancellation, or until every such patient has ceased to be so liable, whichever first occurs.

(3) If the person registered in respect of any such home (not being one of two or more persons so registered) dies at a time when any patient is liable to be so detained, the registration shall continue in force until the expiry of the period of two months beginning with the death, or until every such patient has ceased to be so liable, or until a person other than the deceased has been registered in respect of the home, whichever first occurs.

(4) A registration continued in force by virtue of subsection (3) above shall continue in force—

   (*a*) as from the grant of representation to the estate of the deceased, for the benefit of the personal representative of the deceased; and
   (*b*) pending the grant of such representation, for the benefit of any person approved for the purpose by the Secretary of State.

(5) For the purposes of this Part of this Act, a person for whose benefit the registration continue in force by virtue of subsection (3) above shall be treated as registered in respect of the home.

1–215

DEFINITIONS
mental nursing home: s.22.
mental disorder: s.55.

GENERAL NOTE

1–216   This section provides for the temporary continuation of the registration of a mental nursing home on the death of the registered person or on the registration authority cancelling the registration of the home under s.28. It only applies if the home is caring for residents who are detained under the Mental Health Act 1983 at the relevant time.

Subs. (1)

1–217   This subsection provides that this section shall only apply to a mental nursing home that informed the registration authority at the time that the registration took place that it intended to care for patients who are detained under the Mental Health Act 1983. Under s.23(5), the registration authority has to specify such an intention in the certificate of registration.

Subs. (2)

1–218   *Liable to be detained in the home:* The patient need not necessarily be resident in the home at the relevant time because a patient would continue to be "liable to be detained in the home" even though he had been granted leave of absence from the home by his responsible medical officer under s.17 of the 1983 Act.

Two months beginning with: i.e. including the date of the cancellation (subs. (2)) or death (subs. (3)) (*Hare* v. *Gocher* [1962] 2 All E.R. 765). A "month" means a calendar month (Interpretation Act 1978, s.5, Sched. 1).

Cease to be so liable: The registration authority has power to discharge the patient from his detention under s.23(3) of the 1983 Act.

Subs. (3)

1–219   *Person:* Or corporation (Interpretation Act 1978, s.5, Sched. 1).

Subs. (5)

1–220   *This Part of this Act:* i.e. ss.21 to 38.

Miscellaneous and supplemental

Power to exempt Christian Science homes

1–221   **37.**—(1) The Secretary of State may grant exemption from the operation of the provisions of this Part of this Act in respect of any nursing home or mental nursing home as respects which he is satisfied that it is being, or will be, carried on in accordance with the practice and principles of the body known as the Church of Christ Scientist.

(2) It shall be a condition of any exemption granted under this section that the home in question shall adopt and use the name of Christian Science house.

(3) An exemption granted under this section may at any time be withdrawn by the Secretary of State if it appears to him that the home in question is no longer being carried on in accordance with the said practice and principles.

DEFINITIONS
nursing home: s.21.
mental nursing home: s.22.

GENERAL NOTE

1–222   This section gives the registration authority power to exempt Christian Science homes from the need to register as nursing homes or mental nursing homes.
Secretary of State: See the General Note to this Part.

Ancillary provisions of Mental Health Act 1983

1–223   **38.** So far as section 125 (inquiries), 126 (forgery, false statements, etc.) or 139 (protection for acts done) of the Mental Health Act 1983 applied immediately before the commencement of this Part of this Act in relation to any provision re-enacted by this Part of this Act, those sections shall apply in relation to the corresponding provision of this Act.

GENERAL NOTE

If any of s.125, 126 or 139 of the Mental Health Act 1983 applied to a provision which has been consolidated in this Part, this section provides that the relevant section shall continue to apply to the corresponding provision of this Act. **1–224**
Commencement: See s.59(2).
Corresponding provision of this Act: See the Table of Derivations, at para. 1–284.

PART III

REGISTERED HOMES TRIBUNALS

GENERAL NOTE

This Part establishes a system of Registered Homes Tribunals which supersede the tribunals previously constituted under the Child Care Act 1980 to hear appeals relating to the registration of children's homes. The Tribunals also takes over from magistrates' courts the responsibility for hearing appeals relating to the registration of residential care homes, nursing homes and mental nursing homes. Appeals under this Act can be heard in respect of a registration authority's decision to refuse a registration application, to grant a registration subject to conditions, or to cancel or amend a registration. The Tribunals will also hear appeals against orders made by magistrates under the urgent procedures set out in ss.11 and 30. Registered Homes Tribunals derive their existence and authority from this Act and the Registered Homes Tribunal Rules 1984. They have no inherent jurisdiction. **1–225**

In *R.* v. *Humberside County Council, ex p. Bogdal* (1992) 11 B.M.L.R. 46, Brooke J. applied *R.* v. *Birmingham City Council, ex p. Ferrero Ltd.* [1993] 1 All E.R. 530, C.A. in holding that it is only in an exceptional case that application should be brought for the judicial review of a decision of a registration authority as a perfectly satisfactory alternative remedy of an appeal procedure to a Registered Homes Tribunal had been provided by this Act. In any event it is wrong to allow judicial review before the remedy by way of an appeal to a tribunal has been exhausted (*R.* v. *Leicestershire County Council, ex p. Thompson* (unreported, April 19, 1991)).

The decision of a Tribunal is based on the facts of the case before it and it does not create a precedent. Decisions are not therefore binding on other Tribunals. However, Tribunal decisions are of persuasive value as they provide useful guidance on the interpretation of this Act and the Residential Homes Regulations and the Nursing Homes and Mental Nursing Homes Regulations. This guidance helps towards establishing a degree of uniformity in the decisions of registration authorities, proprietors and applicants. For a discussion on the operation of the Registered Homes Tribunal System, see R. Brooke Ross, *The Registered Homes Act 1984 and the Registered Homes Tribunal* (Social Care Association, 1987). Also see Emlyn Cassam, "Home Sweet Home", *Social Services Insight*, May 1, 1987, pp. 12–14 and paras. 17 to 22, Annex B to DHSS Circular No. HC (84)21. A report on the first 96 cases of the Registered Homes Tribunal can be found in H. and S. Harman, *No Place Like Home* (NALGO, 1989). A second edition of this publication which reviews a further 11 decisions of the Registered Homes Tribunal was compiled by H. Harman and L. Winn and published in 1991.

An appeal on a point of law against a decision of a Registered Homes Tribunal may be made to the High Court under s.11(1) of the Tribunals and Inquiries Act 1992. A rule of court has been made under Ord. 94, r.9 pursuant to power given in s.11(3) of the 1992 Act which enables the Tribunal of its own motion to state in the course of proceedings before it in the form of a special case for decision of the High Court any question of law arising in the proceedings. Registered Homes Tribunals act under the general supervision of the Council on Tribunals by virtue of s.1, Sched. 1 of the 1992 Act.

The procedure to be followed in proceedings before a Registered Homes Tribunal is contained in the Registered Homes Tribunal Rules 1984 (S.I. 1984 No. 1346). As the Tribunal has no power to award costs each party bears its own costs, regardless of the outcome. Legal aid is not available for proceedings before a Registered Homes Tribunal. The address of the Tribunal Secretariat is Room B1601, Alexander Fleming House, Elephant and Castle, London, SE1 6BY.

Department of Health Circular No. LAC (89)10 informed registration authorities of the publication of a booklet on the procedures of Registered Homes Tribunals. Copies of the booklet, which has the title "Registered Homes Tribunals Procedure", may be obtained from the Leaflets Unit, P.O. Box 21, Stanmore, Middlesex, HA7 1AY, priced £1.00. The circular supplements the booklet with the following additional guidance:

"Reasons for authorities' decisions

The reasons for an authority's formal decision should be recorded at the time that it is taken. **1–226**

To avoid unnecessary appeals, a registration authority should explain, in their letter notifying a formal decision, the reasons for the decision. The legislation requires an authority to give the person their reasons for a proposed decision but following the hearing of representations additional reasons may be specified and the individual needs to know them.

The reasons on which the authority based their *formal* decision need to be included in the statement of reasons submitted to a Tribunal under rule 5(2) of the Registered Homes Tribunals Rules 1984. The authority should ensure that these reasons are comprehensive as the authority may be confined to them at the hearing of the appeal.

Advice to potential appellants

1–227 When an authority informs a person that there is a right of appeal to a Registered Homes Tribunal against a decision that they are notifying or against an order that a justice of the peace has made under the urgent procedure, they should also:
  (a) say there is a procedure booklet on appeals and where it may be purchased (as at the end of this circular);
  (b) ask him, if he decides to appeal, to explain concisely the reasons why he is doing so when he sends in his appeal notice.
  (c) ask him to send a copy of the appeal to the Registered Homes Tribunals Secretariat whose address is given at paragraph 9 below.

Legal representation

1–228 An Authority will no doubt have brought their legal adviser into the matter at an earlier stage than the receipt of the appeal. He would need to be involved in drawing up the reasons for the authority's decision in the first place as well as in considering any representations against it. Similarly the legal adviser will need to be informed of an appeal directly it is received.

When the appellant is not going to be represented by a lawyer, the authority should offer to prepare the agreed bundle of letters exchanged between them and the appellant.

Action

1–229 Authorities should:
  (a) bring to the notice of their staff operating the Registered Homes Act 1984 the publication of the booklet on the procedure of the Registered Homes Tribunals and what is said about communicating authorities' reasons for decisions under the Act that could result in an appeal and about legal representation;
  (b) arrange for potential appellants to these Tribunals to be informed of this booklet and certain other matters specified in paragraph 5 above."

Preliminary

1–230 **39.** The following are relevant enactments for the purposes of this Part of this Act—
  [(a) the Children Act 1989]; and
  (c) Parts I and II of this Act.

AMENDMENT
Para. (a) was substituted for paras. (a) and (b) by the Children Act 1989, s.108(5), Sched. 13, para. 49.

GENERAL NOTE

1–231 *This Part of this Act: i.e.* ss.39 to 45.
Parts I and II of this Act: i.e. ss.1 to 20 (Pt. I) and ss.21 to 38 (Pt. II).

Constitution of panels for chairmen and members

1–232 **40.**—(1) For the purpose of enabling a tribunal to hear an appeal under a relevant enactment to be constituted as occasion may require there shall be—
  (a) a panel appointed by the Lord Chancellor (in this Part of the Act referred to as "the legal panel") of persons available to act as chairmen of any such tribunals; and
  (b) a panel appointed by the Lord President of the Council (in this Part of this Act referred to as "the panel of experts") of persons available to act as members.

(2) Tribunals constituted under this Part of this Act are to be known as Registered Homes Tribunals.

(3) No person shall be qualified to be appointed to the legal panel unless he possesses such legal qualifications as the Lord Chancellor considers suitable.

(4) No person shall be qualified to be appointed to the panel of experts unless he has had experience in social work, medicine, nursing or midwifery or such other experience as the Lord President of the Council considers suitable.

(5) No officer of a government department may be appointed to either panel.

(6) A person appointed to a panel shall hold office subject to such conditions as to the period of his membership and otherwise as may be determined by the person appointing him.

GENERAL NOTE

This Act does not create standing Registered Homes Tribunals. This section therefore establishes a legal panel and a panel of experts for the purpose of appointing members to sit on Tribunals as and when the occasion demands.

1-233

Subs. (1)

Relevant enactment: Defined in s.39.

Panel of experts: The members of this panel are required to have had experience in a related dicipline (subs. (4)). They are not required to have gained any particular qualifications.

1-234

Constitution of tribunals—general

41.—(1) A Registered Homes Tribunal shall consist of a chairman and two other members.

1-235

(2) The chairman shall be a member of the legal panel appointed to the tribunal by the Lord Chancellor.

(3) The other two members shall be members of the panel of experts appointed to the tribunal by the Lord President of the Council.

GENERAL NOTE

This section requires appeals to be heard by a Tribunal consisting of a legally qualified chairman appointed by the Lord Chancellor and two expert members appointed by the Lord President of the Council.

1-236

Subs. (2)

Legal panel: Constituted under s.40(1)(*a*).

1-237

Subs. (3)

Panel of experts: Constituted under s.40(1)(*b*).

1-238

Tribunal for appeals relating to nursing homes (including maternity homes) and mental nursing homes

42.—(1) A Registered Homes Tribunal to hear an appeal relating solely to registration under Part II of this Act shall include a registered medical practitioner.

1-239

(2) Such a tribunal shall also include—
  (*a*) if the appeal relates to registration of a maternity home, a registered midwife; and
  (*b*) in any other case, a qualified nurse.

(3) A tribunal which is constituted to hear both an appeal relating to registration under Part I of this Act and an appeal relating to registration under Part II shall include a person selected in accordance with subsection (2) above.

(4) In this part of this Act "qualified nurse" means a person who—

(a) is for the time being registered under the Nurses, Midwives and Health Visitors Act 1979; and

(b) would have been qualified to be registered under section 2(1) of the Nurses Act 1957.

DEFINITIONS
maternity home: ss.55, 21(1)(b).
registered homes tribunal: s.40(2).

GENERAL NOTE

1–240   This section stipulates that a Tribunal hearing an appeal relating solely to a nursing home or a mental nursing home must include in its membership a medical practitioner (subs. (1)) and a qualified nurse or midwife (subs. (2)). Where the appeal relates to an establishment which is registered both as a residential care home and as a nursing home or mental nursing home one of the expert members will be a qualified nurse or midwife (subs. (3)).

Procedure of tribunals

1–241   **43.**—(1) The Secretary of State may by statutory instrument make rules as to the practice and procedure to be followed with respect to the constitution of Registered Homes Tribunals, and as to proceedings before such tribunals and matters incidental to or consequential on such proceedings; and without prejudice to the generality of this section such rules may make provision—

(a) requiring particulars to be supplied of matters relevant to the determination of an appeal;

(b) enabling two or more appeals to be heard together; and

(c) as to representation before a tribunal, by counsel or a solicitor or otherwise.

(2) Rules under this section shall be subject to annulment in pursuance of a resolution of either House of Parliament.

(3) The Arbitration Act 1950 shall not apply to any proceedings before Registered Homes Tribunals except so far as any provision of that Act may be applied to such tribunals with or without modifications by rules made under this section.

DEFINITION
registered homes tribunal: s.40(2).

GENERAL NOTE

1–242   The Registered Homes Tribunals Rules 1984 (S.I. 1984 No. 1346) prescribe the procedure to be followed in proceedings before a Registered Homes Tribunal. An account of Tribunal procedure is contained in the General Note to s.15.

Staff for tribunals

1–243   **44.** The Secretary of State shall assign such staff as may from time to time be required for Registered Homes Tribunals.

Fees, allowances and expenses

1–244   **45.** The Secretary of State may—

(a) pay to members of Registered Homes Tribunals such fees and allowances as he may, with the consent of the Treasury, determine; and

(b) defray the expenses of such tribunals up to such amount as he may with the like consent determine.

Part IV

Offences

GENERAL NOTE

A local authority exercising its powers under s.21 of the National Assistance Act 1948 to provide residential accommodation cannot under the community care arrangements arrange for such accommodation to be provided by a person who has been convicted of an offence under this Act (or any enactment repealed by this Act): see s.26(1E) of the 1948 Act.

A conviction for an offence under Pt. I or II of this Act is a ground for cancelling the registration of a person in respect of a home: see ss.10(c) and 28(b).

1–245

Failure to register

46.—(1) A person guilty of an offence under section 2 above shall be liable on summary conviction to a fine of an amount not exceeding level 5 on the standard scale.

1–246

(2) A person guilty of an offence under section 23(1) above shall be liable on summary conviction to a fine of an amount not exceeding the statutory maximum or on conviction on indictment to a fine.

DEFINITIONS
standard scale: s.55.
statutory maximum: s.55.

GENERAL NOTE

Subs. (1)
Person: Or corporation (Interpretation Act 1978, s.5, Sched. 1).

1–247

Subs. (2)
Offence under section 23(1): Which can be tried summarily or on indictment. For proceedings for an offence under s.23(1) relating to a nursing home, see s.53(1).
Conviction on indictment to a fine: Which has no statutory maximum.

1–248

Failure to affix certificate of registration

47.—(1) A person guilty of an offence under section 5(6) above shall be liable on summary conviction to a fine of an amount not exceeding level 2 on the standard scale and to a further fine not exceeding £5 for each day on which the offence continues after conviction.

1–249

(2) A person guilty of an offence under section 23(6) above shall be liable on summary conviction—

(a) to a fine of an amount not exceeding level 2 on the standard scale; and

(b) subject to subsection (3) below, to a further fine not exceeding £5 for each day on which the offence continues after conviction.

(3) The court by which a person is convicted of an original offence under subsection (2) above may fix a reasonable period from the date of conviction for compliance with any directions given by the court; and where the court has fixed such a period the daily penalty prescribed by that subsection shall not be recoverable in respect of any day before the expiry of that period.

DEFINITION
standard scale: s.55.

TRANSITIONAL PROVISIONS
See s.57(2), Sched. 2, para. 3.

General Note

Subs. (1)

1–250   *Person:* Or corporation (Interpretation Act 1978, s.5, Sched. 1).

Subs. (2)

1–251   *Offence under section 23(6):* For proceedings for an offence under s.23(6) relating to a nursing home, see s.53(1).

Breach of conditions as to registration

1–252   **48.** A person guilty of an offence under section 5(5) or 29(4) above shall be liable on summary conviction to a fine of an amount not exceeding level 4 on the standard scale.

Definition
standard scale: s.55.

General Note

1–253   *Person:* Or corporation (Interpretation Act 1978, s.1, Sched. 5).

Contravention of regulations

1–254   **49.** A person guilty of an offence against regulations made under section 16, 26 or 27 above shall be liable on summary conviction to a fine of an amount not exceeding level 4 on the standard scale.

Definition
standard scale: s.55.

General Note

1–255   *Person:* Or corporation (Interpretation Act 1978, s.1, Sched. 5).

Contravention of section 24

1–256   **50.** A person guilty of an offence under section 24 above shall be liable on summary conviction to a fine of an amount not exceeding level 3 on the standard scale.

Definition
standard scale: s.55.

General Note

1–257   *Person:* Or corporation (Interpretation Act 1978, s.1, Sched. 5).

Obstruction

1–258   **51.**—(1) A person guilty of an offence under section 17(6) above shall be liable on summary conviction to a fine of an amount not exceeding level 4 on the standard scale.

(2) A person guilty of an offence under section 35(5) or (6) above shall be liable on summary conviction to imprisonment for a term not exceeding three months or to a fine not exceeding level 4 on the standard scale, or to both such imprisonment and fine.

Definition
standard scale: s.55.

General Note

1–259   *Subs. (1)*
Person: Or corporation (Interpretation Act 1978, s.1, Sched. 5).

1–260   *Subs. (2)*
Offence under section 35(5) or (6): Proceedings may be instituted by a local authority: see s.53(2).

Bodies corporate and their officers

52. Where an offence under this Act or any regulations under it which has been committed by a body corporate is proved to have been committed with the consent or connivance of, or to be attributable to any neglect on the part of, the director, manager, secretary or other similar officer of the body corporate, or any person purporting to act in any such capacity, he as well as the body corporate shall be deemed to be guilty of that offence and shall be liable to be proceeded against and punished accordingly.

1–261

General Note

This section states that if an offence under this Act is committed by a company, not only the company itself but also any officer of the company to whom the offence is attributable shall be liable to a penalty.

1–262

Proceedings

53.—(1) Proceedings in respect of an offence under section 23(1) or (6) above relating to a nursing home shall not, without the written consent of the Attorney General, be taken by any person other than a party aggrieved or the Secretary of State.

1–263

(2) A local social service authority may institute proceedings for any offence under section 35(5) or (6) above.

Definitions
   local social services authority: s.55.
   nursing home: s.21.

General Note

1–264

Subs. (1)
   Relating to a nursing home: Note that this provision does not apply in relation to a mental nursing home.
   Secretary of State: See the General Note to Pt.II.

Part V

Supplementary

Service of documents

54.—(1) Any notice or other document required under this Act to be served on a person carrying on, or intending to carry on, a residential care home, or a nursing home or mental nursing home may be served on him by being delivered personally to him, or being sent by post to him in a registered letter or by the recorded delivery service.

1–265

(2) For the purposes of section 7 of the Interpretation Act 1978 (which defines "service by post") a letter to a person carrying on a residential care home or a nursing home or mental nursing home enclosing a notice or other document under this Act shall be deemed to be properly addressed if it is addressed to him at the home.

(3) Any such notice or other document required to be served on a body corporate or a firm shall be duly served if it is served on the secretary or clerk of that body or a partner of that firm.

(4) For the purposes of this section, and of section 7 of the Interpretation Act 1978 in its application to this section, without prejudice to subsection (2) above, the proper address of a person, in the case of a secretary or clerk of a body corporate, shall be that of the registered or principal office of that body, in the case of a partner of a firm shall be that of the principal office of the firm, and in any other case shall be the last known address of the person to be served.

DEFINITIONS
    residential care home: s.1(1), (2).
    nursing home: s.21.
    mental nursing home: s.22.

GENERAL NOTE

Subs. (1)

1–266   *May be served:* Note that this provision does not prevent the notice or document being sent by ordinary post.

Subs. (2)

1–267   *Person:* Or corporation (Interpretation Act 1978, s.5, Sched. 1).

Subs. (4)

1–268   *Registered or principal office:* Every company is required to have a registered office (Companies Act 1985, s.287). The principal office of a company is the place at which the business of the company is controlled and managed as a whole (*Palmer* v. *Caledonian Railway Co.* [1892] 1 Q.B. 823).

Interpretation—general

1–269   **55.** In this Act—

"local social services authority" means a council which is a local authority for the purposes of the Local Authority Social Services Act 1970;

"maternity home" has the meaning given by section 21 above;

"mental disorder" means mental illness, arrested or incomplete development of mind, psychopathic disorder, and any other disorder or disability of mind;

"mental nursing home" has the meaning given by section 22 above;

"nursing home" has the meaning given by section 21 above;

"psychopathic disorder" means a persistent disorder or disability of mind (whether or not including significant impairment of intelligence) which results in abnormally aggressive or seriously irresponsible conduct on the part of the person concerned;

"the standard scale" means the standard scale as defined in section 75 of the Criminal Justice Act 1982; and

"the statutory maximum" means the statutory maximum as defined in section 74 of that Act.

GENERAL NOTE

1–270   *Local social services authority:* The local authorities for the purposes of the Local Authority Social Services Act 1970 are the councils of non-metropolitan counties, metropolitan districts and the London Boroughs and the Common Council of the City of London; *ibid.* s.1.

Mental disorder: This definition is taken from s.1 of the Mental Health Act 1983.

Standard scale: Section 37(2) of the Criminal Justice Act 1982, as amended by s.17(1) of the Criminal Justice Act 1991, sets out a standard scale of maximum fines for offences triable only before a magistrates' court. The scale is:

    Level 1—£200
    Level 2—£500
    Level 3—£1,000
    Level 4—£2,500
    Level 5—£5,000

The statutory maximum: Is the maximum fine that can be imposed by a magistrates' court in respect of an offence which is triable either summarily or on indictment. The current maximum is £5,000: see s.32(9) of the Magistrates' Courts Act 1980, as amended by s.17(2)(*c*) of the Criminal Justice Act 1991.

Regulations and orders

1–271   **56.**—(1) Any regulations or order under this Act shall be made by statutory instrument.

(2) Any such statutory instrument, except an instrument containing an order under section 59(2) below, shall be subject to annulment in pursuance of a resolution of either House of Parliament.

(3) The power to make regulations conferred on the Secretary of State by section 27 above shall, if the Treasury so directs, be exercisable by the Treasury and the Secretary of State acting jointly.

(4) Any power conferred by this Act to make regulations may be exercised—
   (a) either in relation to all cases to which the power extends, or in relation to all those cases subject to specified exceptions, or in relation to any specified cases or classes of case; and
   (b) so as to make, as respects the cases in relation to which it is exercised—
      (i) the same provision for all cases in relation to which the power is exercised, or different provision for different cases or different classes of case, or different provision as respects the same case or class of case for different purposes;
      (ii) any such provision either unconditionally or subject to any specified condition;
and includes power to make such incidental or supplemental provision in the regulations as the persons making them consider appropriate.

Consequential amendments, transitional provisions, savings and repeals

57.—(1) The enactments specified in Schedule 1 to this Act shall have effect subject to the amendments there specified, being amendments consequential upon the provisions of this Act. **1–272**

(2) The transitional provisions and savings contained in Schedule 2 to this Act shall have effect.

(3) Subject to the provisions of Schedule 2, the enactments specified in Schedule 3 to this Act are hereby repealed to the extent specified in the third column of that Schedule.

(4) Nothing in this Act shall be taken as prejudicing the operation of section 16(1) of the Interpretation Act 1978 (which relates to the operation of repeals).

Extent

58.—(1) This Act does not extend to Scotland or Northern Ireland. **1–273**

(2) The Secretary of State may by order direct that so much of this Act as relates to nursing homes and mental nursing homes shall extend to the Isles of Scilly, subject to such exceptions, adaptations and modifications as may be specified in the order, but except as so directed so much of this Act as relates to nursing homes and mental nursing homes shall not extend to the Isles.

(3) Subject to subsection (2) above, this Act shall, in its application to the Isles of Scilly, have effect subject to such extensions, adaptations and modifications as the Secretary of State may by order prescribe.

DEFINITIONS
   mental nursing home: s.22.
   nursing home: s.21.
   qualified nurse: s.25(2).

GENERAL NOTE

Subs. (2)
   May by order: No order has been made. **1–274**

Short title and commencement

59.—(1) This Act may be cited as the Registered Homes Act 1984. **1–275**

(2) This Act shall come into force on such day as the Secretary of State may by order appoint and different days may be so appointed for different provisions and for different purposes.

GENERAL NOTE

Subs. (2)

1–276   S.I. 1984 No. 1348 brought into force, all on January 1, 1985, the provisions of this Act except in so far as it relates to an establishment which is a school referred to in s.1(15)(*f*). Section 1, so far as it relates to such an establishment, was brought into force by S.I. 1984 No. 1348 on January 1, 1986.

SCHEDULES

Section 57   SCHEDULE 1

1–277   CONSEQUENTIAL AMENDMENTS

[*Not reproduced.*]

Section 57   SCHEDULE 2

1–278   TRANSITIONAL PROVISIONS AND SAVINGS

1. Where a person's registration in respect of a home was in force immediately before 1st August 1981, the Secretary of State shall not cancel the registration on any ground mentioned in paragraph (*f*) or (*g*) of subsection (1) of section 25 above before the expiration of the period of 3 months beginning with the day on which the relevant notice is served on him under subsection (2) or (3) of that section.

2.—(1) In the case of a nursing home which was in existence on 1st July 1928 the registration of a person in respect of that home shall not be cancelled on the ground that the provision of paragraph (*f*) or (*g*) of section 25 above are not complied with unless, in the case of a nursing home not being a maternity home, the nursing of the patients in the home is not under the superintendence of a qualified nurse who is resident in the home.

(2) For the purpose of sub-paragraph (1) above, a nursing home shall not be deemed to be a home which was in existence on 1st July 1928 if, in the case of a home which was carried on at that date by an individual, it has ceased since that date or ceases to be carried on by that individual solely, or, in the case of a home which was carried on at that date by a body corporate, it has ceased since that date or ceases to be under the charge of the individual under whose charge it was at that date.

3. Where an offence, for the continuance of which a penalty was provided, has been committed under any of the enactments repealed by the Nursing Homes Act 1975 or this Act proceedings may be taken under this Act in respect of the continuance of the offence after the commencement of this Act, in the same manner as if the offence had been committed under the corresponding provision of this Act.

4.—(1) The Secretary of State may—
   (*a*) by regulations make such transitional provision as he considers necessary or expedient in connection with any enactment contained in this Act which derives—
      (i)   from Part I or III of Schedule 4 to the Health and Social Services and Social Security Adjudications Act 1983; or
      (ii) from the amendments to the Nursing Homes Act 1975 made by Part II of that Schedule;
   (*b*) by order repeal any provision of a local Act passed on or before 13th May 1983 if it appears to him that the provision is inconsistent with or has become unnecessary in consequence of any such enactment or of regulations made under any such enactment;
   (*c*) by order amend any provision of such an Act if it appears to him that the provision requires amendment in consequence of any such enactment or of regulations made under any such enactment or of any repeal made by virtue of this sub-paragraph.

(2) An order made in pursuance of sub-paragraph (1) above may include such incidental or transitional provisions as the Secretary of State considers are appropriate in connection with the order.

(3) It shall be the duty of the Secretary of State, before he makes an order in pursuance of sub-paragraph (1) above amending or repealing any provision of a local Act, to consult each local authority which he considers would be affected by the amendment or repeal of that provision.

DEFINITIONS
  nursing home: s.21.
  maternity home: ss.55, 21(1)(b).

GENERAL NOTE

Para. 1

Person: Or corporation (Interpretation Act 1978, s.5, Sched. 1). 1–279

Paras. 2, 3

1st July 1928: The commencement day of the Nursing Homes Registration Act 1927. 1–280

Para. 3

Commencement of this Act: See s.59. 1–281

Para. 4

Regulations: The Residential Care Homes Regulations 1984 (S.I. 1984 No. 1345) and the Nursing Homes and Mental Nursing Homes Regulations 1984 (S.I. 1984 No. 1578) have been made under para. 4(1)(a). No regulations have been made under para. 4(1)(b) or (c). 1–282

13th May 1983: The day on which the Health and Social Services and Social Security Adjudications Act 1983 received the Royal Assent.

Section 57   SCHEDULE 3

                              REPEALS   1–283

                          [*Not reproduced.*]

TABLE OF DERIVATIONS

Notes:

1. The following abbreviations are used in this Table:—   1–284

1975	=	The Nursing Homes Act 1975 (1975 c.37)
1976	=	The Health Services Act 1976 (1976 c.83)
1977(1)	=	The Criminal Law Act 1977 (1977 c.45)
1977(2)	=	The National Health Service Act 1977 (1977 c.49)
1979	=	The Nurses, Midwives and Health Visitors Act 1979 (1979 c.36)
1980	=	The Health Services Act 1980 (1980 c.53)
1982	=	The Mental Health (Amendment) Act 1982 (1982 c.51)
1983(1)	=	The Mental Health Act 1983 (1983 c.20)
1983(2)	=	The Health and Social Services and Social Security Adjudications Act 1983 (1983 c.41)
R (followed by a number)	=	The recommendation set out in the paragraph of that number in the Appendix to the Report of the Law Commission (Cmnd. 9115)

2. In 1980, section 16 and Part I of Schedule 4 made numerous amendments to 1975. Where the Table mentions 1980 but the reference is merely to a numbered paragraph, it is a reference to the paragraph of that number in that Schedule.

3. Where the Table mentions 1983(2) but the reference is merely to a numbered paragraph, it is a reference to the paragraph of that number in Schedule 4 to that Act.

4. For "the standard scale" see the definition in section 55. The terminology derives from section 37 of the Criminal Justice Act 1982 (c.48).

Section of 1984 Act	Derivations
1	1983(2) para. 1.
2	1983(2) para. 4.
3	1983(2) para. 5.
4	1983(2) para. 6.
5	1983(2) para. 7.
6	1983(2) para. 8.
7	1983(2) para. 9.
8	1983(2) para. 10.
9	1983(2) para. 11.
10	1983(2) para. 12.
11	1983(2) para. 13.
12	1983(2) para. 14.
13	1983(2) para. 15.
14	1983(2) para. 16.
15	1983(2) para. 17.
16	1983(2) para. 19.
17	1983(2) para. 20.
18	1983(2) para. 22.
19	1983(2) para. 3.
20	1983(2) para. 2.
21	1975 s.1; 1980 para. 2(1); 1983(2) para. 24.
22	1975 s.2; 1977(2) s.129 and Sch. 15 para. 66; 1980 Sch. 1 para. 27; 1982 s.63(2).
23	1975 s.3; 1983(1) s.148 and Sch. 4 para. 43; 1983(2) para. 25.
24	1975 s.3A; 1983(2) para. 26.
25	1975 s.4; 1976 s.19(1)(*a*) and (2); 1979 s.23(4) and Sch. para. 23; 1980 para. 3(1), (2) and 5.
26	1975 s.5; 1983(2) para. 27.
27	1975 s.6; 1983(1) s.120(5); 1983(2) para. 28.
28	1975 s.7; 1983(2) paras. 29 and 30.
29	1975 s.8; 1980 para. 4(1) and (2); 1983(2) para. 31.
30	1975 s.8A; 1983(2) para. 32.
31	1975 s.8B; 1983(2) para. 32.
32	1975 s.8C; 1983(2) para. 32.
33	1975 s.8D; 1983(2) para. 32.
34	1975 s.8E; 1983(2) para. 32.
35	1975 s.9.
36	1975 s.10; 1983(1) s.148 and Sch. 4 para. 43.
37	1975 s.18.
38	1975 s.21; 1983(1) s.148 and Sch. 4 para. 43.
39	1983(2) para. 49.
40	1983(2) para. 50.
41	1983(2) para. 51.
42	1983(2) para. 52.
43	1983(2) paras. 53 and 54.
44	1983(2) para. 55.
45	1983(2) para. 56.
46	1975 s.12; 1976 s.19(4); 1983(3) para. 4.
47	1975 s.13; 1977(1) s.31 and Sch. 6; 1983(2) paras. 7 and 34.
48	1975 s.15; 1977(1) s.31 and Sch. 6; 1983(2) para. 7.
49	1975 s.14; 1977(1) s.31 and Sch. 6; 1983(2) para. 19.
50	1975 s.13A; 1983(2) para. 35.
51	1975 s.16; 1977(1) s.31 and Sch. 6; 1983(2) para. 20.
52	1975 s.17; 1983(2) paras. 21 and 36; R.1.
53	1975 s.11.
54	1975 s.10A; 1983(2) paras. 18 and 33.
55	1975 ss.1, 2 and 20(1); 1983(2) para. 2(1).
56	1975 s.19; 1980 para. 5; 1983(2) para. 23; R.2 and 3.
57	—
58	1975 s.23; 1983(2) s.33 and para. 37.
59	—
Sch. 1	—
Sch. 2	—

TABLE OF DESTINATIONS

Nursing Homes Act 1975

1975	1984		1975	1984		1975	1984
s.1	ss.21, 55		s.8B	s.31		s.13A	s.50
2	22, 55		8C	32		14	49
3	s.23		8D	33		15	48
3A	24		8E	34		16	51
4	25		9	35		17	52
5	26		10	36		18	37
6	27		10A	54		19	56
7	28		11	53		20(1)	55
8	29		12	46		21	38
8A	30		13	47		23	58

Health Services Act 1976

1976	1984
s.19(1)(a), (2)	s.25
(4)	46

Criminal Law Act 1977

1977	1984
s.31	ss.47, 48, 49, 51
Sch. 6	47, 48, 49, 51

National Health Service Act 1977

1977	1984
s.129	s.22
Sch. 15, para. 66	22

Nurses, Midwives and Health Visitors Act 1979

1979	1984
s.23(4)	s.25
Sch. 7, para. 23	25

Health Services Act 1980

1980	1984
Sch. 1, para. 27	s.22
Sch. 4, Pt. I, para.	
2(1)	21
3(1), (2)	25
4(1), (2)	29
5	ss.25, 26

Mental Health (Amendment) Act 1982

1982	1984
s.63(2)	s.22

Mental Health Act 1983

1983	1984
s.120(5)	s.27
148	ss.23, 36, 38
Sch. 4, para. 43	23, 36, 38

Health and Social Services and Social Security Adjudications Act 1983

1983	1984	1983	1984	1983	1984
s.33	s.58	Sch. 4,		Sch. 4,	
Sch. 4		para. 15	s.13	para. 31	s.29
para. 1	1	16	14	32	ss.30–34
2	20	17	15	33	s.54
(1)	55	18	54	34	47
3	19	19	ss.16, 49	35	50
4	ss.2, 46	20	17, 51	36	52
5	s.3	20	s.51	37	58
6	4	21	52	49	39
7	ss.5, 47, 48	22	18	50	40
8	s.6	23	56	51	41
9	7	24	21	52	42
10	8	25	23	53, 54	43
11	9	26	24	55	44
12	10	27	26	56	45
13	11	28	27		
14	12	29, 30	28		

Recommendation in Appendix to Report of Law Commission (Cmnd. 9115)

1983	1984
para. 1	s.52
paras. 2, 3	56

PART 2

RESIDENTIAL CARE HOMES REGULATIONS 1984

(S.I. 1984 No. 1345)

Dated August 22, 1984, and made by the Secretary of State for Social Services under the Registered Homes Act 1984 (c. 23), ss.5(1), 8, 16, 17(4) and 57(2), Sched. 2, para. 4(1)(a)(i). **2–001**

ARRANGEMENT OF REGULATIONS

REG.
1. Citation, commencement and interpretation.
2. Particulars to be supplied on application for registration.
2A. Documentary evidence to be supplied on application for registration.
3. Registration fees.
4. Time limit for registration.
5. Annual fee.
6. Records.
7. Registers.
8. Consultation with fire authority.
9. Conduct of homes.
10. Provision of facilities and services.
11. Visits by parents, guardians, etc.
12. Religious observance.
13. Notification of arrival of children.
14. Notification of death, illness, or accident.
15. Notice of absence.
16. Notice of termination of accommodation.
17. Information for residents as to method of making complaints.
18. Inspection of homes.
19. Visits by person in control of the home.
20. Offences.
21. Form and service of notices.
22. Compliance with regulations.
23. Appeals.
24. Exemption from registration in respect of certain small homes.
25. Annual returns.

SCHEDULES
1. Information to be supplied on an application for registration.
2. Records to be kept in a home.
3. Particulars to be recorded in the registers kept by registration authorities.
4. Information to be supplied in the annual return.

GENERAL NOTE

These Regulations make provision in relation to the registration of persons in respect of, and the conduct of, residential care homes under Pt. I of the Registered Homes Act 1984. Many of the matters covered by these Regulations are discussed in the Centre for Policy on Ageing publication *Home Life*: see the General Note to the 1984 Act. A procedure for securing compliance with the Regulations is set out in reg. 20. **2–002**

The residents of a residential care home cannot by agreement relieve the registered person or the registration authority of their statutory duties. This is not to say that the resident's agreement should be ignored: see *Tribunal Decision* No. 55.

AMENDMENTS

The amendments to these Regulations were made by S.I. 1986 No. 457, S.I. 1988 No. 1192, S.I. 1991 No. 2502, S.I. 1992 No. 2007 and S.I. 1992 No. 2241. The amendments made by S.I. 1992 No. 2241 are considered in Department of Health Circular No. LAC (92)10.

Citation, commencement and interpretation

2–003 1.—(1) These regulations may be cited as the Residential Care Homes Regulations 1984 and shall come into operation on January 1, 1985.

(2) In the these regulations, unless the context otherwise requires—

"the Act" means the Registered Homes Act 1984;

"the 1980 Act" means the Residential Homes Act 1980;

["care authority", in relation to a child, means the local authority who is looking after the child within the meaning of section 22(1) of the Children Act 1989];

["care order" has the meaning assigned to it in section 105 of the Children Act 1989];

"child" means a resident under the age of 18 years and any resident who has attained that age and is the subject of a care order;

"fire authority", in relation to a home, means the authority discharging in the area in which the home is situated, the function of fire authority under the Fire Services Act 1947;

"home" means a residential care home;

["independent visitor" means a person appointed as a visitor pursuant to paragraph 17 of Schedule 2 to the Children Act 1989];

"local social services authority" means a council which is a local authority for the purposes of the Local Authority Social Services Act 1970;

"mental handicap" means a state of arrested or incomplete development of mind which includes impairment of intelligence and social functioning;

"person registered" means any person registered in respect of the home;

"relevant date" means the date on which the Act and the repeal of the 1980 Act by Schedule 10 to the Health and Social Services and Social Security Adjudications Act 1983 came into force;

"resident" means any person in the home who is in need of personal care by reason of old age, disablement, past or present dependence on alcohol or drugs, or past or present mental disorder.

Particulars to be supplied on application for registration

2–004 2. On any application for registration made under section 5 of the Act, the applicant shall supply in writing to the registration authority information in regard to the matters mentioned in Schedule 1 to these regulations, and such other information as the registration authority may reasonably require [, except that an applicant for registration in respect of a small home need not supply information in regard to the matters mentioned in paragraphs 3(c), (e), (l), (m) or (n) of that Schedule.]

GENERAL NOTE

2–005 *Application:* "The wording of registration forms should make it clear that *all* convictions should be disclosed, not just those relating to another registration authority. Applicants' attention also needs to be drawn to the effect of the Rehabilitation of Offenders Act 1974 (Exceptions) Order 1975—para. A22 of the guidance notes issued with LAC (84)15 dealt with this. Authorities may wish to consult their legal advisers on the wording of the forms ": (DHSS Circular No. LAC (88)15, para. 14).

Reasonably require: i.e. reasonably require to enable the authority to perform its registration functions.

[Documentary evidence to be supplied on application for registration

2–006 2A. An applicant for registration under Part I of the Act shall, if the registration authority so requires, supply to that authority such birth certificate and such other documentary evidence as is specified by that authority as being necessary to substantiate the information supplied in accordance with paragraphs 1(*a*) or 2(*a*)(i) of Schedule 1 to these regulations.]

GENERAL NOTE

This regulation makes provision for the supply by applicants for registration of documentary evidence to substantiate details as to their identity at the request of the registration authority.

2–007

Registration fees

3.—(1) Subject to paragraph (2) of this regulation, the registration fee to accompany an application for registration made under section 5 of the Act shall be—

2–008

(*a*) in the case of an application in respect of the manager or intended manager of the home who is not the person in control of it (whether as owner or otherwise), [£230];

(*b*) in the case of an application in respect of the person in control of the home, [£840].

[(2) The registration fee to accompany an application for registration under Part I of the Act of a person in respect of a small home shall be £230.]

GENERAL NOTE

Under s.5(2A) of the 1984 Act the registration authority can waive the whole or part of the registration fee in respect of a small home. Also see paras. 6 and 7 of Annex A to Department of Health Circular No. LAC (92)10.

2–009

Authorities should keep separate accounts of their costs and income arising from the Registered Homes Act 1984 (DHSS Circular No. LAC (88)15, para. 7). Guidance on the compilation of registration accounts is contained in Department of Health Circular No. LAC (89)14.

As neither these Regulations nor the 1984 Act specifically refer to a fee payable where there is to be a change to a registered home (other than a change of owner or manager) a registration authority has no power to charge a fee when agreeing to vary a condition of registration on the application of the registered person. This issue was investigated by the Local Ombudsman in Complaint No. 89/C/0268 against Cleveland County Council. In para. 8 of her report the Ombudsman refered to para. A25 of the Guidance Notes attached to DHSS Circular No. LAC (84)15 which states that "no registration fee is payable if there is a change at the home but no change in its ownership or in the manager". The Department of Health advised the Ombudsman that this guidance remains in force. "The Department's view is that no fee should be charged where there are changes to the home but no change in the identity of the owner or manager. They say that the condition about the number of residents should be changed by way of amendment (rather than by requiring a new application). The Department says that the annual fee levied on the next renewal after amendment would reflect the higher number of residents": *ibid.* para. 8.

Under s.5(4) of the 1984 Act a registration authority is not legally obliged to entertain an application by a registered owner to vary a condition of registration. If an authority is faced with such a request its response should be conditioned by the nature and extent of the proposed changes. The following approach could be adopted:

(1) If the authority does not agree with the proposed changes it should refuse to entertain the application. The registered person has no right of appeal to a Registered Homes Tribunal against such a refusal (*Coombs* v. *Hertfordshire County Council* (1991) 89 L.G.R. 774, noted under s.5(4) of the 1984 Act) and his only recourse would be to submit a full registration application, incorporating the proposed changes, to the authority. The authority is obliged to consider the application by virtue of s.5(2) of the 1984 Act and if the application is refused the owner can appeal to a Tribunal under s.15 of the Act.

(2) If the authority agrees with the proposed changes and considers them to be minor and unlikely to affect the basic nature and purpose of the home, it should amend the certificate of registration without charging a fee.

(3) If the authority considers that the proposed changes are substantial and are likely to affect the basic nature and purpose of the home, it should refuse to entertain a request to vary the conditions of registration. The registered owner could then submit a full registration application incorporating the proposed changes.

Time limit for registration

2–010   **4.**—(1) Where—
      (*a*) immediately before the relevant date a person was not required to be registered under the 1980 Act in respect of an establishment; and
      (*b*) on that date he is required to be registered under Part I of the Act in respect of that establishment,
he shall within six months of that date apply to the registration authority for registration under that Part and until that application is determined he shall for the purposes of the Act be deemed to be registered under that Part in respect of that establishment.

    (2) A person who immediately before the relevant date was registered under the 1980 Act in respect of an establishment and who on that date is required to be registered in respect of that establishment under Part I of the Act shall for the purposes of the Act and of these regulations be deemed to be registered under that Part in respect of that establishment.

GENERAL NOTE

Para. (2)

2–011   *Be deemed to be registered:* In a form as closely appropriate as possible to the form in which the person was registered under the Residential Homes Act 1980. In *Decision* No. 43 the Tribunal said that "registration as a residential care home for persons in need of personal care by reason of old age is entirely appropriate for a home registered [under the 1980 Act] for the 'aged or infirm but not otherwise handicapped' ".

Annual fee

2–012   [**5.**—(1) A person registered in respect of a residential care home as being the person in control of it shall pay an annual fee, of an amount determined in accordance with paragraphs (2) to (4) of this regulation, within one month of the date on which the certificate of registration was issued and thereafter in each year no later than the day before the anniversary of that date.

    (2) Where the home is not a small home, the annual fee shall, subject to paragraph (4) of this regulation, be of an amount equal to £41 multiplied by the maximum number of persons specified (in accordance with section 5(3) of the Act) in the certificate of registration in respect of the home.

    (3) Where the home is a small home, the annual fee shall be £30.

    (4) Where the home is not a small home, but an annual fee was payable in respect of the immediately preceding year and was that payable in accordance with paragraph (3) of this regulation because the home was then a small home and no application for re-registration under section 5(1) of the Act has been made and accompanied by the registration fee, the amount of the annual fee determined in accordance with paragraph (2) of this regulation shall be increased by £610.]

GENERAL NOTE

2–013   Under s.8(2) of the 1984 Act a registration authority can waive the whole or part of the registration fee in respect of a small home. Also see para. 8 of Annex A to Department of Health Circular No. LAC (92)10.

Records

2–014   **6.**—(1) [Subject to paragraph (1A) of this regulation] the person registered shall compile the records specified in Schedule 2 to these regulations and shall keep them in the home at all times available for inspection by any person authorised in that behalf by the registration authority or, as the case may be, the Secretary of State.

    [(1A) A person registered in respect of a small home need not compile the records specified in—

(a) paragraphs 8 to 16 of Schedule 2 to these regulations;
(b) paragraph 4 of that Schedule, except to the extent that it relates to any medicines administered to a resident; or
(c) in paragraph 7 of that Schedule to the extent that it relates to any visits by persons authorised to inspect the home.]

(2) The person registered shall keep in a safe place in the home the case record of each resident compiled in accordance with paragraph 4 or 5 of the said Schedule 2.

(3) Any person who is deemed by virtue of regulation 4(2) of these regulations to be registered under Part I of the Act in respect of a home shall within three months of the relevant date compile the records specified in the said Schedule 2.

(4) Every record compiled in accordance with this regulation shall be retained for a minimum of three years from the date of the last entry in it.

General Note

A registered person who contravenes this regulation commits an offence: see reg. 20.   2–015

For examples of poor record-keeping being a contributory factor in the decision to cancel a registration, see *Tribunal Decisions* No. 94, 95 and 195. An owner's lack of understanding of the purposes of and the necessity for records was a contributory factor in the Tribunal's decision to confirm a cancellation of registration in *Decision* No. 147. The Tribunal said in this case that residents "are at risk because the records give them inadequate protection, inadequate continuity of care and inadequate quality of life". Also see *Decision* No. 219, where the Tribunal said that records "are not simply a description of what is happening. Good, accurate and reliable records are essential to, and indicative of, the whole process of care in a well run Home. Only with accurate, meaningful records can the Respondents know what is going on in the Home, how the residents are progressing, whether there are matters which should be investigated, and so forth. Further, for continuity of care of residents, all the staff need to have clear records to which they can turn, so that, *e.g.* absences of staff or incidents with residents do not take anyone by surprise".

Registers

7. The registers kept by a registration authority for the purposes of Part I   2–016
of the Act shall contain the particulars specified in Schedule 3 to these regulations.

Consultation with fire authority

8. The person registered shall [except in respect of a small home] at such   2–017
times as may be agreed with the fire authority, consult that authority on fire precautions in the home.

Conduct of homes

9.—(1) The person registered shall arrange for the home to be conducted   2–018
so as to make proper provision for the welfare, care and, where appropriate, treatment and supervision of all residents.

(2) In reaching any decision relating to a resident the person registered shall give first consideration to the need to safeguard and promote the welfare of the resident and shall, so far as practicable, ascertain the wishes and feelings of the resident and give due consideration to them as is reasonable having regard to the resident's age and understanding.

(3) Every home shall be maintained on the basis of good personal and professional relationships between the person registered and persons employed at the home and the residents.

[(4) The person registered shall ensure that corporal punishment is not used as a sanction in relation to any child in the home.]

General Note

Para. (1)

Welfare: "Good care practise does not require a home to be run like an over hearty holiday   2–019
camp, but it does require that residents be treated as individuals and helped to follow their individual interests": *per* the Tribunal in *Decision* No. 147.

Care: An analysis of the uses and abuses of restraint in residential care and nursing homes for older people can be found in *What if they hurt themselves* (Counsel and Care, 1992). (The appellant's failure to seek any assessment or advice before implementing her decision to employ the physical restraint and sedation of a resident was a factor which led the Tribunal in *Decision* No. 98 to confirm an order made under s.11 of the 1984 Act.) Counsel and Care has also published a report on privacy for residents, *Not Such Private Places—A Study of Privacy and the Lack of Privacy for Residents in Private and Voluntary Residential and Nursing Homes in Greater London* (1991) and, on risk taking in residential settings, *The Right to Take Risks* (1993). A further report on privacy, *From Home to Home*, was published by Counsel and Care in 1992. The address of Counsel and Care is Twyman House, 16 Bonny Street, London NW1 9PG.

Supervision: In *Decision* No. 195, the Tribunal said that it regarded the use of electronic listening devices in a residential care home as "being a very serious breach of the right to privacy of staff and residents".

Para. (2)

2–020 *First consideration:* Where there is a conflict between action that is considered to be in the interests of the welfare of the resident and any wishes expressed by the resident, the resident's welfare will prevail.

Para. (4)

2–021 "The ban on corporal punishment of a child is a ban on punishment of that kind. It does not prevent a person taking necessary physical action to avert an immediate danger of personal injury to the child, or another person, nor to avoid immediate danger to property. A 'child' is defined at reg. 1(2) ... as a resident under the age of 18 or one who is older and is the subject of a care order": DHSS Circular No. LAC (88)15, para. 9.

Provision of facilities and services

2–022 **10.**—(1) [Subject to paragraphs (1A) and (1B) of this regulation,] the person registered shall having regard to the size of the home and the number, age, sex and condition of residents—

(a) employ by day and, where necessary, by night suitably qualified and competent staff in numbers which are adequate for the well being of residents;

(b) provide for each resident such accommodation and space by day and by night as is reasonable;

(c) provide adequate and suitable furniture, bedding, curtains, floor covering and, where necessary, equipment and screens in rooms occupied or used by residents;

(d) provide for the use of residents a sufficient number of water closets, and of wash-basins, baths and showers fitted with a hot and cold water supply, and any necessary sluicing facilities;

(e) make such adaptations and provide such facilities as are necessary for residents who are physically handicapped;

(f) provide adequate light, heating and ventilation in all parts of the home occupied or used by residents;

(g) keep all parts of the home occupied or used by residents in good structural repair, clean and reasonably decorated;

(h) take adequate precautions against risk of fire, including the provision of adequate means of escape in the event of fire, and make adequate arrangements for detecting, containing and extinguishing fires, for the giving of warnings and for the evacuation of all persons in the home in the event of fire and for the maintenance of fire precautions and fire fighting equipment;

(i) make arrangements to secure by means of fire drills and practises that the staff in the home and, so far as practicable, residents know the procedure to be followed in the case of fire including the procedure for saving life;

(j) take adequate precautions against the risk of accidents including the training of staff in first aid;

(k) provide sufficient and suitable kitchen equipment, crockery and cutlery together with adequate facilities for the preparation and storage of food and, so far as may be reasonable and practicable in the circumstances, adequate facilities for residents to prepare their own food and refreshments;
(l) supply suitable, varied and properly prepared wholesome and nutritious food in adequate quantities for residents;
(m) make, after consultation with the local environmental health officer, suitable arrangements for maintaining satisfactory conditions of hygiene in the home;
(n) arrange for regular laundering of linen and clothing and, so far as may be reasonable and practicable in the circumstances, provide adequate facilities for residents to do their own laundering;
(o) make arrangements for any person authorised by the registration authority or, as the case may be, by the Secretary of State, to interview in private any resident;
(p) make arrangements, where necessary, for residents to receive medical and dental services, whether under Part II of the National Health Service Act 1977, or otherwise;
(q) make suitable arrangements for the recording, safekeeping, handling and disposal of drugs;
(r) make suitable arrangements for the training, occupation and recreation of residents including the provision of play and educational facilities for children;
(s) provide a place where the valuables of residents may be deposited for safekeeping.

[(1A) Sub-paragraph (i) of paragraph (1) of this regulation shall not apply in respect of a small home.

(1B) Sub-paragraphs (h), (j) and (m) of paragraph (1) of this regulation shall apply in respect of a small home with the following modifications—
(a) in sub-paragraph (h) as if the words after the words "risk of fire" were omitted;
(b) in sub-paragraph (j) as if the words after the word "accidents" were omitted;
(c) in sub-paragraph (m) as if the words ", after consultation with the local environmental health officer," were omitted.]

(2) The person registered shall arrange for the home to be connected to a public telephone service and shall, so far as may be reasonable and practicable in the circumstances, make arrangements for residents to communicate with others in private by post or telephone.

GENERAL NOTE

The following advice to registration authorities on the provision of facilities and services is given in paras. 7 and 8 of DHSS Circular No. LAC (86)6: **2–023**

"Authorities should be broadly consistent about standards across the public and private sectors and, as indicated in the Secretaries of State's foreword to *Home Life*, should not expect higher standards in registered homes than they have in their own homes. The general guidance given in *Home Life* deliberately avoided a detailed prescriptive approach in the knowledge that what might constitute appropriate levels of care in one home would be unnecessary or unworkable in another. For these reasons, the Residential Care Homes Regulations 1984 give authorities discretion in deciding whether the services and facilities provided in a registered home are appropriate to its size and to the number, age, sex and condition of the residents. In exercising this discretion, authorities need to take account of each establishment's objectives and character. For example, where an establishment aims to foster its residents' self-reliance or to prevent the development of avoidable dependence the staffing and other facilities and services may need to be of a different kind or order from those of a home caring for heavily dependent residents.

When requiring a person already registered to make changes in his home a reasonable time should be allowed for the changes to be arranged and made."

In *Decision* No. 219, the Tribunal observed that "standards by Respondent authorities are being, and should be, constantly improved. It accepts that in the early days of the running of the Home it is likely that standards were tolerated which today would not be so tolerated. Far from this being reprehensible, this is to be applauded. Standards should always go up rather than down, *a fortiori* where the client group is so very vulnerable and needs the protection of the State. The more recent Respondents' officers clearly had higher standards and rightly sought to encourage and promote these".

For the application of this regulation to small homes, see paras. 3 to 5 of Annex A to Department of Health Circular No. LAC (92)10.

A registered person who contravenes this regulation commits an offence: see reg. 20.

Para. (1)(a)

2–024   *Employ:* In *Decision* No. 190, the Tribunal made the following comments on staff rotas:

"Much was made by the Respondents as to the lack of reliable records as to who was on duty at what time. The Tribunal finds that rotas are a valuable and important management tool, essential for a large establishment where forward-planning (for days off, holidays, substitutions in case of illness or other emergencies etc.) can be difficult/complicated. In such an establishment it would be very rare for a planned rota to remain unchanged. For a proprietor a properly kept note as to who is on duty, who on stand-by and so forth, is an orderly plan for the future, a record of the past and an *aide-memoire* for the payment of wages and such related matters. For local authority supervisory staff such a record is probably of doubtful value in isolation from other records since it can so easily be 'fudged'."

And, where necessary, by night: There is no absolute requirements that night staff should be employed. The decision would depend upon the client group and the level of dependency although night staff should always be employed where there are elderly residents (*Tribunal Decisions* No. 33 and 42). The criteria for employing *waking* night staff was considered by the Tribunal in *Decisions* No. 55 and 117. In *Decision* No. 117 the Tribunal agreed with the registration authority that for residential care homes providing accommodation for more than eight people "a waking member of staff must always be preferable to two sleeping members of staff". The Tribunal identified the advantages of having a waking member of staff as follows:

"As a general principle, unrelated to any formula of numbers, a waking member of staff can make periodic inspections (and the Tribunal does not consider that this could ever constitute an intrusion on the privacy of residents), thus being aware of emergencies, helping with personal tasks (*e.g.* taking someone to the lavatory) and giving that comfort and tremendous feeling of security to residents who find themselves sleepless, frightened or lonely. Just to know that someone else is awake gives very great comfort in these circumstances."

See further *Home Life*, para. 5.5.

Suitably qualified and competent staff: In *Decision* No. 53 one of the factors which led the Tribunal to dismiss an owner's appeal against the registration authority's decision to cancel her registration was that it "was clear from her evidence that she regarded the obtaining of references as a tiresome formality insisted upon by [the registration authority] and that the fact that one of her staff might have produced forged references was to her of no significance". For examples of lack of suitable staffing being a contributory factor in the decision to cancel a registration, see *Tribunal Decisions* No. 46, 93, 95, 132 and 219.

Adequate: For staffing of small homes, see para. 5 of Annex A to Department of Health Circular No. LAC (92)10. In *Decision* No. 95 the Tribunal said that a residential care home for the elderly "should not be left unattended by a member of staff on duty for period of time, either by day or by night". In *Decision* No. 147 the Tribunal said that staffing levels should be "designed to ensure that staff have sufficient time to care for residents and not just to meet their physical needs". Also see the notes to reg. 12(1)(a) of the Nursing Homes and Mental Nursing Homes Regulations 1984.

Para. (1)(b)

2–025   *Accommodation:* In *Decision* No. 57 the Tribunal rejected a submission that accommodation in double bedrooms was in all respects superior to accommodation in single bedrooms for elderly people. The reasons for single rooms being preferred are set out in para. 2.5.1 of *Home Life*. The subdivision of large and attractive rooms was criticised by the Tribunal in *Decision* No. 52.

"Registration authorities and the Tribunal have a duty to ensure that the accommodation in Homes comes up to an objective standard. The fact that a particular resident chose and is happy in a particular room is evidence, but not conclusive evidence, of the suitability of the room. We accept it as a salutory reminder that, in seeking the welfare of residents, objective standards are not the only criterion. Residents' wishes must also be taken into account" (*Tribunal Decision* No. 112).

A decision by a registration authority as to the maximum percentage of double rooms which will be allowed in a residential care home must not be allowed to harden into a fixed rule, or even into a rule from which the authority will only depart in exceptional cases: see *Tribunal Decision* No. 56 where the Tribunal considered the factors which should guide a registration authority when it is considering what proportion of double rooms should be permitted in a particular home. This issue was also considered by the Tribunal in *Decision* No. 106. In *Decisions* No. 51, 52, 56, 57 and 143 the Tribunal supported the policy of the Birmingham City Council that double bedrooms should normally form no more than 25 per cent. of the total bedrooms in a home. The policy of Trafford Borough Council of working towards 80 per cent. single occupancy for new homes was supported by the Tribunal in *Decision* No. 142. In *Decision* No. 169 the Tribunal commended the recommendation of the Dudley Metropolitan Borough Council that "not more than 10 per cent. of rooms (or two if this is greater) should be shared". Such a recommendation was stated to represent "good practice" and was accepted by the Tribunal as "being a sound policy". In *Decision* No. 71 the Tribunal upheld the registration authority's policy of phasing out multi-occupancy rooms and said that the authority "has both the right and the duty to seek to implement those standards set out in [*Home Life*], standards which strive to attain the good rather than . . . the acceptable". Also note the following passage from *Tribunal Decision* No. 99:

"We uphold the principles stated in paras. 2.5.1 and 3.5 of *Home Life*. We stress, however, that if a registration authority formulates rigid guidelines, particularly concerning matters such as occupancy and space, it must nevertheless take account of the totality of each situation presented and be ready to apply them flexibly in an appropriate case. Such an approach was visualised in para. 9 of Local Authority Circular (86)6 by the statement: 'Decisions on the size and occupancy of bedrooms will need to take account not only of the design and construction of the premises but also of the levels of dependency of prospective residents and their likely needs for privacy and care.' We appreciate the conflicting considerations often faced by a registration authority; on the one hand it is expected positively and confidently to apply its policies without suspicion of weakness or favouritism, but on the other hand it has to do so in a sensible way that takes account of the circumstances of each individual case, and therefore may appear to be discriminatory. The final decision must always be a matter of judgment and not, as it rather appears to have been in this case, one of purely arithmetical calculation."

Evidence of the registration authority's own standards relating to multiple occupancy rooms was admitted in *Decisions* No. 16, 24 and 25.

The risk of undertaking alterations to a home without prior consultation with the registration authority was emphasised by the Tribunal in *Decision* No. 75: see the note on reg. 10(1)(*b*) of the Nursing Homes and Mental Nursing Homes Regulations 1984.

Also see the note on "accommodation" in s.9(*b*) of the 1984 Act.

By day: In *Decision* No. 139 the Tribunal agreed with the appellants that "because of the size and nature of residents' individual rooms the standard guidelines laying down the amount of communal space required for each resident was less applicable to [this] Home than they are to a home with smaller bedrooms".

Para. (1)(c)

Adequate and suitable furniture: In *Decision* No. 30 some residents' clothing was kept in a "locker" outside the bedroom. All bedrooms in the home were large enough to take a wardrobe but the owner objected to wardrobes as they "cluttered up" the bedrooms and reduced living space. The Tribunal found that there should be wardrobes in all of the bedrooms as this enabled residents to at least have some say in what they wear, even though some may not be capable of exercising a rational choice. There was no objection to winter clothing being stored elsewhere in the summer and *vice versa*. The Tribunal concluded its decision by stating that what it had said about wardrobes "should relate to all residential care homes, and if the principle resulted in some cases to reducing a bedroom to an unacceptable size, this was a matter for the relevant local authority to consider when registration was applied for". The physical features of a residential care home are considered by *Home Life* at paras. 3 *et seq.* Note that the term "adequate" is not defined: *cf.* reg. 2(1) of the Nursing Homes and Mental Nursing Homes Regulations 1984.

2–026

Para. (1)(e)

This regulation does "not preclude local authorities from supplying individual aids such as walking frames and dressing aids to residents in private and voluntary homes provided such items are supplied individually for their personal use on the same basis as for other people living in the community": DHSS Circular No. LAC (86)6, para. 11.

2–027

Para. (1)(f)

Adequate light: The sufficiency of the natural lighting in a resident's room was at issue in *Tribunal Decision* No. 142.

2–028

Para. (1)(j)

2–029 A failure to conduct any fire drills during a period of 15 months was one of the reasons to cancel registration in *Tribunal Decision* No. 201.

Para. (1)(k)

2–030 *Food:* Residential care homes are subject to the provisions of the Food Safety Act 1990.

Para. (1)(l)

A failure to supply residents with suitable, varied and properly prepared wholesome food in sufficient quantities was proved in *Tribunal Decision* No. 219.

Para. (1)(p)

2–031 *Medical . . . services:* "Family Practitioner Committees [now Family Health Services Authorities] have been asked to pay particular attention in preparing their short term plans to collaborating with appropriate bodies to ensure that there are adequate family practitioner services for elderly people in residential care homes. This will give a registration authority the opportunity to draw attention to any deficiencies in the coverage of the homes in the area, so that the Family Practitioner Committee can consider what arrangements may be needed to remedy them": DHSS Circular No. LAC (18)15, para. 15.

"The principle is well established and strongly supported by the Government that people in residential care homes have the same general entitlement to national health service and community nursing services as people living in their own homes": *per* the Parliamentary Under-Secretary of State for Health speaking on the Standing Committee of the Community Care (Residential Accommodation) Bill (Standing Committee E, June 18, 1992, col. 55).

Local authority and National Health Service responsibilities for funding community health services for residents of residential care and nursing homes who have been placed in those homes by local authorities are set out in Department of Health Circular No. LAC (92)24.

Para. (1)(q)

2–032 *Recording:* The person registered has a duty to compile records relating to the administration of drugs under reg. 6, Sched. 2, paras. 4, 6.

Drugs: Concern about the handling, maintenance, administration and recording of drugs was a factor in the decision to confirm registration cancellations in *Tribunal Decisions* No. 95, 110, 132 and 144. The administration of drugs is considered by *Home Life* at para. 2.7.3. For the application of this provision to small homes, see para. 26 of Annex A to Department of Health Circular No. LAC (92)10.

Visits by parents, guardians, etc.

2–033 **11.**—(1) The person registered shall provide suitable facilities for visits to the home by parents, guardians, friends or other visitors of any resident and by any officer of a local authority whose duty it is to supervise the welfare of that resident, but the use of such facilities, times of visiting and other arrangements connected with the visits shall be as the person registered may, after consultation with the registration authority, decide [, except that no such consultation is required in respect of a small home.]

(2) The person registered shall ensure that there are facilities in the home whereby residents may, if they so desire, communicate in private with their visitors.

(3) [Except in respect of a small home,] the person registered shall keep affixed in a conspicuous place in the home a notice stating the times during which visits may be made and he shall, at the request of any person wishing to visit a resident, make available to that person details of such times.

GENERAL NOTE

2–034 A registered person who contravenes this regulation commits an offence: see reg. 20.

In *Decision* No. 79 the Tribunal urged registration authorities to ensure that the relatives and friends of residents are given information on how to contact the local social services. This could be done by providing relatives and friends with a simple information sheet or a duplicate of the residents' contract.

Religious observance

2–035 **12.** The person registered shall ensure that every resident under the age of 18 years has so far as practicable in the circumstances the opportunity to attend such religious services and to receive such instruction as may be appropriate to the religious persuasion to which the resident belongs.

Notification of arrival of children

13. The person registered shall as soon as practicable notify the registration authority and the District Health Authority in whose district the home is situated of the date of arrival of each child in the home and the expected duration of his stay.

GENERAL NOTE

A registered person who contravenes this regulation commits an offence: see reg. 20.

Notification of death, illness, or accident

14.—(1) The person registered shall notify the registration authority not later than 24 hours from the time of its occurrence—
   (a) of the death of any resident under the age of 70 and of the circumstances of his death;
   (b) of the outbreak in the home of any infectious disease which in the opinion of any registered medical practitioner attending persons in the home is sufficiently serious to be so notified, or of any serious injury to or serious illness of any person residing in the home;
   (c) of any unexplained absence of a child from the home;
   (d) of any event in the home which affects the well-being of any resident; and
   (e) of any theft, burglary, fire or accident in the home.

(2) Where a child is in the home, the person registered shall not later than 24 hours from the time of the occurrence of any of the events specified in paragraph (1)(a) to (d) of this regulation also notify the occurrence of that event to the following persons—
   (a) his parent or guardian;
   (b) if the child is in the care of a care authority not being the registration authority, that authority;
   (c) if the child is the subject of a care order, his independent visitor (if any); and
   (d) any person or organisation who or which has accepted responsibility wholly or partly for the cost of that child's maintenance in the home.

(3) The person registered shall notify the Secretary of State not later than 24 hours from the time of its occurrence of the death of any child in the home and of the circumstances of his death.

GENERAL NOTE

A registered person who contravenes this regulation commits an offence: see reg. 20.

Notice of absence

15.—(1) Subject to paragraph (5) of this regulation, where the person in control of the home or, as the case may be, the manager of it proposes to be absent from the home for a period of four weeks or more the person in control of the home shall give notice in writing to the registration authority of the proposed absence.

(2) Except in the case of an emergency, the notice referred to in paragraph (1) above shall be given no later than one month before the proposed absence or within such shorter period as may be agreed with the registration authority and the notice shall specify—
   (a) the length or expected length of the proposed absence;
   (b) the reason for that absence;
   (c) the arrangements which have been made for the running of the home during that absence; and
   (d) the name, address and qualifications of the person who will be responsible for the home during that absence.

(3) Where the absence arises as a result of an emergency, the person in control of the home shall give notice of the absence within one week of its occurrence and the notice shall specify the matters referred to in subparagraphs (*a*) to (*d*) of paragraph (2) of this regulation.

(4) The person in control of the home shall notify the registration authority in writing of his return or, as the case may be, the return of the manager of the home within one week of that return.

(5) The provisions of this regulation shall not apply where it is not proposed to accommodate any resident in the home during the absence of the person in control or, as the case may be, the manager of the home.

GENERAL NOTE

2–041   A registered person who contravenes this regulation commits an offence: see reg. 20.

Para. (1)

2–042   In *Decision* No. 213, the Tribunal considered that this paragraph, "correctly construed, does not require the giving, by a person in control, of notice of his absence in a case where there is a manager. In other words, it is only in a case where there is no manager that a person in control must give notice of his own absence".

Notice of termination of accommodation

2–043   **16.**—(1) The person registered shall, before terminating any arrangements for the accommodation of a child, give his parent or guardian or, as the case may be, his care authority reasonable notice of his intention to terminate those arrangements.

(2) Where arrangements for the accommodation of a resident are terminated the person registered shall notify the person who appears to him to be the resident's next of kin and, where the resident is under the supervision of an officer of a local social services authority, the person registered shall also notify that officer.

GENERAL NOTE

2–044   A registered person who contravenes this section commits an offence: see reg. 20.

Para. (1)

2–045   *Reasonable notice:* The obligation to give notice of intention to terminate accommodation is confined to cases where the resident is a child, *i.e.* a person under 18 or subject to a care order (reg. 1(2)). Whether prior notice is given in other cases will depend upon the terms of the contractual relationship between the home and the resident.

Information for residents as to method of making complaints

2–046   **17.**—(1) The person registered shall inform every resident in writing of the person to whom and the manner in which any request or complaint relating to the home may be made and the person registered shall ensure that any complaint so made by a resident or a person acting on his behalf is fully investigated.

(2) The person registered shall also inform every resident in writing of the name and address of the registration authority to which complaints in respect of the home may be made by a resident or a person acting on his behalf.

GENERAL NOTE

2–047   "The 1984 Regulations already require the registered person to inform every resident in writing how a complaint about the home can be made, and that a complaint may be made to the registering authority. Authorities should also ask the registered person to:
   (*a*) include in the information supplied to residents an explanation about the role of the Local Commission for Administration and the method of access to him: the authority should inform the registered person how a complaint has to be made to the Local Commissioner;

(b) ensure that the information is readily available at all times to residents and persons acting on their behalf": DHSS Circular No. LAC (88)15, para. 13.

Inspection of homes

[**18.** The registration authority shall ensure that any home other than a small home is inspected pursuant to section 17 of the Act not less than twice in every period of 12 months.]

2–048

General Note

This regulation is considered in paras. 29 and 30 of Annex A to Department of Health Circular No. LAC (92)10.

Small home: For the inspection of small homes, see paras. 9 and 10 of Annex A to Department of Health Circular No. LAC (92)10.

Inspected: "Authorities should carry out at least one inspection a year without prior notice": DHSS Circular No. LAC (88)15, para. 11.

Not less than twice: This is a minimum and registration authorities may inspect or "visit" more often if the situation warrants it.

2–049

Visits by person in control of the home

19.—(1) Where the person in control of the home is not also the manager of the home he shall at least once in every month visit the home or arrange for another person to visit the home on his behalf and to report in writing to him on the conduct of the home.

(2) Where the person in control of the home is a company, society, association or other body or firm, the directors or other persons responsible for the management of the body or the partners of the firm shall arrange for one or more of their number to visit the home at least once in every month and to report in writing to them on the conduct of the home.

2–050

General Note

A registered person who contravenes this regulation commits an offence: see reg. 20.

2–051

Offences

20.—(1) Subject to paragraph (3) of this regulation, where the registration authority consider that the person registered has contravened or failed to comply with regulation 6, 10, 11, 13, 14, 15, 16 or 19 of these regulations, the authority may serve a notice on the person registered specifying—
  (a) in what respect in their opinion the person registered has failed or is failing to comply with the requirements of that regulation;
  (b) what action, in the opinion of the registration authority, the person registered should take so as to comply with that regulation; and
  (c) the period, not [exceeding] three months, within which the person registered should take action.

(2) Where notice has been given in accordance with paragraph (1) of this regulation and the period specified in the notice, beginning with the date of the notice, has expired, the person registered who contravenes or fails to comply with any provision of these regulations mentioned in the notice shall be guilty of an offence against these regulations.

(3) The provisions of this regulation shall not apply where the registration authority has applied to a justice of the peace for an order under section 11 of the Act or while such an order is in force.

2–052

General Note

A local authority exercising its powers under s.21 of the National Assistance Act 1948 to provide residential accommodation cannot, under the community care arrangements, arrange for such accommodation to be provided by a person who has been convicted of an offence under these regulations: see s.26(1E) of the 1948 Act.

2–053

A conviction for an offence under these regulations is a ground for cancelling the registration of a person in respect of a home: see s.10(c) of the 1984 Act.
Person registered: If more than one person is registered in respect of a home, reg. 22 applies.

Para. (1)

2–054   *Serve a notice:* See reg. 21. The notice must comply with paras. (a), (b) and (c).

Form and service of notices

2–055   **21.**—(1) Any notice which is required under these regulations to be given to any person shall be in writing and may be served on him by being delivered personally to him or by being sent by post to him in a registered letter or by the recorded delivery service.

(2) For the purposes of section 7 of the Interpretation Act 1978 (which defines "service by post") a letter to a person registered enclosing a notice under regulation 20 of these regulations shall be deemed to be properly addressed if it is addressed to him at the home.

Compliance with regulations

2–056   **22.** Where there is more than one person registered in respect of a home, anything which is required under the foregoing provisions of these regulations to be done by the person registered in respect of the home shall, if done by one of the persons so registered, not be required to be done by any other person registered in respect of the home.

Appeals

2–057   **23.** Where a person aggrieved by an order made under section 3 of the 1980 Act before the relevant date—

(a) had appealed before that date to a magistrates' court under section 4 thereof and that appeal has not been determined by that date the provisions of the 1980 Act shall, notwithstanding the repeal thereof, continue to have effect for the purposes of the determination of that appeal;

(b) desires to appeal against the order after that date but within the period of 21 days from the date on which the copy of that order was served upon him, the appeal shall lie to a Registered Homes Tribunal and the provisions of Part III of the Act shall apply for the purposes of the determination of that appeal as if the appeal were an appeal under Part I of that Act.

[Exemption from registration in respect of certain small homes

2–058   **24.**—(1) Registration under Part I of the Act is not required in respect of a small home if the only person or persons for whom it provides residential accommodation with both board and personal care are—

(a) a child or children in need of personal care by reason of disablement, past or present dependence on alcohol or drugs, or past or present mental disorder, who are accommodated pursuant to any of the provisions specified in paragraph (2) of this regulation;

(b) a child or children to whom paragraph (1)(a) of this regulation applies and a person or persons falling within section 1(4)(a) of the Act.

(2) The provisions referred to in paragraph (1)(a) of this regulation are—

(a) section 23(2)(a) of the Children Act 1989 (foster placement by a local authority);

(b) section 59(1)(a) of the Children Act 1989 (foster placement by a voluntary organisation);

(c) Part IX of the Children Act 1989 (private arrangements for fostering children).]

GENERAL NOTE

This regulation makes provision for exemption from registration in respect of circumstances governed by the Children Act 1989. Also see paras. 19 to 21 of Annex A to Department of Health Circular No. LAC (92)10.

2–059

[Annual returns

25.—(1) The person registered in respect of a small home shall make to the registration authority an annual return containing the information referred to in Schedule 4.

2–060

(2) The annual return in respect of a home shall be made each year on or before the anniversary of the date on which the certificate of registration relating to the home was issued, and shall be—
  (*a*) in the case of the first return, for the period beginning with the date on which the application was made and ending with the date on which the return is made; and
  (*b*) in the case of subsequent returns, for the period since the last return was made until the date on which the subsequent return is made.]

GENERAL NOTE

This regulation places an obligation on the person registered in respect of a small home to make an annual return containing information specified in Schedule 4.

2–061

Regulation 2   SCHEDULE 1

INFORMATION TO BE SUPPLIED ON AN APPLICATION FOR REGISTRATION

1. Where the application for registration is made by the manager or intended manager of the home and he is not the person in control of it (whether as owner or otherwise) he shall supply in writing to the registration authority the following information—
  (*a*) his full name, date of birth, address and telephone number (if any);
  (*b*) details of his professional or technical qualifications and experience (if any) of running a home;
  (*c*) the names and addresses of his previous employers and of two referees;
  (*d*) the name, address and telephone number of the home in respect of which registration is required; and
  (*e*) if the registration authority so requests, a report by a registered medical practitioner on the state of the applicant's health.

2–062

2. Where the application for registration is made by the person in control of the home—
  (*a*) that person shall, in a case other than one specified in sub-paragraph (*b*) of this paragraph, supply to the registration authority the following information—
    (i) his full name, date of birth, address and telephone number (if any),
    (ii) details of his professional or technical qualifications and experience (if any) of running a home,
    (iii) the names and addresses of his previous employers and of two referees,
    (iv) the name, address and telephone number of the home in respect of which registration is required [, and in the case of a small home if different the name, address and telephone number of the person to whom enquiries are to be made,] and
    (v) if the registration authority so requests, a report by a registered medical practitioner on the state of the applicant's health;
  (*b*) that person shall, in the case of a company, society, association or other body or firm supply to the registration authority the following information—
    (i) the address of the registered office or principal office of the body or firm and the full names, dates of birth and addresses of the chairman and secretary of the company, or other persons responsible for the management of the body or the partners of the firm, and
    (ii) if the registration authority so requests, details of their professional or technical qualifications and experience (if any) of running a home.

[2A. An applicant for registration who is the intended manager of the home (whether or not he is in control of it) shall—

(a) supply in writing to the registration authority details with respect to his criminal convictions (if any);
(b) where the registration authority ask him for details of any criminal convictions which are spent convictions within the meaning of section 1 of the Rehabilitation of Offenders Act 1974 and inform him at the time the question is asked that, by virtue of the Rehabilitation of Offenders Act 1974 (Exceptions) Order 1975, spent convictions are to be disclosed, supply in writing to the registration authority details of those convictions.]

3. An applicant to whom paragraph 2 of this Schedule applies shall also supply to the registration authority the following information—
  (a) the name, address and telephone number of the home in respect of which registration is required;
  (b) the address of any other home or of any nursing home or mental nursing home within the meaning of Part II of the Act or any voluntary home within the meaning of the Child Care Act 1980, or any children's home within the meaning of the Children's Homes Act 1982 in which the applicant has or had a business interest, and the nature and extent of his interest;
  (c) the situation of the home and its form of construction and, where requested by the registration authority, details of any comments made by the local fire authority or local environmental health authority;
  (d) the accommodation available for residents and for persons employed at the home;
  (e) the date on which the home was established or is to be established;
  (f) whether any other business is or will be carried out in the same premises as the home and whether the home is also required to be registered under Part II of this Act;
  (g) the number, sex and categories of residents for whom the home is proposed to be used indicating the various categories by reference to the following code—

old age [(not falling within any other category)]	I
mental disorder, other than mental handicap, past or present	MP
mental handicap	MH
alcohol dependence, past or present	A
drug dependence, past or present	D
physical disablement	PH

  add if the resident is—
  (i) over 65 years of age [(but not within the category of old age)]   E
  (ii) a child   C

  (h) the full names, dates of birth, qualifications and experience (if any) of persons employed, or proposed to be employed, in the management of the home (apart from a person to whom paragraph 1 of this Schedule applies) and whether they reside or are to reside in the home;
  (i) the number, sex, position and relevant qualifications of staff excluding any teaching staff and those referred to in sub-paragraph (h) of this paragraph, employed or proposed to be employed at the home distinguishing between resident staff and non-resident staff and those employed on a full-time and part-time basis, and indicating the number of hours per week for which it is intended to employ part-time staff;
  (j) a statement of the aims and objectives of the home, of the care and attention to be provided in the home and of any arrangements for the supervision of residents;
  [(k) details of any special arrangements made or other services available for any particular category of resident and, except in the case of a small home, details of equipment and facilities and services to be provided in the home;]
  (l) the arrangements made or proposed to be made for medical and dental supervision and treatment and for nursing care in cases of minor ailments;
  (m) the arrangements for the handling and administration of medicines;
  (n) details of the scale of charges payable by residents.
  [(o) in the case of a small home the number of persons who are participating in the management or running of the home or providing personal care in the home on an informal basis (including any such person who is a relative of the person registered) and their sex, relevant qualifications and position in the home.]

GENERAL NOTE

Para. 1(e)

In Local Ombudsman's Complaint No. 88/C/0776 the Council had delayed registration partly because they insisted that medical references should be taken up on members of the company which was seeking registration. The Ombudsman concluded that "[t]here seems to be no valid reason for the Council to seek medical references for officers of a company if those officers are not to be concerned with the day-to-day running of the home. The need for medical references is specifically mentioned in the Regulations with regard to applications by individuals but is not so mentioned with regard to owners of companies".

This adjudication is reported in [1991] J.S.W.F.L. 170.

Para. 2A

2–064 This paragraph introduces a statutory requirement on applicants who intend themselves to manage a home to provide details of any criminal convictions to the registration authority.

"The requirement on applicants to declare criminal convictions, including those which would for other purposes be regarded as spent, underpins the procedure described in Annex A to Circular LAC (91)4 (on the disclosure of criminal background, and police checks). Authorities' existing registration procedures may need little or no adjustment as a result of the provisions made in the amendment regulations therefore: a requirement to declare past convictions and to provide proof of identity may already be placed on applicants. In these instances the regulations will give added weight to a system which, although unlikely ever to be completely watertight, should ensure that checks against criminal records and the national list of cancelled and refused registrations and by other means are not invalidated because an assumed name is used" (Department of Health Circular No. LAC 91(18), para. 5).

Also see Department of Health Circular No. LAC (91)4.

Para. 3(g)

2–065 "The classification of residential care homes by the main categories of residents that the home is intended to care for is to assist people seeking accommodation and to enable registration authorities to judge whether the facilities and services to be provided are appropriate to the home's objectives. More recently the classification has been used for supplementary benefit purposes. Where an establishment provides accommodation for people aged over 65, consideration needs to be given to whether the residents require personal care on account of physical disablement, mental disorder, or dependence on alcohol or drugs. If so, the home should be classified in whichever of these categories is appropriate (*e.g.* PH, MP, MH, A or D with the suffix E). Only if the care is not provided specifically for one or more of those conditions but on account of old age should the classification 'old age' be applied. This is being made clear by the amending regulations. In this connection the condition of many 'elderly mentally infirm' residents would constitute a 'mental disorder', as defined at s.55 of the Registered Homes Act 1984.

A home may be classified for more than one category of residents (*e.g.* category Codes I and MP). In the course of time the number in each category may fluctuate and the registration authority should review the situation each year to see whether the registration conditions need to be varied to take account of the changes. However, the situation in a home may change substantially during the course of a year and the registration authorities may have to act quickly to adjust the registration conditions": DHSS Circular No. LAC (86)6, paras. 18, 19.

Regulation 6(1)   SCHEDULE 2

RECORDS TO BE KEPT IN A HOME

2–066 The records to be kept under the provisions of paragraph (1) of regulation 6 of these regulations shall be—

1. A copy of the statement of the aims and objectives of the home, of the care and attention to be provided in the home and of any arrangements for the supervision of residents, which statement has in accordance with paragraph 3(*j*) of Schedule 1 to these regulations been supplied to the registration authority and has been agreed with that authority.

2. A daily register of all residents (excluding persons registered or persons employed at the home and their relatives) which register shall, where applicable, include in respect of each resident the following particulars—
   (*a*) the name, address, date of birth and marital status of the resident and whether he is the subject of any court order or other process;
   (*b*) the name, address and telephone number of the resident's next of kin or of any person authorised to act on his behalf;
   (*c*) the name, address and telephone number of the resident's registered medical practitioner and of any officer of a local social services authority whose duty it is to supervise the welfare of that person;
   (*d*) the date on which the resident entered the home;
   (*e*) the date on which the resident left the home;

(f) if the resident is transferred to a hospital or nursing home, the date of, and reasons for, the transfer and the name of the hospital or nursing home to which the resident is transferred;
(g) if the resident died in the home, the date, time and cause of death;
(h) if the resident is a child in the care of a care authority, the name, address and telephone number of the care authority, of any officer of the authority whose duty it is to supervise the welfare of the child and of the child's independent visitor (if any);
(i) if the resident is an adult who is subject to the guardianship of a local social services authority, the name, address and telephone number of that authority and of any officer of the authority whose duty it is to supervise the welfare of that resident;
(j) the name, and address of any authority, organisation or other body which arranged the resident's admission to the home;
(k) if the resident is a child, the name of any school which he is attending or any other place where he may be receiving education or vocational training.

3. In homes accommodating children—
(a) a statement of the sanctions used in the home to control bad behaviour and a book in which shall be entered a record of any sanction administered to a child and the name of that child;
(b) a register in which shall be entered the date on which each child's arrival was notified to the district health authority in whose district the home is situated and, except where the home is an independent school within the meaning of the Education Act 1944, to the local education authority for that district.

4. A case record in respect of each resident which shall include details of any special needs of that resident, any medical treatment required by him including details of any medicines administered to him, and any other information in relation to him as may be appropriate including details of any periodic review of his welfare, health, conduct and progress; and, in the case of a child who is the subject of a care order, such details of any review by the care authority as may have been notified by that authority to the person registered.

5. A record in respect of each child who has special educational needs within the meaning of section 1 of the Education Act 1981 and of the special educational provision within the meaning of that section which is being made in relation to him.

6. A record of all medicines kept in the home for a resident and of their disposal when no longer required.

7. A record book in which shall be recorded the dates of any visits by persons authorised to inspect the home and the occurrence of any event to which regulation 14(1) of these regulations refers.

8. Records of the food provided for residents in sufficient detail to enable any person inspecting the record to judge whether the diet is satisfactory and of any special diets prepared for particular residents.

9. A record of every fire practice, drill or fire alarm test conducted in the home and of any action taken to remedy defects in fire alarm equipment.

10. A statement of the procedure to be followed in the event of fire.

11. A statement of the procedure to be followed in the event of accidents or in the event of a resident becoming missing.

12. A record of each person employed at the home to provide personal care for residents, which record shall include that person's full name, date of birth, qualifications, experience and details of his position and dates of employment at the home and the number of hours for which that person is employed each week.

13. A record of any relatives of the registered person or of persons employed at the home who are residents.

14. A statement of facilities provided in the home for residents and of the arrangements made for visits by their parents, guardians, friends and other visitors.

15. A copy of any report made in accordance with the provisions of regulation 19(2) of these regulations.

16. A record of the scale of charges from time to time applicable including any extras for additional services not covered by that scale and of the amounts paid by or in respect of each resident.

17. A record of all money or other valuables deposited by a resident for safekeeping [or received on the resident's behalf] specifying the date on which such money or valuables were deposited [or received] and the date on which any sum or other valuable was returned to a resident or used, at the request of the resident, on his behalf and the purpose for which it was used.

[18. In the case of a small home a record of each person, whether employed or not, at the home who is providing personal care for residents which record shall include that person's full name, date of birth, qualifications, experience and position in the home.]

General Note

Para. 2(g)
Under s.46(1) of the Public Health (Control of Disease) Act 1984 it is the duty of the relevant district council or London Borough Council "to cause to be buried or cremated the body of any person who has died or been found dead in their area, in any case where it appears to the authority that no suitable arrangements for the disposal of the body have been or are being made otherwise than by the authority". A power to claim reimbursement is contained in s.46(5).

2–067

Para. 17
"The 1984 Regulations required the registered person to keep a record of money or other valuables deposited by a resident. The amendment to Schedule 2 . . . now requires the registered person to keep a record showing for each individual resident *any money or other valuables received on his behalf and how it has been spent or disposed of by the registered person*. As recommended in the code of practice *Home Life* those involved in running homes should not normally become involved with the handling and management of residents' financial affairs. However there will be exceptional cases where residents, because they are incapable of managing their affairs and because it has proved impossible to find an alternative, have had the registered person appointed to act on their behalf in relation to their social security benefit. Local offices of the DHSS are being instructed to notify registration authorities of these exceptional cases. Authorities should ensure that an individual record is being kept by the registered person for each of the residents that they are notified of. The registered person should allow the resident or his representative to have access to the account": DHSS Circular No. LAC (88)15, para. 12.

2–068

The Law Commission states that this provision "offers the opportunity through the local social services authority of monitoring those cases where the registered person is the appointee in order to ensure that any benefits received are being used in the interest of intended beneficiaries": Consultation Paper No. 128, p.49

Regulation 7   SCHEDULE 3

Particulars to be Recorded in the Registers Kept by
Registration Authorities

1. The full name and address of the person registered in respect of the home and, where both the manager and person in control of the home are registered in respect of it, their full names and addresses.

2–069

2. Where the person registered is a company, society, association or other body or firm the address of its registered office or principal office and the full names and addresses of the directors, or other persons responsible for the management of that body or the partners of the firm.

3. The name, address and telephone number of the home [and in the case of a small home if different the name, address, and telephone number of the person to whom enquiries are to be made.]

4. The number, sex and categories of residents (excluding persons registered or persons employed at the home and their relatives) indicating the various categories by reference to the following code:—

    old age [(not falling within any other category)]   I
    mental disorder, other than mental handicap,
        past or present   MP
    mental handicap   MH
    alcohol dependence, past or present   A
    drug dependence, past or present   D
    physical disablement   PH
    add if the resident is—
        (i) over 65 years of age [(but not within the
            category of old age)]   E
        (ii) a child   C

5. The date of registration and of the issue of the certificate of registration and, where applicable, the date of any cancellation of registration.

6. The details of any conditions imposed on registration and of any addition to those conditions or variation thereof.

[7. Whether the certificate of registration issued relates to a small home.]

GENERAL NOTE

Para. 3

2–070   *Small home:* See para. 14 of Annex A to Department of Health Circular No. LAC (92)10.

Para. 4

2–071   "The duty imposed by para. 4 of Sched. 3 may well be a duty to keep particulars of the residents taken in by category. This clearly imposes an onerous task on an authority as there are likely to be continuous changes in at least the number and sex of residents, if not in the categories as well. The respondent Authority in this case (as we understand is so with many other authorities) comply with para. 4 by keeping particulars of the maximum number of residents in any particular category who may be accommodated in a Home" (*Tribunal Decision* No. 43).

It is submitted that the practice of keeping particulars of the maximum number of residents in any particular category who may be accommodated in a home is sufficient to meet the requirements of this paragraph.

Para. 7

2–072   *Small home:* See para. 13 of Annex A to Department of Health Circular No. LAC (92)10.

[Regulation 25

2–073

SCHEDULE 4

INFORMATION TO BE SUPPLIED IN THE ANNUAL RETURN

1. (a) The name, address and telephone number of the home, and the name and address of the person registered, indicating which if any of these items of information is different from that previously supplied;
   (b) the number, sex and category of residents cared for in the home, indicating which if any of these items of information is different from that previously supplied;
   (c) the number of residents who have left the home since the later of the date of registration or the date when information was previously supplied;
   (d) the date and cause of death of any resident who has died in the home since the later of the date of registration or the date when information was previously supplied;
   (e) the number of residents who are permanently confined to bed indicating any change since the later of the date of registration or the date when information was previously supplied;
   (f) the full names and dates of birth of the persons other than residents who are living in the home, whether or not employed in the management or running of the home or in the provision of care in the home, indicating which if any of these items of information is different from that previously supplied;
   (g) the full names and dates of birth, qualifications and experience of the persons employed in the management or running of the home or in the provision of care in the home, whether living in the home or not, and of the persons assisting informally in the management or running of the home or in the provision of care in the home but not living in the home, indicating which if any of these items of information is different from that previously supplied;
   (h) any criminal convictions details of which have not been previously supplied, including, where the registration authority ask for details of any criminal convictions which are spent convictions as mentioned in paragraph 2A(*b*) of Schedule 1 to these Regulations, and inform the person registered as mentioned in that paragraph, details of those spent convictions.
2. In this Schedule "previously supplied" means—
   (a) where no annual return has previously been made, supplied in the application for registration;
   (b) in relation to any other return supplied in the last annual return made.]

GENERAL NOTE

2–074   See paras. 11 and 12 of Annex A to Department of Health Circular No. LAC (92)10.

NURSING HOMES AND MENTAL NURSING HOMES REGULATIONS 1984

(S.I. 1984 No. 1578)

Dated October 5, 1984, and made by the Secretary of State for Social Services under the Registered Homes Act 1984 *(c.* 23), *ss.*21(4), 23(3)(*b*), 26, 27, 29(3)(*a*), 35(3), 56(4), *and Sched.* 2, *para.* 4(1)(*a*).

2–075

ARRANGEMENT OF REGULATIONS

REG.
1. Citation and commencement.
2. Interpretation.
3. Specially controlled techniques.
4. Registration.
5. Annual fees.
6. Variation of conditions of registration.
7. Records.
8. Notices in respect of deaths.
9. Absence of person in charge from the home.
10. Inspection of nursing homes.
11. Frequency of inspection of homes.
12. Provision of facilities and services.
13. Conduct of nursing homes using specially controlled techniques.
14. Transitional provisions.
15. Offences.

SCHEDULES
1. Fees to accompany applications.
2. Particulars required to be furnished by an applicant.
3. Annual fees.
4. Records.

GENERAL NOTE

These Regulations replace the Nursing Homes and Mental Nursing Homes Regulations 1981 (as amended) and the Nursing Homes (Lasers) Regulations 1984 (S.I. 1984 No. 958), which were made under the Nursing Homes Act 1975. Guidance on the interpretation of these Regulations is contained in the handbook published by the National Association of Health Authorities, *Registration and Inspection of Nursing Homes* (1985). A supplement to this work was published in 1988. A procedure for securing compliance with the regulations is set out in reg. 15.

2–076

The residents of a nursing home or a mental nursing home cannot by agreement relieve the registered person or the registration authority of their statutory duties. This is not to say that the residents's agreement should be ignored: see *Tribunal Decision* No. 55.

AMENDMENTS

The amendments to these Regulations were made by S.I. 1986 No. 456, S.I. 1988 No. 1191, S.I. 1990 No. 2164, and S.I. 1991 No. 2532.

Citation and commencement

1. These regulations may be cited as the Nursing Homes and Mental Nursing Homes Regulations 1984 and shall come into operation on January 1, 1985.

2–077

Interpretation

2.—(1) In these regulations unless the context otherwise requires—
 "the Act" means the Registered Homes Act 1984;
 "adequate" means sufficient and suitable;
 "application" means an application for the registration of a person in respect of a home under Part II of the Act and "applicant" shall be construed accordingly;

2–078

"child" means any person under the age of 18 and any person who has attained that age and is the subject of care order [within the meaning of the Children Act 1989];

"class 3B laser product" and "class 4 laser product" have the meanings assigned to them in Part I of British Standard 4803:83 (Radiation safety of laser products and systems) as effective on March 31, 1983;

"dentist" means a person registered in the dentists' register under the Dentists Act 1984;

"fire authority", in relation to a home, means the authority discharging, in the area in which the home is situated, the function of fire authority under the Fire Services Act 1947;

"health authority", in relation to a home, means the District Health Authority, within the meaning of the National Health Service Act 1977, for the district in which the home is situated;

"home" means a nursing home or mental nursing home;

"medical practitioner" means a fully registered person within the meaning of section 55 of the Medical Act 1983;

"patient" means a patient in a home;

"person authorised" means a person authorised by the Secretary of State to exercise powers under regulation 11;

"person registered" means a person registered in respect of a home under Part II of the Act;

"record" means any record kept or retained in pursuance of regulation 7 including any book, card, form, tape, computerised record, film or notes;

"specially controlled technique" means a technique specified in regulation 3.

(2) Unless the context otherwise requires any reference in these regulations to a numbered regulation or a numbered Schedule is a reference to the regulation in or Schedule to these regulations which bears that number and any reference in a regulation or in a Schedule to a numbered paragraph is a reference to the paragraph which bears that number in that regulation or Schedule.

(3) The provisions contained in section 54 of the Act (service of documents) shall apply for the purposes of these regulations as though any reference in that section to a notice or other document under, or required to be served under, the Act were a reference to a notice under, or required to be given or served under, these regulations.

GENERAL NOTE

Para. (1)

2–079   *Adequate:* The definition of this term has been criticised as being "hardly conducive to a recognisable and mutually acceptable schedule of criteria. It is a position that can only be reached by negotiation": see C. Vellenoweth, "Fresh Start Needed" [1985] *Health Service Journal* 1200.

Specially controlled techniques

2–080   **3.** Any technique of medicine or surgery (including cosmetic surgery) involving the use of a class 3B laser product or a class 4 laser product (being a technique of medicine or surgery as to which the Secretary of State is satisfied that its use may create a hazard for persons treated by means of it or for the staff of any premises where the technique is used) is hereby specified as subject to control for the purposes of the Act.

GENERAL NOTE

2–081   See the note on s.21(4) of the 1984 Act.

Registration

4.—(1) An application shall be made to the Secretary of State in writing and sent or delivered to the health authority and shall be accompanied by a fee provided for in Schedule 1.

(2) In making an application an applicant shall furnish the particulars specified in Schedule 2 and such other information, including details of any comments made by the fire authority in relation to the home, as the Secretary of State may reasonably require.

[(3) Where the Secretary of State so requires an applicant shall also furnish such birth certificate and such other documentary evidence as is specified by the Secretary of State as being necessary to substantiate the particulars specified in paragraphs 1 or 2 of Schedule 2.]

Annual fees

5. An annual fee of an amount calculated in accordance with Schedule 3 shall be paid by a person registered, within the appropriate time specified in that Schedule, for each home in respect of which he is registered.

GENERAL NOTE

"Since the fees are being increased for the express purpose of recovering full costs, receipts and expenditure must be monitored carefully to see how far receipts from the new fees off-set expenditure. Authorities are therefore reminded to complete Memorandum Trading Accounts (MTA) categorising the various activities involved": DHSS Circular No. HC (88)48, para. 5. Guidance on the completion of MTAs is given in the Annex to Circular No. HC (88)48 and in DHSS Circular No. HC (86)5.

Variation of conditions of registration

6.—(1) The Secretary of State may vary any condition for the time being in force in respect of a home by giving notice in writing to that effect to the person registered.

(2) A notice given under paragraph (1) shall specify a date, which shall be reasonable in the circumstances, on which the variation specified in the notice shall have effect.

(3) Where it is a condition that the number of persons kept at any one time in the home shall not exceed a specified number ("the original maximum") and the Secretary of State varies that condition by specifying a lower number, he shall specify that the original maximum shall continue to apply so long as all the patients in the home are patients who were resident there at the date on which notice of the variation was given under paragraph (1).

Records

7.—(1) The person registered shall keep a record in the form of a register of all patients, which register shall, in respect of each patient, and as from the date when the patient enters the home, include the particulars specified in Part I of Schedule 4, and, in the case of a maternity home, the additional particulars specified in Part II of Schedule 4.

(2) The person registered shall keep a separate record in the form of a register of—
  (a) all surgical operations performed in the home which register shall include the name of the medical practitioner or dentist who performed the operation and the name of the anaesthetist in attendance;
  (b) where the home is a nursing home, any occasion on which a specially controlled technique is used, the nature of that technique, the name of the person using it and, where that person is not a medical practitioner or dentist, the name of the medical practitioner

or dentist in accordance with whose directions the technique was used.

(3) Any record in the form of a register kept under paragraph (1) or (2) shall be retained for a period of not less than one year beginning with the date on which the last entry was made in the register.

(4) The person registered shall keep a case record in the home in respect of each patient which shall include the following particulars:—
   (a) an adequate daily statement of the patient's health and condition; and
   (b) details of any investigations made, surgical operations carried out and treatment given.

(5) In the case of a maternity home, in addition to the register and case records kept under paragraphs (1), (2) and (4), the person registered shall keep a case record of each child born to a patient in the home which shall include the particulars specified in Part III of Schedule 4.

(6) The case records kept under paragraphs (4) and (5) shall be retained for a period of not less than one year beginning with the date on which the patient to whom, or to whose child, they relate ceases to be a patient in the home.

(7) The person registered shall keep a record of the staff employed at the home which shall include the name, date of birth and details of position and dates of employment at the home of each member of staff and, in respect of the nursing staff, details of their qualifications.

(8) The person registered shall keep a record of—
   (a) all fire practices which take place at the home;
   (b) all fire alarm tests carried out at the home together with the result of any such test and the action taken to remedy defects; and
   (c) the procedure to be followed in the event of fire.

(9) The person registered shall keep a record of maintenance carried out on medical, surgical and nursing equipment in the home.

(10) Any records which are required to be made under the Mental Health (Hospital, Guardianship and Consent to Treatment) Regulations 1983 and which relate to the detention or treatment of a patient in a mental nursing home shall be kept for a period of not less than five years beginning with the date on which the person to whom they relate ceases to be a patient in that home.

GENERAL NOTE

2–087   Any person who fails to keep or retain any record which he is required to keep or retain under this regulation or under Sched. 4 commits an offence: see reg. 15(1)(a).

An alteration of medical records which was effected to deceive the registration authority was regarded as a "very serious" matter and contributed to the decision of the Tribunal in *Decision No. 204* to confirm the cancellation of the home's registration.

Notices in respect of deaths

2–088   8.—(1) If a patient, or a child born to a patient, dies in the home, the person registered shall give notice in writing of the death to the health authority not later than 24 hours after it occurs.

(2) For the purposes of paragraph (1), no account shall be taken of any part of a period of 24 hours which falls on a Saturday, Sunday, Christmas Day, Good Friday or on a bank holiday in England and Wales within the meaning of the Banking and Financial Dealings Act 1971.

GENERAL NOTE

2–089   Any person who fails to give to a health authority notice of a patient's death commits an offence: see reg. 15(1)(b).

Absence of person in charge from the home

9.—(1) The person registered shall give notice to the health authority in writing of any period of more than four weeks during which he or, if he is not in charge of the home, the person who is in charge of it, proposes to be absent from the home.

(2) The notice referred to in paragraph (1) shall be given not later than one month before the beginning of the proposed absence except—
  (*a*) where the health authority agrees to a shorter period, in which case notice shall be given not later than the beginning of that period, or
  (*b*) in an emergency, in which case the notice shall be given not later than one week after the start of the absence unless it is impracticable to do so, in which case it shall be given as soon as possible thereafter.

(3) The person registered or the person in charge as the case may be shall, within one week from the date of his return to the home after an absence of which notice was required to be given in accordance with paragraph (1), give notice to the health authority in writing that he has returned.

(4) The notice referred to in paragraph (1) shall contain the following information—
  (*a*) the length or expected length of the proposed absence from the home;
  (*b*) the arrangements which the person registered will make or has made for the running of the home during the proposed absence, including the name, address and qualifications of the person in charge of the home during that absence.

2–090

General Note

A registered person who fails to give to the health authority the notice required by this section commits an offence: see reg. 15(1)(*b*).

2–091

Inspection of nursing homes

10.—(1) Subject to the following provisions of this regulation any person authorised, on producing (if asked to do so) a duly authenticated document showing that he is so authorised, may enter and inspect any premises which are used, or which he reasonably believes to be used, as a nursing home, and in the course of such inspection may require the production of records.

(2) Subject to [paragraphs (3) and (4)], a person authorised may require the person registered to furnish such information in relation to the nursing home as may reasonably be required for the purposes of inspection.

(3) Nothing in this regulation authorises any person other than a medical practitioner in the service of the Crown or of a health authority to inspect any clinical record relating to a patient in a home.

[(4) Nothing in this regulation is to be taken as requiring or authorising the person registered to disclose information contrary to the provisions of section 33(5) of the Human Fertilisation and Embryology Act 1990 (restrictions on disclosure of information).]

2–092

General Note

Guidance on the inspection of nursing homes is given in paras. 19 and 20 of Health Circular No. HC (81)8.

Section 80 of the Children Act 1989 provides the Secretary of State with an additional power to inspect any nursing home required to be registered under the 1984 Act and used to accommodate children (subs. (1)). This power is supplemented by a power to inspect the children (subs. (6)) and by powers to direct the person carrying on the home to provide specific information (subss. (4) and (5)), to inspect records (subs. (7)) and to enter the home (subs. (8)). It is an offence intentionally to obstruct entry (subs. (10)) and if entry is refused a

2–093

warrant can be obtained under s.102 of the 1989 Act. Section 86 of the 1989 Act places a duty on the person carrying on a nursing home to notify the relevant local authority about children who are being accommodated in the home. The local authority has a duty to safeguard the children's welfare (subs. (3)) and also has a duty under s.24 of the 1989 Act to provide such children with advice and assistance with a view to providing for their long-term welfare. An owner who provides day care for children under the age of eight in a registered nursing home is exempted from the registration requirements of Pt. X of the 1989 Act which deals with childminding and day care for young children: see *ibid.* s.71(1)(*b*) and Sched. 9, para. 4(1)(*d*).

Para. (1)

2–094 Any person who refuses to allow an authorised person to inspect any premises or any record under this provision commits an offence: see reg. 15(2).

Person authorised: By the relevant district health authority: see reg. 2(1) and the General Note to Part II of the 1984 Act. The authorised person need not necessarily be an officer of the health authority.

Enter and inspect: See the General Note on s.17 of the 1984 Act and reg. 11. District health authorities have been directed to seek out unregistered homes: see the note on s.27 of the 1984 Act.

Para. (2)

2–095 *Furnish such information:* A person who fails to provide this information commits an offence: see reg. 15(1)(*c*).

Para. (4)

2–096 This paragraph states that the person registered in respect of a nursing home is not required or authorised to disclose information contrary to s.33(5) of the Human Fertilisation and Embryology Act 1990 (which prohibits persons to whom licences under Sched. 2 to that Act apply or have applied and persons to whom directions have been given under s.23 of that Act from disclosing certain information).

Frequency of inspection of homes

2–097 **11.** Inspection of a home pursuant to section 35 of the Act or to regulation 10 may be made on such occasions and at such intervals as the Secretary of State may decide but he shall cause every home to be inspected not less than twice in every period of 12 months.

General Note

2–098 *Secretary of State:* Who has delegated his functions to district health authorities: see the General Note to Pt. II of the 1984 Act.

Provision of facilities and services

2–099 **12.**—(1) The person registered shall, having regard to the size of the home and the number, age, sex and condition of the patients therein—
  (*a*) provide adequate professional, technical, ancillary and other staff;
  (*b*) provide for each patient in the home adequate accommodation and space, including, where appropriate, day-room facilities;
  (*c*) provide adequate furniture, bedding, curtains and where necessary adequate screens and floor covering in rooms occupied or used by patients;
  (*d*) provide and maintain adequate medical, surgical and nursing equipment and adequate treatment facilities;
  (*e*) provide for the use of patients adequate wash basins and baths supplying hot and cold water and adequate water closets and sluicing facilities;
  (*f*) provide adequate light, heating and ventilation in all parts of the home occupied or used by patients;
  (*g*) keep all parts of the home occupied or used by patients in good structural repair, clean and reasonably decorated;
  (*h*) take adequate precautions against the risk of fire, including the provision of adequate means of escape in the event of fire and make

adequate arrangements for detecting, containing and extinguishing fires, for the giving of warnings and for the evacuation of all persons in the home in the event of fire and for the maintenance of fire fighting equipment;
(*i*) make adequate arrangements to secure by means of fire drills and practices that the staff in the home and, so far as practicable, patients know the procedure to be followed in the case of fire including the procedure for saving life;
(*j*) provide adequate kitchen equipment, crockery and cutlery and adequate facilities for the preparation and storage of food;
(*k*) supply adequate food for every patient;
(*l*) arrange adequate laundering facilities;
(*m*) make adequate arrangements for the disposal of swabs, soiled dressings, instruments and similar substances and materials;
(*n*) make adequate arrangements for patients in the home where necessary to receive medical and dental services, whether under Part II of the National Health Service Act 1977 or otherwise;
(*o*) make adequate arrangements for the recording, safe keeping, handling and disposal of drugs;
(*p*) provide adequate arrangements for the prevention of infection, toxic conditions, or spread of infection at the home;
(*q*) make adequate arrangements where appropriate for the training or occupation and recreation of patients and play and education facilities for children;
(*r*) provide adequate facilities for patients to receive visitors in private;
(*s*) take adequate precautions against the risk of accident;
(*t*) provide adequate facilities for any person authorised to interview in private any patient in the home.
(2) The person registered shall—
(*a*) provide for the home to be connected to a public telephone service;
(*b*) where the home is a maternity home or a home in which surgical operations are undertaken or life support systems used, provide such electrical supply as during interruption of public supply is needed to safeguard the lives of the patients;
(*c*) at such times as may be agreed with the fire authority, consult that authority on fire precautions in the home;
(*d*) make adequate arrangements either with the health authority or otherwise for the care of patients, and children born to patients, in medical emergencies;
(*e*) make adequate arrangements for the running of the home while he, or if he is not in charge of the home, the person who is in charge of it is absent from the home.

GENERAL NOTE

Any person who fails to comply with any provision of this regulation (other than reg. 12(2)(*c*)) commits an offence: see reg. 15(3).

In *Decision* No. 124 the Tribunal considered the qualities that a registered nursing home should provide:

"First and foremost there should be a warm and homely atmosphere in which the patients should have freedom of choice, personal privacy and proper opportunities to retain their individuality and self-respect. Secondly, and seen against the above criteria, such a Home should be comfortable, clean, safe and with areas of privacy and it should provide proper care for these most vulnerable residents."

For reports on the uses and abuses of restraint on residents and the protection of residents' privacy, see the note on reg. 9 of the Residential Care Homes Regulations 1984.

2–100

Para. (1)(a)

2–101 *Adequate:* See reg. 2(1). A failure to provide for adequate professional staff on isolated occasions was not considered to be a sufficient ground to confirm the cancellation of a registration in *Tribunal Decision* No. 149. In this case the Tribunal said that "of itself failure to provide fully adequate [staff] facilities would not normally lead to the closure of a Home".

Staff: The employment of unfit staff is a ground for refusing or cancelling a registration: see ss.25(1)(a) and 28(a) of the 1984 Act. Also see the comment on the Rehabilitation of Offenders Act 1974 in the General Note to the 1984 Act.

Para. (1)(b)

2–102 *Accommodation and space:* The risk of undertaking alterations to the home without prior consultation with the registration authority was emphasised by the Tribunal in the following extract from *Decision* No. 75: "If, without previously consulting the health authority, the owner of a Home carries out significant alterations to the Home, she may be creating a situation in which the health authority will feel obliged to cancel the registration because of the unsuitability of the Home in its altered state."

Account must be taken of the wishes of residents when the question of accommodation is under consideration: see *Tribunal Decision* No. 112, noted under reg. 10(1)(b) of the Residential Care Homes Regulations 1984.

Day-room facilities: In *Decision* No. 28 the Tribunal did "not disagree in principle with a requirement that the amount of day room space be related to the total number of registered beds". Also see *Decision* No. 75 where the Tribunal acknowledged the fact that "if patients do not have a particular facility, such as an attractive lounge, they do not miss it and do not think they want it. But if it is there they use it and benefit from it". Day-room facilities were found to be inadequate in *Decision* No. 124 and in *Decision* No. 175 the Tribunal said that it was no answer to an allegation of insufficient day space to say that "many of the patients are/will be bedridden and will not choose to use the day room. They must always be offered the choice of where to sit and where to eat . . . ".

Para. (1)(c)

2–103 *Furniture:* The use of folding beds in the particular circumstances of the home was approved by the Tribunal in *Decision* No. 75.

Para. (1)(e)

2–104 *Water closets:* The inadequacy of the number of lavatories available for patients and staff and an over reliance on the use of commodes for residents was commented upon by the Tribunal in *Decision* No. 8.

Sluicing facilities: These were found to be inadequate by the Tribunal in *Decision* No. 124. Also see *Decision* No. 75 where the Tribunal said that nothing short of an enclosed sluice in a separate room can be considered satisfactory.

Paras. (1)(h), (i)

2–105 *Fire:* Also see reg. 12(2)(c).

Para. (1)(j)

2–106 *Storage of food:* Arrangements for the storage of food were found to be unacceptable by the Tribunal in *Decision* No. 124. Nursing homes and mental nursing homes are subject to the provisions of the Food Safety Act 1990.

Para. (1)(n)

2–107 *Arrangements:* The purpose of this paragraph is to safeguard a patient's freedom of choice by preventing the imposition of a medical or dental practitioner on a patient by the management against the patient's wishes.

Local authority and National Health Service responsibilities for funding community health services for residents of residential care and nursing homes who have been placed in those homes by local authorities are set out in Department of Health Circular No. LAC (92)24.

Para. (1)(o)

2–108 *Drugs:* Guidance on this paragraph and on the provision of drugs and medicines generally is contained in the 1988 Supplement to the NAHA handbook, *Registration and Inspection of Nursing Homes*, pp. 23–28. For an example of an inadequate administration of drugs and medicines policy, see *Tribunal Decision* No. 154.

Para. (1)(q)

2–109 *Children:* Advice on the care of children in nursing homes is contained in para. 48 of DHSS Circular No. HC (81)8.

Para. (1)(s)
Precautions: Also see reg. 7(9). 2-110

Para. (2)(e)
Absent: Also see reg. 9. 2-111

Conduct of nursing homes using specially controlled techniques
13. The person registered shall ensure that any treatment (including 2-112 diagnosis) by specially controlled technique in a nursing home is carried out only by a person who is, or who is acting in accordance with the directions of, a medical practitioner or a dentist.

GENERAL NOTE
A person who fails to comply with this regulation commits an offence: see reg. 15(6). 2-113

Transitional provisions
14.—(1) This regulation applies where an applicant or person registered 2-114 is aggrieved by a decision of the Secretary of State made under regulation 5(4) of the Nursing Homes and Mental Nursing Homes Regulations 1981 ("the 1981 Regulations") before January 1, 1985 and before that date—
  (a) he has appealed to a magistrates' court under regulation 5(5) of the 1981 Regulations and the appeal has not been determined, or
  (b) he has not so appealed and the period referred to in regulation 5(5) of the 1981 Regulations has not expired.
(2) Where paragraph (1)(a) applies the appeal shall be determined as though regulation 5 of the 1981 Regulations were still in force.
(3) Where paragraph (1)(b) applies an appeal against a decision of the Secretary of State made under regulation 5(4) of the 1981 Regulations shall be to a Registered Homes Tribunal and shall be made within the period of 21 days beginning with the date on which the decision was received.

Offences
15.—(1) Any person who fails without reasonable cause— 2-115
  (a) to keep or retain any record which he is required to keep or retain under regulation 7 or Schedule 4; or
  (b) to give to a health authority any notice which he is required to give under regulation 8 or 9; or
  (c) to furnish any information which he is required to furnish under regulation 10(2),
shall be guilty of an offence against these regulations.
(2) Any person who without reasonable cause refuses to allow a person authorised to inspect any premises or any record under regulation 10(1) shall be guilty of an offence against these regulations.
(3) Any person who fails to comply with any provision of regulation 12, other than regulation 12(2)(c), shall be guilty of an offence against these regulations.
(4) Subject to paragraph (5), the Secretary of State shall not bring proceedings against a person in respect of any failure referred to in paragraph (1) or (3) unless—
  (a) he has served on that person a notice in writing specifying—
    (i) the provision of these regulations with which that person, in the Secretary of State's opinion, has failed or is failing to comply,
    (ii) the respect in which, in the Secretary of State's opinion, that person has failed or is failing to comply with that provision,
    (iii) the action which, in the Secretary of State's opinion, should be taken by that person so as to comply with that provision, and

(iv) the period within which such action should be taken; and
(b) the period referred to in sub-paragraph (a)(iv) of this paragraph has expired.

(5) Paragraph (4) shall not apply where, at the time proceedings relating to a home are brought—
(a) the Secretary of State has applied to a justice of the peace for an order under section 30(1) of the Act (urgent procedure for cancellation of registration etc.) relating to that home and that application has not yet been determined; or
(b) such an order is in force.

(6) Any person who fails to comply with regulation 13 shall be guilty of an offence against these regulations.

GENERAL NOTE

2–116 A conviction for an offence against these regulations is a ground for cancelling the registration of the person in respect of a home: see s.28(d) of the 1984 Act.

A local authority exercising its powers under s.21 of the National Assistance Act 1948 to provide residential accommodation cannot, under the community care arrangements, arrange for such accommodation to be provided by a person who has been convicted of an offence under these regulations: see s.26(1E) of the 1948 Act.

Para. (4)(a)

2–117 *Notice:* There is no right of appeal to a Registered Homes Tribunal against the terms of such a notice.

Regulation 4(1)   SCHEDULE 1

FEES TO ACCOMPANY APPLICATIONS

2–118 1. Subject to paragraph 2, the fee to accompany an application shall be [£678].

2. Where, by reason of a proposed change of ownership in the home, an application is made in respect of the person intended to take over the ownership of the home, the fee to accompany an application shall, if there are otherwise no changes in relation to the home, be [£410].

Regulation 4(2)   SCHEDULE 2

PARTICULARS REQUIRED TO BE FURNISHED BY AN APPLICANT

2–119 1. The full name, address and telephone number and professional or technical qualifications (if any) of the applicant.

[1A. Where the application is made by any individual (whether or not he is the person in charge of the home or the person intended to be in charge of the home) details of any criminal convictions he has including, where the Secretary of State asks him for details of any criminal convictions which are spent convictions within the meaning of section 1 of the Rehabilitation of Offenders Act 1974 and informs him at the time the question is asked that by virtue of the Rehabilitation of Offenders Act 1974 (Exceptions) Order 1975 spent convictions are to be disclosed, details of any spent convictions he has.]

2. Where the application is made by a company, society, association or body, the address of its registered office or principal place of business and the full names and addresses and technical qualifications (if any) of the directors or partners.

3. The address of any other home, residential care home, voluntary home within the meaning of [section 60 of the Children Act 1989] or children's home within the meaning of [section 63 of that Act] in which the applicant has or had a business interest and the nature and extent of his interest.

4. The situation of the home and its form of construction.

5. The telephone number of the home.

6. The accommodation available, and the equipment and facilities provided or to be provided in the home.

7. The date on which the home was established or is to be established.

8. Whether any other business is or will be carried on in the same premises as the home, whether the premises or any part of the premises are or have been registered as a residential care home and whether the applicant proposes to register the premises as a residential care home under Part I of the Act.

9. The type of home (*i.e.* mental nursing home, maternity home, clinic catering for day-patients only, acute hospital etc.).

10. The number of patients for whom the home is proposed to be used distinguishing between different categories of patients and indicating the age-range of patients in each category.

11. The full names, ages, qualifications and experience of persons employed or proposed to be employed in the management of the home and whether they are or will be resident in the home.

12. The arrangements for the management and control of the home.

13. The full names and qualifications of any resident or non-resident employed medical practitioners.

14. The full names and (where appropriate) qualifications and grades of the nursing and other professional, technical, administrative and ancillary staff (other than staff included under paragraph 13) employed or proposed to be employed in the home distinguishing between resident and non-resident staff.

15. The number of hours in each week which the staff referred to in paragraphs 14 and 15 are or are to be required to work.

16. The details of arrangements made or proposed to be made in pursuance of any matters mentioned in regulation 12.

17. The arrangements made for the supply of blood and blood products.

18. The arrangements made for the provision of pathology and radiology services.

GENERAL NOTE

Para. 1A

See the note to para. 1A of Sched. 1 to the Residential Care Homes Regulations 1984 and Department of Health Circular No. LAC (91)4.   2–120

Para. 10

Different categories: In *Tribunal Decision* No. 61 the registration certificate categorised the patients whose reception into the home was to be authorised as "Medical, Chronic Sick, Convalescent and One Terminal Bed". The Tribunal suggested that the expression "One Terminal Bed" is "not only unnecessary, but undesirable for inclusion in a document that nursing home proprietors have a statutory duty to display in a conspicuous place in the Home (s.23(6))".   2–121

Regulation 5   SCHEDULE 3

ANNUAL FEES

1. Subject to paragraph 3, the annual fee in respect of a home in which beds are provided for the use of patients at night shall be an amount equal to [£22] multiplied by the maximum number of patients.   2–122

2. In paragraph 1 the "maximum number of patients" means the number specified in the certificate of registration as being the maximum number of patients who may be kept in the home at any one time.

3. For the purposes of paragraph 1, no account shall be taken of cots provided for the use of children born to women who are patients in the home.

4. The annual fee for a home in which no beds are provided for the use of patients at night shall be [£190].

5. Subject to paragraph 6, the annual fee shall be payable within one month of the date on which the certificate of registration was issued and thereafter shall be payable each year on or before the anniversary of the date on which that certificate was issued.

6. A person who immediately before January 1, 1985 was registered in respect of a home under the Nursing Homes Act 1975 shall pay the annual fee within three months of that date and thereafter shall pay it each year on or before the anniversary of the date of that payment.

Regulation 7   SCHEDULE 4

RECORDS

PART I

PARTICULARS TO BE INCLUDED IN THE REGISTER OF PATIENTS

1. The name, address, date of birth and marital status of each patient.   2–123

2. The name, address and telephone number, if any, of the patient's next of kin or any person authorised by the patient to act on the patient's behalf.

3. The name, address and telephone number of the patient's medical practitioner.

4. Where the patient is a child, the name and address of the school which he attends or attended before entering the home.

5. Where a patient has been received into guardianship under the Mental Health Act 1983, the name, address and telephone number of the guardian and if the guardian is a local social services authority the name, address and telephone number of any officer of the authority required to supervise the welfare of the patient.

6. The name and address of any public body which arranged the patient's admission to the home.

7. The date on which the patient entered the home.

8. If the patient has left the home, the date on which he left it.

9. If the patient is transferred to hospital, the date of and reasons for the transfer and the name of the hospital to which the patient is transferred.

10. If the patient died in the home, the date, time and cause of death.

GENERAL NOTE

Para. 10

2–124 See the note on para. 2(*g*) of Sched. 2 to the Residential Care Homes Regulations 1984.

PART II

ADDITIONAL PARTICULARS TO BE INCLUDED IN THE REGISTER OF
PATIENTS IN A MATERNITY HOME

2–125 1. The date and time of delivery of each patient, the number of children then born to the patient, their sex and whether born alive or dead.

2. The name and qualifications of the person who delivered the patient.

3. The date and the time of any miscarriage occurring in the home.

4. The date on which any child born to a patient left the home.

5. If any child born to a patient died in the home, the date and time of the death.

PART III

PARTICULARS TO BE INCLUDED IN THE CASE RECORD OF A CHILD BORN
IN A MATERNITY HOME

2–125 1. Details of the weight and condition of the child at birth.

2. A daily statement of the child's health.

3. If any paediatric examination is carried out involving any of the following procedures:—
 (*a*) examination for congenital abnormalities including congenital dislocation of the hip;
 (*b*) measurement of the circumference of the head of the child;
 (*c*) measurement of the length of the child;
 (*d*) screening for phenylketonuria;
details of such examination.

PART 3

REGISTERED HOMES TRIBUNAL RULES 1984

(S.I. 1984 No. 1346)

Dated August 22, 1984, *and made by the Secretary of State for Social Services under* **3–001**
the Registered Homes Act 1984 (*c.* 23) *s*.43.

Arrangement of Rules

RULE
1. Citation and commencement.
2. Interpretation.
3. Address for service.
4. Appointment of tribunal.
5. Notice of hearing, etc.
6. Representation.
7. Proceedings in public.
8. Adjournment of hearing.
9. Procedure at hearing.
10. Evidence.
11. Decisions.
12. Withdrawal of appeal.
13. Multiple appeals.
14. Extension of time limits.
15. General.

Schedule

General Note

These Rules prescribe the procedure to be followed in proceedings before a Registered **3–002**
Homes Tribunal constituted under Pt. III of the Registered Homes Act 1984 to hear appeals
relating to the registration of residential care homes under Pt. I of, and nursing homes and
mental homes under Pt. II of, that Act. The decision of a Tribunal does not create a
precedent: see the General Note to Pt. III of the 1984 Act. Judicial comment on the procedure
to be adopted by a Registered Homes Tribunal is contained in the General Note to s.15 of the
1984 Act.

Citation and commencement

1. These rules may be cited as the Registered Homes Tribunal Rules **3–003**
1984 and shall come into operation on January 1, 1985.

Interpretation

2. In these rules, unless the context otherwise requires, **3–004**
"the Act" means the Registered Homes Act 1984;
"appellant" means a person who under any of the relevant enactments
is entitled to appeal or being so entitled has appealed to a tribunal;
"registration authority" means—
(a) in relation to a home under Part VI of the Child Care Act 1980, the
Secretary of State;
(b) in relation to a home under the Children's Homes Act 1982, the
local authority for the area in which the home is or is to be situated;
(c) in relation to a home under Part I of the Act, the registration
authority as defined in section 20(1) of that Part of the Act; and

(d) in relation to a home under Part II of the Act, the District Health Authority for the district in which the home is or is to be situated;

"relevant enactments" means the enactments specified in section 39 of the Act;

"tribunal" means a Registered Homes Tribunal constituted under Part III of the Act.

Address for service

3–005 **3.**—(1) An appellant shall state in the notice of appeal which he is required under any of the relevant enactments to give to a registration authority an address at which any notice, order or other document may be served upon him.

(2) Where the registration authority is not the Secretary of State, the authority shall on receipt of the notice of appeal send it to the Secretary of State within seven days.

GENERAL NOTE

Para. (1)

3–006 *Notice of appeal:* There is no prescribed notice of appeal.

Para. (2)

3–007 *Send it to the Secretary of State:* "Your covering letter should give the following
(a) the client group classification of the home, *e.g.* physically disabled or mental nursing home;
(b) whether the appeal is against the refusal of an application, a condition of registration, or the cancellation or alteration of a registration;
(c) whether the appeal is against an order of the justice of the peace under Sections 11 or 30 of the 1984 Act (the urgent procedure)" (*Registered Homes Tribunals Procedure* (Department of Health, 1989), para. 3.3).

Appointment of tribunal

3–008 **4.**—(1) The Secretary of State shall on receipt of the notice of appeal request the Lord Chancellor and the Lord President of the Council respectively to appoint the chairman and members of the tribunal.

(2) The Secretary of State shall appoint a person to act as secretary of the tribunal for the purposes of the appeal.

Notice of hearing, etc.

3–009 **5.**—(1) The chairman of the tribunal shall, so far as practicable within 28 days of his appointment, fix a date, time and place for the hearing of the appeal and shall serve upon the appellant not less than 42 days before the date so fixed notice in the form set out in the Schedule hereto and shall at the same time send a copy of the notice to the registration authority.

(2) Where the appeal is against a decision of the registration authority, the authority shall not less than 30 days before the date fixed for the hearing of the appeal send to the secretary of the tribunal four copies of a statement of the reasons for the decision and shall at the same time serve a copy of the statement upon the appellant.

(3) Where the appeal is against an order made by a justice of the peace under section 11 or, as the case may be, 30 of the Act, the registration authority shall not less than 30 days before the date fixed for the hearing send to the secretary of the tribunal four copies of the statement which supported the authority's application for the order.

(4) The appellant shall not less than 21 days before the date fixed for the hearing send to the secretary of the tribunal four copies of a statement, signed by or on behalf of the appellant of the grounds of the appeal, and

shall at the same time send a copy of the statement to the registration authority.

General Note

The hearing will usually be about seven weeks after the Registered Homes Tribunal Secretariat receive the notice of appeal (*Registered Homes Tribunals Procedure* (Department of Health, 1989), para. 1.10). The time limits set out in this rule may be extended by the Chairman of the Tribunal under r. 14.

3–010

Para. (1)

Place: In *Decision* No. 153 the Tribunal rejected the appellant's submission that the use by the Tribunal of a venue owned and controlled by the registration authority (the Town Hall) breached the rules of natural justice. In the opinion of the Tribunal:

"an ordinary reasonable man, in attending the hearing at the Town Hall, being premises owned, controlled or occupied by the Respondents, or reading afterwards about the hearing at that venue, would not suspect, for that reason, that the Tribunal did not conduct itself fairly and properly. In reaching this decision the Tribunal also took into account the fact that a Town Hall is an official centre for all local citizens where everyone has easy and equal access to public areas."

3–011

Para. (2)

Statement of the reasons: Which should not include the detailed evidence on which the registration authority relied. "Four copies of the authority's guidelines on registration issued to the appellant should be supplied with the statement" (*Registered Homes Tribunals Procedure*, para. 3.4).

3–012

Representation

6.—(1) The appellant may appear before the tribunal in person or he may be represented by counsel or a solicitor or by any other person authorised by him to act on his behalf.

3–013

(2) The registration authority may be represented before the tribunal by an officer or servant of the authority or by counsel or a solicitor.

General Note

Represented: "One of the reasons that Registered Homes Tribunals were set up was so that appeals could be heard less formally than in a magistrates' court. In practice, a considerable degree of formality has been unavoidable. You do not have to be legally represented, though the authority normally will be. You can present your case to the Tribunal yourself or arrange for someone else to represent you. You are advised to seek legal advice or advice from a local advice agency. You may be eligible under the Legal Advice and Assistance Scheme (the 'Green Form' scheme) which would allow a solicitor to give you legal advice costing up to £50 but would not pay for the cost of legal representation at a hearing. Legal aid for the cost of being represented at a hearing is not available for cases before the Registered Homes Tribunals. If you belong to an association of home owners, they may be able to give you advice about an appeal" (*Registered Homes Tribunals Procedure*, para 2.3).

3–014

Proceedings in public

7.—(1) The tribunal shall sit in public unless for any reason the tribunal determines that the hearing or any part of it shall be in private.

3–015

(2) A member of the Council on Tribunals may be present in his capacity as such at a hearing before a tribunal notwithstanding that the hearing is not in public and he may remain present during the deliberations of the tribunal but shall take no part in those deliberations.

General Note

Para. (1)

Reason: The fact that criminal proceedings were pending against the appellants was not considered to be a sufficient reason to hold the hearing in private in *Decision* No. 87. In *Decision* No. 138 the appellant's argument that a public hearing could have a prejudicial effect on two other nursing homes that he owned and which were located in the same town as the nursing home under appeal did not persuade the Tribunal to sit in private. The Tribunal in *Decision*

3–016

No. 162 ordered that the hearing of witnesses be heard in private because "it was apparent that much of the evidence was of a highly personal and intimate nature" and that the main witness for the registration authority "in particular needed protection of her privacy and dignity, particularly in view of her vulnerability". Paragraph 4.17 of the Department of Health's *Registered Homes Tribunals Procedure* (1989) states that a "Tribunal will agree to a private hearing only in exceptional circumstances".

Adjournment of hearing

3–017   **8.**—(1) The tribunal may at any time, whether before or after the beginning of the hearing, adjourn the hearing and when so doing may either fix the date, time and place at which the hearing is to be resumed or leave the date, time and place to be determined later by the tribunal but the tribunal shall not be resumed at that date, time or place unless the tribunal is satisfied that the appellant and the registration authority have been given at least 14 days' notice thereof.

(2) If either the appellant or the registration authority fails to appear or be represented by one of the persons referred to in rule 6 above at the time fixed for the hearing of the appeal the tribunal may take such action whether by proceeding with or adjourning the hearing or otherwise as may appear to the tribunal to be just and expedient.

GENERAL NOTE

Para. (1)

3–018   *The Tribunal:* It is the Tribunal, not the chairman, which determines the question of adjournments.
May: The Tribunal has a discretion. In *Tribunal Decision* No. 87 the appellants applied for an adjournment of the hearing because criminal proceedings were being brought against them. As the same witnesses were to be relied on in both sets of proceedings the appellants argued that it was therefore highly undesirable to proceed with the civil matter before the adjudication of the criminal proceedings. The Tribunal dismissed the application on the ground that the potential prejudice to the appellants was outweighed by the prejudice which would be caused to the parties, their families and others by delaying the matter. Also see *Tribunal Decision* No. 144 where the appellant applied for an adjournment, first, on the ground that her insurers had not confirmed that they would accept responsibility for the costs of her representation and, secondly, on the ground that there had been no contact between her and her solicitors for the month preceding the hearing. The application was refused. In *Tribunal Decision* No. 147 the appellant's unsuccessful application for an adjournment was made on the ground that he was in touch with potential purchasers and was anxious to sell the home as a going concern.
Paragraph 4.20 of the Department of Health's *Registered Homes Tribunal Procedure* states that the "Tribunal will be most reluctant to defer a hearing particularly if the appeal is against an authority's decision to cancel the registration. This is because there will be residents or patients in the home whose health or welfare may be at risk, and it may not be possible to fix a fresh date for sometime".

Para. (2)

3–019   *Or otherwise:* "In our opinion the words 'or otherwise' . . . confer power to allow or dismiss an appeal summarily in default of appearance, but only if that appears to a tribunal to be 'just and expedient' " (*Tribunal Decision* No. 121).

Procedure at hearing

3–020   **9.**—(1) The appellant and the registration authority shall have the right to address the tribunal, to give evidence and to call witnesses and to examine or cross-examine any person giving evidence before the tribunal.

(2) The chairman of the tribunal may require the attendance of further witnesses in addition to those called by or on behalf of the appellant and the registration authority.

(3) The chairman of the tribunal may permit evidence to be given by affidavit but may at any stage of the proceedings require the personal attendance of any deponent for examination and cross-examination.

GENERAL NOTE

3–021   It is open to the parties to negotiate a settlement during the course of the Tribunal proceedings and to ask the Tribunal to consent to the terms of the settlement: see *Decision* No. 89.

In *Lyons* v. *East Sussex County Council, The Times,* July 27, 1987, Farquharson J. said that "while the Tribunal has the power to regulate its own procedure, the sensible course . . . is for the authority to present its case first so that the appellant is not taken by surprise": see further the note to s.15 of the 1984 Act. This procedure was not followed in *Decision* No. 106 where the Tribunal, in responding to the particular circumstances of the appeal, allowed the appellants to both open and close. The Department of Health's *Registered Homes Tribunal Procedure* states at para. 4.12 that the sequence of events at a hearing is usually as follows:

"Registration authority present their case.
Authority call their witnesses.
Appellant may question authority's witnesses.
Appellant states his case.
Appellant can call his witnesses.
Authority may question appellant's witnesses.
Authority make their final statement.
Appellant makes his final statement."

In *Decision* No. 68, an appeal from a magistrate's order under s.11, the chairman of the Tribunal invited counsel to address her on the issue of whether the appellant should have the right to the final word to the Tribunal. The following ruling was made: "The party who has the burden of proving the allegation, and who thus has the right to begin, has the right to the final word. In short, the respondent authority both began and ended, making their final submission *after* counsel for the appellant summed up."

"The Tribunal may decide to visit the home. This depends upon the nature of the points at issue and is at the discretion of the Tribunal. It is usual for the Tribunal to go on its own and not to be accompanied by the representatives of the parties, though the appellant himself would go with the Tribunal" (*Registered Homes Tribunals Procedure*, para. 4.18).

For comment on the lack of a preliminary hearing in these Rules, see the General Note on s.15 of the 1984 Acts.

Para. (1)

Evidence: In *Decision* No. 147 both parties asked the Tribunal to take into account matters **3–022** arising between the date of the registration authority's decision and the date of the hearing. The Tribunal concluded that it would be appropriate to take account of such matters in circumstances where both parties agreed to this course of action.

The Tribunal: Conducts appeals by way of a re-hearing.

Evidence

10.—(1) The provisions of section 12(3) and (4) of the Arbitration Act **3–023** 1950 (administration of oaths, summoning of witnesses etc.) shall apply to proceedings before the tribunal and the chairman of the tribunal shall have the same powers under those provisions as if he were an arbitrator or a party to a reference under an arbitration agreement.

(2) The appellant, the registration authority or any witness may produce in evidence any document or information notwithstanding that such document or information would be inadmissible in a court of law and the tribunal may receive in evidence such document or information if the chairman of the tribunal is satisfied that it is desirable in the interests of justice to receive it.

(3) The chairman of the tribunal may before or after the beginning of the hearing call for such further information or reports as he thinks desirable, and may give directions as to the manner in which and the persons by whom such material is to be furnished.

GENERAL NOTE

The admissibility of evidence before a Tribunal was considered by Farquharson J. in *Lyons* **3–024** v. *East Sussex County Council, The Times,* July 27, 1987. The relevant extracts from his Lordship's judgment are set out in the General Note to s.15 of the 1984 Act.

Paragraphs 4.4 and 4.8 of the Department of Health's *Registered Homes Tribunals Procedure* (1989) provide guidance on evidence:

"The parties to the appeal will find it convenient for reducing the length of the hearing, if they prepare and exchange statements of the witnesses that they intend to call and provide copies for the tribunal not less than *14 days* before the hearing. If it is intended to rely on affidavit evidence, copies of any affidavit should be made available to the Secretariat and to the other party *14 days* before the hearing . . .

If you have difficulty in persuading someone to give evidence on your behalf, the Tribunal may be prepared to grant your permission to obtain an order requiring the witness to attend the Tribunal hearing and produce documents. You should apply to the Secretariat for a subpoena order no less that *14 days* before the hearing. If you do this, you must explain exactly what evidence that person could give, state his full name and full address and say why he will not attend."

Although it is desirable for witness statements to be exchanged prior to the hearing, these Rules do not require such statements to be served.

Para. (1)

3–025 This paragraph provides the Chairman of the Tribunal with a power to administer oaths to, or take the affirmation of, parties and witnesses and to sue out a writ of *subpoena ad testificandum* (compelling a person to attend the Tribunal to give evidence) or a writ of *subpoena duces tecum* (compelling a person to bring documents or papers for examination by the Tribunal). Under the terms of s.12(4) of the Arbitration Act 1950 "no person shall be compelled under any such writ to produce any document which he could not be compelled to produce on the trial of an action".

Para. (2)

3–026 *Document:* "So that neither party is taken by surprise at the hearing, each should disclose to the other all the documents that they intend to rely upon at the hearing. All letters exchanged between parties should be prepared as an agreed separate bundle (bundle means all the pages therein should be *firmly* bound, stapled or otherwise secured) in date order with numbered pages. You should provide the Secretariat with four copies of this at least *14 days* before the hearing" (*Registered Homes Tribunals Procedure*, para. 4.3).

The Tribunal may receive: In *Decision* No. 80 the record of the inquest into the death of a resident and the statements taken by the police were admitted as evidence by the Tribunal under this rule. Statements taken by the registration authority from more than 30 persons were not admitted on the ground that it was not desirable in the interests of justice to receive them. The reason given for this decision was that, where the statements did not overlap with evidence given at the inquest or statements given to the police, they were insufficiently relevant to the question whether closure of the home under s.11 of the 1984 Act was justified, which was the issue before the Tribunal.

In *Tribunal Decision* No. 160 some of the evidence in the proofs of evidence comprised first-hand complaints by residents. The Tribunal decided to admit this evidence even though the residents would not give evidence before the Tribunal. In considering the analogous position relating to the reports of children to others used in wardship proceedings the Tribunal decided to follow the approach adopted by Butler-Sloss L.J. in the following passage from *Re W. (Minors)* [1990] 1 F.L.R. 203 at 214:

"In wardship therefore, the rules as to the reception of statements made by children to others . . . may be relaxed and the information may be received by the judge. He has a duty to look at it and consider what weight, if any, he should give to it. The weight which he places upon the information is a matter for the exercise of his discretion. He may totally disregard it. He may wish to rely upon some or all of it. Unless uncontroversial it must be regarded with great caution. In considering the extent to which, if at all, a judge would rely on the statements of a child made to others, the age of the child, the context in which the statement was made, the surrounding circumstances, previous behaviour of the child, opportunities for the child to have knowledge from other sources, any knowledge, as in this case, of a child's predisposition to tell untruths or to fantasise, are among the relevant considerations."

Also see *Decision* No. 68 where hearsay evidence received by the Tribunal was "either totally disregarded or afforded little weight" and *Decision* No. 163 where it was said that the "Tribunal's hearing is *de novo* at which all the evidence can be heard and tested and afforded the appropriate weight".

In *Tribunal Decision* No. 152 the appellant objected to the admission of a statement of evidence on the ground that the registration authority failed to make the statement available to him 14 days before the hearing in conformity with para. 4.4 of the booklet *Registered Homes Tribunal Procedure* published by the Department of Health in June 1989. In dismissing the objection the Tribunal said that

"failure to comply with para. 4.4 is not of itself a fatal defect in the presentation of a case. The booklet is intended to facilitate the expeditious hearing of appeals, and the question in each case must be whether a failure to comply with the timetable of events has placed the other party under a disadvantage. If it has, the Tribunal may in a proper case grant an application for a postponement, but it will not refuse to hear relevant evidence simply because that evidence is tendered on short notice or even without notice".

Inadmissible in a court of law: The Tribunal is not bound by the rules of evidence and it may receive any information or document in evidence if the Chairman of the Tribunal considers that to do so would be in the interests of justice.

Decisions

11.—(1) The decision of the tribunal on any appeal shall be the decision of the majority.

(2) The chairman of the tribunal shall, as soon as possible after the hearing, notify the appellant and registration authority in writing of the decision and the reasons for the decision.

(3) Where the appeal was against an order made by a justice of the peace under section 11 or, as the case may be, 30 of the Act the chairman of the tribunal shall also notify him in writing of the decision and the reasons for the decision.

GENERAL NOTE

Para. (1)
A Tribunal does not have the power to order a stay of execution of its decision or to award costs against either party.

"The decision of the Tribunal with reasons will be sent to each of the parties. This is usually about four weeks after the hearing. Occasionally it is possible to announce the Tribunal's decision at the end of the hearing. This will be followed later by the formal written confirmation with the reasons for that decision" (*Registered Homes Tribunals Procedure* (Department of Health, 1989), para. 4.23).

Para. (2)
Reasons for the decision: "That reasons have to be given for the exercise by a Tribunal of a power, even a discretionary power, is not in dispute ... But it is not necessary, in my judgment, that the decision-maker should tabulate in his decision each and every factor either way which he took into account in reaching his decision, with the consequence that the decision can be challenged if it can be suggested that anything not actually specified in the decision as taken into account could have been relevant": *per* Dillon L.J. in *Harrison* v. *Cornwall County Council* (1991) 90 L.G.R. 81 at 94, 95, C.A.

Withdrawal of appeal

12. An appellant may at any time give notice in writing to the secretary of the tribunal that he desires to withdraw his appeal and thereupon the appeal shall be deemed to be dismissed.

GENERAL NOTE

"We express the opinion that the proper construction of r. 12 requires that a written notice of withdrawal must be—(*a*) unambiguous in its terms, and (*b*) immediate in its effect, and (*c*) authenticated by each of the appellants in a case where there are several" (*Tribunal Decision* No. 121). Following this decision the Tribunal in *Decision* No. 171 were "satisfied that a notice of withdrawal expressed to be subject to a condition to be fulfilled at some time in the future is not effective". Also see the notes on s.15(4), (5) of the 1984 Act.

The appeal shall be deemed to be dismissed: The effect of a withdrawal under this rule is to confirm the decision of the registration authority.

Multiple appeals

13.—(1) A tribunal may, with the consent of the appellant and the chairman of the tribunal, hear two or more appeals in respect of the same home together.

(2) A tribunal may also hear two or more appeals in respect of different homes together where—
   (*a*) the appellant in respect of each of the appeals is the same; and
   (*b*) both the appellant and the chairman of the tribunal consent to the appeals being heard together.

(3) For the purpose of enabling two or more appeals to be heard together, the tribunal may adjourn the proceedings in relation to any appeal.

3-034 GENERAL NOTE

Para. (1)
Consent of the appellant: All appellants must agree to the appeals being heard together.

Extension of time limits

3-035 **14.** The time appointed by these rules for the doing of any act may be extended by the chairman of the tribunal upon such terms (if any) as may seem just notwithstanding that the time appointed has expired before an application for extension is made.

General

3-036 **15.** Subject to the provisions of Part III of the Act and of these rules, the tribunal may regulate its own procedure.

GENERAL NOTE

3-037 In *Decision* No. 120 the Tribunal interpreted this rule "as widely as it thought proper" by allowing an appeal against the cancellation of a residential care home to be dealt with by written submissions rather than by an oral hearing. This decision was made because of the "wholly exceptional circumstances", *i.e.* the appellant had fully complied with the outstanding matters which were the cause of the cancellation, and because both parties, each of whom had been legally represented, had stated that they were in agreement with the matter being dealt with by written submissions.

Rule 5(1)   SCHEDULE

3-038 TAKE NOTICE that your appeal against—
(a) the decision of *(here insert the registration authority)* under *(here insert the relevant enactment)*
or
(b) the order made by the justice of the peace under *(here insert the relevant enactment)*
in relation to the premises at *(here insert the address of the premises)* will be heard by the Registered Homes Tribunal sitting at   on the   day of   19   , at   o'clock.
Delete (a) or *(b)* as appropriate.

If for any reason you do not wish, or are unable, to attend at the above time and place, you should IMMEDIATELY inform me in writing at the address mentioned at the head of this notice stating the reasons for your inability to attend.

(Signed)
Chairman

PART 4

CIRCULAR No. HC (81)8

Dated July 1981 and issued by the Department of Health and Social Security

HEALTH SERVICE MANAGEMENT
REGISTRATION AND INSPECTION OF PRIVATE NURSING HOMES AND MENTAL NURSING HOMES (INCLUDING HOSPITALS)

4–001

General Note

Although this Circular deals with amendments that were made to the Nursing Homes Act 1975, it is reproduced here, in part only, because the advice it gives to health authorities on their registration functions is still relevant: see para. 8 of DHSS Circular No. (84)21. The statutory references are out of date and should be disregarded.

* * * *

Part III

General Guidance on Registration and Inspection

16. The 1975 Act is concerned with the maintenance of standards of care and facilities in all premises which are required to be registered under the Act. (Responsibility for the medical treatment of individual patients remains with the practitioner concerned.) The registration and inspection of functions set out in the legislation remain delegated to the area health authorities and their successor district health authorities.

4–002

17. Authorities should develop clear procedures for handling applications for registration and for use in monitoring homes once registered. These procedures should be approved by the authority. The procedures should include detailed guidelines, for use both by the authority and applicants, on staffing and accommodation standards, and should be available to the public. Most authorities already have such guidelines; these should be revised in accordance with the new legislation. A copy of the revised guidelines should be sent to DHSS for information.

18. Within the authority, responsibility for registration matters should be clearly defined; although several disciplines are likely to be involved in registration and inspection of a particular home, it would be advisable for one officer to have overall responsibility for registration policy and procedures.

Inspection of nursing homes and mental nursing homes

19. Authorities are empowered to enter and inspect any premises which they have reason to believe are being using as a nursing home or mental nursing home. They may be premises whose purpose is unclear (*e.g.* establishments providing convalescent care or long-term care for the elderly) and authorities may enter such premises to establish whether or not they should be registered under the Act. In such cases authorities should act in consultation with the local social services department, who are responsible for the registration of residential homes.

4–003

20. The new regulations require authorities to inspect all homes *at least* twice every 12 months; previously this was required only in respect of mental nursing homes. (Authorities may of course visit at more frequent intervals where this is felt necessary.) It is for the authority to determine the timing of an inspection—whether it should be during or outside normal working hours—and whether or not the visit should be made by prior arrangement. In most cases relations with homes should enable visits of inspection to be carried out without unnecessary formality, but, to guard against any possible misunderstanding, officers carrying out inspections should carry some form of written authorisation from the authority.

Overlap between nursing homes and residential homes

21. There are various types of accommodation providing long-term care in the private sector, which are subject to different legislative controls; nursing homes are covered by the 1975 Act and residential homes registered with local authorities under the Residential Homes

4–004

Act 1980. It is essential that the two registering authorities should liaise closely on general registration matters, particularly when either is in doubt about the proper registration of a particular home. Where this is the case it is recommended that the two authorities might make joint inspections to help them determine the appropriate registration.

Complaints

4–005 22. It may be necessary from time to time to visit a home to investigate complaints about the standard of care or facilities provided in a registered home. The responsibility of the authority with regard to such complaints is to ensure that there has been no breach of the registration requirements. If complaints relate to such matters as possible ill-treatment of patients or misappropriation of patients' monies it may be necessary for the authority to refer the complaint to the police. If such a complaint involves the "person-in-charge" of a home and is upheld, it may ultimately lead the authority to decide that the individual concerned is not a fit person to be in charge of a home, and to consider cancelling the registration. (Where a complaint relates to the professional conduct of nurses and midwives working in registered premises the authority may need to consider referring the matter to the General Nursing Council for England and Wales or the Central Midwives Board (or, in the case of a nurse or midwife registered or enrolled in Scotland or Northern Ireland, the relevant statutory body)).

23. It is not the responsibiity of the authority to investigate complaints relating to medical treatment. A grievance against a general medical or dental practitioner should be directed to the Family Practitioner Committee if the practitioner concerned was undertaking the care of the patient as part of his NHS contract. Otherwise the matter is between the patient and the practitioner. Patients complaining of unprofessional conduct by a doctor or a dentist in a registered home should be referred to the General Medical Council or the General Dental Council respectively.

24. This guidance does not of course apply to complaints from NHS patients in registered homes under contractual arrangements. These should be dealt with in accordance with existing NHS procedures for the handling of complaints.

Community Health Councils

4–006 25. Community Health Councils do not have any general remit to visit or inspect private hospitals or nursing homes registered under the 1975 Act. Different considerations will however apply in the case of registered premises where NHS patients receive services under contractual arrangements. Representatives of the private health sector have agreed that CHCs should have access to registered premises where the NHS has contractual arrangements and on similar terms to those on which they now visit NHS premises. Any complaints received by CHCs from non-NHS patients in registered homes should be referred to the relevant registering authority.

Refusal or cancellation of registration

4–007 26. The authority has power to cancel registration or to refuse to register a home. Cancellation is clearly a final resort. In most cases where problems arise they can be identified quickly through frequent and effective inspection, and resolved by discussion. Decisions to refuse or cancel a registration should only result after the authority has concluded that there has been a serious breach of the registration requirements and that the "person registered" was either unwilling or unable to meet and maintain the standards required.

27. It is important that authorities establish clear procedures for dealing with registration problems and especially the refusal or cancellation of a registration. When difficulties arise which may lead to refusal or cancellation, the authority should ensure, at the outset, that the applicant or "person registered" is given a clear explanation, in writing, of the requirements they are failing to fulfil and the steps to be taken to rectify the situation. This statement should indicate a timescale for meeting the requirements, giving the applicant or "person registered" reasonable time to fulfil the requirements.

28. Where an authority proposes to refuse or cancel a registration, the Regulations (regulation 5(1)) require that the applicant or "person registered" should be given notice of this intention and the reasons for it. The applicant or person registered may then make representations to the authority as to why the decision should not be made. The authority should have clear procedures for handling any such challenge to a decision. Information on rights of appeal to the Courts against such decisions to refuse or cancel registrations and the timetable for appeals set out in the Regulations should be included in the guidelines on nursing home registration.

29. Where a registration in respect of more than one person (*e.g.* a partnership) is cancelled, the cancellation must apply to all persons covered by the registration.

Variation of conditions of registration

30. The Regulations provide for changes to be made in the conditions of registration without the home being required to go through the full registration procedure again. Such variations may be requested by either the "person registered" or the registering authority. Where the authority wishes to change the condition, there should of course be full prior discussions with the home. The Department's view is that this provision should be used for minor changes only. It is for authorities to decide whether a proposed variation is so substantial that it is necessary for the "person registered" in respect of the home to apply to be re-registered. 4–008

Management of a home

31. Management arrangements in registered homes will vary according to the size and function of the premises. Authorities should keep in mind the two functions which are set out in the legislation:— 4–009
  (a) The *"person registered"* is the person who applies for registration; whose name appears on the registration certificate; and who is ultimately responsible to the registering authority for ensuring that the requirements of the Act and the related Regulations are fulfilled. The Act contained *no* professional or other requirements as to qualifications for the "person registered".
  (b) The *"person-in-charge"* of a home is the person who is responsible for the day to day running of a registered home and who has overall responsibility for the care of the patients. The "person-in-charge" must be a registered medical practitioner, a registered nurse, or in the case of maternity home, a registered nurse or certified midwife.

These two functions are quite separate, although they may often be performed by the same person, *e.g.* in a small nursing home. At the other end of the scale, in a large private hospital the management functions may be divided further. Ownership and management will often be quite separate, and often there will be an administrative manager in addition to the "person-in-charge". Where there is separation of functions in the management of a home, the authority should ensure that the functions of "person registered" and "person-in-charge" are clearly identified within the management structure. Homes should be asked to notify the authority of any proposed changes in the management of a home.

32. The enployment of staff in nursing homes is the responsibility of the owners; however the registering authority needs to ensure that those managing or employed in homes are fit persons. This is particularly important in the case of the two functions of "person registered" and "person-in-charge"; the authority will need to ensure that those filling these posts are fit persons to do so (see section 4(1)(a) of the 1975 Act). In considering the fitness of any person proposing to manage or likely to be employed in a home registered under the 1975 Act authorities should note that they may seek information from them about previous convictions (including "spent" convictions within the meaning of the Rehabilitation of Offenders Act 1974).

Requirement to re-register

33. Re-registration is required wherever there is a change in the "person registered" in respect of a home. Where the "person registered" employs someone else as "person-in-charge" of the home re-registration would not be required if the "person-in-charge" was changed (although an authority could consider cancelling a registration if it did not regard the prospective employee as a fit person). Similarly if the "person registered" is not the owner, a change in ownership does not require re-registration. It should be suggested to home owners, where they are also the "person registered" and where a change in ownership would lead to re-registration, that completion of the transaction should be made conditional upon and not effective until the home is re-registered. This will avoid the home having to cease operations under the new owners until the new registration is granted. 4–010

Applications for registration from companies

34. Applications for registration under the 1975 Act may be received from companies as well as from individuals. A company which is incorporated under the Companies Act has a legal personality entirely separate from that of its shareholders and directors. Thus the company itself can be the "person registered" under the 1975 Act. An application for registration from a company should be signed by a director of the company or the company secretary. 4–011

35. Given the separate status of the company, when there is a change in the ownership or control of a company the need for re-registration will not normally arise. However, when considering an application made by a company, a registering authority will need to consider the fitness of those controlling the company and may refuse registration on the grounds that,

by reason of the unfitness of the persons who control the company, the company is not a fit person to carry on the nursing homes. Similar considerations may arise where there is a change of control or ownership of a company already registered under the 1975 Act. Although re-registration is not necessary in such situations, the authority may decide to cancel the registration on the grounds that by reason of the unfitness of the persons who control the company, the company is no longer a fit person. Where this arises the authority will need to be in a position to adduce substantial evidence that due to changes in the ownership of the company it is no longer a fit person to carry on the home.

Role of authority members

4–012   36. Normally work relating to registration and inspection of homes will be carried out by offices of the authority, although this does not prevent members from being authorised to visit a home if it were considered appropriate. Applications for registration should be brought to the attention of authority members as soon as possible and they should make the final decision to approve or refuse registration. Where serious difficulties arise with a home already registered, which might result in cancellation of the registration, the authority members should be informed at an early stage.

37. Where an authority proposes to refuse or cancel a registration, and the person involved exercises their right under paragraph 5(2) of the new Regulations to show cause why the decision should not be made, members should be involved in consideration of their representations, both oral and written.

Standards of facilities in registered homes

4–013   38. It is not proposed to give authorities detailed guidance on levels of staffing and standards of accommodation and facilities required in homes registered under the 1975 Act. The following paragraphs set out some general principles and highlight possible difficulties and the special needs of particular groups of patients in nursing homes and mental nursing homes.

39. The legislation provides the basic requirements which registered homes must fulfil, but within this framework authorities have the discretion to determine adequate levels of staffing and accommodation which a particular home must meet, bearing in mind the number and category of patients using the home. This local determination of standards allows a measure of flexibility which is necessary given the wide variety of establishments covered by the Act. Authorities' discretion however should not lead to the imposition of unnecessarily onerous or widely differing requirements. In determining the staffing and accommodation standards required of premises registered under the Act, authorities should have regards to standards prevailing generally in the NHS. Relating requirements to such standards may also be of value in circumstances where the registration requirements are challenged. Ultimately if there is an appeal against a decision to withhold or cancel a registration, or against a condition of variation of registration, the decision whether the requirements or conditions are justified will be for the Courts to determine.

Staffing

4–014   40. The calibre of the "person-in-charge" of a home is likely to be the key determinant of the standards of care provided in that home. He or she is responsible for the day to day management of the home, and has ultimate responsibility for the care of the patients. The new provisions in the 1975 Act remove the requirement that the "person-in-charge" should be resident in the home. However, it would be expected that they should be in regular attendance at the home. When the "person-in-charge" is absent (*e.g.* on holiday) it should be made clear who is to be responsible for the day to day running of the home.

41. Where the "person-in-charge" is a nurse, the Secretary of State has issued a Direction that it shall be a registered nurse (copy attached to Annex A). The new provisions give authorities discretion to determine which type of registered nurse is appropriate in any particular case bearing in mind the category of patients in the home. Thus where the home is a mental nursing home, catering predominantly though not necessarily wholly for the mentally ill or handicapped, the authority may decide that it would be appropriate for a RMN or RNMS to be the "person-in-charge", or where the home is a maternity home catering wholly or mainly for maternity patients that a certified midwife should be in charge. The requirements as to the qualifications of the nurse in charge must be set out in a notice issued by the authority under the terms of the new section 4(2) of the 1975 Act, and will constitute a condition of registration.

Nursing staff

4–015   42. The amendments to section 4 of the 1975 Act give authorities greater discretion in determining the numbers and qualifications of nursing staff in a home, and when they should be on duty. In exercising that discretion authorities are under a statutory duty to have regard to the category and the number of patients for whom the premises are to be used. These conditions will vary considerably—a hospital carrying out major surgery or a home accommodating very elderly and frail patients will need 24 hour nursing cover whereas a clinic carrying out surgery on a day care basis only will obviously not. Once determined these staffing requirements will also be a condition of registration set out in a notice under section 4(3), which may not be reduced without the permission of the authority. Where the premises are fully occupied the nurse staffing must be maintained at least at the level specified in the notice.

Superintendence of nursing staff

43. Where the "person-in-charge" of a home is not a nurse or in the case of a maternity home a midwife, the authority will need to ensure that there is a suitably qualified nurse, or practising midwife, to superintend the nursing services. The qualification of the nurse will be a matter for the authority to determine bearing in mind the size of the home, the type of patients using it, and the number and roles of the nursing staff. **4–016**

Supervision of midwives

44. Regional Health Authorities are responsible, under the Midwives Act 1951, for the supervision of *all* certified midwives practising with the region. This function may, and in most cases is, delegated to the AHA (see HSC (IS)15). The local Supervisor of Midwives has the right of access to all premises, including private nursing homes, for the purpose of ensuring that midwifery practice and procedures meet the requirements of the 1951 Act. The Supervisor of Midwives should also be involved in the registration of a maternity home. **4–017**

Nurse training

45. Continuing training and education is an important factor in maintaining professional standards of nursing care. Authorities might consider inviting nurses in registered homes to participate in NHS nurse education programmes. Any financial arrangements involved would be a matter of agreement between the authority and the home. Training is particularly important for the staff in smaller homes, who have perhaps less opportunity than those in the larger independent hospital to meet professional colleagues and keep abreast of new ideas and nursing practices. Where the home is involved in specialist care (*e.g.* nursing elderly patients) for which courses are available under the auspices of the Joint Board of Clinical Nursing Studies, it may be helpful to draw these to the attention of the "person-in-charge". **4–018**

Elderly people in nursing homes

46. The particular needs of elderly people in private nursing homes will be to a large extent be determined by their degree of dependency. It is important that the organisation of a home and the attitude of staff reflect the need for patients to achieve and maintain maximum independence. Provision should be made, where appropriate, for occupational and recreational activities; this is a requirement of the revised Regulations (Regulation 10(i)(*p*)). Authorities might wish to consider making known to those concerned with the management of homes caring for elderly patients the training package "Improving Geriatric Care" which was issued under cover of NH (79)35. Although it was designed for use within the NHS, much of its content is of direct relevance to the care of elderly patients in private nursing homes, and those concerned should find it of considerable value. It might be necessary to make minor adaptations for implementation in private homes, but if the philosophy and objective is explained this should not present difficulty. Copies of the relevant materials can be purchased from the Training Aids Unit at Hydestile Hospital, Godalming, Surrey (Tel. 04868 23703/4). **4–019**

Children in nursing homes

48. It is understood that an increasing number of children are being cared for in private nursing homes. The revised Regulations reflect the special needs of children. Wherever possible sick children in private nursing homes should be accommodated separately from adults, should come under the general care of a consultant paediatrician and be looked after by registered sick children's nurses. Arrangements should also be made to allow parents unrestricted visiting and enable them, particularly mothers, to stay with their children. It is vital that children's links with their homes are maintained, especially when they must spend a long time away from home. Where a child has been in a nursing home for some time and there is a possibility of loss of contact with the family the authority may need to consult the local social services department about the child's future. If children are likely to be accommodated **4–020**

in a home the home should provide play facilities and, for school-age children, arrangements should be made (normally through the Local Education Authority) to ensure continuing education. Authorities might also involve the Local Education Authority when making inspection visits to homes catering for children. It might be useful to refer the person in charge to the following Department guidance: HM (71)22 Hospital Facilities for Children; HC (76)5 Play for Children in Hospital; DS (82)74 Long Stay Children in Hospital; and HC (78)28 Children in Hospital: Maintenance of Family Links.

Mother and baby homes

4–021   49. The definition of a maternity home includes a small number of establishments, normally referred to as "mother and baby homes", which provide care and support for a wide range of women, including in particular teenage mothers. The mothers will normally be admitted to hospital to have their babies and will return to the home with the baby after delivery. For this group and their babies pregnancy and delivery carry a much higher than average degree of risk and this is particularly so during the perinatal period. Authorities will need to keep this in mind when considering the staffing needs of mother and baby homes. The level of midwifery provision needed in the home will depend on the nature of the home and its occupants and its links with the local maternity and other health services. The mothers and their children should receive health care from the primary health services, including in particular the health visitor, and other child health services. Mother and baby homes should also have close links with the local social services department and, since some of the mothers will be under school-leaving age, with the local education service. Registration and inspection of mother and baby homes should be carried out in consultation with the local authority.

Mentally ill and mentally handicapped patients

4–022   50. It is important that nursing homes accommodating *any* mentally ill or mentally handicapped patients are correctly registered as *mental nursing homes*. These are additional provisions for mental nursing homes within the legislation (*i.e.* the power given in section 9(2) of the 1975 Act to persons authorised by the authority to examine patients). Mental nursing homes should provide a range of occupational and recreational activies. Where these facilities cannot be provided within the home itself, the home should be advised to explore the possibility of making arrangements with the local social services department or hospital day centre. For both the mentally ill and mentally handicapped (and particularly mentally handicapped children), it is important that each patient's development needs should be regularly assessed and a planned programme of activities designed to meet their particular requirements. This programme should be supervised by staff with the appropriate skills; also it is important that a proportion of the staff should be Registered Mental Nurses. There should be clear written policy guidelines for the staff on the treatment of patients, including procedures for dealing with patients requiring psychiatric treatment. Patients should be treated with the minimum degree of security but where some security is necessary, *e.g.* where patients are detained under the Mental Health Act, adequate security arrangements will be required.

Approval of nursing homes for the treatment of patients for termination of pregnancy

4–023   51. Authorities are reminded that a registered nursing home cannot admit patients for the termination of pregnancy, except in an emergency, without special approval by the Secretary of State under the Abortion Act 1967. Application for this approval must be made by the proprietors to the Department of Health or to the Welsh Office. The granting of such approval carries with it additional requirements on the proprietors on various aspects of the organisation of the nursing home, including facilities, staffing, records and inspection.

Retention of records

4–024   52. There is a new requirement in the Regulations (Regulations 6(4) and 6(7)) that registered homes keep records and registers for at least *one* year: in the case of registers one year from the date of the last entry and individual patient records one year from death or discharge. This requirement is concerned *only* with the needs of registration and inspection under the 1975 Act and should ensure that officials of the registering authority inspecting a home would see all records at least twice. The "person registered" however may wish to retain some records for longer periods of time, particularly patient case records, which could be required as evidence in legal actions. (Authorities should bring to their attention the guidance given to the NHS on this matter in HC (80)7.) In the case of a maternity home the "person registered" will also need to bear in mind the Rules of the Central Midwives Board, which require midwives to maintain records of their professional attendance on patients.

Safekeeping of medicines

53. Under the Medicines Act 1968, persons carrying on the business of a nursing home are **4–025**
permitted to obtain by way of wholesale dealing the prescription only medicines (POM) and
other medicines which they need to supply or administer to patients in the course of the
business. However, actually selling or supplying medicines to a patient is normally permitted
only (a) in the case of a POM, in accordance with the *written directions of a doctor or dentist*, and
(b) in the case of any other medicine, for administration to the patient in accordance with the
directions of a doctor or dentist. Injections may be *administered* only by a doctor or dentist or by a
person acting in accordance with the directions of a doctor or dentist, or by those for whom
exemptions are provided.

54. When looking at the arrangements for storing medicines in premises covered by the 1975
Act, authorities should keep in mind the points set out below:
   (*a*) All medicines that have not been issued for use should be stored under the control of a
   pharmacist, or, if there is no pharmaceutical department, under the control of a
   responsible person designated for the purpose by the "person-in-charge" of the home
   after consultation with the health authority; and the medicines should be stored in one
   or more lockable cupboards or rooms which should be kept locked so far as is
   reasonably practicable.
   (*b*) Medicines that have been issued for use should, so far as is reasonably practicable, be
   kept in a locked cupboard or trolley or other secure receptacle, under the control of a
   nurse or some other responsible person designated by the "person-in-charge".
   (*c*) Every place within the home where medicines are stored should be inspected regularly
   by a pharmacist.
   (*d*) No medicine should be issued for use (*i.e.* transferred from the main pharmacy store)
   except in accordance with a written order signed by a doctor or dentist or by some
   responsible person (*e.g.* a nurse) designated to perform that function by the "person-in-
   charge" of the home.

55. Registered premises are also subject to the legislation relating to the storage of controlled
drugs.

Fire precautions

56. Regulation 10(i)(*h*) of the new Regulations requires all nursing homes to "take adequate **4–026**
precautions against the risk of fire and make adequate arrangements for detecting, containing
and extinguishing fires, and giving warning for the evacuation of patients and staff in the event
of fire". (The differences between this regulation and the previous regulation dealing with fire
precautions are explained in Annex C.) There is no statutory requirement for private hospitals
and nursing homes to be inspected and certified by local fire authorities but, in the exercise of
their powers under the 1975 Act, registering authorities may ask the local fire authority to
advise on fire precautions arrangements in such premises and may authorise an officer of the
fire authority to inspect for that purpose. It is recommended that, as a matter of normal
practice, the fire authority should be asked to advise before a home is registered, or re-
registered, and where possible to inspect the premises at least once every twelve months
thereafter. The possibility of more frequent inspections, either generally or in particular cases,
should be discussed with the fire authority. The registering authority is ultimately responsible
for deciding, in the light of such advice as is received, whether the fire precautions
arrangements comply with the requirements in the Act.

57. The changes in the Regulations follow the recommendations in the Home Office Fire
Department Report on the fire at Hartopp Court Nursing Home in 1979. The Report was
circulated to authorities under cover of NH (80)17 which asked authorities to bring its
recommendations to the attention of those homes registered with them. The Health Notice also
drew attention to the Home Secretary's statement of 23 April 1980 in which he announced that
the Home Office would be issuing guidance setting out basic standards for means of escape
and related fire precautions in hospitals and personal social services residential homes. The
statement also referred to a joint DHSS/Home Office supplementary memorandum of
guidance on fire precautions in hospitals which would highlight the most urgent features of the
hospital guide and cover other important aspects such as staffing, staff training and
furnishings. Both guides and memorandum will be helpful to authorities' consideration of fire
precautions in premises registered under the 1975 Act and authorities may wish to consider
taking the priorities identified for the NHS as priorities to be applied to comparable private
sector premises.

58. It is important when considering the application of fire precautions to the private sector
to bear in mind factors such as the cost and the limitations of adapted accommodation. Also
the demands of fire precautions should be carefully weighed against the effect such measures
may have on the quality of patients' lives and the care they receive; this is particularly
important when dealing with fire precautions in premises which cater for patients requiring
long-term care.

59. Fire authorities have a statutory duty to respond to requests for advice on fire precautions and an approach for advice may come directly from the person carrying on a nursing home or hospital. In such cases in order to avoid confusion it is advisable for all three parties concerned in fire precautions in private homes and hospitals (the fire officer, the "person registered" or "person-in-charge" and the registering authority) to be kept fully informed of what advice is being sought. Where appropriate authorities might also discuss with proprietors the range of possible alternatives for meeting the fire precautions requirements.

60. Private institutions are also subject to the relevant building regulations and other legislation which has a bearing on fire precautions. Where the fire precautions requirements of such legislation relate to matters for which the registering authority has powers under the 1975 Act it may make compliance with these requirements a condition of registration.

Other relevant legislation and information

4–027   61. In addition to the Nursing Homes Act 1975, other laws and regulations apply to nursing homes and others, whilst not directly applicable, can have a bearing on the conduct of nursing homes. Registering authorities have *no* responsibility for ensuring that any other laws or regulations are complied with by nursing homes. It is for owners and managers to acquaint themselves with the contents of any such legislation. However, in contravening other legislation, the homes may also be in contravention of the 1975 Act or the related Regulations. Therefore authorities should take whatever opportunities are presented (*e.g.* preliminary discussions before application) to ensure the persons carrying on the home are aware of other legislation. In addition there is health service guidance and other codes of practice which will be of value to home owners, and which authorities could make available to them. it is particularly important that authorities pass to nursing homes and hospitals Hazard Notice Circulars and other information issued to the NHS about the health and safety of staff and patients. Authorities may wish to consider making arrangements with registered homes to pass on relevant information: some authorities already have such arrangements involving some contribution from the homes to cover costs such as postage.

ANNEXES A TO C
[*Not Reproduced*]

CIRCULAR No. LAC (84)15

Dated August 31, 1984 *and issued by the Department of Health and Social Security*

REGISTRATION OF RESIDENTIAL HOMES AND REGISTERED HOMES TRIBUNALS

Summary

4–028   This Circular notifies authorities of the coming into force of the Registered Homes Act 1984 and the associated Regulations and code of practice relating to the registration and inspection of residential care homes. It also notifies some amendments to the legislation regulating the registration of voluntary children's homes and certain other children's homes.

Residential care homes

4–029   1. With effect from January 1, 1985 the Registered Homes Act 1984 is generally brought into force by means of the Registered Homes Act 1984 (Commencement) Order 1984 (S.I. 1984/1348). However, for certain independent schools a later date is prescribed in the Order.

2. The Registered Homes Act 1984 broadly supersedes the registration provisions of the Residential Homes Act 1980 and the provisions of the Nursing Homes Act 1975, as amended, relating to residential care homes and nursing homes. In detail what is happening is that the provisions of the Health and Social Services and Social Security Adjudications Act 1983 relating to the registration of homes are being brought into force from January 1, 1985 by the Health and Social Services and Social Security Adjudications Act 1983 (Commencement No. 5) Order 1984 (S.I. 1984 No. 1347) but those provisions are being repealed and replaced immediately by the provisions of the 1984 Act, which is being brought into force by its own commencement order. The 1984 Act is purely a consolidation and makes no substantive changes to the provisions of the 1983 Act.

3. Residential care homes will have an increasingly valuable role to play in the development of care in the community to complement the provision made by public services. Authorities are under statutory obligation to register and inspect homes. It is in the interests of those cared for in the homes as well as of authorities themselves that the registration and inspection processes be carried out in such a way as to enable the safeguards in the statutory registration system to be effective. Authorities will have additional income through the setting of a *substantial* registration fee (formerly only £1) and from the introduction of an annual fee and this should meet the cost of necessary adjustments to their *present* arrangements for the registration and inspection of these homes. Until the new arrangements have had time to come into operation, it will not be possible to make a realistic assessment of their cost. *The fees have therefore been set provisionally at a level which will be reviewed within the first year and periodically thereafter.*

4. The main changes made by the new legislation to the arrangements for registering residential care homes are as follows:—

—The *definition of establishment* has been amended so that registration is required if the specified minimum number (4) of elderly, disabled, mentally disordered or certain other dependent people are cared for. These establishments will be known as "residential care homes".

—The *person registered*, where a home is operated by an organisation, is that organisation as well as the manager.

—The *registration fee* has been increased and an *annual fee* introduced.

—*Penalties for offences.* The maximum fine for operating an unregistered home has been raised from £500 to £2,000.

—*Appeals*, which have formerly been to the magistrates' courts, will in future be to the newly established registered homes tribunals.

—*Inspections* have to occur no less frequently than once a year.

—Nursing homes are no longer excluded from registration as residential care homes, *i.e.* dual *registration* is possible.

—Notice is required of a prolonged *absence of the registered person.*

5. At the same time as the statutory provisions are implemented the following regulations and rules relating to the registration of residential care homes become operative:—

—Residential Care Homes Regulations 1984, dealing with both the registration and the conduct of homes and any necessary transitional measures.

—Registered Homes Tribunals Rules 1984.

6. Additionally the Secretaries of State have endorsed, *as a guide to good practice, Home Life*, a code of practice relating to residential care homes which was published by the Centre for Policy on Ageing in May this year. Local authorities are asked to regard the code in the same light as general guidance that is issued from time to time under powers at Section 7 of the Local Authority Social Services Act 1970.

7. Guidance on the new legislation, the code of practice *(Home Life)*, and the registered homes tribunals is given in the notes enclosed with this Circular.

8. *Corporal punishment of children.* This is still under consideration and will be the subject of a later circular.

9. Ministry of Health Circular 86/49 (registration and inspection of disabled and old persons' homes) is cancelled.

Children's homes

10 to 13. [*Not reproduced.*]   **4–030**

Nursing homes

14. A Health Circular—HC (84)21—giving matching guidance on changes in the provisions for nursing homes registered by district health authorities is being issued and will be available on request from the address shown at the foot of the last page of this Circular.   **4–031**

15. As well as certain nursing homes that will have to be dually registered, there are believed to be a number of homes improperly registered as residential homes which should be registered solely as nursing homes. Section 24 of the Registered Homes Act 1984 makes it an offence for a person, with intent to deceive, to describe premises in a way to indicate they are registered as a nursing home or mental nursing home, unless they are so registered.

16. District health authorities are empowered to enter and inspect establishments believed to be functioning as nursing homes or mental nursing homes. Health authorities will need the close co-operation of local social services authorities to enable them to identify people who should be registered under Part II of the Registered Homes Act 1984. This co-operation should arise in the normal course of taking joint action in connection with dual registration but special action may be needed in some cases where there are suspicions that those running a particular home are attempting to conceal the true nature of the care provided. The Secretary of State has exceptionally issued a direction to district health authorities requiring them to make inspections for this purpose.

Action

4–032　17. Local social services authorities are to take such steps as they think appropriate in their areas to implement the new arrangements for residential care homes and bring them to the attention of those who are, or might be, affected by them.

18. They are also to draw up new local guidelines on registration in consultation with district health authorities in the light of the revised legislation, the guidance issued with this Circular and the recommendations in the code of practice, *Home Life*.

19. Local social services authorities are to co-operate with district health authorities where a special programme of inspections by health authorities is necessary of establishments registered as residential care homes though providing a type of care for which there should be registration as a nursing home or mental nursing home.

Enquiries

4–033　20. Enquiries about this Circular and the enclosures should be directed as below:—

Residential Care Homes	—Community Services Division CSIA Alexander Fleming House 01–407 5522 (Ext. 6341 or 7349).
Voluntary and other Children's Homes	—Children's Division of CHA4 Alexander Fleming House 01–407 5522 (Ext. 7387 or 7634)

ANNEX TO LAC (84)15

GUIDANCE NOTES ON REGISTRATION SYSTEM FOR RESIDENTIAL CARE HOMES AND ON REGISTERED HOMES TRIBUNALS

4–034

Contents

Introduction.

Part A

Residential Care Homes

Operative date.
Definition of residential care home and of personal care.
Registered persons and information about cancelled registrations.
Prolonged absence of registered person.
Registration and annual fees.
Responsibility to register.
Registration procedures.
Conduct of homes (including code of practice).
Fire safety.
Inspection and support.
Penalties.

Part B

Dual Registration as a Residential Care Home and Nursing Home

Part C

National List of Cancelled Registrations and the Children's Consultancy Service

Quarterly lists.
Removal of names from national list.
Children's consultancy service.

Part D

Appeals and the Registered Homes Tribunals

Annexes

Annex I — Educational establishments exempt from registration as residential care homes:
  Part 1—Further education establishments receiving grants under section 100(1)(b) of the Education Act 1944.
  Part 2—Education establishments substantially dependent for maintenance upon local education authorities.
Annex II — National list of cancelled registrations.
Annex III—Flow charts of registration etc. procedures for residential care homes:
  Table 1—Procedure for granting registration application.
  Table 2—Procedure for refusing registration application.
  Table 3—Procedure for cancelling or altering registration.

Introduction

These Notes give guidance on the alterations being made to the registration procedures for residential care homes, and on the unified appeal system. Details of the new legislation are set out in LAC (84)15 forwarding these Notes. Generally they operate from January 1, 1985 but for certain independent schools they apply from January 1, 1986. References to "Sections" and "the 1984 Act" are all references to the Registered Homes Act 1984 and references to "the Regulations" and to "Regulations" are to the Residential Care Homes Regulations 1984 unless otherwise stated.

4–035

Part A

Residential Care Homes

Operative date

4–036 A1. The amended system of registration for residential care homes is brought into operation by the Registration Homes Act 1984 (Commencement) Order 1984 (S.I. 1984 No. 1348) from January 1, 1985 but see paragraph A3 below about certain independent schools.

A2. Establishments (apart from those mentioned in the next paragraph) in existence at January 1, 1985 which did not have to be registered under the Residential Homes Act 1980 immediately before that date and now become registerable as a residential home under Part I of the Registered Homes Act 1984 are required by the Residential Care Homes Regulations 1984 (S.I. 1984 No. 1345) to apply for registration within six months of that date. Establishments registered under the Residential Homes Act 1980 immediately before January 1, 1985 will have the registration carried over as a residential care home without further application, subject to the payment of the annual fee within three months (Regulation 5(C)) and continuing to meet the conditions for registration (Regulation 4).

A3. The application of Part I of the Registered Homes Act 1984 to certain independent boarding schools is deferred by Article 2(2) of the Registered Homes Act 1984 (Commencement) Order 1984 until January 1, 1986. The schools involved are those which at the date of the Commencement Order had applied to the Secretary of State for Education, or for Wales, under Section 11(3)(a) of the Education Act 1981 for approval and a decision on their application has not been given.* This deferment is to allow time for those approval applications to be processed and the requisite inspections to be carried out. If the application is approved, the school will not be subject to registration as a residential care home. Should the application be disallowed, the school becomes registerable as a residential care home, if it fulfils the requirements for such registrations—see paragraph A14 below.

Definitions of residential care home and of personal care

4–037 A4. The amended criteria for registration of residential homes, to be known as "residential care homes", are set out in Section 1 of the 1984 Act. The term "residential care home" replaces the terms "disabled persons' or old persons' home" and "residential home for mentally disordered persons". Accommodation for people with a past or present dependence on alcohol or drugs is explicitly covered, provided, of course, the other criteria for registration are fulfilled. Among the definitions in Section 20(1) and Section 55 are ones of "disablement" and "mental disorder" with the linked definition of "psychopathic disorder".

A5. A fundamental change from the previous legislation is that registration is required for any establishment where four or more people (excluding relatives of the registered person or of the staff) in the dependent categories are cared for. Previously a minimum number was not specified and the dependent people had to constitute more than half of those resident on the premises for registration to arise.

A6. For registration purposes it does not matter what an establishment calls itself, whether a rest home, a hotel, a boarding house or guest house, or a school (unless so registered). The notes that follow are given by way of guidance. It is for registration authorities to decide in the first instance whether an establishment fulfils the requirements for registration. Definitive interpretation of the law on this matter is for the courts which are able to impose a maximum fine at level 5 on the standard scale (at present £2,000) for failing to register in respect of a residential care home. (See paragraph A54 below.)

A7. The distinguishing feature of a residential care home is that the establishment itself provides both *"personal care"* and residential accommodation *with board*. The term "personal care" is defined at Section 20(1). It is a difficult term to define comprehensively in legislation. The definition makes it clear that it may include assistance with bodily functions but not necessarily so. Emotional support counselling by the establishment's personnel could also be included as could assistance from social workers on the staff of the establishment. What the term is intended to include can be seen more clearly by what is said at paragraph 3 of the Memorandum on Health Care issued with LAC (77)13: HC (77)25 and Welsh Office Circular 117/77: WHC (77)30:

"3. Residential Homes are primarily a means of providing a greater degree of support for those elderly people no longer able to cope with the practicalities of living in their own homes even with the help of the domiciliary services. The care provided is limited to that

---

* Information about schools in England that have applied for approval may be obtained from the Department of Education and Science (Special Educaiton Division), Elizabeth House, York Road, London SE1 7PH.

appropriate to a residential setting and is broadly equivalent to what might be provided by a competent and caring relative able to respond to emotional as well as physical needs. It includes for instance help with washing, bathing, dressing; assistance with toilet needs; the administration of medicines and, when a resident falls sicks, the kind of attention someone would receive in his own home from a caring relative under guidance of the general practitioner or nurse member of the primary health care team. However, the staff of a home are not expected to provide the professional kind of health care that is properly the function of the primary health care services. Nor should residential homes be used as nursing homes or extensions of hospitals."*

This extract relates particularly to elderly people for whom the majority of residential care homes are provided. But registration as a residential care home is equally applicable to establishments providing similar personal care for handicapped people, including homes for handicapped children.

A8. At some establishments registered as residential care homes there will be persons resident whose care does not fall within criteria for such registration. For example, holiday makers at a hotel, or some (possibly the majority) of the children at an independent school not needing "personal care", as explained in the preceding paragraph. The services and facilities provided for their use would not fall within the registration and inspection processes for residential care homes, unless those services and facilities were also used by persons provided with "personal care". Additionally at a school those processes would not apply to matters falling within the purview of the Education Acts.

A9. "Old Age" is not defined in the legislation. Whether or not a person receives "personal care" in a residential setting does not depend upon the attainment of a specified age, but on his need for that care. Often, it is not until after age 75 that care of this kind is needed. On the other hand younger people may need it. They could, for example, be suffering from disablement or mental disorder, conditions which also give rise to the need for registration where the registration criteria in other respects are met. Old age and these conditions are not exclusive.

A10. *Group homes* etc. As with other establishments, whether registration as a residential care home is required will depend upon the particular situation. Where four or more dependent people, perhaps recovering from a mental illness or developing the ability to live independently, are livng together and looking after themselves with the minimum of support (*e.g.* from voluntary workers or visiting staff with sleeping-in arrangements) in what are sometimes called "group homes", it is unlikely that the premises would fall to be registered. This is because the establishment running the home would not be providing both "board" as well as "personal care" for the residents.

A11. *Alcohol dependence* is a condition where a person experiences social, psychological, or physical problems related to intoxication or dependence as a consequence of his own repeated drinking of alcohol.

12. *Drug dependence* is a condition where a person experiences social, psychological, physical or legal problems related to intoxication or regular excessive consumption or dependence as a consequence of his own use of drugs or other chemical substances (other than alcohol or tobacco).

A13. *Royal Charter homes.* Homes incorporated by Royal Charter continue to be exempted under Section 1(5)(j) from registration. Authorities will no doubt be aware that the designation "Royal" is not confined to bodies incorporated by Royal Charter.

A14. *Schools.* Independent schools, with residential accommodation for 50 or fewer children under age 18 where four or more in the dependent categories are resident, are registrable as residential care homes if they have not been approved by the Secretary of State for Education and Science or the Secretary of State for Wales under Section 11(3)(a) of the Education Act 1981.** All other schools are exempt (Section 1(5)(f) and 1(6) of the 1984 Act—see paragraph A3 above for operative date in relation to certain schools).

A15. *Further educational establishments* in receipt of maintenance grants under regulations made in accordance with Section 100(1)(b) of the Education Act 1944 are exempted from registration by Section 1(5)(g) and 1(7) of the 1984 Act; a list of such establishments so maintained at present is at Part 1 of Annex I.

A16. As well as educational establishments managed by local authorities, those substantially dependent for their maintenance on assistance from local education authorities are exempted from registration under Section 1(5)(j) of the 1984 Act. The latter are covered by the term "provided by a local authority" and those so exempted are listed as Part 2 of Annex I.

---

* unless, in future, the home is dually registered.
** A list of schools in England approved under the 1981 Act may be obtained from the Department of Education and Science (Special Education Division), Elizabeth House, York Road, London SE1 7PH.

A17. *Holiday accommodation for dependent people.* It would be impracticable to register premises accommodating the occasional group of people in the specified dependent categories. However, establishments, whatever their description, which make a practice of regularly (*e.g.* for more than a month a year) accommodating such people for holidays, even though individuals may stay no longer than a week or two, would require to be registered, if the registration criteria are met in other respects.

Registered persons and information about cancelled registrations

4–038   A18. In future both the manager of a residential care home, and if different, the person or organisation which controls the establishment (whether as owner or otherwise) are to be registered (Section 3 of the 1984 Act.).

A19. Precise qualifications for the person to be registered are not prescribed in the legislation. Apart from the fact that organisations and owners as well as managers will be registerable, the objective of these homes is to provide, as indicated in note A7 above, care broadly equivalent to what a competent and caring relative would provide.

A20. The Department is setting up a national list of persons whose registration in respect of a residential care home, nursing home or children's home is cancelled after January 1, 1985. Information about this and about the Department's Consultancy Service in relation to children's services is given in Part C below.

A21. The maintenance of this national list of cancelled registrations supplements, but does not replace, the procedure that registration authorities would be expected to apply in the normal way to satisfy themselves that a person could be registered. They should continue to take up relevant references and carefully check qualifications and periods of service or occupations with particular attention to unexplained gaps in the person's past history or periods of self-employment or any time spent outside this country. In this way they are more likely to pick up aliases against which the national list is unlikely to be a full safeguard.

A22. It should not be overlooked that a person may be required to declare a "spent" conviction when applying for registration in relation to a residential care home. Under the Rehabilitation of Offenders Act 1974 a person who received a non-custodial sentence, or a custodial sentence of not more than 30 months, and is not reconvicted during a specified period, becomes a rehabilitated person. His conviction then becomes spent *i.e.* it is regarded in law for most purposes as never having occurred. However, there are certain occupations listed in the Rehabilitation of Offenders Act 1974 (Exceptions) Order 1975 (S.I. 1975, No. 1023) where this does not apply, provided that, when asked about previous convictions, the person is told that by virtue of the Order spent convictions must be declared. Running a residential care home is one of these occupations.

Prolonged absence of registered person

4–039   A23. Regulation 15 requires the person registered in respect of a home normally to give the registration authority at least a month's notice of his intended absence from duty at the home for more than four weeks. This is not necessary if no person in need of "personal care" is to be accommodated there during the registered person's absence (*e.g.* if a school is to be closed during the summer holidays). Provision is made for shorter notice at the discretion of the registration authority and, in the case of an emergency, for notice to be given within one week afterwards. Adequate arrangements for running the home are required during the period of absence. Notice also has to be given within a week of the return of the registered person to duty at the home. If the home and its staff are well known to the registration authority's officers responsible for registration and inspection, the written notice may be sufficient to satisfy the authority that the arrangements are adequate. If not, it would normally be advisable for the proposed arrangements to be discussed with the registered person, or persons. If the proposed arrangements are clearly unsatisfactory and no agreement can be reached on improving them, the registration authority would need to consider whether action should be taken to cancel the registration.

Registration and annual fees

4–040   A24. The increased registration fees along with the new annual fees are set out at Regulations 3 and 5. These fees have been fixed *provisionally* at a level expected to defray the costs of the registration and inspection arrangements of registration authorities. *Until, however, the new arrangements have come into operation and have been operating for some time, it will not be possible to make a realistic assessment of the additional costs. A review of the new registration arrangements will therefore be carried out during the first year and the fees will be adjusted in due course to take the findings into account.*

A25. An application for registration of a person who owns the establishment is to be accompanied by the £100 registration fee. A manager who is not the owner and has to be registered pays a registration fee of £75 which is additional to the fee paid by the owner. Where there is a change of ownership but no substantial change in the home, a registration fee of £75 is payable. No registration fee is payable if there is a change at the home but not change in its ownership or in the manager.

A26. An annual fee becomes payable within one month of the registration being granted. Subsequent payments of the annual fee will be payable no later than the anniversary date of the grant of the registration by the registration authority. If the annual fee is not paid in time the registration may be cancelled (Section 10(*b*) of the 1984 Act).

A27. *Existing registration.* Persons who have been registered under the Residential Homes Act 1980 immediately prior to January 1, 1985 are required by Regulation 5(2) to pay the first annual fee within 3 months of that date. Subsequent payments of the annual fee for these homes will have to be made within 12 months of the date on which the first annual fee was paid. It is important that adequate notice is given to each home of its new liability, the amount in question and the final date for payment.

Responsibility to register

A28. The 1984 Act (Section 2) continues to place a responsibility for applying for registration upon the person running the establishment. At the same time registration authorities have a responsibility for seeing that the registration requirements are known and, if necessary, of seeking out anyone who fails to register. This is supported by authorities' power (Section 17) to enter and inspect any premises that it has reasonable cause to think should be registered as a residential care home.

4–041

Registration procedures

A29. The general procedures for handling a registration application and for cancelling or altering a registration are set out in Sections 12–14 of the 1984 Act. These procedures are described in the immediately following paragraphs and are depicted in the algorithms at Annex III. Additionally there is an urgent procedure for cancelling or amending a registration in exceptional circumstances which is also described below. This is shown in the algorithm as well.

4–042

A30. *Ordinary procedure.* An application for registration is granted subject to the conditions set out in Section 5(3). *If the proposed conditions accord with the applciation or have been agreed with the applicant,* the authority can proceed to grant the registration subject to the conditions, without first giving the applicant notice that they intend to do so. The registration authority's decision to do this has immediate effect (Sections 12(2) and 13(3)).

A31. In *other circumstances*, the authority has to inform the applicant in writing that they intend to impose conditions in accordance with Section 5 and say why. The applicant then has 14 days to notify the authority whether he wants to make representations. If he does not want to, the authority can grant the registration with the conditions. On the other hand if he wishes to make representations, the registration authority's decision has to be deferred until they have been made. The authority should allow him a reasonable time to make them and should inform him how long they are allowing. If the applicant wants to make oral representations, he has to have the opportunity of having them heard by a committee, or sub-committee, of the authority. Should the representations not be made within the time allowed, the authority can proceed to grant the registration with the conditions. In any event an authority's decision to impose conditions does not have effect for 28 days, or until an appeal, if made, is decided, or abandoned (Sections 12(1), (2) and (5), 13 and 14).

A32. *Refusal of application.* When an authority intend to refuse a registration application, they have to inform the applicant in writing before so deciding that they are going to do this and why. The applicant then has 14 days to notify the authority whether he wants to make representations. If he does not want to, the authority can refuse the application. On the other hand if he wishes to make representations, the registration authority's decision has to be deferred until they have been made. The authority should allow him a reasonable time to make them and should inform him how long they are allowing. If the applicant wants to make oral representations, he has to have the opportunity of having them heard by a committee, or sub-committee, of the authority. Should the representations not be made within the time allowed, the authority can proceed to refuse the application. A decision to refuse an application has immediate effect (Sections 12(3) and (5), 13 and 14).

A33. *Cancellation or amendment of registration.* When an authority intend to cancel a registration or alter the conditions of one, they have to inform the registered person in writing before so deciding that they are going to do this and say why. The registered person then has 14 days to notify the authority whether he wants to make representations. If he does not want to, the authority can cancel the registration or alter the conditions. On the other hand if he wishes to make representations, the registration authority's decision has to be deferred until they have been made. The authority should allow him a reasonable time to make them and should inform him how long they are allowing. If the applicant wants to make oral representations, he has to have the opportunity of having them heard by a committee, or sub-committee, of the authority. Should the representations not be made within the time allowed, the authority can proceed to cancel the registration or alter the conditions. In any event an authority's decision to cancel a registration, or alter the conditions, does not have effect for 28 days, or until an appeal, if made, is decided or abandoned (Sections 12(4) and (5), 13 and 14).

A34. *Urgent procedure.* A registration may be cancelled, or amended, under the urgent procedure at Section 11. This procedure is intended to be used only in extreme cases where there would be a *serious* risk to the life, health or well-being of the residents in a registered home if the ordinary procedure for cancelling or altering a registration were followed. The authority has to apply in writing to a justice of the peace stating the circumstances. The authority should, if it is practicable, inform the registered person that it is proposing to take such action. The justice, if satisfied that there is this risk, can make an order cancelling or amending the registration. Such an order can be made, whether or not a magistrates' court is sitting, and it has immediate effect. As soon as practicable afterwards the registration authority has to inform the registered person that it has been made and what its terms are, and also supply a copy of the statement setting out the authority's reasons for seeking the order.

A35. [*This paragraph was cancelled by para. 3 of Department of Health Circular No. LAC (89)12.*]

Conduct of homes (including code of practice)

A36. The way a residential care home is to be run and the services and facilities to be available are governed by the Regulations. These are complemented by the code of practice, *Home Life*. It is of the utmost importance that the home should run in such a way as to enable those living there to fulfil themselves to the fullest extent they are capable of. There should be adequate and appropriate opportunities for the physical, emotional, social and intellectual development of residents. Apart from giving guidance on the general needs of residents, Section 4 of *Home Life*, the code of practice, gives useful guidance on the needs of individual client groups.

A37. A person guilty of an offence against the Regulations can be convicted by a magistrates' court and required to pay a fine up to level 4 on the standard scale (Sections 16(2) and 49)—see paragraph A54 below. Such a conviction can be a ground for cancelling a registration (Section 10(*c*)(i)). Alternatively a breach of the Regulations could be reason itself for cancelling the registration without first securing a conviction. For example, inadequate staffing could be a ground for withdrawing a registration by reason of Section 10(*a*) linked with Section 9(*b*). However, it should be noted the only method for taking action against a person who is not conducting the home in accordance with Regulation 9 is, if it would give grounds for action under Section 10, to cancel the registration; it would not be appropriate for such a failure to give rise to a criminal action in view of the terms of the regulation.

A38. The value of issuing a notice under Regulation 20 should not be overlooked. This may be sufficient to secure improvement without resorting to the procedure to cancel a registration or seeking a conviction.

A39. As well as the code of practice, *Home Life*, the following existing general guidance issued by the Departments is applicable to these homes:
—Memorandum on Health Care in Residential Homes for the Elderly; and on the Custody, Administration and Disposal of Medicines in these Homes and in Residential Homes for the Mentally Disordered (issued with LAC (77)13: HC (77)25) and Welsh Office Circular 117/77: WHC (77)30, as amended by the Health and Safety Commission's "The Safe Disposal of Clinical Waste".
—Draft Guide to Fire Precautions in Existing Residential Care Premises (issued with LAC (83)4: HC (83)5 and Welsh Office Circular 9/83).
—Local Authority Building Note No. 2—Residential Accommodation for Elderly People.
—Local Authority Building Note No. 8—Residential Accommodation for Mentally Handicapped Adults.
—LASSL (75)19 and Welsh Office Circular 145/75—Residential Accommodation for Physically Handicapped People.
—LAC 13/74 and Welsh Office Circular 46/74 and LAC 1974 and Welsh Office Circular 100/74—deal with local authority sponsorship of elderly, disabled and mentally disordered people in residential homes.
—"Catering in Homes for Elderly People" (1975).
—LASSL (78)20—Safe Temperatures for Heated Surfaces and Hot Water.
—DSWS (83)5—enclosing Health Technical Memorandum (HTM) No. 87—Fire Safety in Health Care Premises—Furniture, Furnishings, Bed Assemblies, Apparel.

A40. The code of practice, *Home Life*, is intended to provide a framework that will help registration authorities in their registration, inspection and support functions, and assist those running homes to clarify their aims and objectives. Local authorities are asked to regard the code in the same light as general guidance that is issued from time to time under powers at Section 7 of the Local Authority Social Service Act 1970. The recommendations in the code are discretionary rather than mandatory for authorities. However, when considering applications for registration, or when inspecting premises, registration authorities should take these recommendations into account along with other relevant guidance to see whether the statutory provisions and those in the Regulations governing registration are met, for example, that the accommodation and the space allotted to each resident for their care by day and by night is reasonable.

A41. Where housing association schemes are developed in accord with the standards contained in the Housing Corporation's Design and Contract Criteria-Shared Housing Supplement, these standards should be acceptable to the registration authority where registration as a residential care home is required.

A42. *Case records* required by the Regulations have to be kept in a secure place (Regulation 6(2)). At a school the requirement to maintain a case record only applies to children in the dependent categories boarding there who are provided with "personal care".

Fire safety

A43. In registered residential care premises, control over fire safety is exercised essentially through the statutory provisions relating to registration. However, in certain cases other statutory provisions may apply and there could be overlap between the legislation. This is explained in the following paragraphs. It is for the appropriate authorities to decide which statutory provisions should apply in any particular case. In considering the appropriate fire safety standards for such premises the fire authority will normally have regard to the recommendations in the Home Office Draft Guide to Fire Precautions in Existing Residential Care Premises, which was issued in January 1983. Separate guidance is being prepared on new homes for the elderly.

4–044

A44. In a limited number of cases the Fire Precautions Act 1971 by reason of the Fire Precautions (Hotels and Boarding Houses) Order 1972 (S.I. 1972 No. 238) may also apply. This could happen where the "residential care home" also caters for holiday makers and travellers as well as for persons in need of "personal care", as defined for registration as a residential care home.

A45. Doubt could also arise whether the housing legislation governing the provision of means of escape from fire in houses in multiple occupation should also apply to a registered residential care home. However, as suggested by the joint Department of the Environment Circular 25/82, Home Office Circular 91/82 and Welsh Office Circular 41/82, where there is more clearly applicable legislation, such as that referred to in paragraphs A43 and A44 above, this should be used and the Housing Act powers would not be invoked.

Inspection and support

A46. The powers of inspection conferred by Section 17 of the 1984 Act are an important part of the registration system. Apart from enabling the authority to satisfy itself that acceptable standards are being maintained in registered homes and that continued registration is justified, they also enable authorised persons to enter and inspect any premises which are used, or which they have reasonable cause to believe are used, for the purposes of a residential care home.

4–045

A47. Inspection may be undertaken by a person authorised by the registration authority or by the Secretary of State. Inspection may be carried out at any time of the day or night and advance notice does *not* have to be given. The inspector must, if requested to do so, produce his authority for entering and inspecting (Sections 17(1), (2) and (5)). Inspectors should let residents have an opportunity of seeing them in private.

A48. Regulation 18 requires an authority to inspect a registered home at least once every 12 months. This should be regarded as a minimum and authorities should inspect more frequently if the situation in the home warrants it. When inspecting an independent school for the purposes of the registration system for residential care homes, care should be taken not to deal with matters falling within the purview of the Education Act.

A49. Advice is given in Part B of these Notes about joint inspection by the health and the local authority of homes registered as both nursing homes and residential care homes.

A50. Occasion can also arise when it would be appropriate for the local authority to arrange with the health authority for joint inspection of homes registered only as residential care homes. In some areas authorities already operate in this way. This is useful to see that the type of care provided in homes merits the registration status and adequate arrangements are made for the control of medicines. Collaboration in this way is part of the duty placed upon health authorities and local authorities by Section 22 of the National Health Service Act 1977, to cooperate. A general procedure for such inspections should be agreed between the two types of authority through the standing joint consultative machinery or otherwise. Social services departments also need to consider whether further arrangements need to be made by them with appropriate authorities for advice on other matters affecting these homes such as fire precautions, environmental health, electrical installations.

A51. There is often likely to be a need for two types of visit. Local authorities should carry out inspections within the statutory period to satisfy themselves that standards in the home are acceptable for registration purposes. If, however, the authority is to be concerned with more than just physical facilities, its staff need to be able to gauge the atmosphere of the home and the quality of life of its residents. For this purpose they might need to visit a home on other occasions when those registered could be given advice informally on various aspects of home management. Many authorities already operate in this way.

A52. Whenever an inspection is carried out for the purposes of the legislation (whether a yearly visit or at another occasion), it is essential that a written report should be made and submitted to social services senior management. The registered person should be given a copy of the report or made aware in writing of its principal contents as happens in some areas at present. In this way the registered person would know how well he was performing and whether any deficiencies needed to be remedied.

A53. The registration authority and the registered person should be able to see the registration and inspection system as more than a negative policing procedure. It should be part of a partnership in providing residential care in the authority's area. As well as pointing out failings the authority could—as many authorities do at present—actively endeavour to maintain and improve standards of care as well as facilities. There are no doubt some individuals or organisations registered who wish to distance themselves from the registration authority, but there are many who would be receptive to advice and support. This could take many forms. Registered persons and their staff (whether or not professionally trained) could be offered opportunities—as some already are—to attend local and health authorities' formal training courses; seminars and study days on appropriate subjects; and informal discussions with the local authorities' own homes staff. Residents could also benefit from support given to homes through the provision of the day care or training facilities. This aspect is dealt with in more detail in *Home Life*.

Penalties

4–046   A54. The maximum fines that may be imposed by the courts for registration offences are expressed in terms of the levels of the standard scale prescribed in the Criminal Justice Act 1982. Currently they are as below for each level mentioned in the Registered Homes Act 1984:
Level 2 £   100
Level 4 £1,000
Level 4 £2,000
The Home Secretary is empowered by the 1982 Act to alter these sums by order. This will enable them to be kept in line with changes in the value of money. The amounts mentioned came into effect from May 1, 1984—The Criminal Penalties etc. (Increase) Order 1984 (S.I. 1984/447).

Part B

Dual Registration as a Residential Care Home and Nursing Home

4–047   B1. A feature of the new legislation is that in certain circumstances a home has to be registered both as a residential care home and as a nursing home. Previously this was not so (Sections 1(3), (5)(*a*) and 23(2) of the 1984 Act). The main objective is to avoid the need for transfers between different types of homes when a resident's condition changes after admission by enabling the widest possible range of care to be provided in a single establishment with the statutory safeguards attaching to registration for both types of home. However, for this to be successfully accomplished there will be a need within the legal framework for as much flexibility as possible to meet as far as practicable the particular need for care of individuals in the homes.

B2. From the start it has to be recognised that the line between nursing proper which is appropriate to a nursing home and personal care which is appropriate to a residential care home is difficult to draw. This is particularly so for some elderly physically or mentally handicapped and mentally ill people. The distinction between the criteria for registration as a residential care home or as a nursing home is dealt with in paragraph A7 of the Notes. Any uncertainties in this area should be discussed with the nursing officer of the district health authority with responsibility for registration and inspection as only she can decide which residents need nursing care and whether it should be provided by the community nursing services or by nurses included in the staff establishment.

B3. The whole of a home will be dually registered. However, this need not prevent the two different types of care being provided in separate parts of a home, whether in a distinct wing or on different floors. But equally the two types of care (including terminal care) could be provided in a resident's own room, if appropriate.

B4. The effect of this change in the legislation is that a residential care home with one or more residents requiring the type of care calling for registration under Part II of the 1984 Act will also have to be registered as a nursing home. Those in the home whose care calls for registration under that Part of the Act will have to be in the charge of a registered doctor or first level registered nurse (who need not be the person registered under that Part).

B5. Even though the whole of the home will be dually registered, the number allowed under each registration system has to be stated. This requirement is necessary because, for nursing homes, the number and qualification of nurses is a condition of registration. In the case of residential care home registration this is a condition required by Section 5(3) of the 1984 Act. Schedule 2 of the Regulations also requires a register to be kept at the home showing for each day those there in receipt of residential care home type of care. For example, a home which can care for 20 people in all might have 13 approved under nursing home registration and 7 under that for residential care homes. It is accepted that the condition of those in the home may fluctuate from time to time and the registration authorities should review the situation each year to see whether the registration conditions need to be varied to take account of any changes. However, the situation in a home may change drastically during the course of a year and the registration authorities may have to act quickly to adjust the registration conditions.

B6. A nursing home used *solely* as a nursing home will not be registerable as a residential care home (Section 1(5)(a)). However, a nursing home will *have to be* registered as a residential care home as well if it has *four or more persons* requiring care of a type characteristic of a residential care home which is not incidental to care falling for registration as a nursing home (see Part A of these Notes). Nursing homes with *fewer than four persons* needing care characteristic of a residential care home *may* be registered as such a home if the registered person makes application under Section 4.

B7. Clearly where two types of registration authority are involved with one home there has to be even closer co-operation between them over the registration and inspections and other support. Joint inspections by both registration authorities should be undertaken wherever necessary. There should in particular be agreement between the two types of authority over the standards applied to common areas of a home *e.g.* kitchens and day rooms. For these parts of the home the inspector from one authority may with the other's agreement act for both. In any event at the minimum annual statutory inspection of a dually registered home by the local social services authority for the purpose of registration a a residential care home joint inspection is especially desirable. Joint inspection is also desirable as a means of reducing the demands made on homes by registration authorities.

B8. With a dually registered establishment, the person or persons registered in respect of it as a residential care home may be different from the person registered in respect of it as a nursing home. This can arise where a home is operated, for example, by a corporate body. For residential care home registration, both that body and the manager would be registered, but for registration as a nursing home only the corporate body will be registered. Regardless of this, those in the home whose care calls for nursing home registration will have to be in the charge of a doctor, or nurse, who does not have to be a person registered in respect of the home.

B9. A separate registration fee will be payable by the registered person or persons to the local social services authority and the district health authority, so that at the registration of a new dual purpose establishment run by its proprietor a registration fee of £100 would be paid to the local authority and one of £100 to the district health authority.

B10. The annual fee payable to the local authority and to the health authority would be related to the number of persons approved under each registration system—see paragraph B5 above. In the example given in that paragraph a fee of £70 (7 × 10) would be payable to the local authority and £130 (13 × £10) to the district health authority.

B11. The annual fees in respect of each registration will become payable at the time appropriate to the circumstances of each registration. For example, when the annual fee is payable in respect of registration as a residential care home is governed by what is said in Part A of these Notes.

B12. Existing nursing homes which fulfil the requirements for compulsory dual registration will have to apply to be so registered to the local authority within 6 months of January 1, 1985.

B13. The separate Regulations, the code of practice for residential care home (*Home Life*) and a handbook for nursing homes produced by the National Association of Health Authorities will be applicable to the respective types of care provided in a dually registered home.

PART C

NATIONAL LIST OF CANCELLED REGISTRATIONS AND THE CHILDREN'S CONSULTANCY SERVICE*

4–048 C1. The Department of Health and Social Security will be keeping from January 1, 1985 a list of persons whose registration is cancelled in respect of the following types of homes after that date:
—residential care homes registered under Part I of the 1984 Act
—nursing homes and mental nursing homes registered under Part II of the 1984 Act
—voluntary children's homes registered under the Child Care Act 1980, Part VI
When the Children's Homes Act 1982 is implemented the list will be extended to include the names of persons who had been carrying on a home in relation to which the registration under that Act had been withdrawn.

C2. Authorities in England and Wales having occasion to cancel such a registration after January 1, 1985 are asked to notify the Department at the following address that they have done this:
Department of Health and Social Security (CSIA)
Alexander Fleming House
London SE1 6BY
They should also notify the Department of any registration cancelled by an order of a justice of the peace under the urgent procedure for cancelling a registration (see paragraph A34 above).

C3. Where the registration of a person in relation to a residential care home in England which is also an independent school is cancelled, notification of that should be sent as well to the Department of Education and Science (Special Education Division), Elizabeth House, London SE1 7PH.

C4. The notification should be sent to the Department on the appropriate form, RH1 (specimen at Annex II). Neither this notification nor that sent in the case of independent schools to the Education Department should be sent until the cancellation becomes operative. The order of a justice of the peace has immediate effect, even though there is a right of appeal against it to a Registered Homes Tribunal. However, the decision of a registration authority to cancel does not have effect for 28 days or, if an appeal is brought, until the appeal has been determined or abandoned.

C5. If the registered person is an organisation or a company, its name and the name and address of the chairman and secretary of the board of management should be given on form RH1. Where two persons are registered in respect of a residential care home and both their registrations are cancelled, a separate form RH1 should be sent to each.

C6. Authorities are asked to record on form RH1 any other name that a previously registered person has or had, or any that a person is known to have used. For example, some married women continue to use their maiden name for professional purposes and in that case the married name and the maiden name should be notified. Authorities may also know of an alias used by a person whose registration has been cancelled. This should be given, but care should be taken by the authority that the allegation could be substantiated so as to avoid the risk of an action for defamation.

C7. It is important to identify on form RH1 the precise statutory provision(s) under which the registration has been cancelled. This could be helpful to another registration authority considering a registration application subsequently from the person.

C8. On receipt of a form RH1 the Department will immediately send a copy of it by recorded delivery or similar service to the person at his address, as on the form, and allow him a calendar month in which to notify any correction that may be needed before incorporating his name in the national list.

Quarterly lists

4–049 C9. Once a quarter, starting on April 30, 1985 the Department will send to each registration

---

* "The national list that is maintained of people whose registrations have been cancelled has been extended to include the names of people whose application for registration in respect of a residential care home, nursing home or voluntary children's home has been refused on or after September 1, 1989 on the ground that he was not a fit person to run such a home; the list is not being extended to include refusals on other grounds, such as the suitability of the premises or the services to be provided at them.
The procedure for a cancellation set out at Part C of the guidance notes issued with LAC (84)15 or at paragraphs 23 to 34 of Annex B to HC (84)21 should be followed with suitable adaptations. As a refusal of an application has immediate effect, form RH1 should be sent to the Department directly after an applicant has been notified of the refusal of the registration." Department of Health Circular No. LAC (89)12, paras. 8, 9.

authority (*i.e.* district health authority and local social services authority) in England and Wales a copy of the current list of persons the cancellation of whose registration has been notified to it since January 1, 1985. Allowing for the time that the processing of a registration might be expected to take, it should not be necessary if the procedure explained in paragraphs A21, A22, C11 and C14 is followed for authorities to approach the Department about any cancellations between issues of the quarterly lists. The list will be in the form of RH2 (specimen at Annex II).

C10. An applicant for registration should be informed by the registration authority that a person with the same name as his is entered in the national list, even if there is doubt that they are one and the same person. Authorities will appreciate the sensitive nature of this list and the need to be vigilant in ensuring that persons are not unwittingly prejudiced by entries on it.

C11. The grant of registration should also be explicitly on the basis that misleading information in the application may be a ground for cancelling the registration.

Removal of names from national list

C12. A person's name would be removed from the national list of cancelled registrations if a registration authority subsequently decided to register him in respect of the same category of home, provided, of course, he had declared the cancellation when applying for registration. For example, a person may have had his registration in respect of a nursing home withdrawn but subsequently applied successfully to a district health authority for registration. He would have his name removed from the national list. However, it would not be removed automatically if he was subsequently registered with a local authority. An authority registering a person whose name is on the list should send form RH3 (specimen at Annex II) to the Department at the address mentioned in paragraph C2 above. **4–050**

C13. A person whose name is on the list may also apply to the Department to have his name removed. For example, a registration may have been cancelled because the fire precautions at a nursing home were inadequate. The person may have applied subsequently to be registered in relation to a residential care home where fire precautions were satisfactory and in consequence had been registered. Retention of his name on the list in these circumstances is unlikely to seem justified. However, it could be if his nursing home registration had been cancelled on account of dangerous health procedures (*e.g.* use of stale blood for transfusions).

Children's consultancy service

C14. An authority considering a registration application for a home, where children under the age of 18 are to be accommodated, may also make use of the consultancy services provided by the Department. This has more extensive coverage than the national list of cancelled registrations and would be an additional means for an authority to satisfy themselves whether anything was known about an applicant that might point to his unsuitability for a position of responsibility for children's welfare. Written application for this service should be made to the Department: **4–051**

 The Executive Officer
 Children's Division A2
 Room B1309
 Alexander Fleming House
 Elephant and Castle
 London SE1 6BY

(Details of this service will be given in a forthcoming circular.)

PART D

APPEALS AND REGISTERED HOMES

D1. Registered Homes Tribunals set up under Part III of the 1984 Act supersede the tribunals previously constituted under the Child Care Act 1980 to hear registration appeals by voluntary children's homes. The new Tribunals will hear appeals relating only to these children's homes but also to certain other children's homes when the Children's Homes Act 1982 is implemented. Additionally they will hear appeals relating to residential care homes, nursing homes and mental nursing homes; previously these appeals had been heard by magistrates' courts. Their procedure is governed by the Registered Homes Tribunals Rules 1984 (S.I. 1984 No. 1346) and it is to these Rules that reference is made in this Part of the Notes. **4–052**

D2. Registered Homes Tribunals will hear appeals against authorities' decisions: to refuse a registration application, to the condition for the grant of one or to cancel or amend a registration. They will also hear appeals against an order of a justice of the peace made under the urgent procedure in relation to residential care homes or nursing home.

D3. On a point of law, an appeal against a decision of a Registered Homes Tribunal may be made to the High Court under Section 13(1) of the Tribunals and Inquiries Act 1971, as amended by paragraph 11 of Schedule 9 to the Health and Social Services and Social Security Adjudications Act 1983.

D4. Persons who wish to have an appeal heard by a Registered Homes Tribunal are required to send written notice to this effect to the registration authority concerned (Section 15(2) of the 1984 Act). The authority should send the notice of appeal within 7 days by recorded delivery post to the Secretary of State (rule 3(2)) at the address below that is appropriate:

England:
    Residential Care Homes—Community Services Division 1A
        Alexander Fleming House
        London SE1 6BY

Wales:
    Residential Care Homes—Local Authority Social Services Division 1
        Welsh Office, Cathays Park
        Cardiff CF1 3NQ

D5. Expenses incurred by an appellant attending tribunal hearings, including his witnesses, have to be met by him. Wherever practicable tribunals are expected to be held at a place which is convenient for the parties to the dispute, though the final decision on this will rest with the chairman of the tribunal (rule 5(1)).

D6. Appeals will be heard by a tribunal made up of a chairman appointed by the Lord Chancellor and two expert members appointed by the Lord President of the Council (Section 40 of the 1984 Act). For an appeal involving a nursing home registration as well as a residential care home registration (*i.e.* dual registration) one of the expert members will be a qualified nurse or midwife. The other would be a person experienced in social work. For other types of appeal (*i.e.* registration solely as a residential care home or as a children's home) the expert members would be persons with experience in the field appropriate to the type of home involved (Section 42).

D7. The new tribunals will hear appeals lodged from January 1, 1985 onwards. Appeals made before then to magistrate's court under the Residential Homes Act 1980 or the Nursing Homes Act 1975 will remain with magistrates' courts even though the proceedings may be after that date (Regulation 23 of the Residential Care Homes Regulations 1984).

GENERAL NOTE

Para. D4

4–053

"When sending appeals to the Departments in accordance with paragraph D4 of the guidance notes issued with LAC (84)15 the following information should be given (if not indicated in the notice of appeal):

(*a*) the client group classification of the home *e.g.* physically disabled;
(*b*) whether the appeal is against the refusal of an application, a condition of registration, or the cancellation or alteration of a registration;
(*c*) whether the appeal is against an order of the justice of the peace under Section 11 of the Registered Homes Act 1984 (the urgent procedure).

The notice of the appeal should be sent addressed to:
    Registered Homes Tribunal Secretariat
    Room B1615
    Department of Health and Social Security
    Alexander Fleming House
    Elephant and Castle
    London SE1 6BY

Paragraph D4 of the guidance notes should be amended accordingly": DHSS Circular No. LAC (86)6, paras. 20, 21.

ANNEX I

LIST OF CERTAIN EDUCATIONAL ESTABLISHMENTS EXEMPT FROM REGISTRATION AS RESIDENTIAL CARE HOMES

PART 1

LIST OF FURTHER EDUCATION ESTABLISHMENTS RECEIVING GRANTS UNDER SECTION 100(1)(*b*) OF THE EDUCATION ACT 1944

4–054

Bishop Grossteste College, Lincoln
Cambridge Institute
Chester College
Christ Church College, Canterbury
Coleg Harlech, Gwynedd
College of Ripon and York St. John, North Yorkshire
College of St. Mark and St. John, Plymouth
College of St. Paul and St. Mary, Cheltenham
College of the Sea, London
Co-operative College, Loughborough
De La Salle College, Manchester
Derby Lonsdale College, Derby
Fircroft College, Birmingham
Goldsmith's College, London
Harper Adams Agricultural College, Newport, Shropshire
Hillcroft College, Surbiton
Homerton College, Cambridge
King Alfred's College, Winchester
La Sainte Union College, Southampton
Liverpool Institute of Higher Education
National Sea Training Trust, London
Newman College, Birmingham
Northern College, Nr. Barnsley
Plater College, Oxford
Roehampton Institute of Higher Education
Rolls Royce Technical College, Bristol
Royal College of Nursing, London
Ruskin College, Oxford
St. Martin's College, Lancaster
St. Mary's College, Newcastle-upon-Tyne
St. Mary's College, Twickenham
Seale Hayne Agricultural College, Newton Abbot
Shuttleworth Agricultural College, Biggleswade
Trinity and All Saints College, Leeds
Trinity College, Carmarthen, Dyfed
Trinity College of Music, London
Westhill College, Birmingham
West London Institute of Higher Education
Westminster College, Oxford
West Sussex Institute of Higher Education

PART 2

EDUCATION ESTABLISHMENTS SUBSTANTIALLY DEPENDENT FOR MAINTENANCE UPON LOCAL EDUCATION AUTHORITIES

4–055

Camborne School of Mines, Cornwall
Central School of Speech and Drama, London
City of London Polytechnic
Cordwainers Technical College, London
Dartington College of Arts, Devon
London School of Nautical Cookery
Morley College, London
Polytechnic of Central London
Polytechnic of North London
Polytechnic of the South Bank, London
Rose Bruford College of Speech and Drama, Bexley
Thames Polytechnic, London

ANNEX II

Form RH1 REGISTERED HOMES ACT 1984**

RESIDENTIAL CARE HOMES AND NURSING HOMES

NOTIFICATION OF A CANCELLED OR A REFUSED REGISTRATION

4–056 (Authorities should see Notes at the end *before* completing the form)

1. Give <u>full</u> names and address (including postal code) of person whose registration has been cancelled or refused. Include all other names that person is known by.

2. Give <u>full</u> name and address (including postal code) of premises associated with the cancellation or refusal

3. Registration Authority:—

4. Authority's reference:—

5. Date notice of cancellation or refusal was served

6. If applicable, date of justice of peace order

7. Was an appeal made?   Yes/No* (If Yes go to question 8. If No go to question 9.)

8. If an appeal was made   Yes/No*
   (a) Was the appeal abandoned
   (b) If Yes, give date appeal abandoned
   (c) If No, give date and number of Tribunal's decision

9. Date when cancellation becomes effective (see Notes 2 and 3)

CANCELLATIONS

10. Please tick the statutory provision under which the registration was cancelled.

<u>Residential Care Homes</u>   <u>Nursing Homes, Maternity Homes, Mental Nursing Homes</u>

<u>Section</u> 10(*b*) ☐   <u>Section</u> 28(*a*) ☐

---

* delete as appropriate
** This revised form RH1 was issued as Annex 1 to Department of Health Circular No. LAC (89)12. Forms RH1 for nursing homes as well as residential care homes should be sent to:
   Department of Health (CSIA),
   Alexander Fleming House,
   Elephant and Castle,
   London SE1 6BX.

(Also tick appropriate part of section 9 below)		(Also tick appropriate part of section 25 below)	
10(b)	☐	28(b)	☐
10(c)(i)	☐	28(c)	☐
10(c)(ii)	☐	28(d)	☐
10(c)(iii)	☐	28(e)	☐
If you have ticked section 10(a) also complete this section		If you have ticked section 28(a) also complete this section	
Section 9(a)	☐	Section 25(a)	☐
9(b)	☐	25(b)	☐
9(c)	☐	25(c)	☐
		25(d)	☐
		25(e)	☐
		25(f)	☐
		25(g)	☐
Section 11	☐	Section 30	☐

REFUSALS

11. Please state whether the refusal was made under section 9(a) or section 25(a)

Signed by
Name:
Position:
Address:
Post Code:
Tel. No.:—   Date:

Notes on the Completion of Form RH1

1. A separate form should be submitted for each person whose registration has either been refused because he is considered an unfit person or cancelled in relation to a home.
   If it is a company: give the name of the chairman of the board and the company secretary.
   If it is a partnership: give the names of all the partners.
   If it is an organisation: give the name of the person responsible for the organisation's management.
2. The address of a person for this purpose is his last known address. In the case of a body corporate the address is that of its registered or principal office, and in the case of the partner of a firm, the principal office of the firm.
3. A registration authority's decision to cancel a registration does not come into effect until after 28 days following the notification to the person concerned. However, should an appeal be lodged, the decision does not have effect until the appeal is determined (or abandoned). <u>Form RH1 should not be sent to the Department of Health until the authority's decision has become operative.</u>
4. The order of a justice of the peace and the decision of an authority to refuse an application for registration has immediate effect. However, should an appeal be made, form RH1 should <u>not</u> be sent until it has been determined (or abandoned).
5. A form should only be submitted if a registration has been refused under Sections 9(a) (residential care homes) or 25(a) (nursing homes).

Form RH2
(list dated . . .)

REGISTERED HOMES
NATIONAL LIST OF CANCELLED REGISTRATIONS

NOTE:
An authority wanting more information about any entry on this list should contact the registration authority which cancelled the registration, *not* the Department of Health and Social Security*. The previous registration authority's reference, the date of this list and the number on this list should be quoted.

* However, if the entry relates to a voluntary children's home where registration under the Child Care Act 1980 has been cancelled the Department of Health and Social Security (Children's Division A4) should be contacted.

List No.	Person whose registration has been cancelled	Name and address of Home	Registration Authority which cancelled registration	Statutory Provision under which registration cancelled (*i.e.* as at item 8 of form RH1)	Registration Authority's Reference
(1)	(2)	(3)	(4)	(5)	(6)

Form RH3 REGISTERED HOMES

REGISTRATION OF A PERSON ON
THE NATIONAL LIST OF CANCELLED REGISTRATIONS

4–058

1. Registration authority	
2. Person(s)	Name (Surname) : Christian or Forename (Capitals) Street Town County Postal Code
3. List number on RH2 (Column 1) and the date of RH2 (RH2: the national list of cancelled registrations)	
4. Enactment(s) under which home is now registered: (a) Part I of the Registered Homes Act 1984 (Residential Care Home)	(Tick)
(b) Part II of the Registered Homes Act 1984 (Nursing Home, Maternity Home or Mental Nursing Home)	

Signed by: ....

Name: ....

Address: ....

....

.... Post Code ....

Date ....   Telephone No: ....

ANNEX III

4–059

TABLE 1. GRANT OF REGISTRATION

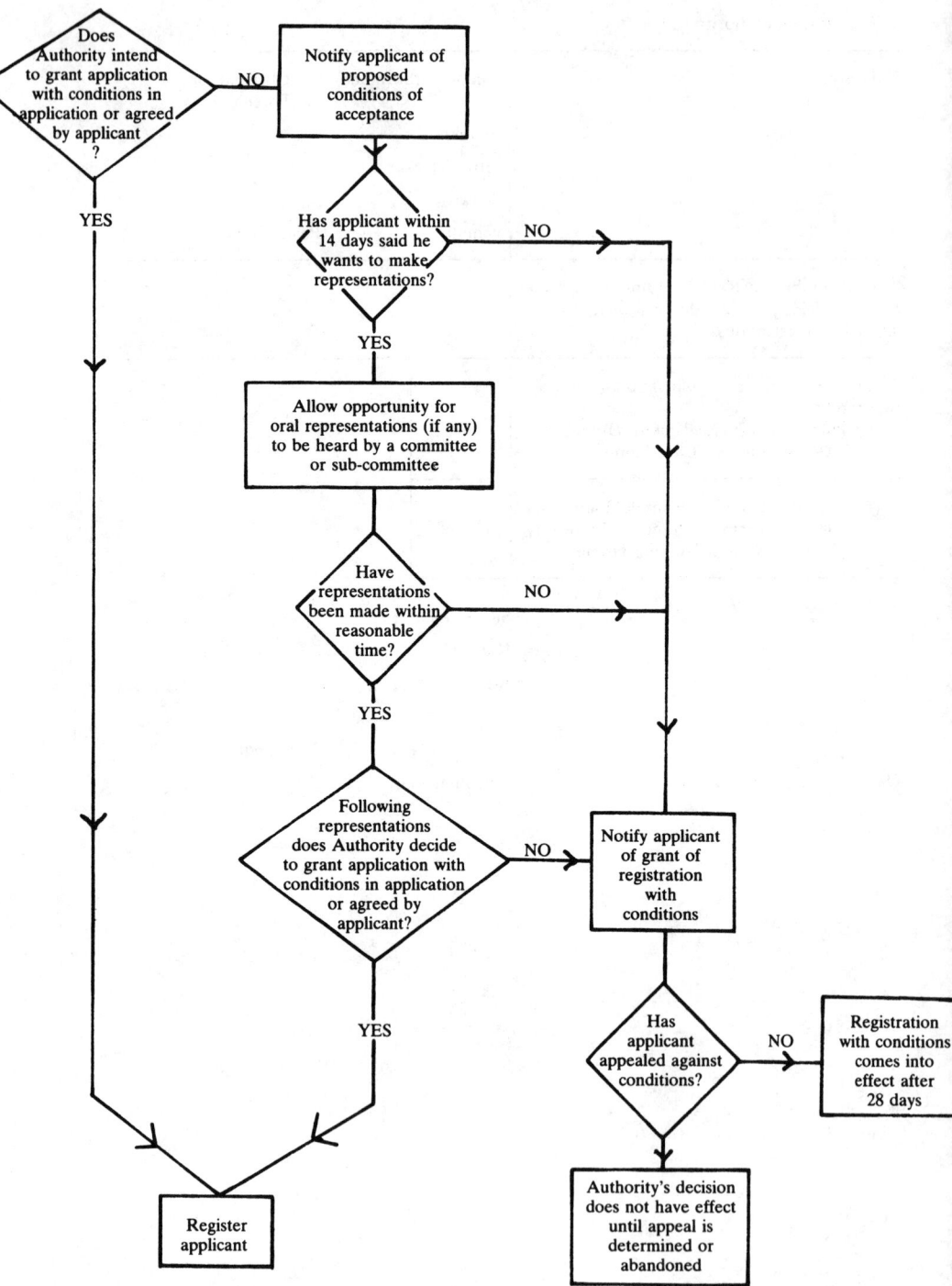

TABLE 2. REFUSAL OF REGISTRATION

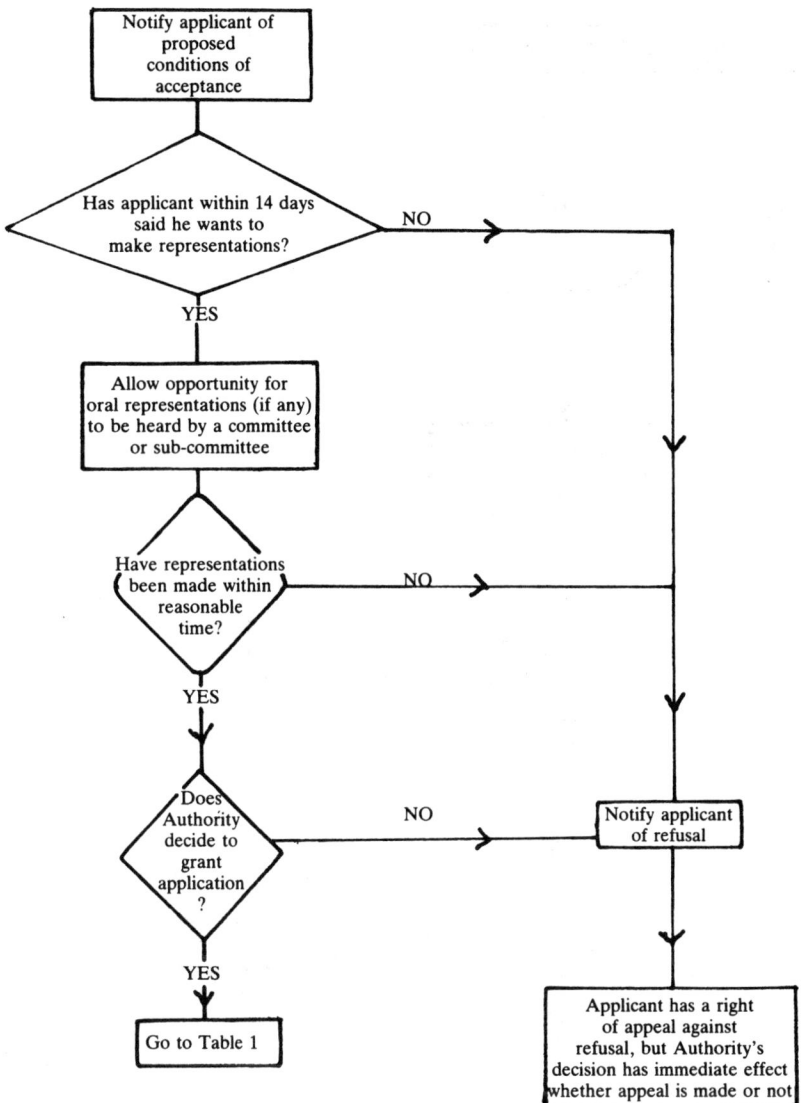

4–060 TABLE 3. CANCELLATION OR ALTERATION OF A REGISTRATION

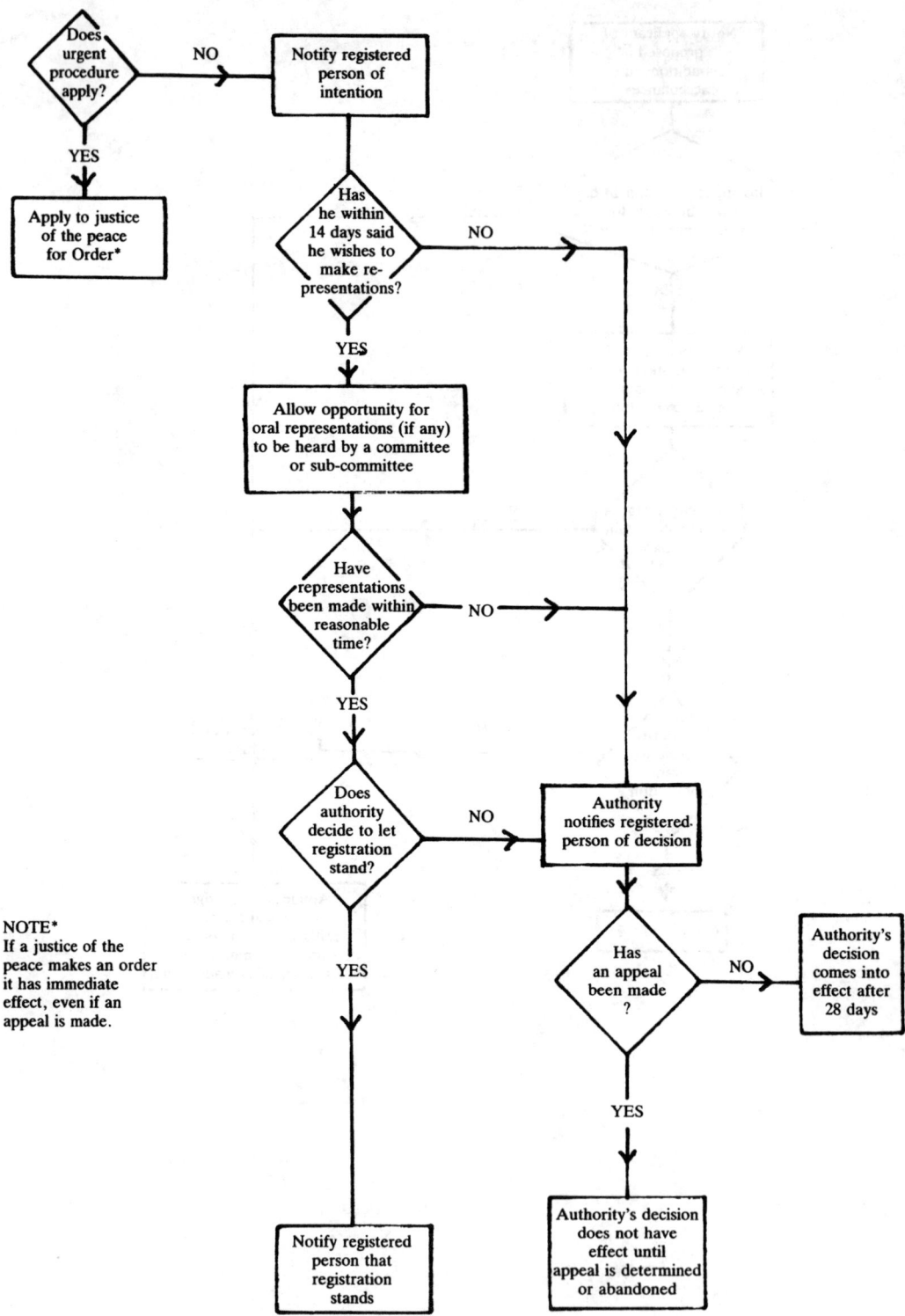

CIRCULAR No. HC (84)21

Dated October 1984, and issued by the Department of Health and Social Security

HEALTH SERVICES MANAGEMENT
REGISTRATION AND INSPECTION OF PRIVATE NURSING HOMES AND MENTAL NURSING HOMES (INCLUDING PRIVATE HOSPITALS)

GENERAL NOTE

This Circular is reproduced subject to the amendments made to it by DHSS Circular No. HC (86)5.

4–061

Summary

This Circular: **4–062**
 (i) notifies authorities of changes in legislation governing the registration and inspection of private nursing homes and hospitals.
 (ii) gives guidance on the new provisions.
 (iii) commends to authorities a handbook on registration and inspection produced by the National Association of Health Authorities in England and Wales.

Introduction

1. The Nursing Homes Act 1975 ("the 1975 Act") as amended by the Health Services Act 1980 and Health and Social Services and Social Security Adjudications Act 1983 ("the HASSASSA Act") provides for registration and inspection of private nursing homes and mental nursing homes (including hospitals) by the Secretary of State for Social Services. This function is delegated to district health authorities. The Nursing Homes Act 1975 and amending legislation, together with legislation relating to residential care homes, has been consolidated in the Registered Homes Act 1984 ("the 1984 Act"). Accompanying the 1984 Act is an amended set of nursing homes regulations to replace the Nursing Homes and Mental Nursing Homes Regulations 1981. The new regulations differ from the 1981 regulations mainly in respect of post HASSASSA Act changes described below. **4–063**

2. A Local Authority Circular LAC (84)15 giving matching guidance on changes in provisions for residential care homes registered by local authorities is available on request from the address shown at the end of this Circular.

3. A comprehensive account of the law on the registration and inspection of nursing homes and guidance on its application prior to HASSASSA Act amendments are given in HC (81)8. This present Circular is concerned principally with changes made by or following the HASSASSA Act. (The 1984 Act, as a consolidating measure, does not itself make any changes.) The changes are described below together with details of a new handbook on registration and inspection to be produced by the National Association of Health Authorities in England and Wales.

Changes to legislation and procedure for the registration and inspection of nursing homes

4. The main changes made by, or following, the HASSASSA Act involve: **4–064**
 (i) extending the scope of controls to premises hitherto unregistered using lasers for medical and surgical purposes (including cosmetic surgery);
 (ii) recognition that there are homes containing residents some of whom require nursing care and others who only require residential care without the nursing component; the Act requires such homes providing both types of care to be registered with both DHAs as nursing homes and with local social services authorities as residential care homes;
 (iii) making it an offence to describe, with intent to deceive, premises not registered with a DHA, as a nursing home, maternity home or mental nursing home;
 (iv) requiring notice of absence of the person in charge of a home;
 (v) increases in initial registration fees and introduction of annual registration fees;
 (vi) the introduction of a new appeals system.

5. Associated with these changes are:
 (i) the creation of a national list of cancelled registrations;
 (ii) a direction from the Secretary of State requiring DHAs to inspect unregistered premises they have reason to believe may be providing nursing care (Annex C);

(iii) a direction from the Secretary of State bringing up-to-date the direction issued with HC (81)8 specifying the qualifications without which a nurse may not be the "person in charge" of a nursing home (Annex C);

(iv) amending regulations to keep requirements for nursing homes and residential care homes in line with each other as may be appropriate.

6. The changes are described in more detail in Annex A with guidance on their implementation in Annex B.

7. Health and local authorities have always been encouraged to co-operate closely in the registration and inspection of homes. The need will now be that much greater a statutory obligation because of dual registration (*i.e.* the provision for homes to be registered as both nursing and residential care homes), the sanction provided by the new offence (see 4(iii) above and Section 24 of the 1984 Act) and action required by the Secretary of State's Direction at Annex C. Joint inspections are recommended in Annex B in appropriate cases.

NAHA Handbook on registration and inspection

4–065
8. Ministers welcome the publication of a new handbook on registration and inspection produced by the National Association of Health Authorities in England and Wales (NAHA). The NAHA Handbook provides comprehensive advice on all aspects of registration and inspection, including the changes described in this Circular. HC (81)8 drew attention to the need for authorities to "develop clear procedures for handling applications for registration and for use in monitoring homes once registered". The NAHA handbook, HC (81)8 and this Circular should provide a good foundation.

9. A copy of the handbook will be distributed by NAHA to each RHA, DHA and SHA for London Postgraduate Hospitals. Further copies may be purchased from NAHA at:

National Association of Health Authorities
Garth House
47 Edgbaston Park Road
Birmingham B15 2RS
(021–471–4444)

NHS Functions (Directions to Authorities and Administration Arrangements) Amendment Regulations 1984 (SI 1984 No. 1577)

4–066
10. NHS Functions Regulations are the means by which health authorities are directed to undertake duties and exercise powers conferred by statute upon the Secretary of State for Social Services. Consolidation of the legislation relating to registration and inspection of nursing homes in the Registered Homes Act 1984 requires that amendment regulations be made referring to the new statutory powers. A copy of the Regulations was sent to health authorities on publication.

11. The broad scope and purpose of the revised functions regulations remain much the same as before and reference should be made to HC (82)8 for a general statement of the principles involved. The opportunity has been taken to effect a further minor amendment to Regulation 3, to enable a limitation to be directed by an instrument in writing, as was the case from 1974 to 1982.

Action

4–067
12. Regional Health Authorities are asked to issue revised directions to DHAs in respect to these functions to be exercised by them from January 1, 1985, when the NHS Functions (Directions to Authorities and Administrative Arrangements) Amendment Regulations 1984 come into force.

13. District Health Authorities are asked to:—

(i) take note of the new provisions incorporated in the 1984 Act and the 1984 Regulations and bring these to the attention of officers concerned with registration and inspection;

(ii) bring the new requirements to the attention of the "person registered" and "the person-in-charge" of premises which are already registered;

(iii) draw up new local guidelines on registration in consultation with local social services authorities in the light of the revised legislation, guidance on this circular and the NAHA Handbook.

(iv) institute, as required by the Secretary of State's direction, and in co-operation with local social services authorities, a special programme of inspections of premises they have reason to believe may be providing a type of care for which registration as a nursing home is required by law: thereafter to maintain, in co-operation with the local social services authority, a continuing search in their district of such unregistered premises.

Annex A

CHANGES IN LEGISLATION FOR THE REGISTRATION AND INSPECTION OF NURSING HOMES

Introduction

1. This Annex describes in more detail the changes made, by or following the HASSASSA Act, and now incorporated in the Registered Homes Act 1984 ("the 1984 Act"), to the registration and inspection of nursing homes and mental nursing homes. Annex B gives guidance on the implementation of the changes.   **4–068**

The main changes:

The scope of controls

2. The definitions of nursing home in Section 21 of the 1984 Act includes premises in which treatment by "specially controlled techniques" is provided. Regulations may specify any technique of medicine or surgery (including cosmetic surgery) which may create a hazard for staff or patients, the use of certain types of laser as a "specially controlled technique" has been specified. Guidance on this extention of controls is given in HC (84)15.   **4–069**

Dual registration

3. The Residential Homes Act 1980 excluded from registration by a local authority any premises requiring registration as a nursing home or mental nursing home under the 1975 Act. This restriction is now removed as residents do not fall into neat legislative compartments. A registered nursing home (or mental nursing home) which provides residential care only for four or more of its occupants, as defined in Section 1 of the 1984 Act, will also have to be registered as a residential care home. (Dual registration will be permissible but not mandatory if residential care is provided for fewer than four people.) Existing nursing homes which fulfil the requirements for compulsory dual registration will have to apply to be registered also as residential care homes.   **4–070**

New offence and Secretary of State direction

4. As well as homes which will have to be dually registered there are believed to be a number of homes currently registered as residential care homes which should more appropriately be registered solely as nursing homes. Section 24 of the 1984 Act makes it an offence for a person with intent to deceive to describe premises in such a way as to indicate that they are a nursing home, maternity home or mental nursing home unless they are registered as such. DHAs are already empowered under Sections 27 and 35 of the 1984 Act to enter and inspect any unregistered premises believed to be functioning as nursing homes or mental nursing homes. Annex C reproduces a direction from the Secretary of State *requiring* authorities to make inspections of this kind. The unusual step of issuing a direction has been taken because of concern about the welfare of patients receiving nursing care which is not subject to the rigorous standards applied to registered nursing homes.   **4–071**

5. Any premises which the DHA have reason to believe may be functioning as nursing homes (whatever may be the ground *e.g.* hearsay or otherwise for that belief) must be inspected and any necessary action taken. The important objective, in the interests of the patients accommodated, is that the establishment (if the standards warrant) be quickly registered and that inspection, with all that that term implies, begins without delay. Some residential care homes (aside from those whose circumstances will justify dual registration) may be found to be more appropriately registered wholly and exclusively as nursing homes. The DHA should take action accordingly, keeping the local services authority informed at all stages.

Notice of absence

6. 1984 Regulation 8 made under new powers in Section 26 of the 1984 Act requires the person registered in respect of a home normally to give at least a month's notice of the intended absence of the person-in-charge of the home for more than four weeks. Provision is made for shorter notice at the discretion of the health authority and for notice to be given within one week, if possible, where the absence results from an emergency. Adequate arrangements for running the home are required during the period of absence. Notice also has to be given of the return of the person-in-charge to the home.   **4–072**

Registration fees

4–073 7. Schedule 1 to the 1984 Regulations set out increased fees for initial registration. Schedule 3 introduces annual registration fees, as permitted by Section 27(e) of the 1984 Act.

Urgent procedure for cancellation of registration, etc.

4–074 8. DHAs will have a new power to apply to a justice of the peace for an order cancelling or varying a registration in an emergency, as permitted by Section 30 of the 1984 Act.

New appeals system

4–075 9. Appeals against authorities' decisions on registration will lie to Registered Homes Tribunals, to be serviced by the Department, and not as now to magistrates' courts. Part III of the 1984 Act provides for the new Tribunals, the rules for which are in S.I. 1984 No. 1345. An appeal against a decision of a Registered Homes Tribunal may be made on a point of law to the High Court, under Section 13(1) of the Tribunals and Inquiries Act 1971, as amended by paragraph 5 of Schedule 1 to the 1984 Act.

Cancelled registrations

4–076 10. The Department is introducing a list compiled on a national basis of cancelled registrations as a further saferguard against abuse. Each quarter all registration authorities will be sent the list of people and companies whose registration has been cancelled in respect of nursing homes and mental nursing homes, residential care homes and children's homes since January 1, 1984. Authorities are asked to ensure the prompt notification of cancelled registrations to keep the list up to date.

Secretary of State's direction on nurses qualified to be in charge of registered homes

4–077 11. Annex C reproduces a Direction that takes account of the Nurses, Midwives and Health Visitors (Parts of the Register) Order 1983 S.I. 1983/667. It does not involve any change of substance.

Changes to the Regulations

4–078 12. The 1984 Regulations (S.I. 1984 No. 1578) incorporate a number of amendments to the 1981 Regulations, in addition to those referred to above. In the main the amendments are needed to keep in step with new requirements on residential care homes. But a number of differences remain between the two sets of regulations, reflecting differences in the character and purpose of residential care homes and nursing homes. In summary, the changes, apart from those mentioned elsewhere in this Circular, are:—
  (i) Records: the 1984 Regulations provide for statutory records kept by homes to show in addition to information already required:
      —telephone numbers where appropriate
      —whether patients are in the care of guardianship of a local authority or another public authority (*e.g.* NHS patients admitted under contractual arrangements)
      —[. . .]
      —where the patient is a child the name and address of the school he attends
      —[. . .]
      —the procedure to be followed in the event of fire
      —details of all fire practices and fire alarm tests
      —details of maintenance carried out to medical, surgical and nursing equipment.
  (ii) [. . .]
  (iii) Information which *may* be required by a health authority from applicants for registration: Schedule 2 to the 1984 Regulations shows the following additions to the information which may be required:
      —whether the premises are, have been, or are proposed to be registered also as a residential care home
      —comments made by the local fire authority
      —the telephone number of the home
      —[. . .]
      —the hours worked or proposed to be worked by resident or non-resident staff employed or proposed to be employed in the home.

(iv) Notice to be given for offences related to:
  —record keeping
  —supply of information
  —refusal to allow inspection

Annex B

GUIDANCE ON IMPLEMENTING THE CHANGES

NAHA Handbook

1. The guidance which follows is intended to be read in conjunction with relevant parts of the NAHA Handbook. **4–079**

Registration and inspection of premises using lasers for medical and surgical purposes

2. Detailed guidance is given in HC (84)15. **4–080**

Dual registration

3. A main feature of the new legislation is the provision which enables a home to be registered both as a residential care home and as a nursing home, in appropriate circumstances. Dual registration has been introduced because the boundary between the need for nursing care at a level and frequency greater than can be provided by the community nursing service and personal care and attention is very often not clear, particularly for some elderly physically or mentally handicapped and mentally ill people. Dual registration will allow the widest possible range of care to be provided in a single home (with the statutory safeguards attaching to registration for both types of home). An important objective of dual registration is that there need be no physical transfer from one home to another when a resident's or patient's condition changes. **4–081**

4. The whole of a home will be dually registered. However, this need not prevent the two types of care being provided in separate parts of a home *e.g.* in a separate wing. But, equally, the two types of care (including terminal care) could be provided in a resident's own room, if appropriate. Any home, or part of a home, in which nursing care is provided will, as with all registered nursing homes, have to be in the charge of a registered doctor or qualified nurse. Such dually registered homes should maintain records showing from day to day whether the resident is in residential care or nursing care.

5. The effect of this change in the legislation is that a residential care home with one or more residents requiring the type of care calling for registration under Part II of the Registered Homes Act 1984 will also have to be registered as a nursing home. Those in the home whose care calls for registration under that Part of the Act will have to be in the charge of a registered doctor or first level registered nurse (who need not be the person registered under that Part).

6. Even though the whole of the home will be dually registered, the number allowed under each registration system has to be stated. This requirement is necessary because, for nursing homes, the number and qualification of nurses is a condition of registration. In the case of residential care home registration this is a condition required by regulations. For example, a home which can care for 20 people in all might have 13 approved under nursing home registration and 7 under that for residential care homes. The condition of those in the home may fluctuate from time to time and small temporary changes must be accepted to allow flexibility. It is suggested that the situation be reviewed and, if necessary, registration conditions varied to take account of permanent changes at the time the annual fee becomes payable. When/where the situation in a home changes drastically during the course of a year the registration authorities may have to act quickly to adjust the registration conditions.

7. A nursing home used *solely* as a nursing home will not be registerable as a residential care home. However, a nursing home will *have to be* registered as a residential care home as well, if it has *four or more persons* requiring care of a type characteristic of a residential care home which is not incidental to care falling for registration as a nursing home. Nursing homes with *fewer than four persons* needing care characteristic of a residential care home *may* be registered as such a home, if the registered person makes application to the appropriate local authority.

8. Clearly where two types of registration authority are involved with one home, close cooperation between them will be necessary. Joint inspections should be undertaken wherever necessary. There should, in particular, be agreement over the standards applied to common areas of a home *e.g.* kitchens and day rooms, for such parts of the home, inspection by one authority may, with the other's agreement, suffice for both. It is desirable that the statutory inspection by the local social services authority once a year be made jointly with the health

authority (who have to make two statutory inspections each year). Joint inspection is also desirable as a means of reducing the demands made on home by registering authorities.

9. If a DHA officer has reason to believe that a home registered only as a nursing home or mental nursing home should also be registered as a residential care home, he should inform the person registered in respect of the home and the appropriate local services authority. Officers acting for local social services authorities are being asked to take parallel action for residential care homes which are believed to need registration as a nursing home or mental nursing home. DHAs will not have to wait for such information if they believe that registration as a nursing home is needed.

10. With a dual registered establishment the person or persons registered in respect of it as a residential care home may be different from the person registered in respect of it as a nursing home. This can arise where a home is operated, for example, by a corporate body. For residential care home registration both that body and the manager should be registered but for registration as a nursing home either the corporate body or the manager, but not both, may be registered.

11. A separate registration fee will be payable by the registered person or persons to the local social services authority and the district health authority, to that at the registration of a new dual purpose establishment run by its proprietor a registration fee of £100 would be paid to the local authority and one of £100 to the district health authority.

12. The annual fee payable to the local authority and to the health authority would be related to the number of persons approved under each registration system—see paragraph 6. In the example given in that paragraph a fee of £70 (7 × £10) would be payable to the local authority and £130 (13 × £10) to the district health authority.

13. The annual fees in respect of each registration will become payable at the time appropriate to the circumstances of each registration. It is, however, important that adequate notice is given to each home of its new liability, the amount in question and the final date for payment.

The new offence and action required by the Secretary of State's Direction

4–082 14. Close co-operation with local social services authorities will also be necessary for DHAs wishing to identify people who are attempting to deceive the public into believing that unregistered premises are a nursing home *and* for the programme of inspections of unregistered homes believed to be providing nursing care, required by the Secretary of State's Direction. There will be an overlap with joint action taken in connection with dual registration. But special action may be called for in places where there are suspicions that the owners and operators of particular homes are attempting to conceal the true nature of care they are providing, and the way they represent it, from local authority and/or DHA inspectors.

Notice of absence

4–083 15. In a written notice to the DHA of the intended absence of the person-in-charge of a home, details have to be given of arrangements for running the home during the period of absence. If the home and its staff are well known to the DHA officers responsible for registration and inspection the written notice may be sufficient to satisfy the DHA that the arrangements are "adequate". If, however, there has been reason for less than complete satisfaction with the arrangements it would be advisable for the proposed arrangements to be discussed with the person-in-charge and an ad hoc inspection of the home may be called for. If the proposed arrangements are clearly unsatisfactory and no agreement can be reached on improving them the DHA may be obliged to consider cancelling the registration. If such circumstances develop and time is running short, the DHA may have to apply to a justice of the peace under the "urgent" procedure for cancellations of the registration (see Section 30(1)(a) of the Registered Homes Act and para. 16 below).

Urgent procedure for cancellation of registration etc.

4–084 16. DHAs will have a new power to apply to a justice of the peace for an order cancelling registration, or, less drastically, varying a registration or imposing an additional condition, in an emergency. Section 30 of the 1984 Act sets out the procedure and that such an application can only be successful if the justice is satisfied that "there will be serious risk to the life, health or well-being of the patients in the home". In the event of an appeal to the Registered Homes Tribunal from a justice's order, the DHA would have to substantiate its case. An application to a justice of the peace can be made at any reasonable time and not necessarily to a magistrates' court. The application can be made to a justice's home at weekends, evenings etc. where the urgency warrants it. An order made under this procedure takes immediate effect, although the person registered has 28 days in which to appeal to a Registered Homes Tribunal against such a decision.

New appeals system

17. The new appeals system and associated procedural changes differ entirely from the appeal provisions in 1981 Regulation 5. The system should prove more rigorous and involve greater professional input than the existing procedure. In revising their own procedure DHAs are asked to ensure that there is full compliance with the requirements in Sections 31 to 34 of the 1984 Act. The important changes are: **4–085**

   (i) an applicant or person registered who receives a DHA notice granting a registration subject to conditions, refusing registration, cancelling, varying or applying additional conditions to an existing registration will have *fourteen days* in which to make written or oral representations about any matter which he wishes to dispute.

  (ii) a person wishing to make oral representations as in (i) has to be given an opportunity of appearing before someone specially appointed by the DHA for this purpose. It would not be appropriate for the person hearing the representations to have been already associated with the case. This apart, the person appointed could be a member or officer of the DHA or another suitably qualified person not connected with the DHA. The person appointed should be asked to provide a written account of all representations but should not himself make an recommendations or decisions on the representations. The report of the representations may have to be produced to the appeal Tribunal if the DHA's decision is appealed against.

 (iii) applicants or persons registered have 28 days in which to appeal against decisions made by a DHA or an order made under the urgent procedure; an authority's decision will not take effect until this period has elapsed or, if appealed against, until the appeal is determined or abandoned. An order made under the urgent procedure takes effect immediately.

18. Appeals will lie to the new Registered Homes Tribunals. A person who wishes to appeal is required to send a written notice to this effect to the registration authority concerned. The authority should send the notice of appeal in respect of a nursing home within 7 days by recorded delivery post to: DHSS Health Services Division 3A, Room 1220, Hannibal House, London SE1 6TE. The procedure for appeals to the Tribunal is set out in the Registered Homes Tribunals Rules (S.I. 1984 No. 1346).

19. Expenses incurred by an appellant attending Tribunal hearings, including witnesses, have to be met by him. Wherever practicable Tribunals are expected to be held at a place convenient for the parties to the dispute, though the final decision on this will rest with the chairman of the Tribunal.

20. Appeals will be heard by a Tribunal made up of a chairman appointed by the Lord Chancellor and two expert members appointed by the Lord President of the Council. For appeals involving only a nursing home registration one of the experts has to be a qualified nurse or midwife and the other a registered medical practitioner. Where a residential care home registration is also involved (*i.e.* dual registration) one of the experts will be a qualified nurse or midwife and the other a person experienced in social work.

21. The new Tribunals will hear appeals lodged from January 1, 1985 onwards. Appeals made before then will remain with magistrates' courts.

22. On a point of law, an appeal against a decision of a Registered Homes Tribunal may be made to the High Court under Section 13(1) of the Tribunals and Inquiries Act 1971, as amended by para. 5(*b*) of Schedule 1 to the 1984 Act.

National list of cancelled registrations*

23. The Department will be keeping from January 1, 1985 a list of persons whose registration is cancelled in respect of the following types of home after that date: **4–086**
—residential care homes registered under Part I of the Registered Homes Act 1984
—nursing homes registered under Part II of the Registered Homes Act 1984
—voluntary children's homes registered under the Child Care Act 1980, Part VI

---

* "The national list that is maintained of people whose registrations have been cancelled has been extended to include the names of people whose application for registration in respect of a residential care home, nursing home or voluntary children's home has been refused on or after September 1, 1989 on the ground that he was not a fit person to run such a home; the list is not being extended to include refusals on other grounds, such as the suitability of the premises or the services to be provided at them.

    The procedure for a cancellation set out at Part C of the guidance notes issued with LAC (84)15 or at paragraphs 23 to 34 of Annex B to HC (84)21 should be followed with suitable adaptations. As a refusal of an application has immediate effect, form RH1 should be sent to the Department directly after an applicant has been notified of the refusal of the registration": Department of Health Circular No. LAC (89)12, paras. 7, 8.

When the Children's Homes Act 1982 is implemented the list will be extended to include the names of persons who had been carrying on a home in relationto which the registration under that Act had been withdrawn.

24. District health authorities in England and Wales having occasion to cancel such a registration after January 1, 1985 are asked to notify the Department at the following address that they have done this:

Department of Health and Social Security (HS3A)
Room 1220
Hannibal House
London
SE1 6TE

25. They should also notify the Department of any registration cancelled by an order of a justice of the peace under the urgent procedure for cancelling a registration.

26. The notification should be sent to the Department on the appropriate form, RH1 (specimen at Annex D). It should *not* be sent until the cancellation becomes operative. The order of a justice of the peace has immediate effect, even though there is a right of appeal against it to a Registered Homes Tribunal. However, the decision of a registration authority to cancel does not have effect for 28 days or, if an appeal is brought, until the appeal has been determined or abandoned. If the registered person is an organisation or a company, its name and the name and address of the chairman and secretary of the board of management should be given on form RH1.

27. Authorities are asked to record on form RH1 any other name that a previously registered person has or had, or any that the person is known to have used. For example, some married women continue to use their maiden name for professional purposes and in that case the married name and the maiden name should be notified. Authorities may also know of an alias used by a person whose registration has been cancelled. This should be given, but care should be taken by the authority that the allegation could be substantiated so as to avoid the risk of an action for defamation.

28. It is important to identify on form RH1 the precise statutory provision(s) under which the registration has been cancelled. This could be helpful to another registration authority considering a registration application subseqently from the person.

29. On receipt of a form RH1 the Department will immediately send a copy of it by recorded delivery or similar service to the person at his address, as on the form, and allow him a calendar month in which to notify any correction that may be needed before incorporating his name in the national list.

30. *Quarterly lists.* Once a quarter starting on April 1, 1985 the Department will send to each registration authority (*i.e.* district health authority and local social services authority) in England and Wales a copy of the current list of persons the cancellation of whose registration has been notified to it since January 1, 1985. Allowing for the time that the processing of a registration might be expected to take, it should not be necessary for authorities to approach the Department about any cancellations between issues of the quarterly lists: the list will be in the form of RH2 (specimen at Annex E).

31. *Normal procedures.* The maintenance of this national list of cancelled registrations supplements, but is not intended to replace, the procedure that registration authorities would be expected to apply in the normal way to satisfy themselves about the fitness for registration of an applicant. They should continue to take up relevant references and carefully check qualifications and periods of service or occupations with particular attention to unexplained gaps in the person's past history or periods of self-employment or any time spent outside this country. In this way they are more likely to pick up aliases against which the national list is unlikely to be a safeguard. An applicant should be informed by the registration authority if a person with the same name is entered in the national list even if there is doubt that they are one and the same person. Authorities will appreciate the sensitive nature of this list and the need to be vigilant in ensuring that persons are not unwittingly prejudiced by entries on it.

32. In registering a home, the DHA should make it clear that inaccuracy in the application may result in the cancellation of registration.

33. *Removal of names from national list.* A person's name would be removed from the national list of cancelled registrations, if a registration authority, aware that he had had a registration withdrawn, had subsequently decided to register him in respect of the same category of homes from which his registration had previously been withdrawn. For example, a person whose registration in respect of a nursing home had been withdrawn and who subsequently applied successfully to a DHA for registration of a nursing home would have his name removed from the national list. However, it would not be removed automatically if the subsequent registration had been with a local authority in respect of a residential care home. An authority registering a person whose name is on the list should send form RH3 (specimen at Annex F) to the Department at the address in paragraph 24 above.

34. A person whose name is not automatically removed from the list in the way mentioned in the preceding paragraph could apply to the Department to have it removed. For example, a

registration may have been cancelled because the fire precautions at a nursing home were considered inadequate. The person concerned may have applied subsequently with success to be registered in relation to a residential care home where fire precautions were satisfactory. Retention of his name on the list in such circumstances would be unlikely to be justified. However, it could if his nursing home registration had been cancelled because of activities which were dangerous to patients (*e.g.* use of stale blood for transfusions).

Children's consultancy service

35. An authority considering a registration application for a home, where children under the age of 18 are to be accommodated, may also make use of the consultancy services provided by the Department. This has more extensive coverage than the national list of cancelled registrations and would be an additional means for an authority to satisfy themselves whether anything was known about an applicant that might point to his unsuitability for a position of responsibiity for children's welfare. Written application for this service should be made to the Department:

4–087

    Children's Division A2
    Room B1309
    Alexander Fleming House
    Elephant and Castle
    London SE1 6BY

ANNEX C

DIRECTION

NATIONAL HEALTH SERVICE ACT 1977

REGISTERED HOMES ACT 1984

The Secretary of State for Social Services, in exercise of the powers conferred on him by Section 17 of the National Health Service Act 1977 and all other powers enabling him on that behalf, hereby gives the following Directions:—

4–088

1. Each District Health Authority is hereby directed, in the exercise of the functions relating to nursing homes and mental nursing homes which it has been directed to exercise:—
   (1) to secure that there shall be inspected any premises in its district which are not registered as a nursing home or a mental nursing home under Part II of the Registered Homes Act 1984 and which it has reason to believe should be so registered;
   (2) to specify in any notice service under Section 25(2) of the Registered Homes Act 1984, as a qualification which a nurse shall possess, that the nurse shall be registered in Part 1, 3, 5, 8 or 10 of the register maintained under the Nurses, Midwives and Health Visitors Act 1979(a).
2. The Nursing Homes (Qualifications of Nurses) Directions 1981 are hereby revoked.

Signed by authority of the
Secretary of State for
Social Services

A B BARTON
an Assistant Secretary of
the Department of Health
and Social Security

September 1984

ANNEXES D, E AND F

[*Forms RH1, RH2 and RH3 are reproduced in Annex II to the Guidance Notes issued with DHSS Circular No. (84)15.*]

4–089

CIRCULAR No. LAC (91)4

Dated March, 1991, and issued by the Department of Health, the Home Office (HOC 22/91) and the Welsh Office (WOC 12/91)

DISCLOSURE OF CRIMINAL BACKGROUND PROPRIETORS AND MANAGERS OF RESIDENTIAL CARE HOMES AND NURSING HOMES

This Circular will be cancelled on March 31, 1986.

Summary

4–090 This circular introduces procedures for checking with the police the possible criminal background of applicants for registration as owners or managers of residential care homes, nursing homes and mental nursing homes, and of applicants for managerial posts in local authority care homes.

Annex A explains the procedure; Annex B sets out a model local policy statement; Annex C is a model request for a police check; Annex D is a form of indemnity.

Action

4–091 The procedure described in Annex A comes into effect immediately. Local authorities and health authorities responsible for the registration of homes are asked to adopt it for gaining access to the police records described, and to nominate a senior officer to liaise with the police. The name of the nominated officer should be given to the police as soon as possible.

Background

4–092 1. These arrangements result from the decision to allow registration authorities access to criminal records held by the police. They are intended to reinforce the protection that registration and employing authorities give to people accommodated in care homes and nursing homes. They have been drawn up in consultation with representatives of health authorities, local authorities and the Association of Chief Police Officers.

2. In so far as it applies to local authorities this Circular is guidance issued under section 7(1) of the Local Authority Social Services Act 1970.

3. These new arrangements add to those already in place dealing with employees and others with access to children. The provisions of LAC (88)19[1] and HC (88)9[2] are reflected in this guidance to the extent that they apply in the context of residential care homes and nursing homes.

4. Some local authorities, including all those in Wales, have agreed terms with their local police forces under which requests for criminal records to be checked are accepted as part of the care home registration process. These local arrangements have been of value to the authorities concerned, who will need to compare the terms of their existing arrangements with the national scheme. Where local arrangements fall short of that scheme they should be revised. Local schemes need not be constrained by the national agreement if the authority and police force concerned agree on additional provisions consistent with the principles set out in this guidance.

Enquiries

4–093 5. Contact points for enquiries are:
From local authorities
 Community Services Division 1A
 Department of Health
 Room B1601
 Alexander Fleming House
 Elephant and Castle
 London SE1 6BY
 Tel: 071 972 4033

---

[1] Issued as a joint Circular by the Home Office (HOC 102/88), Department of Education and Science (DES 12/88), Department of Health (LAC (88)19, and the Welsh Office (WOC 45/88).

[2] Issued as a joint Circular by the Department of Health (HC (88)9), the Home Office (HOC 8/88), and the Welsh Office (WHC (88)10).

From health authorities:
    Priority and Health Services Division 4A
    Department of Health
    Room 313
    Eileen House
    89/94 Newington Causeway
    London SE1 6EF
    Tel: 071 972 2760

From Welsh authorities:
    Social Care Division
    Welsh Office
    Cathays Park
    Cardiff CF1 3NQ
    Tel: 0222 823096

From the police:
    Mr F E Whittaker
    F2 Division
    Home Office
    50 Queen Anne's Gate
    London SW1H 9AT
    Tel: 071 273 3716

Annex A

DISCLOSURE OF CRIMINAL BACKGROUND: PROPRIETORS AND MANAGERS OF RESIDENTIAL CARE HOMES

Scope

1. Subject to the restrictions set out in paragraphs 3 and 9 health authorities and local authorities with responsibilities under the Registered Homes Act 1984 ("the Act") may ask the police to undertake a check on
   - any applicant for registration under Part I of the Act (residential care homes);
   - any applicant for registration under Part II of the Act (nursing homes) including the person proposed by the applicant to be in charge of the nursing home;
   - any applicant for appointment as an officer in charge[1] of a residential care home established under Part III of the National Assistance Act 1948 or Section 21 of the National Health Service Act 1977;

where the application was received on or after April 2, 1991 or was under consideration at that date.

2. Checks may also be made in exceptional circumstances on such persons already in post or already registered under the Act. The use of this facility is governed by certain conditions. These are explained in paragraph 17.

3. As a general rule, checks should *not* be sought on people such as directors or senior staff of established national or regional voluntary organisations or established private companies with an interest in the provision of nursing or residential care who may submit an application for registration but who will not themselves be closely involved in the day to day management of the home. It is not intended to stop checks being made—subject to the general constraints imposed by the scheme—
   - where the applicant or company involved is new to health or social care and possibly unknown to the authority, or
   - where there are grounds for concern about a named individual likely to be in contact with residents or with responsibility for residents' affairs.

4. These provisions will apply automatically to residential care homes with fewer than 4 residents if and when the owners of those homes are required to register under the Act.

---

[1] The term officer in charge is used to describe the senior member of staff in a particular local authority home, and any manager with day to day responsibility for running two or more homes.

The police check

4–095 5. In all cases the police check will be made against the index to the national collection of criminal records maintained on the Police National Computer (PNC). These records include details of
- persons convicted of all offences, broadly speaking, for which a term of imprisonment may be given; and
- persons who are to be prosecuted for such offences.

A complete list of the offences reported to the National Identification Bureau and held in the national collection of criminal records is shown in Appendix F to Home Office Circular No 88/1985; and is available separately from the Home Office on request.

6. Subject to paragraph 4 of the main Circular the police will not normally examine
- local police records of minor offences and
- information not recorded nationally.

The structure of local criminal record systems varies and in general information held locally will be of little value to the registration or selection process. Police forces will however consider checking and disclosing such records in specific cases if the authority concerned makes a separate written request stating why a check might yield relevant information about a particular applicant. Any information disclosed will be limited to convictions not recorded centrally or factual information which the police would be prepared to present as evidence before a court or tribunal. Information about acquittals or decisions not to prosecute where the circumstances of the case give cause for concern may also be given. Information from local records, other than details of convictions, should be disclosed only on the authority of a police officer of ACPO rank.

7. In cases where the police agree exceptionally to check local records, the police force handling the request may seek information from other police forces. The check may then take considerably longer to complete.

Senior nominated officer

4–096 8. A senior officer in each local authority or health authority to which these arrangements apply (*e.g.* assistance director of social services) should take responsibility for requesting checks from the police. Authorities should give their local police force details of their senior nominated officer as soon as possible. He or she should be personally responsible for
- overseeing the operation of the checking procedure within the authority,
- ensuring that requests fall within the terms of this Circular,
- ensuring that requests are made at the right time,
- ensuring that information received from the police is released only to those who need to see it, and
- ensuring that records are kept securely and destroyed after use.

Procedure

4–097 9. Police checks must not take the place of normal registration procedures.
- Other checks to establish a person's integrity and fitness to own and manage a home must be carried out first and unexplained gaps in employment satisfactorily accounted for.
- The Department of Health's list of cancelled and refused registrations should be consulted.

A police check should not be made until all other enquiries have been completed, nor should a check be made if an applicant is found unsuitable for other reasons.

10. In considering applications from potential owners and managers of homes, authorities should ask applicants to declare any previous convictions, bringing to their attention these arrangements and the effect of the Rehabilitation of Offenders Act 1974 (Exceptions) Order 1975 which allows authorities, in these circumstances, to ask for spent convictions to be disclosed.

11. An applicant should give his or her permission in writing for a police check to be carried out. It should be made clear to the applicant that refusal could jeopardise the application.

12. Authorities should make every effort to confirm the identity of the applicant before the police are asked to run a check. Verification of identity, date of birth and of any change of name should be obtained. Incomplete or incorrect information may invalidate the police check and lead to a failure to discover relevant convictions.

13. Registration authorities familiar with the child protection arrangements may already use the sample policy statement included as an Annex to Circular LAC (88)19[1]. Authorities may wish to consider making a similar statement available to people who may be subject to a criminal records check under these arrangements. A model statement is offered at Annex B.

14. When a police check is necessary, the request should be sent to the Chief Officer of the police force for the area in which the applicant has applied to work. Requests should be made in a form consistent with the model layout shown at Annex C. Where the senior nominated officer has grounds for requesting a check against local records a letter explaining the reasons for the request should accompany the standard form.

15. The police will reply to the senior nominated officer either indicating that there is no trace on national police records of a record which matches the details provided, or that those details appear identical with the person whose record will be attached. The record will contain details of all convictions recorded nationally against that person.

16. Where
- the information provided by the police differs from that provided by the applicant, and is of significance, the authority must discuss the discrepancy with the applicant before reaching any final decision in which the nature of the information received is a factor;
- there is disagreement, the person should have the opportunity to see the information provided by the police.

A person who believes the information is incorrect and who wishes to make representations to the police should do so in the first place through the senior nominated officer.

Checks on persons already registered or in post

17. Checks should not normally be made on persons already registered or in post. If however serious allegations are made against an owner or manager, or previously unrevealed information comes to light and the senior nominated officer is satisfied that that information cannot be verified in any other way, a police check may be requested. This must not be done without the knowledge of the individual concerned who must be given an opportunity to discuss the outcome of the check. Chief officers of police may wish to ensure that decisions to disclose convictions in these circumstances are taken at a senior level.   **4–098**

Use of information

18. The fact that a person has a criminal record or is known to the police does not necessarily mean that he or she is unfit to run a home. The authority concerned must make a balanced judgment about a person's suitability taking into account only those offences which are considered relevant to the job or situation in question. A person's suitability should be looked at as a whole in the light of all the information available.   **4–099**

19. In deciding the relevance of convictions, authorities will want to bear in mind that offences which took place many years in the past may often have less relevance than recent offences. Similarly, a pattern of unrelated or similar offences over a period of time is more likely to give cause for concern than an isolated minor conviction. In any event the importance of rehabilitation must be weighed against the need to protect those in care.

Storage and destruction of records

20. Any information the police supply will be of a sensitive and personal nature. It must be used only in connection with the application which gave rise to the request for a check to be made. The senior nominated officer must ensure it is kept securely while the registration or appointment process takes its course. Once the process is complete the information should be destroyed. An indication on the permanent record that a check with the police has been carried out may be made but should not refer to specific offences.   **4–100**

Checks on applicants from overseas

21. Other than in exceptional circumstances, the police cannot   **4–101**
- make enquiries about the antecedents of people from overseas or
- establish details of convictions acquired outside the United Kingdom.

Applicants from certain EC countries may, however, be able to produce certificates of good conduct.

---

[1] Issued as a joint circular by the Home Office (HOC 102/88). Department of Education and Science (DES 12/88). Department of Health (LAC (88) 19), and the Welsh Office (WOC 45/88).

Police reporting of convictions as they occur

4–102   22. If a police force is able to identify that the owner or manager of a home has acquired a relevant conviction, it will give details to the local senior nominated officer. This will occur only where the police are aware that a person is registered under the Act or employed as a care home manager and so will not mean that the nominated officer will automatically get information about all relevant convictions.

Police indemnity

4–103   23. The police must be indemnified against any liability incurred as a result of providing information under these arrangements. The indemnity is in Annex D. It differs from that which authorities have given in the past and has been drawn up with the aim of meeting some of the objections levelled against its predecessor: for example, it no longer indemnifies the police against their own negligence. It is intended that the new indemnity will be applied to any new disclosure arrangements agreed by the police service but the police service has emphasised that it cannot undertake to substitute the new indemnity for the old in any existing arrangements outside the scope of this Circular.

Police monitoring

4–104   24. The Home Office and ACPO will monitor the use of these arrangements and where possible forces are asked to collate the following information in respect of each authority with which they deal.
- number of PNC checks requested,
- number of retrospective checks requested,
- number of local records searches requested,
- time taken to process checks,
- number of positives traces, and
- any apparent difficulties with these arrangements.

Additional copies of Home Office list of reportable offences (paragraph 5)

4–105   25. Copies of this list may be obtained from
Miss S.A. O'Donnell
F7 Division
Home Office
Horseferry House
Dean Ryle Street
London SW1P 2AW
Telephone No. 071 217 8148

Enquiries

4–106   26. Contact points for enquiries are:
From local authorities:
Community Services Division 1A
Department of Health
Room B1601
Alexander Fleming House
Elephant and Castle
London SE1 6BY
Telephone: 071 972 4033

From health authorities:
Priority and Health Services Division 4A
Department of Health
Room 313
Eileen House
89/94 Newington Causeway
London SE1 6EF
Telephone: 071 972 2760

From Welsh authorities:
Social Care Division
Welsh Office
Cathays Park
Cardiff CF1 3NQ
Telephone: 0222 823096

From the police:
Mr F E Whittaker
F2 Division
Home Office
50 Queen Anne's Gate
London SW1H 9AT
Telephone: 071 273 3716

Annex B

STATEMENT OF POLICY ABOUT RELEVANT CONVICTIONS
(PARAGRAPH 17)

4–107

Authorities may wish to consider using the following statement suitably adapted to reflect local policy and the circumstances of the different groups of people to whom it will be addressed:

"The job of running a residential care home or nursing home entails substantial contact and involvement with vulnerable people. You are therefore required to declare any convictions or cautions you may have, even if they would otherwise be regarded as 'spent' under the Rehabilitation of Offenders Act 1974. The information you give will be treated in confidence and will only be taken into account in relation to your application [for registration/for the post of . . .] to which the exception from the 1974 Act applies. The [registration] authority is also entitled, under arrangements introduced for the protection of people in residential or nursing home care, to check with the police for the existence and content of any criminal record held in the name of an [applicant/person in charge of a home]. Information received from the police will be kept in strict confidence and will be destroyed immediately the decision on the application [for registration] has been made. The disclosure of a criminal record or other information will not debar you from [appointment/registration] unless the authority considers that the conviction renders you unsuitable. In making this decision the authority will consider the nature of the offence, how long ago and what age you were when it was committed and any other factors which may be relevant.

If you would like to discuss what effect a conviction might have on your application you may telephone [A. N. Other on 12-345-6789] in confidence, for advice."

Annex C

[LOCAL AUTHORITY OR HEALTH AUTHORITY HEADING]

REQUEST FOR POLICE CHECK IN RESPECT OF APPLICATION FOR REGISTRATION UNDER REGISTERED HOMES ACT 1984 (OR EQUIVALENT LOCAL AUTHORITY POST)

4–108

A.   To be completed by applicant in BLOCK CAPITALS.

I have applied for registration under the Registered Homes Act 1984.*

It has been proposed by an applicant for registration under the Registered Homes Act 1984 that I should be the person in charge of a nursing home.*

I have applied for the post of manager of a local authority residential care home.*

[* delete the sentences which do not apply]

I understand that this is a post subject to a police record check. This has been explained to me and I am aware that spent convictions may be disclosed. I hereby declare that the information I have given below is true and I give my consent to a check being made.

.... (Signature) .... (Date)
Surname .... All Forenames ....
Maiden Name .... Any Previous Surnames ....
Date of Birth ..../........./......... Place of Birth .... Sex M/F
Present Address ....

Previous addresses in last 5 years   Date from   and to:
....
....
....

HAVE YOU EVER BEEN CONVICTED AT A COURT OR CAUTIONED BY THE POLICE FOR ANY OFFENCE? YES/NO

If yes provide details overleaf, including approximate date, the offence, and the court or police force which dealt with you.

B. To be completed by the Senior Nominated Officer.

The person identified above satisfies the conditions for requesting a police check set out in Joint Circular LAC (91)4, HC (91)16, WOC 12/91, HOC 22/91. The details provided have been verified and I am satisfied they are accurate.

.... (Signed) .... (Date)

C. For Police Use Only.   Ref.: ─────────

PNC Records have been checked against the above details:

_____ No trace on details supplied   _____ The subject appears identical with the person whose criminal record is attached.

.... (Signed) .... (Date)

ALL FORMS TO BE RETURNED UNDER "CONFIDENTIAL" COVER

ANNEX D

FORM OF INDEMNITY

4–109 1. In consideration of the provision of information in accordance with [*insert details of agreement or arrangement under which information is to be supplied*] [*insert name of authority granting indemnity*] undertakes to indemnify any of the persons or any authority referred to in paragraph 2 below against liability which may be incurred by such person or authority as a result of the provision of such information.

Provided that this indemnity shall not apply:
  (*a*) where the liability arises from information supplied which is shown to have been incomplete or incorrect, unless the person or authority claiming the benefit of this indemnity establishes that the error did not result from any wilful wrongdoing or negligence on his or its part or on the part of any other person or authority referred to in paragraph 2 below;
  (*b*) unless the person or authority claiming the benefit of this indemnity notifies [*insert name of authority granting indemnity*] as soon as possible of any action, claim or demand to which this indemnity applies, permits [*insert name of authority granting indemnity*] to deal with the action, claim or demand by settlement or otherwise and renders [*insert name of authority granting indemnity*] all reasonable assistance in so dealing;
  (*c*) to the extent that the person or authority claiming the benefit of the indemnity makes any admission which may be prejudicial to the defence of the action, claim or demand.
  2. Persons who may claim the benefit of this indemnity are as follows:
  (*a*) any police authority
  (*b*) any chief officer of police
  (*c*) any serving or former member of a police force
  (*d*) any serving or former civilian employee of a police authority,
and in this paragraph the expressions "police authority", "chief officer of police" and "police force" have the same meaning as in section 62 of the Police Act 1964.

CIRCULAR No. LAC (92)10

Dated September 1992, and issued by the Department of Health

REGISTERED HOMES ACT 1984

REGISTERED HOMES (AMENDMENT) ACT 1991 AND COMMENCEMENT ORDER 1992

RESIDENTIAL CARE HOMES (AMENDMENT) (NO. 2) REGULATIONS

Summary

4–110

This Circular gives local authorities guidance about the implementation of the Registered Homes (Amendment) Act 1991 and the Residential Care Homes (Amendment) (No. 2) Regulations 1992. The guidance is issued under Section 7 of the Local Authority Social Services Act 1970 (which places a duty on local authorities to act under the guidance of the Secretary of State). It also explains the effect of amendment of the regulations on inspection.

4–111

I. SMALL RESIDENTIAL CARE HOMES

Provisions of the Act and Regulations

1. The Annex to LASSL (91)7 outlined the provisions of the Registered Homes (Amendment) Act 1991 which removes the general exemption from registration conferred on private and voluntary residential care homes with fewer than four residents by the Registered Homes Act 1984.

2. The Residential Care Homes (Amendment) (No. 2) Regulations 1992 modify the Residential Care Homes Regulations 1984 in their application to small homes (that is homes with fewer than four residents, excluding staff and their relatives). A number of the provisions found in the 1984 Regulations are not extended to small homes in line with the single registration criterion and with Ministers' announced intention to apply a lighter touch to such homes.

3. In addition new regulations are made which apply only to small homes and deal with:
   (*a*) the timing and content of annual returns (Regulation 25 and Schedule 4: Amending Regulations 10 and 14);
   (*b*) the exemption from the requirement to register under the 1991 Act of homes providing residential care for children who are subject to the foster placement provisions of the Children Act 1989 (Regulation 24: Amending Regulation 10).

Timetable for implementation

4–112

4. The Registered Homes (Amendment) Act 1991 Commencement Order 1992 brings the Amendment Act into force on April 1, 1993. From that date it will be an offence to operate an unregistered small residential care home which is not exempt from the requirement to register. Where an application for registration has been made by that date the home will be deemed to be registered until such time as the application has been determined and any appeal rights exhausted (Section 2(3) of the Amendment Act).

5. The Amendment Regulations will take effect on April 1, 1993. By virtue of the Interpretation Act 1978, local authorities can now begin to receive and process registration applications. Any decisions taken will take effect from 1 April 1993 when the Regulations and Act come into force. Appeals can also be dealt with during the interim period although again any decisions will not take effect until April 1, 1993.

Guidance on implementation

4–113

6. Annex A gives guidance on the implementation of the new legislation. Authorities will particularly want to note what is said about the need to publicise the new requirements (paragraph 28 of Annex A).

II. INSPECTION

4–114

7. Paragraphs 29 and 30 of Annex A explain the implications, for residential care homes of all sizes, of the amendment which has been made to Regulation 18 of the Residential Care Homes Regulations 1984, which relates to inspection.

References to regulations

4–115 8. In this Circular unqualified references to a regulation number are to regulations in the Residential Care Homes Regulations 1984, as amended by the present Amending Regulations. References to "Amending Regulation . . . " are to the Residential Care Homes (Amendment) (No. 2) Regulations 1992.

Action

4–116 9. Authorities should take action to implement the Registered Homes (Amendment) Act 1991 and the Residential Care Homes (Amendment) (No. 2) Regulations 1992 drawing on the guidance given in this Circular. They should also take account of the amendment made to Regulation 18 (inspection), which is not restricted to small homes.

Enquiries

4–117 10. Any enquiries about this Circular should be made to:
Community Services 1A (CS1A)
217 Wellington House
133–136 Waterloo Road
London SE1 8UG
Tel: 071–972–4032 or 4033 (direct line)

GUIDANCE ON IMPLEMENTATION OF REGISTERED HOMES (AMENDMENT) ACT 1991 AND THE RESIDENTIAL CARE HOMES (AMENDMENT) (NO. 2) REGULATIONS

4–118   INDEX TO SUBJECTS COVERED

PARA. NO.

I. SMALL RESIDENTIAL CARE HOMES

1, 2	Registration, de-registration.
3, 4	Lighter touch for small homes—application of Regulation 10 and related provisions, caselaw and guidance.
5	Staffing.
6, 7	Waiver or subsidy of fees.
8	Fees on expansion to cater for 4 or more residents.
9–12	Inspection, annual returns.
13, 14	Local authority registers, certificates of registration.
15–17	Adult placement, respite care and similar schemes.
18	Members of religious communities.
19–21	Homes and schools catering for children.
22	Occasional provision of care.
23, 24	Dual registration/nursing homes.
25	Categories of residents catered for.
26	Medicines.
27	Application of other legislation to small homes.
28	Publicity.

II. INSPECTION

29, 30	Inspection.

APPENDICES: SMALL RESIDENTIAL CARE HOMES

1	Draft publicity/information
2.	Sample annual return form

I. SMALL RESIDENTIAL CARE HOMES

Registration, de-registration

4–119 1. The only basis on which registration of a small home may be refused is that a person involved in running that home is not a fit person to do so. Authorities are reminded that in checking on fitness they may make use of the procedures for seeking police checks on criminal records described in Circular LAC (91)4.

2. The grounds on which the registration of a small home may be cancelled are the same as those for larger homes, that is where:
— the reasons for cancellation are reasons which would entitle the registration authority to refuse an application for registration
— the annual fee is not paid on time
— the person registered has been convicted of an offence under the Act, or someone else has been convicted of an offence under the Act in respect of the home
— a condition in force in respect of the home has not been complied with

with the addition of:
— failure to submit an annual return in accordance with the statutory requirements.

While the adequacy of accommodation, staffing, services and facilities are not grounds in themselves for the refusal of registration and cannot therefore automatically form the basis of de-registration it may prove possible to demonstrate that failures in such areas are indicative that the person running the home is not fit to do so. The urgent procedures for cancellation of registration may be used.

Lighter touch for small homes—application of Regulation 10 and related provisions, caselaw and guidance

3. Ministers intend that a lighter touch should be applied to small homes. Following consultation, some provisions applying to larger homes have not been applied to small homes in an attempt to keep, in particular, specific additional requirements on those providing care to a necessary minimum. Authorities are not expected to check routinely on compliance with the remaining part of Regulation 10 or on other requirements about the situation in the home, *e.g.* record-keeping. If they do need to decide for any reason whether such provisions are being complied with they should bear the need for a lighter touch in mind, and make use of the scope Regulation 10 and other Regulations already provide to assess the adequacy of provision in the light of the size of home as well as the numbers and types of residents.   **4–120**

4. The precedents formed by the decisions of the Courts under the 1984 Act will have to be considered in the light of the more limited statutory requirements relating to small homes. Similarly, such considerations will have to underlie the interpretation of the decisions of Tribunals and also the application of guidance such as *Home Life*.

Staffing

5. In small homes care will often be provided mainly by the registered person, perhaps with assistance from members of their family or others on a voluntary basis. Paid staff will not always be employed. Authorities should take account of all such assistance provided when considering whether staffing levels in the home are adequate (Regulation 10(1)(*a*)).   **4–121**

Waiver or subsidy of fees

6. The Amendment Act (Sections 1(4) and (5)) gives local authorities powers to waive registration and annual fees in respect of small homes in whole or in part. The (maximum) fee levels laid down by regulations are intended to reflect local authority costs where they have to carry out in full the relevant checks. The intention is that the scheme should be self-financing. Authorities are likely to be able to waive costs therefore if the action that they need to take in any case is significantly reduced, *e.g.* where they have already made equivalent checks under an adult placement scheme, or there is an application for dual registration and some checks have already been made by the health authority. There is unlikely to be the same scope for cost saving and waiver of annual fees since annual returns are required in respect of all small homes.   **4–122**

7. If authorities instead decide to subsidise the registration function in order to reduce the fees payable by particular groups/organisations or to pay any fees on their behalf, the appropriate financial transfer must be made. Any sums transferred in this way should be included when returns of fee income from small homes are made.

Fees on expansion to cater for 4 or more residents

8. If a home expands to cater for 4 or more residents the registered person must either: **4–123**
(i) apply for a variation in the conditions of registration; *or*
(ii) submit a fresh application for registration (and pay the appropriate registration fee).

Regulation 5 (Amending Regulation 4) provides that where the first option is chosen the next annual fee payable shall be increased by the difference between the registration fee for small homes and that for other homes. This is to meet authorities' costs in carrying out the additional checks involved in the registration of larger homes.

Inspection, annual returns

4–124 9. In view of the single registration criterion and the need to protect the family atmosphere of small homes authorities are neither required nor expected to inspect small homes either on registration or regularly thereafter. Powers of inspection (Section 17 of the Registered Homes Act 1984) apply equally however to small homes and authorities may use them if they consider it appropriate *e.g.* on receipt of a complaint.

10. Where inspection of a small home is proposed liaison with any other authorities (*e.g.* the fire service) which might also need to carry out inspections will be important. The aim should be to keep disruption to residents to a minimum.

11. Authorities will keep in touch with small homes through the return the registered person is required to complete annually. Details of the information to be given in annual returns are in the new Schedule 4 (Amending Regulation 14) and a sample form which authorities may copy or adapt for their own use is at Appendix 2. Authorities may wish to consider including in their covering letter a reminder that registered persons are under an obligation to report various changes as they occur and should not wait for the next annual return before doing so. Authorities should use these returns to help identify matters which might require further investigation *e.g.* has anyone known to be unsuitable moved in or started working there, is the person running it able to cater for the categories of residents? (Authorities cannot insist on the provision of information beyond that specified in Schedule 4 to the Regulations.)

12. The Regulations provide in most cases for the returns to show not only the current position but also whether there has been any change since the last return (or registration in the case of the first annual return) to make authorities task in spotting significant changes easier.

Local authority registers, certificates of registration

4–125 13. Schedule 3 (Amending Regulation 13) requires authorities to indicate in their registers whether the certificate of registration relates to a small home. This is so that it will be clear to those consulting those registers which registration criteria have been applied. Authorities may wish to maintain a separate register for small homes, although this is not a statutory requirement. They may also wish to provide advice about the different requirements applying to small homes. Authorities may want to consider indicating on registration certificates where registration is a small home.

14. Schedule 3 (Amending Regulation 13) provides for contacts for enquiries, other than the home, to be included in registers. This is to help shield carers from unwanted enquiries. They may for instance give an adult placement scheme organiser as the enquiry point.

Adult placement, respite care and similar schemes

4–126 15. Whilst not exempt from the requirement to register, carers who operate within adult placement, respite care or similar schemes managed by a local authority or other organisation only come within the scope of the Registered Homes Act 1984 if they provide not only residential accommodation but also both board and personal care for those in need of personal care for the reasons specified in Section 1 of the Act (see Circular LAC (84)15 for further guidance). Otherwise registration is not appropriate.

16. Where some or all of the homes forming an adult placement scheme satisfy the definition in Section 1 (and so have to be registered) authorities may find that checks already made on individuals carers can—in so far as they cover the same grounds as those they would otherwise make under the Registered Homes Act—safely be taken to satisfy registration requirements. It would clearly be wrong if the registration process duplicated checks already properly made by the registration authority or some other reputable body.

17. While responsibility for compliance with the legislation is necessarily placed on the registered person this does not mean that they cannot be assisted in fulfilling these responsibilities. In the case of adult placement schemes for example the scheme organiser might compile information for them or pay fees in respect of all registered homes in the scheme, or might assist with the investigation of complaints.

Members of religious communities

4–127 18. Authorities are reminded that members of religious communities needing care may be among those who count as relatives under Section 19 of the 1984 Act if they have lived with the person providing care for five years or more.

Homes and schools for children

4–128 19. Section 1(5) of the 1984 Act which exempts those running homes registered under the Children Act 1989 and certain schools from the requirement to register as residential care homes is not altered by the 1991 Amendment Act. By virtue of the 1992 Regulations those running homes catering for three or fewer disabled children are also now exempt from the requirement to register as small homes under the Registered Homes Act where the children are covered instead by Children Act 1989 fostering provisions (new Regulation 24, Amending Regulation 10 refers).

20. This means that children will only come within the provisions of the Registered Homes (Amendment) Act 1991 where the fostering provisions of the Children Act do not apply for any reason, or where there are children and adults requiring care (other than people employed in the home or their relatives) in the same home.

21. Despite the intention to apply a "lighter touch" to small homes, the majority of regulations specific to children have been retained unaltered so as to keep important safeguards for children in line with other legislation relating to children.

Occasional provision of care

22. Authorities are reminded of the guidance in paragraph A17 of the Annex to Circular LAC (84)15 about the impracticability of registering those providing care only occasionally.   **4–129**

Dual registration/nursing homes

23. Section 1(4) of the Registered Homes Act 1984 as amended continues the previous option under which nursing homes having fewer than 4 residential care places could register under Part I of the Act—as if they had more than 4 such places. Where this option is chosen, the fee levels and all other requirements of the Act applying to larger homes will apply to these residential care places in the home concerned. Section 2(4) of the (Amendment) Act deems any nursing home already registered in this way on the day the (Amendment) Act comes into force to have opted not to be treated as a small home in respect of its residential care places. Options may however be changed at a later date.   **4–130**

24. Where homes are already registered as nursing homes the local authority should liaise with the health authority concerned to see for example what checks on fitness have already been made.

Categories of residents catered for

25. Where a home caters for a succession of short stay residents, it may be helpful to register the person running it for the maximum numbers and full range of categories of resident that person is considered fit to cater for, to avoid the need for frequent revision of the conditions of registration.   **4–131**

Medicines

26. In applying Regulation 10(1)(q) (recording, safekeeping, handling and disposal of medicines) and the related provisions in Schedule 2, paragraphs 4 and 6 to small homes authorities should consider how far special arrangements for medicines are necessary in individual homes in view of the needs of the particular residents.   **4–132**

Application of other legislation to small homes

27. The "lighter touch" approach being adopted in the regulation of small homes has resulted in some modification of the regulations under the 1984 Act as applied to such homes. But it should be noted that this does not modify other legislation which is relevant to small homes, for instance that relating to fire precautions and food safety.   **4–133**

Publicity

28. While those affected by the Amendment Act are in law responsible for applying for registration, local authorities should publicise the change in their area. They may like to consider making use of the draft at Appendix 1 which gives basic written information about the Act. Authorities may reproduce this, with or without modifications such as the addition of local details.   **4–134**

II. INSPECTION

29. The Department's re-examination of the Regulations made in 1984 revealed that parts of Regulation 18 go beyond the powers to make regulations provided in Section 17 of the Registered Homes Act 1984. The Amending Regulations therefore replace the existing provisions on inspection by one which retains only the requirement for inspection of homes at least twice a year, which the Act allows. This requirement is not imposed on small homes.   **4–135**

30. Regulation 18(2)—which requires for the registered person to provide such information as the authority might reasonably require as to the conduct of the home on inspection—is effectively revoked by Amending Regulation 9. This should have little effect in practice on the conduct of inspections. Section 17 of the 1984 Act provides that powers of inspection include powers to inspect any records required to be kept under the Act and Regulations, and makes obstruction of inspection an offence.

Draft Publicity/Information About the Act and Regulations

Do you provide residential care for anyone?

4–136 If so this leaflet explains how you may be affected by the Registered Homes (Amendment) Act 1991 which comes into force on April 1, 1993 and the action you may need to take before then.

Who will be affected by the Act?

4–137 * Almost anyone who provides care on a residential basis for between one and three people who need personal care because of old age, disablement, past or present mental disorder or dependence on alcohol or drugs. (Further details of what is meant by "residential care" and about people who do not need to register are given later.)

What do I need to do?

4–138 * Anyone providing the type of residential care outlined must register with their local authority by April 1, 1993. (After that date it will be an offence to run an unregistered small home.)

* Contact your local authority about registration. They will send you the appropriate forms to complete and give you any necessary supporting information. *Do this as soon as possible, as you need to return your completed form by April 1, 1993.* (If the authority has not decided by that date whether your application can be accepted they will treat it as if it has been accepted until a decision has been reached.)

* Most people will need to pay a fee on registration and annually thereafter. The normal registration fee is £230, and the annual fee £30 per home. Your local authority will advise whether there is any basis on which they can reduce or waive the fees in your case—but this is only likely to be possible if they have already checked on you and the home you run for some other reason (*e.g.* if you care for someone for them under a placement scheme).

What conditions do I need to satisfy?

4–139 * The main condition is that you should be a person considered fit to run a home for the number and type of people you intend to care for.

* You also need to comply with the basic rules laid down in regulations about such matters as the way in which the home is run, the accommodation and facilities which should be provided for residents and the records to be kept. These rules have been kept to a minimum to try to avoid placing undue burdens on people providing care, while still giving protection to residents on essential matters. Your local authority can give further details.

What is meant by "residential care"?

4–140 * Residential care is the provision of residential accommodation, food and personal care (help with physical and/or emotional needs) for anyone in the groups listed at the beginning of this leaflet.

* It does not make any difference if the accommodation is provided in your own home or in a special building, whether or not you get paid for providing the care, or if you are part of an adult placement scheme or similar arrangement.

* If you provide nursing care places you should be registered with the health authority as a person running a nursing home. If you provide both nursing care and residential care places you will need to be "dually registered" (that is with both the health authority and the social services authority).

Are there any people who do not have to register?

4–141 * You do not need to register under the Act if the only people you provide care for are relatives (see below), children you are fostering (but you will instead need to comply with rules relating to fostering) or children in certain schools or other establishments. (If you think that any of these exceptions may apply to you, check with your local authority—see below.)

Who count as relatives in the paragraph above?

* Relatives are husbands, wives, sons and daughters, fathers and mothers, brothers and sisters, grandparents or grandchildren and anyone else from whom you are descended, or who is descended from you, and aunts and uncles, nephews and nieces. There are also detailed rules including in some circumstances those living together as husband and wife, step children, and half-blood relationships. In addition people who are not related to you are counted as relatives if they have been ordinarily living with you for the past five years. Please ask your local authority for further details if you think that these special rules might apply to you. **4–142**

Where can I get further information?

* Contact your local authority registration section (often within the inspection unit and part of the social services department) as soon as possible for any further information and advice you need. *Remember to do this in good time to allow them to advise you and for you to submit your application before April 1, 1993.* **4–143**

* You can buy copies of the Registered Homes Act 1984, the Residential Care Homes Regulations 1984, the Registered Homes (Amendment) Act 1991, the Residential Care Homes (Amendment) (No. 2) Regulations 1992, and also if you wish earlier Amendment Regulations made in 1986, 1988, and 1992, from Her Majesty's Stationery Office, or from some local authorities. Or you may be able to consult copies at your local or a central library.

SAMPLE ANNUAL RETURN FORM
(Paragraphs 11 and 12 of Annex A refer)

ANNUAL RETURN   Name of person registered ....

(Regulation 25, Schedule 4 of the Residential Care Homes Regulations 1984, as amended by the Residential Care Homes (Amendment) (No. 2) Regulations 1992.) To be completed by the person registered in respect of a small residential care home.

1. About the home	Current details	Is this a change?* Yes/No	For official use only
(a) Its name			
(b) Its address (including postal code)			
(c) Its telephone number			

2. About residents receiving care

For each resident, please state their sex, age and category.

	SEX	CAT	Under 18 YES/NO	65 or over YES/NO	Bedfast† YES/NO	Is this a change? YES/NO	Is s/he a new resident since the last return?‡ YES/NO
Example	M	I	NO	NO	NO	NO	NO
1							
2							
3							

CATEGORIES:
I = Old age (not falling within any other category)
MP = Mental disorder, other than mental handicap
MH = Mental handicap (learning disability)
A = Alcohol dependence
D = Drug dependence
PH = Physical disablement

* If "yes", in the earlier columns please ring the details which have changed since the last annual return (or application for registration if this is the first annual return).

† i.e. permanently confined to bed (other than because of a short-term illness)

‡ or application for registration if this is the first return

	For official use only
3. <u>People living or working in the home</u> Please complete the separate sheets attached (questions 3a and b).	
4. Since the last return (or application for registration if this is the first annual return), how many residents have: (a) Moved out of the home? .... (b) Died? .... Please give cause of death in each case	
5. I certify that the information in this return (including that on other sheets) is, to the best of my knowledge, accurate and complete. Signature of registered person .... Name in block capitals .... Date	
<u>Other information</u> You may use this space to give any other information you wish to provide to the registration authority.	

I enclose the annual fee of £ .... payable in respect of the home.

(Please give explanation if fee not enclosed.)

3. a) **People involved in the management running or provision of care in the home, whether on a paid or voluntary basis (including family members)**

Full name: forenames, followed by surname (and any previous names in brackets below that)	Date of birth	Relevant qualifications and experience (state type and length)	Changes*	Details of any criminal convictions*	For official use only
1. The registered person in control of the home					

(a) Address & Tel No. if different from that of home:

Tel No.:

180

2. Any separate manager of the home

(b) Address & Tel No. if different from that of home:

Tel No.:

3. Other

* Any changes since the last return (or application for registration if this is the first annual return)—please give any explanatory notes here, and in the earlier columns ring the details which have changed.

* Since the last return or since application for registration in the case of the first annual return. Include details of convictions which would otherwise be regarded as 'spent' under the Rehabilitation of Offenders Act 1984.

3. Cont'd. b) People living in the home not already included at 3(a) above (excluding residents receiving care)

Full name: forenames, followed by surname (and any previous names in brackets below)	Date of birth	Relevant qualifications and experience (state type and length)	Changes*	Details of any criminal convictions*#	For official use only
4.					
5.					
6.					
7.					

* Any changes since the last return (or application for registration if this is the first annual return)—please give any explanatory notes here, and in the earlier columns ring the details which have changed.

Since the last return or since application for registration in the case of the first annual return. <u>Include details of convictions which would otherwise be regarded as 'spent' under the Rehabilitation of Offenders Act 1984.</u>

CIRCULAR No. LAC (92)24

Dated December, 1992, and issued by the Department of Health

LOCAL AUTHORITY CONTRACTS FOR RESIDENTIAL AND NURSING HOME CARE: NHS RELATED ASPECTS

Summary

1. This Circular sets out local authority and NHS responsibilities, from April 1993, for funding community health services for residents of residential care and nursing homes who have been placed in those homes by local authorities. The attached note sets out the responsibilities. It has also been sent to health authorities under cover of HSG (92)50. **4–145**

Action

2. Local authorities are asked to take the following action: **4–146**
   (i) to ensure that the nursing home care that is funded by them includes the provision of all general nursing care services (including incontinence services and aids but not specialist incontinence advice). Their contracts with the independent sector must ensure that general nursing care services are fully provided.
   (ii) to discuss and agree with NHS purchasers the arrangements for supplying specialist nursing (primarily continence advice and stoma care, but also other specialists nursing such as diabetic liaison) and other community health services (primarily physiotherapy, speech and language therapy and chiropody) that will be provided to residents placed in nursing homes by local authorities.

Enquiries

3. Enquiries about this Circular should be made to Mr P. R. Evans, CS4A, Room 215 Wellington House, 133–155 Waterloo Road, London SE1 8UG, tel 071–972–4095. **4–147**

From: Ref: CC10
CS4A
Wellington House
133–155 Waterloo Road
London SE1 8UG
Tel: 071–972–2000

ANNEX TO LAC (92)24

LOCAL AUTHORITY CONTRACTS FOR RESIDENTIAL AND NURSING HOME CARE AFTER APRIL 1993: NHS RELATED ASPECTS

Summary

1. This guidance sets out how local authority contracts for residential and nursing home care from April 1993 should relate to the provision of NHS community health services. **4–148**

Contracts with residential care homes

2. Local authority contracts for independent sector residential care should not include provision of any service which it is the responsibility of the NHS to provide. It will continue to be the responsibility of the NHS to provide where necessary community health services to residents of LA and independent residential care homes on the same basis as to people in their own homes. These services include the provision of district nursing and other specialist nursing services (*e.g.* incontinence advice) as well as provision, where necessary, of incontinence and nursing aids, physiotherapy, speech and language therapy and chiropody. Where such services are provided they must be free of charge to people in independent sector residential care homes as well as to residents of local authority Part III homes. **4–149**

Contracts with nursing and mental nursing homes after April 1993

3. Full implementation of the White Paper "Caring for People" will mean that local authorities will have responsibilities for purchasing nursing home care for the great majority of people who need it and who require to be publicly supported. When, after April 1993, a local **4–150**

authority places a person in a nursing home after joint HA/LA assessment, the local authority is responsible for purchasing services to meet the general nursing care needs of that person, including the cost of incontinence services (*e.g.* laundry) and those incontinence and nursing supplies which are not available on NHS prescription. Health authorities will be responsible for purchasing, within the resources available and in line with their priorities, physiotherapy, chiropody and speech and language therapy, with the appropriate equipment, and the provision of specialist nursing advice, *e.g.* continence advice and stoma care, for those people placed in nursing homes by local authorities with the consent of a DHA. Health authorities can opt to purchase these services through directly managed units, NHS Trusts, or other providers including the nursing home concerned.

General issues

4–151   4. It is the responsibility of the DHA in which the patient is regarded as usually resident, in accordance with existing regulations and guidance,* to purchase appropriate community health services. (Where the patient's GP is a fundholder, the GP fundholder would be responsible for purchasing the services within the terms of the fundholding scheme.)

5. When local and health authorities are both contracting with a nursing home for the provision of services, it may be best for this to be done with a joint LA/HA contract, which could be agreed at the time of the local authority placement.

6. Responsibility for the provision of occupational therapy services varies around the country. Health and local authorities often provide such services for different groups and purposes. They need to discuss and agree at local level appropriate arrangements for occupational therapy services for residents of residential care and local authority controlled nursing home places.

7. Health authorities continue to have the power to enter into a contractual arrangement with a nursing home where a patient's need is primarily for health care. Such placements must be fully funded by the health authority.

8. Health authorities are reminded of the role which the services which they are responsible for providing can play in helping people to live as normal and dignified a life as possible and in preventing a resident's health deteriorating to the point where admission to higher levels of containing care or acute in-patient care is necessary.

9. Health authorities are reminded that good quality community health services involve multidisciplinary working; and that geriatricians and psycho-geriatricians have specialist expertise which should be readily accessible to purchasers when looking at quality assurance. The community health services which health authorities are expected to provide would include advice to homes on issues such as the management of continence, maintenance of mobility and the management of behavioural disorders in elderly people.

10. The extent to which community health services can be provided is a matter for health authorities' judgment taking account of the resources available and competing priorities. In securing such services, health authorities will also need to consider the medium- to long-term resource implications given that the number of people placed in nursing homes by local authorities will increase in future years. Changes in overall levels of provision should be discussed first with the local authority concerned.

---

* A person should be treated as usually resident in one of the following places:
  (i) the address he gives as being the one at which he usually resides;
  (ii) if no such address, the address he gives as his most recent address; and
  (iii) where his usual address cannot be determined under (i) or (ii) he should be treated as usually resident in the region or district where he is.
In practice, the DHA of usual residence will be the nursing home's DHA.

INDEX

Abortions, nursing homes,
approved for, 4–023
Absence, manager, notification of, 2–040
Accidents,
notification of, 2–038
risk of, 2–022
Accommodation,
mental nursing homes, in, 2–099, 2–102
nursing homes, in, 2–099, 2–102
residential care homes, in, 1–056, 2–022
small homes, in, 2–022, 2–025
Accounts, Registered Homes Act, arising from, 2–009
Adjournment, Registered Homes Tribunal, of, 3–017, 3–018
Adult Placement schemes, 1–017, 4–126
Affidavit, evidence by, 3–020
Affirmation, taking of, 3–025
Aids, residents to, residential care homes, in, 2–027
Alcohol dependence, definition of, 4–037
Alcoholics, residential care homes for, 1–013
Annual fee, 1–048 et seq. 2–012, 2–013, 2–083, 2–112, 4–040
Annual return, small home, by, 1–051, 1–052, 2–060, 2–073, 4–124
Appeal, 1–086 et seq., 1–200, 4–085
expenses of appellant, 4–052
grounds of, 3–009
notice of, 3–005, 4–052
point of law, on, 1–225, 4–052
right of, 1–088
withdrawal of, 1–091, 3–031
Appeals, multiple, 3–033
Appellant,
meaning of, 3–004
representation of, 3–013
Applicants, birth certificate of, 2–006
criminal background of, 1–055

Applicants, birth certificate of—*cont.*
refused or cancelled, list of, 1–055
Application,
meaning of, 2–078
residential care home,
registration as a, 2–004
refusal of, 1–033, et seq.
small home, refusal of, 1–1053, 1–058
registration as a, 2–004
variation of condition of registration, for, 1–041
Approved social workers, 1–134
inspection, powers of, 1–209
Attorney General, consent of, 1–263

Bed occupancy, phased reduction of, 1–056
Bedrooms, shared, 2–025
Birth certificate, applicant, supply of, 2–006
Board, meaning of, 1–013
Burden of proof, Registered Homes Tribunals, in, 1–087
Burglary, homes, in, 2–038
Burial, residents, of, 2–067

Cancellation,
registration, of, 1–059 et seq., 1–116 et seq., 4–007
appeal against, 1–086 et seq.
urgent procedure, 1–065 et seq., 1–179 et seq.
Cancelled registrations, national list, of, 1–055, 1–167, 4–048 et seq., 4–086 et seq.
Care, occasional provision of, 4–128
Care authority, meaning of, 2–003
Care order, meaning of, 2–003
Carrying on the home, meaning of, 1–055
Centre for Policy on Ageing, Code of Practice, of, 1–005
Certificate of registration, 1–035, 1–038, 1–040, 1–137, 1–145, 4–125

Child, meaning of, 2–003, 2–078
Children, absence from home, notification of, 2–038
Consultancy Service, 1–055, 4–051, 4–087
  corporal punishment of, 2–018, 2–021
  fostering of, 4–128
  homes, in, 2–022, 2–036, 2–038
  maternity home, born in a, 2–123
  mental nursing homes, in, 1–209, 2–099, 4–128
  nursing homes, in, 1–124, 2–099, 4–020
  records of, 4–043
  residential care homes, in, 1–013, 2–038, 2–043
Children Act 1989, powers under, 1–099
Children's homes, registration and, 1–010, 1–011
Chiropody, homes, in, 4–150
Christian Science homes,
  registration of, power to exempt from, 1–221
Clinical record, patient, of, 2–092
Closed circuit television, residential care homes, in, 1–056
Clywd County Council, registration procedures, of, 1–006
Codes of Practice, function of, 1–005
Community Health Councils, 4–006
Community health services, nursing and residential care homes, and, 1–007, 4–145 *et seq.*
Company, offences by a, 1–261
  registration of a, 1–139, 4–011
  service of document to, 1–265
  visits by, 2–050
Complaints,
  investigation of, 1–211, 4–055
  mentally disordered patient, by, 1–208
  residents, by, 2–046
Conditions of registration, 1–035, 1–040, 1–173 *et seq.*
  additional, 1–035, 1–041
  ambiguity of, 1–042
  breach of, 1–035, 1–042
  Registered Homes Tribunal, power to impose, 1–092
  variation of, 1–035, 1–041, 2–009, 2–085, 4–008

Consultancy service, Department of Health, of the, 1–055, 4–051, 4–087
Convictions,
  fit person, and, 1–055
  manager of, 2–062, 2–064
  relevant, 4–107
  spent, 1–008
Corporal punishment, 2–018, 2–021
Corporations. *See* Company
Council on Tribunals, Registered Homes Tribunal hearing, present at, 3–015
Counselling, personal care, and, 1–013
Criminal background, applicants, of, 1–055
  disclosure of, 4–090 *et seq.*
Criminal proceedings, Registered Homes Tribunal, pending, 3–016

Death, resident of, 2–038, 2–088
Deceive, meaning of, 1–148
Decisions, Registered Homes Tribunal, of, 3–027 *et seq.*
Defences, prosecutions, to, 1–107
Dental services,
  nursing homes, in, 2–099
  residential care homes, in, 2–022
Dentist, meaning of, 2–078
Detained patients,
  death of registered person, effect on, 1–215
  nursing homes, in, 1–137
  power to discharge, 1–209
  records of, 2–086
Department of Health,
  cancelled or refused registrations, list of, 1–055, 4–038, 4–048 *et seq.*, 4–086 *et seq.*
  Children's Consultancy Service, 1–055, 4–051, 4–087
Disablement, meaning of, 1–116, 1–117
District Health Authorities. *See* Health Authorities
Doctor, patient, examination of, 1–208
Documents,
  evidence, as, 3–026
  service of, 1–265
  súbpoena of, 3–025
Double bedrooms, residential care homes, in, 2–025

Dressings, disposal of, 2–099
Drug dependence, definition of, 4–037
Drug misusers, residential care homes, in, 1–013
Drugs
  nursing and mental nursing home, in, 2–099, 2–108
  residential care homes, in, 2–022, 2–032
Dual registration,
  1–004, 4–047, 4–070, 4–081, 4–130
  appeals relating to, 1–239

Educational establishments, registration, exempt from, 4–054
Elderly, meaning of, 1–013
Elderly people. *Also see* Old age
  nursing homes, in, 4–019
Electrical supply, nursing and mental nursing homes, in, 2–099
Emergency procedures,
  cancellation of registration, nursing homes, 1–179 *et seq.*
  residential care homes, 1–065 *et seq.*
Employed, meaning of, 1–152
Equipment,
  medical and nursing, 2–099
  residential care homes, in, 1–054
Establishments,
  holiday accommodation, providing, 1–013
  meaning of, 1–013
  separate, 1–013
Evidence,
  admissibility of, 3–024
  admission of, 1–087
  hearsay, 3–026
  Registered Homes Tribunal, before, 3–020, 3–023 *et seq.*
  residents, by, 3–026
  rules of, 3–026

Fees, 1–142, 4–040
  annual, 1–048 *et seq.* 2–012, 2–013, 2–083
  registration, 1–035, 1–037, 2–008, 2–009, 2–118
  small home, for, 4–122, 4–123
  variation of condition of registration, not payable on, 2–009

Financial viability, home, of running a, 1–013
Fire authority,
  consultation with, 2–017
  meaning of, 2–003, 2–078
Fire drills,
  nursing and mental nursing homes, in, 2–099
  residential care homes and small homes, in, 2–022
Fire precautions, 4–026
  nursing and mental nursing homes, in, 2–099
  residential care homes, in, 4–044
First aid, training, in, 2–022
Fit person, 1–053, 1–055, 1–149, 1–152
Food,
  patients, supply to, 2–099
  residential care homes and small homes, in, 2–022–2–030
Fostering, children, of, 4–128
Furniture,
  mental nursing homes, in, 2–099
  nursing homes, in, 2–099
  residential and small homes, in, 2–022, 2–026

Government, guidance, 1–002
Group homes, 4–037
Guidelines, registration authority, of, 1–005

Habilitation, meaning of, 1–135
Health Authorities,
  cancellation of registration, use of urgent procedure, 1–179 *et seq.*
  complaints, investigation of, 4–005
  decisions of, 1–197
  designated senior nurse, of, 1–013
  detained patients, power to discharge, 1–209
  inspection,
    guidance on, 4–001 *et seq.*
    power of, 1–208
  local authorities, duty to provide services to, 1–013
  meaning of, 2–078
  members, role of, 4–012
  mental nursing home,
    cancellation of registration of, 1–215 *et seq.*

187

Health Authorities—*cont.*
  mental nursing home—*cont.*
    inspection of, 4–031
  nursing care, advice on, 1–013
  nursing homes,
    contractual relationship with, 1–122
    inspection of, 4–031
  nursing staff, determination of, 1–149, 1–157, 1–164
  registration authorities, as, 1–118, 4–001 *et seq.*
  registration, guidance on, 1–119 *et seq.*, 4–001 *et seq.*
  representations to, 1–189 *et seq.*
  resident, interview of, 2–022
  responsibilities of, 4–067
  social services authorities, co-operation with, 1–004, 1–013, 4–032, 4–082
  standards, determination of, 4–013
  unregistered homes, inspection of, 1–138, 1–164, 4–071, 4–083, 4–088
Hearing,
  Registered Homes Tribunal, notice of, 3–009
  procedure at, 3–020 *et seq.*
Hearsay evidence, 3–026
Heating,
  nursing and mental nursing homes, in, 2–099
  residential and small homes, in, 2–022
High Court, injunction, 1–066
Holiday accommodation,
  registration of, 1–013
  residential care homes, as, 4–037
Homeless persons,
  accommodation for, 1–013
Home Life, 1–005, 4–029, 4–043
  manager, definition in, 1–030
  Registered Homes Tribunals, and, 1–005
Homes. *See* Establishments
Hospital,
  meaning of, 1–020, 1–129
  registration not required, for, 1–010 *et seq.*
Household nursing, meaning of, 1–013
Hygiene, homes, in, 2–022

Incontinence services, 4–150

Independent visitor, meaning, of, 2–003
Infection, nursing homes, control of, 2–099
Infectious disease, residential care homes, in, 2–038
Injunction, unregistered home, to close an, 1–066
Inspection,
  guidance on, 1–099
  health authorities, guidance to, 4–001 *et seq.*
  joint, 1–004, 1–013, 1–099, 4–047
  mental nursing homes, of, 1–208 *et seq.*, 4–003, 4–061 *et seq.*
  nursing homes, of, 4–003, 4–061 *et seq.*
  purpose of, 1–006, 4–045
  report, availability of, 4–045
  residential care homes, of, 1–098 *et seq.*, 2–048, 4–045
  small homes, of, 4–124
  unregistered homes, of, 1–164, 4–071, 4–083, 4–088
Interviews,
  facilities for, 2–099
  nursing homes, in, 2–099
  patient, power to, 1–208
  residential care homes, in, 2–022

Joint consultative committee, role of, 1–004
Joint inspections, 1–004, 1–013, 1–099, 4–047
Judicial review, 1–040, 1–147, 1–225
Justice of the peace. *See* Magistrate

Kitchen equipment,
  nursing and mental nursing homes, in, 2–099
Kitchens,
  residential and small homes, in, 2–022, 2–030

Laser products,
  meaning of, 2–078
  use of, 1–132, 2–080, 2–112
Laundering facilities,
  nursing homes and mental nursing homes, in, 2–099
  residential care homes, in, 2–022
Legal Aid, Registered Homes Tribunal, and, 3–014

Legal representatives, Chairman of Registered Homes Tribunal, meeting with, 1–087
Lighting,
  nursing homes and mental nursing homes, in, 2–099
  residential care and small homes, in, 2–022, 2–028
Listening device, residential care homes, in, 2–019
Local authority. *See* Registration authority
Local authority officer, visits by, 2–033
Local Commission for Administration, complaints to, 2–047
Local social services authorities. *Also see* Registration authorities
  meaning of, 1–269, 1–270, 2–003
Lockers, provision of, 2–026

Magistrate,
  Registered Homes Tribunal, appeal to, against decision of, 1–088
  registration, cancellation of, application to, 1–065 *et seq.*, 1–179 *et. seq.*
Manager,
  absence of, 2–040
  criminal background of, 4–090 *et seq.*
  meaning of, 1–030
  "one Home and one manager" policy, 1–030
  qualification of, 1–030
  residential care home, of, 1–029, 1–030
Marriage breakdown, joint proprietors, of, 1–030
Maternity home. *Also see* Mother and baby home
  appeals relating to, 1–239
  child,
    born in a, 2–123
    case records of, 2–086, 2–126
  holding out as a, 1–146 *et seq.*
  meaning of, 1–123, 4–021
  register of patients, 2–123
Matron, residential care homes, in, 1–148
Medical emergencies, nursing and mental nursing homes, in, 2–099

Medical practitioner. *Also see* Doctor
  meaning of, 2–078
Medical records, patients, of, 1–208
Medical services, mental nursing homes, in, 2–099
  nursing homes, in, 2–099
  residential care homes, in, 2–022, 2–031
Medicines. *Also see* Drugs
  safekeeping of, 4–025
  small homes, in, 4–132
Mental disorder, meaning of, 1–269
Mental handicap, meaning of, 2–003
Mental Health Act 1983,
  discharge, powers of, 1–209
  managers under, the, 1–143
  mental nursing home, continuation of registration on death of registered person, 1–215 *et seq.*
  patients detained under, 1–134, 1–137, 1–144, 1–167, 1–209, 1–215
  provisions of, 1–223
Mental Health Act Commission, 1–134
  powers of, 1–209
Mental nursing homes. *Also see* Nursing homes
  accommodation, in, 2–099, 2–102
  annual fee, 2–083, 2–112
  appeals relating to, 1–239
  applicant for registration, 1–143
  application for registration, fee for, 2–119
  cancellation of registration, urgent procedure, 1–179 *et seq.*
  certificate of registration, 1–137, 1–145
  children, in, 1–209, 2–099
  community health services for, 2–031
  conditions of registration, variation of, 2–085, 4–008
  conduct of, 1–159 *et seq.*
  detained patients accommodated, in, 1–134, 1–137, 1–144, 1–209, 1–215
  drugs, in, 2–099, 2–108
  dual registration of, 1–004
  facilities, in, 2–099 *et seq.*, 4–013
  fire precautions, in, 4–026

Mental Nursing Homes—*cont.*
furniture in, 2–099
health authority functions, 1–118
holding out as a, 1–146 *et seq.*
inspection of, 1–208 *et seq.*,
  4–003, 4–061 *et seq.*
  joint, 1–004
management of, 4–009
meaning of, 1–133 *et seq.*
medical records, inspection of,
  1–208
medical services, in, 2–099
medicines, safekeeping of, 4–025
NHS responsibilities, in, 4–145 *et seq.*
nursing staff, in a, 1–149, 1–157,
  1–164
person in charge, 1–155
  absence of, 2–090, 2–099
records, and, 2–086, 4–024
registered person, death of, 1–215
  et seq.
registration of, 1–137 *et seq.*,
  1–184, 2–082, 4–022, 4–065 *et seq.*
  application for, 2–119
  cancellation of, 1–150, 1–166 *et seq.*, 1–215 *et seq.*, 4–007
  conditions of, 1-173 *et seq.*
  refusal of, 1–149 *et seq.*, 4–007
regulations, 1–159 *et seq.*
repair of, 2–099
services in, 2–099 *et seq.*
small home, registration as a,
  1–031 *et seq.*
staffing of, 2–099, 2–101, 4–014
treatment facilities, in, 2–099
unregistered, 1–013
  inspection of, 1–138, 1–164
Mentally disordered patient,
medical examination of, 1–208
mental nursing home, detained
  in, 1–137
nursing homes, in, 4–022
offences on, 1–013
visiting of, 1–208
Mentally disordered people,
residential care homes for, 1–013
Midwives, supervision of, 4–017
Money, residents, record of, 2–066
Mother and baby Homes. *Also see* Maternity homes
meaning of, 1–126, 4–021
Multiple appeals, Registered
  Homes Tribunal, to, 3–033

Multiple occupancy rooms. *See* shared bedrooms

NAHA, handbook, 1–005,
  1–118, 1–190, 4–065
National Assistance Act 1948,
  action under the, 1–066
National Health Service, nursing
  homes and residential care
  homes, responsibilities in, 4–145
  et seq.
Natural justice, rules of, 1–077
Notices, service of, 2–055
Nurses,
qualifications of, 1–149, 1–156,
  1–157, 1–164
training of, 4–018
Nursing,
definition of, 1–013, 1–125
personal care, compared with,
  1–013
specialist, 4–150
Nursing care, personal care, and,
  1–013
Nursing home care, definition of,
  1–013
Nursing homes,
abortions, approved for, 4–023
accommodation, in, 2–099, 2–102
annual fee, 2–083, 2–112
appeals relating to, 1–120, 1–239
applicant for registration, 1–143
application for registration, fee
  for, 2–118
certificate of registration, 1–137,
  1–145
children in, 1–124, 2–099, 4–020
Code of Practice. *See* NAHA
  handbook
community health services, and,
  1–007, 2–031
complaints, 4–005
conditions of registration,
  variation of, 2–085, 4–008
dayroom facilities, 2–099
death in, notice of, 2–088
dental services in, 2–099
dressings, etc. disposal of, 2–057
drugs, in, 2–099, 2–108
dual registration of, 1–004,
  1–031, 4–047, 4–130
elderly people in, 1–135, 4–019
electricity supply to, 2–099
facilities in, 2–099 *et seq.*, 4–013

Nursing homes—*cont.*
  facilities in—*cont.*
    standards of, 4–013
  fire precautions in, 4–026
  furniture in, 2–099
  health authorities, contractual arrangements with, 1–122
  holding out as, 1–146 *et seq.*
  infection, prevention of, 2–099
  inspection of, 2–092 *et seq.*, 4–003, 4–061 *et seq.*
    joint, 1–004
  laser products, use in, 1–132, 2–080, 2–086, 2–112
  laundering facilities, 2–099
  management of, 4–009
  meaning of, 1–123 *et seq.*
  medical services, in, 2–099
  medicines, safekeeping of, 4–025
  mentally handicapped people, in, 4–022
  mentally ill people, in, 4–022
  NHS responsibilities in, 4–145 *et seq.*
  nursing, in, 1–013
  nursing staff, in, 1–149, 1–157, 1–164
  operations performed in, 2–086
  patients,
    interviewing of, 2–099
    numbers in, 1–173
  person in charge, 1–149, 1–155
    absence of, 2–090
  person registered, 1–137, 1–143, 2–099
  records, in, 2–086, 2–092, 4–024
  registered person, absence of, 4–072, 4–083
  registers, particulars in, 2–123 *et seq.*
  registration of, 1–137 et seq., 2–082, 4–061 *et seq.*
    amendment of, urgent procedure, 1–179
    application for, 2–119
    cancellation of, 1–150, 1–166 *et seq.*, 4–007
      urgent procedure, 1–179 *et seq.*
    conditions of,
      additional, 1–173
      variation of, 1–173, 2–085
    procedure, 1–184
    refusal of, 1–149 *et seq.*, 4–007

Nursing homes—*cont.*
  regulations as to conduct of, 1–159 *et seq.*
  repairs of, 2–099
  residential care homes,
    overlap with, 4–004
    registration as, 1–019
  Secretary of State's functions, 1–118
  services in, 2–099 *et seq.*
  small home, registration as, 1–031 *et seq.*
  specially controlled techniques, in, 2–122
  staffing, 2–099, 2–101, 4–014
  telephone service, 2–099
  treatment facilities, in, 2–099
  unregistered, 1–013, 1–020, 4–031, 4–071, 4–083, 4–088
    inspection of, 1–138, 1–164
  visitors to, 2–099
Nursing skills, 1–013
Nursing staff, 4–015, 4–016

Oath, administration of, 3–025
Obstruction, offence of, 1–098, 1–106, 1–258
Offences, 1–162, 1–165, 1–166, 1–169, 1–208, 1–245 *et seq.*, 2–052
  carrying on a home without registration, 1–027, 1–137
  certificate of registration, failure to exhibit, 1–035, 1—043, 1—249
  companies, by, 1–261
  conditions of registration, breach of, 1–035, 1–042, 1—173, 1—252
  defences to, 1–107
  failure to register, 1–246
  holding out, of, 1–146 *et seq.*
  nursing home and mental nursing home, relating to, 2–115
  obstruction, 1–098, 1–106, 1–258
  proceedings in respect of, 1–263
  regulations, contravention of, 1–252
  unregistered home, 1–027
Offenders, Registered Homes Act, and, 1–008
Old age. *Also see* Elderly people
  definition of, 1–013, 4–037
Ombudsman. *See* Local Commission for Administration

Owners, meaning of, 1–030
Ownership, change of, reduction in number of residents in, 1–056

Patients,
  categories of, 1–173
  death of, 2–088
  detained under the Mental Health Act, 1–134, 1–137, 1–144, 1–209, 1–215
  examination of, 1–208
  interview of, 2–099
  medical records of, 2–092
  nursing and mental nursing home, in, numbers of, 1–173
  occupation of, 2–099
  privacy of, 2–019
  records of, 2–086
  recreation of, 2–099
  register of, 2–123
  risks, and, 2–019
  training of, 2–099
  visiting of, 1–208 et seq., 2–099
Person in charge, nursing home, qualifications of, 1–137, 1–149 et seq.
Person in control,
  absence of, 2–040, 2–090, 2–099
  registration of, 1–029 et seq.
  visits by, 2–050
Person registered, meaning of, 2–003
Personal care,
  meaning of, 1–013, 1–116, 1–117, 4–037
  nursing, compared with, 1–013
Physical restraint, resident, of, 2–019
Physiotherapy, homes, in, 4–150
Police checks, 4–090 et seq.
Post,
  residential care homes, arrangements for, 2–022
  service of documents by, 1–265
Privacy, residents, of, 2–033
Private residential care, extent of, 1–012
Professional nursing, meaning of, 1–013
Proof, burden of, 1–087
Proprietor. *Also see* Registered person
Proprietors,
  marriage breakdown of, 1–030

Psychopathic disorder, meaning of, 1–269
Publicity, small homes, on, 4–134, 4–136 et seq.

Records,
  child born in a maternity home, of, 2–086, 2–123
  clinical, inspection of, 2–092
  meaning of, 2–078
  mental nursing homes, in, 2–086, 4–024
  nursing homes, in, 2–086, 2–092, 4–024
  registration authority, of, 2–069
  residential care and small homes, in, 2–014, 2–066, 4–043
  retention of, 4–024
  small homes, in, 2–014
References, medical, 2–063
  staff, for, 2–024
Refused registrations, national list of, 1–055, 4–038, 4–048 et seq., 4–086 et seq.
Registered Homes Act,
  accounts relating to, 2–009
  background to, 1–002
  commencement of, 1–009
  Derivations, Table of, 1–284
  Destinations, Table of, 1–285
  extent of, 1–009
  Parliamentary debates, 1–009
  publications on, 1–002
  transitional provisions, 1–009, 1–278
Registered Homes Tribunals, 1–255 et seq., 4–028 et seq.
  adjournment, criminal proceedings pending, 3–016, 3–018
  admissability of evidence, 1–087
  affidavits, exchange of, 1–087
  appeal against decision of, 1–225, 4–052
  appeals to, 1–086 et seq., 1–200, 1–225, 4–052
  grounds for, 3–009
  multiple, 1–241, 3–033
  notice of, 4–052
  withdrawal of, 1–091, 3–031
  appellants, advice to, 1–227
  criminal proceedings pending against, 3–016
  appointment of, 3–008

Registered Homes Tribunals—cont.
  burden of proof, 1–087
  cancellation of registration,
    urgent procedure, attitude
    toward, 1–066
  chairman of, meeting with legal
    representatives, 1–087
  conditions, power to impose,
    1–092
  constitution of, 1–232 et seq.,
    1–239
  costs, 1–225
  decisions, 1–225, 3–027 et seq.
  evidence,
    admission of, 1–087
    before a, 3–020, 3–023 et seq.
  financial viability of running a
    home, attitude towards, 1–013
  fit person, adjudications on,
    1–055
  guidelines, attitude toward,
    1–005
  hearing,
    adjournment of, 3–017, 3–018
    date of, 3–009
    private, in, 3–015, 3–016
    procedure at, 3–020, 3–021
    venue for, 3–011
  High Court, usurping the
    functions of, 1–088
  Home Life, and, 1–005
  homes, visits to, 3–021
  judicial review, and, 1–225
  legal representation, 1–228
  magistrate, decision of, appeal
    against, 1–088
  members of, fees for, 1–244
  potential residents, taking
    account of needs of, 1–040
  powers of, 1–091, 1–200
  preliminary hearing, lack of,
    1–087
  procedure of, 1–087, 1–241,
    3–036, 3–037
  proprietor's future intentions,
    regard to, 1–056
  representation before, 3–013
  residential care homes,
    financial viability of, 1–013
  Secretariat, 1–225
    address of, 1–088
  settlement, negotiation of, 3–020
  staff, 1–243
  statement of reasons, 3–009

Registered Homes Tribunals—*cont.*
  time limits, extension of, 3–035
  witnesses, calling of, 3–020
  written submissions, use of,
    3–037
Registered Homes Tribunal Rules,
  3–001 et seq.
Registered person,
  absence of, 4–039
  absence of person in charge,
    notice of, 2–090
  complaints, information to
    residents, 2–046, 2–047
  criminal background of, 4–090 et
    seq.
  death of, 1–044, 1–045
  duty to notify death, illness or
    accident, 2–038
  duty to promote welfare of
    residents, 2–018 et seq.
  fire authority, consultation with,
    2–017
  marriage breakdown of, 1–030
  meaning of, 2–003
  nursing home,
    absence from, 2–090, 4–072,
      4–083
    duty to provide services and
      facilities, 2–099
    records in, 2–086
  residential care homes,
    duty to provide services and
      facilities, 2–014
    records in, 2–014
  residents, duty toward, 2–018
  visitors, duty to make
    arrangements for, 2–033
  visits to residential care homes,
    2–050
Registered proprietor. *See*
  Registered person
Register of patients, 2–123
Registers,
  inspection of, 1–046, 1–047
  registration authority, kept by,
    2–016, 4–125
Registration,
  annual fee for, 1–048, 2–012,
    2–013, 2–083, 2–122
  application for, 1–035 et seq.,
    1–137 et seq., 2–004, 2–062,
    2–082, 2–119
  cancellation of, 1–059 et seq.,
    1–150, 1–166 et seq.

Registration—*cont.*
  cancellation of—*cont.*
    urgent procedure, 1–065 *et seq.*, 1–179 *et seq.*, 4–042
  cancelled, national list of, 4–048 *et seq.*, 4–086 *et seq.*
  carrying on home without, 1–027, 1–028
  certificate of, 1–035, 1–038
  conditions of, 1–035, 1–040, 1–149, 1–173
    power of Registered Homes Tribunal to impose, 1–092
  consultation prior to, 1–037
  definition of, 1–036
  establishments not requiring, 1–016 *et seq.*
  expenditure prior to, 1–006
  fee, 1–035, 2–008, 2–009, 4–040
  financial viability, and, 1–013
  health authorities, guidance to, 4–001 *et seq.*
  holiday accommodation, and, 1–013
  homeless people, and, 1–013
  "in principle", 1–036
  local authorities, guidance to, 4–028 *et seq.*, 4–110 *et seq.*
  mental nursing home, 1–137, 2–082, 4–061 *et seq.*
    application for, 1–137, 2–119
    cancellation of, 1–166, 1–172, 4–007
    refusal of, 1–149 *et seq.*, 4–007
  nursing home, 1–137 *et seq.*, 2–082, 4–061 *et seq.*
    application for, 1–137, 2–119
    cancellation of, 1–166, 1–179, 4–007
    refusal of, 1–149 *et seq.*, 4–007
  preliminary inquiries, 1–119
  procedures, 1–006, 1–184, 4–042
  purpose of, 1–006
  refusal of,
    grounds for, 1–053 *et seq.*, 1–149 *et seq.*
  refused, national list of, 4–048 *et seq.*, 4–086 *et seq.*
  residential care homes, 1–010 *et seq.*, 1–070 *et seq.*, 4–028 *et seq.*
    conditions of, 1–070 *et seq.*
    procedure for cancelling, 1–070 *et seq.*
    procedure for imposing additional conditions, 1–070 *et seq.*

Registration—*cont.*
  residential care homes—*cont.*
    procedure for varying condition of, 1–070 *et seq.*
  responsibility for, 4–041
  role of, 1–006
  schools, of, 1–022, 1–023
  small homes, 1–003, 1–016, 1–017, 1–031 *et seq.*, 1–035 *et seq.*, 4–119 *et seq.*
    cancellation of, 4–119
    exemption from, 2–058
    refusal of, 1–053, 1–058
  time limit for, 2–010, 2–011
  urgent cancellation of, appeal against, 1–086 *et seq.*
Registration authorities, accounts, 2–009, 2–084
  cancellation of registration, application for, 1–065 *et seq.*
    power to move residents, on a, 1–066
  certificate of registration, 4–125
  complaints to, 2–046
  decision of, 1–083 *et seq.*
    appeal against, 1–086 *et seq.*
  definition of, 1–010
  guidance, consultation on, 1–005
  guidelines of, 2–025
  health authorities, co-operation with, 4–031
  joint inspections by, 1–099
  judicial manner, duty to act in a, 1–077
  meaning of, 1–116, 1—117
  mental nursing homes, and, 1–013
  nursing homes, and, 1–013
  potential residents, taking account of needs of, 1–040
  procedures, procedural defects in, 1–088
  records kept by, 2–069
  registers, 2–016, 4–125
    inspection of, 1–046, 1–047
  registration,
    cancellation by, 1–659 *et seq.*
    refusal by, 1–053 *et seq.*
  representations, 3–013
    duty to hear, 1–076
    right to make, to, 1–076 *et seq.*
  residents, interview of, 2–022
  responsibilities of, 1–036
  standards of, 2–025

Registration authorities, accounts
—*cont.*
  standards of—*cont.*
    in own homes, 2–023, 2–025
Registration officers, role of, 1–036
Regulations,
  compliance with, 2–056
  enforcement of, 2–052, 2–115
  mental nursing homes, conduct of, 1–159 *et seq.*
  nursing homes, conduct of, 1–159 *et seq.*
  power to make, 1–271
  residential care homes, as to, 1–093 *et seq.*
Rehabilitation of Offenders Act 1974, 1–008, 2–004
Relatives,
  meaning of, 1–111 *et seq.*
  members of religious communities, and, 4–127
Relevant date, meaning of, 2–003
Relevant enactments, meaning of, 3–004
Religious communities, members of, 1–127
Religious observance, homes, in, 2–035
Report, inspection, availability of, 4–045
Representations,
  procedure for making, 1–077
  right to make, 1–076 *et seq.*, 1–189 *et seq.*
Re-registration, requirement of, 4–010
Residence,
  place, of, guidance on, 4–151
  removal of person from place of, 1–066
Residential accommodation, 1–013
Residential care, private, extent of, 1–012
Residential care homes,
  accidents in, 2–022, 2–038
  accommodation in, 1–056, 2–022, 2–025
  additional condition of registration, procedure for imposing, 1–070 *et seq.*
  alcoholics, for, 1–013
  annual fee, for, 1–048 *et seq.* 4–040
  bedrooms, shared, in, 2–025

Residential care homes—*cont.*
  cancellation of registration, procedure for, 1–059 *et seq.*, 1–065 *et seq.*
  care, occasional provision of, 4–128
  carrying on without registration, 1–027
  case records, in, 4–043
  categorisation of, 2–062
  children, in, 1–013, 2–022, 2–036
  close circuit television in, 1–056
  Codes of Practice, and, 1–005
  community health services, and, 1–006
  conditions of registration,
    breach of, 1–035 *et seq.*
    fee for variation of, 2–009
  conduct of, 1–011 *et seq.*, 2–018, 2–019, 4–043
  day places in, 1–013
  death of registered person, 1–044
  decoration of, 2–022
  definition of, 1–010, 1–011, 4–037
  dental services, in, 2–022
  description of, 1–012, 1–014
  double bedrooms in, 2–025
  drug misusers, for, 1–013
  drugs, in, 2–022, 2–032
  dual registration of, 1–004, 1–031, 4–047
  educational establishments, exempt from registration as, 4–054
  equipment in, 1–056
  facilities in, 2–022 *et seq.*
  fee, registration, 2–008, 2–009
  financial viability of, 1–013
  fire drills in, 2–022
  fire safety in, 4–044
  first aid, training in, 2–022
  food in, 2–022, 2–030
  furniture in, 2–022, 2–026
  future residents of, 1–087
  general practitioners, and, 1–013
  holiday accommodation, and, 1–013, 4–037
  hygiene, in, 2–022
  illness in, 2–038
  infectious diseases in, 2–038
  inspection of, 1–098 *et seq.*, 2–048, 4–045
  isolation of, 1–056
  joint inspection of, 1–004

Residential care homes—*cont.*
  kitchens in, 2–022, 2–030
  lighting of, 2–022
  listening device in, 2–019
  manager of, 1–029, 1–030, 2–040
  medical services in, 2–022, 2–031
  mentally disordered, for, 1–013
  NHS responsibilities in, 4–145 *et seq.*
  naming of, 1–012, 1–014
  numbers in, 1–035, 1–040
  nursing in, 1–013
  nursing homes, overlap with, 4–004
  person in control, visits by, 2–050
  physically handicapped residents in, 2–099
  records in, 2–014, 2–044
  registered person, absence of, 4–039
  registration,
    annual fee, for, 2–012, 2–013, 4–040
    application for, 1–035 *et seq.*, 2–004, 2–062
    cancellation of, 1–059 *et seq.*
    conditions of, 1–070 *et seq.*
    procedure, 1–010 *et seq.*, 1–035 *et seq.*, 1–070 *et seq.*, 4–028 *et seq.*, 4–042
    refusal of, 1–033 *et seq.*
    responsibility for, 4–041
    time limit for, 2–010, 2–011
  regulations relating to, 1–093 *et seq.*, 2–001 *et seq.*
  residents,
    intention of, 1–013
    numbers in, 1–040, 1–056
    removal from, 1–066
  sale of, 1–028
  separate establishments as, 1–013
  services in, 2–022 *et seq.*
  situation of, 1–056
  staffing of, 1–054, 2–022, 2–024
  standards in, 1–002
  telephones in, 2–022
  unregistered, 1–027, 1–028
    closure of, 1–066
  variation of condition of registration, procedure for, 1–070 *et seq.*
  visits to, 2–033
  welfare of residents, 2–018 *et seq.*

Residential Care Homes Regulations, 2–001 *et seq.*
Residents,
  accidents to, 2–038
  aids for, 2–027
  board for, 1–013
  burial of, 2–067
  cancellation of registration, position on a, 1–066
  categories of, 1–035, 2-062, 2–065
    small homes, in, 4–131
  clothing, choice of, 2–027
  communal space for, 2–025
  complaints by, 2–046
  death of, 2–038
  evidence of, 3–026
  health of, 1–013
    illness of, 2–038
  intention of, 1–013
  interview of, 2–022
  lockers for, 2–026
  meaning of, 1–040, 2–003
  money of, 2–066
  numbers of, reduction of, 1–056
  physically handicapped, 2–022
  physical restraint of, 2–019
  privacy of, 2–033, 2–019
  regligious observance by, 2–035
  residential care homes,
    choice of location, 1–056
    numbers in, 1–056
    removal from, 1–066
  risks, and, 2–019
  rooms for, 2–022, 2–025
  serious illness of, 2–038
  short stay of, 1–013
  statutory duties in respect of, waiving of, 1–036
  temporary, 1–040
  valuables of, 2–022
  visiting of, 2–033
  welfare of, 2–018, 2–020
  wishes and feelings of, 2–018
Respite care schemes, 4–126
Risk taking, 2–019
Rooms, residents for, 2–022, 2–025
Rotas, staff, 2–024
Royal charter, bodies established under, 1–010, 1–011, 1–024

Schools,
  registration of, 1–010, 1–011, 1–022, 1–023
  residential care homes, and, 4–128

Secretary of State,
  direction to inspect unregistered premises, 1–164
  nursing homes, delegation of functions relating to, 1–118
  residential care homes, power to inspect, 1–098 et seq.
Serious risk, meaning of, 1–067
Service, address for, 3–005
Situation, residential care homes, of, 1–056
Sluicing facilities,
  nursing and mental nursing homes, in, 2–099
  residential care homes and small homes, in, 2–022
Small homes,
  accommodation in, 2–022, 2–025
  annual fee, 1–048 et seq.
  annual return by, 1–051, 1–052, 2–060, 2–073, 4–124
  children, in, 2–022, 2–036
  decoration of, 2–022
  definition of, 1–010, 1–011
  dental services, in, 2–022
  drugs, in, 2–022, 2–032
  facilities, in, 2–022 et seq.
  fees, 4–122, 4–123
    registration, 2–008
  fire drills, in, 2–022
  food, in, 2–022—2–030
  furniture, in, 2–022, 2–026
  hygiene, in, 2–022
  inspection of, 1–099, 2–048, 4–124
  kitchens, in, 2–022, 2–030
  lighting of, 2–022
  medical services, in, 2–022, 2–031
  medicines, in, 4–132
  person in control, visits by, 2–050
  publicity on, 4–134, 4–136 et seq.
  records in, 2–014, 2–066
  registration, 1–003, 1–016, 1–017, 1–031 et seq., 1–035 et seq., 4–119 et seq.
    application for, 2–004, 2–062
    cancellation of, 1–059 et seq., 4–119
    exemption from, 2–058
    fee for, 1–035, 1–039
    refusal of, 1–053, 1–058
  residents, categories of, 4–131

Small homes—cont.
  services, in, 2–022 et seq.
  staffing of, 2–022, 2–024, 4–121
  telephones, in, 2–022
  visits to, 2–033
Specially controlled techniques,
  meaning of, 1–123
  nursing homes, in, 2–122
Speech therapy, homes, in, 4–150
Staff,
  mental nursing homes, in, 2–099, 2–101, 4–014
  might, 2–024
  nursing homes, in, 2–099, 2–101, 4–014
  references for, 2–024
  residential care homes, in, 1–056, 2–022, 2–024
  rotas, 2–024
  small home, in, 4–121
Standard of proof. See Burden of proof
Standards, guidance on, 1–002
Standard scale, meaning of, 1–269
Statement of reasons, service of, 3–009
Statutory maximum, meaning of, 1–269, 1–270
Subpoena,
  documents, of, 3–025
  witness, attendance of, 3–024, 3–025
Swabs, disposal of, 2–099

Telephone service,
  nursing and mental nursing homes, in, 2–099
  residential care and small homes, in, 2–022
Termination of pregnancies. See Abortions
Theft, residential care and small homes, in, 2–038
Time limits, extension of, 3–035
Training, nurses, of, 4–018
Treatment, meaning of, 1–123
Treatment facilities,
  mental nursing homes, in, 2–099
  nursing homes, in, 2–099
Tribunal. See Registered Homes Tribunal

University, registration not required, 1–010

Unregistered homes, closure of, 1–064
Unregistered nursing homes, 4–071, 4–083, 4–088
   inspection of, 1–122
Urgent procedure, cancellation of registration, for the, 1–065 *et seq.*, 1–179 *et seq.*, 4–042

Valuables, residents', safe keeping of, 2–022
Ventilation,
   nursing and mental nursing homes, in, 2–099
   residential care homes and small homes in, 2–022

Visiting,
   facilities for, 2–033
   local authority officer, by, 2–033
   patients, of, 1–208 *et seq.*, 2–099
   residents, of, 2–033
Visitors, privacy for, 2–099
Visits, person in control, by, 2–050

Water closets, nursing and mental nursing homes, in, 2–099
Witness, subpoena of, 3–024, 3–025
Witnesses, Registered Homes Tribunal, calling of, 3–020
Witness statements, exchange of, 3–024, 3–025